PENGUIN BO

CIVILIZATI

'Provocative, entertaining and important' Jack Straw, *Prospect*

'Brings history alive for the reader with a dazzling knowledge . . .
peerless' *Independent on Sunday*

'Stiffens the sinews and summons the blood of a civilization which has
lost its way' Andrew Marr, *Financial Times*

'The most original, entertaining and argumentative historian writing in
English today . . . a delightfully provocative book' *Mail on Sunday*

'Thoughtful and engaging. . . with flashes of humour' *Literary Review*

'Tackles a large and complex subject in a way that could hardly be
more accessible' *Independent*

'Informed, enlightening and frightening . . . packed with arresting
observations' *Glasgow Sunday Herald*

'An academic pugilist . . . captivating' *Metro*

NIALL FERGUSON

Civilization
The Six Killer Apps of Western Power

PENGUIN BOOKS

PENGUIN BOOKS

Published by the Penguin Group
Penguin Books Ltd, 80 Strand, London WC2R ORL, England
Penguin Group (USA), Inc., 375 Hudson Street, New York, New York 10014, USA
Penguin Group (Canada), 90 Eglinton Avenue East, Suite 700, Toronto, Ontario, Canada M4P 2Y3
(a division of Pearson Penguin Canada Inc.)
Penguin Ireland, 25 St Stephen's Green, Dublin 2, Ireland (a division of Penguin Books Ltd)
Penguin Group (Australia), 250 Camberwell Road, Camberwell, Victoria 3124, Australia
(a division of Pearson Australia Group Pty Ltd)
Penguin Books India Pvt Ltd, 11 Community Centre, Panchsheel Park, New Delhi – 110 017, India
Penguin Group (NZ), 67 Apollo Drive, Rosedale, Auckland 0632, New Zealand
(a division of Pearson New Zealand Ltd)
Penguin Books (South Africa) (Pty) Ltd, 24 Sturdee Avenue, Rosebank, Johannesburg 2196, South Africa

Penguin Books Ltd, Registered Offices: 80 Strand, London WC2R ORL, England

www.penguin.com

First published by Allen Lane 2011
Published in Penguin Books 2012
003

Printed in Great Britain by Clays Ltd, St Ives plc

A CIP catalogue record for this book is available from the British Library

978-0-141-04458-3

www.greenpenguin.co.uk

MIX
Paper from
responsible sources
FSC™ C018179

Penguin Books is committed to a sustainable
future for our business, our readers and our planet.
This book is made from Forest Stewardship
Council™ certified paper.

ALWAYS LEARNING   **PEARSON**

For Ayaan

Contents

List of Illustrations

List of Maps

List of Figures

Preface to the UK Edition

I am trying to remember now where it was, and when it was, that it hit me. Was it during my first walk along the Bund in Shanghai in 2005? Was it amid the smog and dust of Chongqing, listening to a local Communist Party official describe a vast mound of rubble as the future financial centre of South-west China? That was in 2008, and somehow it impressed me more than all the synchronized razzamatazz of the Olympic opening ceremony in Beijing. Or was it at Carnegie Hall in 2009, as I sat mesmerized by the music of Angel Lam, the dazzlingly gifted young Chinese composer who personifies the Orientalization of classical music? I think maybe it was only then that I really got the point about the first decade of the twenty-first century, just as it was drawing to a close: that we are living through the end of 500 years of Western ascendancy.

The principal question addressed by this book increasingly seems to me the most interesting question a historian of the modern era can ask. Just why, beginning around 1500, did a few small polities on the western end of the Eurasian landmass come to dominate the rest of the world, including the more populous and in many ways more sophisticated societies of Eastern Eurasia? My subsidiary question is this: if we can come up with a good explanation for the West's past ascendancy, can we then offer a prognosis for its future? Is this really the end of the West's world and the advent of a new Eastern epoch? Put differently, are we witnessing the waning of an age when the greater part of humanity was more or less subordinated to the civilization that arose in Western Europe in the wake of the Renaissance and Reformation – the civilization that, propelled by the Scientific Revolution and the Enlightenment, spread across the Atlantic and as far as the Antipodes, finally reaching its apogee during the Ages of Revolution, Industry and Empire?

The very fact that I want to pose such questions says something about the first decade of the twenty-first century. Born and raised in Scotland, educated at Glasgow Academy and Oxford University, I assumed throughout my twenties and thirties that I would spend my academic career at either Oxford or Cambridge. I first began to think of moving to the United States because an eminent benefactor of New York University's Stern School of Business, the Wall Street veteran Henry Kaufman, had asked me why someone interested in the history of money and power did not come to where the money and power actually were. And where else could that be but downtown Manhattan? As the new millennium dawned, the New York Stock Exchange was self-evidently the hub of an immense global economic network that was American in design and largely American in ownership. The dotcom bubble was deflating, admittedly, and a nasty little recession ensured that the Democrats lost the White House just as their pledge to pay off the national debt began to sound almost plausible. But within just eight months of becoming president, George W. Bush was confronted by an event that emphatically underlined the centrality of Manhattan to the Western-dominated world. The destruction of the World Trade Center by al-Qaeda terrorists paid New York a hideous compliment. This was target number one for anyone serious about challenging Western predominance.

The subsequent events were heady with hubris. The Taliban overthrown in Afghanistan. An 'axis of evil' branded ripe for 'regime change'. Saddam Hussein ousted in Iraq. The Toxic Texan riding high in the polls, on track for re-election. The US economy bouncing back thanks to tax cuts. 'Old Europe' – not to mention liberal America – fuming impotently. Fascinated, I found myself reading and writing more and more about empires, in particular the lessons of Britain's for America's; the result was *Empire: How Britain Made the Modern World* (2003). As I reflected on the rise, reign and probable fall of America's empire, it became clear to me that there were three fatal deficits at the heart of American power: a manpower deficit (not enough boots on the ground in Afghanistan and Iraq), an attention deficit (not enough public enthusiasm for long-term occupation of conquered countries) and above all a financial deficit (not enough savings relative to investment and not enough taxation relative to public expenditure).

In *Colossus: The Rise and Fall of America's Empire* (2004), I warned that the United States had imperceptibly come to rely on East Asian capital to fund its unbalanced current and fiscal accounts. The decline and fall of America's undeclared empire might therefore be due not to terrorists at the gates, nor to the rogue regimes that sponsored them, but to a financial crisis at the very heart of the empire itself. When, in late 2006, Moritz Schularick and I coined the word 'Chimerica' to describe what we saw as the dangerously unsustainable relationship – the word was a pun on 'chimera' – between parsimonious China and profligate America, we had identified one of the keys to the coming global financial crisis. For without the availability to the American consumer of both cheap Chinese labour and cheap Chinese capital, the bubble of the years 2002–7 would not have been so egregious.

The illusion of American 'hyper-power' was shattered not once but twice during the presidency of George W. Bush. Nemesis came first in the backstreets of Sadr City and the fields of Helmand, which exposed not only the limits of American military might but also, more importantly, the naivety of neo-conservative visions of a democratic wave in the Greater Middle East. It struck a second time with the escalation of the subprime mortgage crisis of 2007 into the credit crunch of 2008 and finally the 'great recession' of 2009. After the bankruptcy of Lehman Brothers, the sham verities of the 'Washington Consensus' and the 'Great Moderation' – the central bankers' equivalent of the 'End of History' – were consigned to oblivion. A second Great Depression for a time seemed terrifyingly possible. What had gone wrong? In a series of articles and lectures beginning in mid-2006 and culminating in the publication of *The Ascent of Money* in November 2008 – when the financial crisis was at its worst – I argued that all the major components of the international financial system had been disastrously weakened by excessive short-term indebtedness on the balance sheets of banks, grossly mispriced and literally overrated mortgage-backed securities and other structured financial products, excessively lax monetary policy on the part of the Federal Reserve, a politically engineered housing bubble and, finally, the unrestrained selling of bogus insurance policies (known as derivatives), offering fake protection against unknowable uncertainties, as opposed to quantifiable risks. The globalization of financial institutions that were of Western origin had been supposed to usher in a new era of reduced economic volatility. It took historical knowledge to foresee how an old-fashioned liquidity crisis might bring the whole shaky edifice of leveraged financial engineering crashing to the ground.

The danger of a second Depression receded after the summer of 2009, though it did not altogether disappear. But the world had nevertheless changed. The breathtaking collapse in global trade caused by the financial crisis, as credit to finance imports and exports suddenly dried up, might have been expected to devastate the big Asian economies, reliant as they were said to be on exports to the West. Thanks to a highly effective government stimulus programme based on massive credit expansion, however, China suffered only a slow-down in growth. This was a remarkable feat that few experts had anticipated. Despite the manifest difficulties of running a continental economy of 1.3 billion people as if it were a giant Singapore, the probability remains better than even at the time of writing (December 2010) that China will continue to forge ahead with its industrial revolution and that, within the decade, it will overtake the United States in terms of gross domestic product, just as (in 1963) Japan overtook the United Kingdom.

The West had patently enjoyed a real and sustained edge over the Rest for most of the previous 500 years. The gap between Western and Chinese incomes had begun to open up as long ago as the 1600s and had continued to widen until as recently as the late 1970s, if not later. But since then it had narrowed with astonishing speed. The financial crisis crystallized the next historical question I wanted to ask. Had that Western edge now gone? Only by working out what exactly it had consisted of could I hope to come up with an answer.

What follows is concerned with historical methodology; impatient readers can skip it and go straight to the introduction. I wrote this book because I had formed the strong impression that the people currently living were paying insufficient attention to the dead. Watching my three children grow up, I had the uneasy feeling that they were learning less history than I had learned at their age, not because they had bad teachers but because they had bad history books and even worse examinations. Watching the financial crisis unfold, I realized that they were far from alone, for it seemed as if only a handful of people in the banks and treasuries of the Western world had more than the sketchiest information about the last Depression. For roughly thirty years, young people at Western schools and universities have been given the idea of a liberal education, without the substance of historical knowledge. They have been taught isolated 'modules', not narratives, much less chronologies. They have been trained in the formulaic analysis of document excerpts, not in the key skill of reading widely and fast. They have been encouraged to feel empathy with imagined Roman centurions or Holocaust victims, not to write essays about why and how their predicaments arose. In *The History Boys*, the playwright Alan Bennett posed a 'trilemma': should history be taught as a mode of contrarian argumentation, a communion with past Truth and Beauty, or just 'one fucking thing after another'? He was evidently unaware that today's sixth-formers are offered none of the above – at best, they get a handful of 'fucking things' in no particular order.

The former president of the university where I teach once confessed that, when he had been an undergraduate at the Massachusetts Institute of Technology, his mother had implored him to take at least one history course. The brilliant young economist replied cockily that he was more interested in the future than in the past. It is a preference he now knows to be illusory. There is in fact no such thing as the future, singular; only futures, plural. There are multiple interpretations of history, to be sure, none definitive – but there is only one past. And although the past is over, for two reasons it is indispensable to our understanding of what we experience today and what lies ahead of us tomorrow and thereafter. First, the current world population makes up approximately 7 per cent of all the human beings who have ever lived. The dead outnumber the living, in other words, fourteen to one, and we ignore the accumulated experience of such a huge majority of mankind at our peril. Second, the past is really our only reliable source of knowledge about the fleeting present and to the multiple futures that lie before us, only one of which will actually happen. History is not just how we study the past; it is how we study time itself.

Let us first acknowledge the subject's limitations. Historians are not scientists. They cannot (and should not even try to) establish universal laws of social or political 'physics' with reliable predictive powers. Why? Because there is no possibility of repeating the single, multi-millennium experiment that constitutes the past. The sample size of human history is one. Moreover, the 'particles' in this one vast experiment have consciousness, which is skewed by all kinds of cognitive biases. This means that their behaviour is even harder to predict than if they were insensate, mindless, gyrating particles. Among the many quirks of the human condition is that people have evolved to learn almost instinctively from their own past experience. So their behaviour is adaptive; it changes over time. We do not wander randomly but walk in paths, and what we have encountered behind us determines the direction we choose when the paths fork – as they constantly do.

So what can historians do? First, by mimicking social scientists and relying on quantitative data, historians can devise 'covering laws', in Carl Hempel's sense of general statements about the past that appear to cover most cases (for instance, when a dictator takes power instead of a democratic leader, the chance increases that the country in question will go to war). Or – though the two approaches are not mutually exclusive – the historian can commune with the dead by imaginatively reconstructing their experiences in the way described by the great Oxford philosopher R. G. Collingwood in his 1939 *Autobiography*. These two modes of historical inquiry allow us to turn the surviving relics of the past into history, a body of knowledge and interpretation that retrospectively orders and illuminates the human predicament. Any serious predictive statement about the possible futures we may experience is based, implicitly or explicitly, on one or both of these historical procedures. If not, then it belongs in the same category as the horoscope in this morning's newspaper.

Collingwood's ambition, forged in the disillusionment with natural science and psychology that followed the carnage of the First World War, was to take history into the modern age, leaving behind what he dismissed as 'scissors-and-paste history', in which writers 'only repeat, with different arrangements and different styles of decoration, what others [have] said before them'. His thought process is itself worth reconstructing:

a) 'The past which an historian studies is not a dead past, but a past which in some sense is still living in the present' in the form of traces (documents and artefacts) that have survived.

b) 'All history is the history of thought', in the sense that a piece of historical evidence is meaningless if its intended purpose cannot be inferred.

c) That process of inference requires an imaginative leap through time: 'Historical knowledge is the re-enactment in the historian's mind of the thought whose history he is studying.'

d) But the real meaning of history comes from the juxtaposition of past and present: 'Historical knowledge is the re-enactment of a past thought incapsulated in a context of present thoughts which, by contradicting it, confine it to a plane different from theirs.'

e) The historian thus 'may very well be related to the nonhistorian as the trained woodsman is to the ignorant traveller. "Nothing here but trees and grass," thinks the traveller, and marches on. "Look," says the woodsman, "there is a tiger in that grass."' In other words, Collingwood argues, history offers something 'altogether different from [scientific] rules, namely insight'.

f) The true function of historical insight is 'to inform [people] about the present, in so far as the past, its ostensible subject matter, [is] incapsulated in the present and [constitutes] a part of it not at once obvious to the untrained eye'.

g) As for our choice of subject matter for historical investigation, Collingwood makes it clear that there is nothing wrong with what his Cambridge contemporary Herbert Butterfield condemned as 'present-mindedness': 'True historical problems arise out of practical problems. We study history in order to see more clearly into the situation in which we are called upon to act. Hence the plane on which, ultimately, all problems arise is the plane of "real" life: that to which they are referred for their solution is history.'

A polymath as skilled in archaeology as he was in philosophy, a staunch opponent of appeasement and an early hater of the *Daily Mail*,* Collingwood has been my guide for many years, but never has he been more indispensable than in the writing of this book. For the problem of why civilizations fall is too important to be left to the purveyors of scissors-and-paste history. It is truly a practical problem of our time, and this book is intended to be a woodsman's guide to it. For there is more than one tiger hidden in this grass.

In dutifully reconstructing past thought, I have tried always to remember a simple truth about the past that the historically inexperienced are prone to forget. Most people in the past either died young or expected to die young, and those who did not were repeatedly bereft of those they loved, who did die young. Consider the case of my favourite poet, the Jacobean master John Donne, who lived to the age of fifty-nine, thirteen years older than I am as I write. A lawyer, a Member of Parliament and, after renouncing the Roman Catholic faith, an Anglican priest, Donne married for love, as a result losing his job as secretary to his bride's uncle, Sir Thomas Egerton, the Lord Keeper of the Privy Seal.† In the space of sixteen impecunious years, Anne Donne bore her husband twelve children. Three of them, Francis, Nicholas and Mary, died before they were ten. Anne herself died after giving birth to the twelfth child, which was stillborn. After his favourite daughter Lucy had died and he himself had very nearly followed her to the grave, Donne wrote his *Devotions upon Emergent Occasions* (1624), which contains the greatest of all exhortations to commiserate with the dead: 'Any man's *death* diminishes *me*, because I am involved in *Mankinde*; And therefore never send to know for whom the *bell* tolls; It tolls for *thee*.' Three years later, the death of a close friend inspired him to write 'A Nocturnal upon St Lucy's Day, Being the Shortest Day':

---

* Which he called 'the first English newspaper for which the word "news" lost its old meaning of facts which a reader ought to know ... and acquired the new meaning of facts, or fictions, which it might amuse him to read'.
† After he was briefly arrested for defying her father, she quipped: 'John Donne – Anne Donne – Un-done.' No wonder he loved her.

Study me then, you who shall lovers be
At the next world, that is, at the next spring;
  For I am every dead thing,
    In whom Love wrought new alchemy.
      For his art did express
A quintessence even from nothingness,
From dull privations, and lean emptiness;
He ruin'd me, and I am re-begot
Of absence, darkness, death – things which are not.

Everyone should read these lines who wants to understand better the human condition in the days when life expectancy was less than half what it is today.

The much greater power of death to cut people off in their prime not only made life seem precarious and filled it with grief. It also meant that most of the people who built the civilizations of the past were young when they made their contributions. The great Dutch-Jewish philosopher Baruch or Benedict Spinoza, who hypothesized that there is only a material universe of substance and deterministic causation, and that 'God' *is* that universe's natural order as we dimly apprehend it and nothing more, died in 1677 at the age of forty-four, probably from the particles of glass he had inhaled doing his day-job as a lens grinder. Blaise Pascal, the pioneer of probability theory and hydrodynamics and the author of the *Pensées*, the greatest of all apologias for the Christian faith, lived to be just thirty-nine; he would have died even younger had the road accident that reawakened his spiritual side been fatal. Who knows what other great works these geniuses might have brought forth had they been granted the lifespans enjoyed by, for example, the great humanists Erasmus (sixty-nine) and Montaigne (fifty-nine)? Mozart, composer of the most perfect of all operas, *Don Giovanni*, died when he was just thirty-five. Franz Schubert, composer of the sublime String Quintet in C (D956), succumbed, probably to syphilis, at the age of just thirty-one. Prolific though they were, what else might they have composed if they had been granted the sixty-three years enjoyed by the stolid Johannes Brahms or the even more exceptional seventy-two years allowed the ponderous Anton Bruckner? The Scots poet Robert Burns, who wrote the supreme expression of egalitarianism, 'A Man's a Man for A' That', was thirty-seven when he died in 1796. What injustice, that the poet who most despised inherited status ('The rank is but the guinea's stamp, / The Man's the gowd [gold] for a' that') should have been so much outlived by the poet who most revered it: Alfred, Lord Tennyson, who died bedecked with honours at the age of eighty-three. Palgrave's *Golden Treasury* would be the better for more Burns and less Tennyson. And how different would the art galleries of the world be today if the painstaking Jan Vermeer had lived to be ninety-one and the over-prolific Pablo Picasso had died at thirty-nine, instead of the other way round?

Politics, too, is an art – as much a part of our civilization as philosophy, opera, poetry or painting. But the greatest political artist in American history, Abraham Lincoln, served only one full term in the White House, falling victim to an assassin with a petty grudge just six weeks after his second inaugural address. He was fifty-six. How different would the era of Reconstruction have been had this self-made titan, born in a log cabin, the author of the majestic Gettysburg Address – which redefined the United States as 'a nation, conceived in liberty, and dedicated to the proposition that all men are created equal', with a 'government of the people, by the people, for the people' – lived as long as the polo-playing then polio-stricken grandee Franklin Delano Roosevelt, whom medical science kept alive long enough to serve nearly four full terms as president before his death at sixty-three?

Because our lives are so very different from the lives of most people in the past, not least in their probable duration, but also in our greater degree of physical comfort, we must exercise our imaginations quite vigorously to understand the men and women of the past. In his *Theory of Moral Sentiments*, written a century and half before Collingwood's memoir, the great economist and social theorist Adam Smith defined why a civilized society is not a war of all against all – because it is based on sympathy:

As we have no immediate experience of what other men feel, we can form no idea of the manner in which they are affected, but by conceiving what we ourselves should feel in the like situation. Though our brother is on the rack, as long as we ourselves are at our ease, our senses will never inform us of what he suffers. They never did, and never can, carry us beyond our own person, and it is by the imagination only that we can form any conception of what are his sensations. Neither can that faculty help us to this any other way, than by representing to us what would be our own, if we were in his case. It is the impressions of our own senses only, not those of his, which our imaginations copy. By the imagination, we place ourselves in his situation.

This, of course, is precisely what Collingwood says the historian should do, and it is what I want the reader to do as she encounters in these pages the resurrected thoughts of the dead. The key point of the book is to understand what made their civilization expand so spectacularly in its wealth, influence and power. But there can be no understanding without that sympathy which puts us, through an act of imagination, in their situation. That act will be all the more difficult when we come to resurrect the thoughts of the denizens of other civilizations – the ones the West subjugated or, at least, subordinated to itself. For they are equally important members of the drama's cast. This is not a history of the West but a history of the world, in which Western dominance is the phenomenon to be explained.

In an encyclopaedia entry he wrote in 1959, the French historian Fernand Braudel defined a civilization as:

first of all a space, a 'cultural area' ... a locus. With the locus ... you must picture a great variety of 'goods', of cultural characteristics, ranging from the form of its houses, the material of which they are built, their roofing, to skills like feathering arrows, to a dialect or group of dialects, to tastes in cooking, to a particular technology, a structure of beliefs, a way of making love, and even to the compass, paper, the printing press. It is the regular grouping, the frequency with which particular characteristics recur, their ubiquity within a precise area [combined with] ... some sort of temporal permanence ...

Braudel was better at delineating structures than explaining change, however. These days, it is often said that historians should tell stories; accordingly, this book offers a big story – a meta-narrative of why one civilization transcended the constraints that had bound all previous ones – and a great many smaller tales or micro-histories within it. Nevertheless the revival of the art of narrative is only part of what is needed. In addition to stories, it is also important that there be questions. 'Why did the West come to dominate the Rest?' is a question that demands something more than a just-so story in response. The answer needs to be analytical, it needs to be supported by evidence and it needs to be testable by means of the counterfactual question: if the crucial innovations I identify here had not existed, would the West have ruled the Rest anyway for some other reason that I have missed or under-emphasized? Or would the world have turned out quite differently, with China on top, or some other civilization? We should not delude ourselves into thinking that our historical narratives, as commonly constructed, are anything more than retro-fits. To contemporaries, as we shall see, the outcome of Western dominance did not seem the most probable of the futures they could imagine; the scenario of disastrous defeat often loomed larger in the mind of the historical actor than the happy ending vouchsafed to the modern reader. The reality of history as a lived experience is that it is much more like a chess match than a novel, much more like football game than a play.

It wasn't all good. No serious writer would claim that the reign of Western civilization was unblemished. Yet there are those who would insist that there was nothing whatever good about it. This position is absurd. As is true of all great civilizations, that of the West was Janus-faced: capable of nobility yet also capable of turpitude. Perhaps a better analogy is that the West resembled the two feuding brothers in James Hogg's *Private Memoirs and Confessions of a Justified Sinner* (1824) or in Robert Louis Stevenson's *Master of Ballantrae* (1889). Competition and monopoly; science and superstition; freedom and slavery; curing and killing; hard work and laziness – in each case, the West was father to both the good and the bad. It was just that, as in Hogg's or Stevenson's novel, the better of the two brothers ultimately came out on top. We must also resist the temptation to romanticize history's losers. The other civilizations overrun by the West's, or more peacefully transformed by it through borrowings as much as through impositions, were not without their defects either, of which the most obvious is that they were incapable of providing their inhabitants with any sustained improvement in the material quality of their lives. One difficulty is that we cannot always reconstruct the past thoughts of these non-Western peoples, for not all of them existed in civilizations with the means of recording and preserving thought. In the end, history is primarily the study of civilizations, because without written records the historian is thrown back on spearheads and pot fragments, from which much less can be inferred.

The French historian and statesman François Guizot said that the history of civilization is 'the biggest of all ... it comprises all the others'. It must transcend the multiple disciplinary boundaries erected by academics, with their compulsion to specialize, between economic, social, cultural, intellectual, political, military and international history. It must cover a great deal of time and space, because civilizations are not small or ephemeral. But a book like this cannot be an encyclopaedia. To those who will complain about what has been omitted, I can do no more than quote the idiosyncratic jazz pianist Thelonious Monk: 'Don't play everything (or every time); let some things go by ... What you don't play can be more important than what you do.' I agree. Many notes and chords have been omitted below. But they have been left out for a reason. Does the selection reflect the biases of a middle-aged Scotsman, the archetypal beneficiary of Western predominance? Very likely. But I cherish the hope that the selection will not be disapproved of by the most ardent and eloquent defenders of Western values today, whose ethnic origins are very different from mine – from Amartya Sen to Liu Xiaobo, from Hernando de Soto to the dedicatee of this book.

A book that aims to cover 600 years of world history is necessarily a collaborative venture and I owe thanks to many people. I am grateful to the staff at the following archives, libraries and institutions: the AGI Archive, the musée départemental Albert Kahn, the Bridgeman Art Library, the British Library, the Charleston Library Society, the Zhongguo guojia tushuguan (National Library of China) in Beijing, Corbis, the Institut Pasteur in Dakar, the Deutsches Historisches Museum in Berlin, the Geheimes Staatsarchiv Preussischer Kulturbesitz at Berlin-Dahlem, Getty Images, the Greenwich Observatory, the Heeresgeschichtliches Museum in Vienna, the Irish National Library, the Library of Congress, the Missouri History Museum, the musée du Chemin des Dames, the Museo de Oro in Lima, the National Archives in London, the National Maritime Museum, the Başbakanlık Osmanlı Arşivleri (Ottoman Archives) in Istanbul, PA Photos, the Peabody Museum of Archaeology and Ethnology at Harvard, the Archives Nationales du Sénégal in Dakar, the South Carolina Historical Society, the School of Oriental and African Studies, the Süleymaniye Manuscript Library and of course Harvard's incomparable Widener Library. It would be wrong not to add an additional line of thanks to Google, now an incomparable resource for speeding up historical research, as well as Questia and Wikipedia, which also make the historian's work easier.

I have had invaluable research assistance from Sarah Wallington, as well as from Daniel Lansberg-Rodriguez, Manny Rincon-Cruz, Jason Rockett and Jack Sun.

As usual, this is a Penguin book on both sides of the Atlantic, edited with customary skill and verve by Simon Winder in London and Ann Godoff in New York. The peerless Peter James did more than copy-edit the text. Thanks are also due to Richard Duguid, Rosie Glaisher, Stefan McGrath, John Makinson and Pen Vogler, and many others too numerous to mention.

Like four of my last five books, *Civilization* was from its earliest inception a television series as well as a book. At Channel 4 Ralph Lee has kept me from being abstruse or plain incomprehensible, with assistance from Simon Berthon. Neither series nor book could have been made without the extraordinary team of people assembled by Chimerica Media: Dewald Aukema, a prince among cinematographers, James Evans, our assistant producer for films 2 and 5, Alison McAllan, our archive researcher, Susannah Price, who produced film 4, James Runcie, who directed films 2 and 5, Vivienne Steel, our production manager, and Charlotte Wilkins, our assistant producer for films 3 and 4. A key role was also played in the early phase of the project by Joanna Potts. Chris Openshaw, Max Hug Williams, Grant Lawson and Harrik Maury deftly handled the filming in England and France. With their patience and generosity towards the author, my fellow Chimericans Melanie Fall and Adrian Pennink have ensured that we remain a pretty good advertisement for the triumvirate as a form of government. My friend Chris Wilson once again ensured that I missed no planes.

Among the many people who helped us film the series, a number of fixers also helped with the research that went into the book. My thanks go to Manfred Anderson, Khadidiatou Ba, Lillian Chen, Tereza Horska, Petr Janda, Wolfgang Knoepfler, Deborah McLauchlan, Matias de Sa Moreira, Daisy Newton-Dunn, José Couto Nogueira, Levent Öztekin and Ernst Vogl.

I would also like to thank the many people I interviewed as we roamed the world, in particular Gonzalo de Aliaga, Nihal Bengisu Karaca, Pastor John Lindell, Mick Rawson, Ryan Squibb, Ivan Touška, Stefan Wolle, Hanping Zhang and – last but by no means least – the pupils at Robert Clack School, Dagenham.

I am extremely fortunate to have in Andrew Wylie the best literary agent in the world and in Sue Ayton his counterpart in the realm of British television. My thanks also go to Scott Moyers, James Pullen and all the other staff in the London and New York offices of the Wylie Agency.

A number of eminent historians generously read all or part of the manuscript in draft, as did a number of friends as well as former and current students: Rawi Abdelal, Ayaan Hirsi Ali, Bryan Averbuch, Pierpaolo Barbieri, Jeremy Catto, J. C. D. Clark, James Esdaile, Campbell Ferguson, Martin Jacques, Harold James, Maya Jasanoff, Joanna Lewis, Charles Maier, Hassan Malik, Noel Maurer, Ian Morris, Charles Murray, Aldo Musacchio, Glen O'Hara, Steven Pinker, Ken Rogoff, Emma Rothschild, Alex Watson, Arne Westad, John Wong and Jeremy Yellen. Thanks are also due to Philip Hoffman, Andrew Roberts and Robert Wilkinson. All surviving errors are my fault alone.

At Oxford University I would like to thank the Principal and Fellows of Jesus College, their counterparts at Oriel College and the librarians of the Bodleian. At the Hoover Institution, Stanford, I owe debts to John Raisian, the Director, and his excellent staff. This book has been finished at the London School of Economics IDEAS centre, where I have been very well looked after as the Philippe Roman Professor for the academic year 2010–11. My biggest debts, however, are to my colleagues at Harvard. It would take too long to thank every member of the Harvard History Department individually, so let me confine myself to a collective thank-you: this is not a book I could have written without your collegial support, encouragement and intellectual inspiration. The same goes for my colleagues at Harvard Business School, particularly the members of the Business and Government in the International Economy Unit, as well as for the faculty and staff at the Centre of European Studies. Thanks are also due to my friends at the Weatherhead Centre for International Affairs, the Belfer Centre for Science and International Affairs, the Workshop in Economic History and Lowell House. But most of all I thank all my students on both sides of the Charles River, particularly those in my General Education class, Societies of the World 19. This book started life in your presence, and greatly benefited from your papers and feedback.

Finally, I offer my deepest thanks to my family, particularly my parents and my oft-neglected children, Felix, Freya and Lachlan, not forgetting their mother Susan and our extended kinship group. In many ways, I have written this book for you, children.

It is dedicated, however, to someone who understands better than anyone I know what Western civilization really means – and what it still has to offer the world.

London   December 2010

Introduction: Rasselas's Question

> He would not admit *civilization* [to the fourth edition of his dictionary], but only *civility*. With great deference to him, I thought *civilization*, from *to civilize*, better in the sense opposed to *barbarity*, than *civility*.
>
> James Boswell

> All definitions of civilization ... belong to a conjugation which goes: 'I am civilized, you belong to a culture, he is a barbarian.'
>
> Felipe Fernández-Armesto

When Kenneth Clark defined civilization in his television series of that name, he left viewers in no doubt that he meant the civilization of the West – and primarily the art and architecture of Western Europe from the Middle Ages until the nineteenth century. The first of the thirteen films he made for the BBC was politely but firmly dismissive of Byzantine Ravenna, the Celtic Hebrides, Viking Norway and even Charlemagne's Aachen. The Dark Ages between the fall of Rome and the twelfth-century Renaissance simply did not qualify as civilization in Clark's sense of the word. That only revived with the building of Chartres cathedral, dedicated though not completed in 1260, and was showing signs of fatigue with the Manhattan skyscrapers of his own time.

Clark's hugely successful series, which was first broadcast in Britain when I was five years old, defined civilization for a generation in the English-speaking world. Civilization was the chateaux of the

Loire. It was the palazzi of Florence. It was the Sistine Chapel. It was Versailles. From the sober interiors of the Dutch Republic to the ebullient façades of the baroque, Clark played to his strength as an historian of art. Music and literature made their appearances; politics and even economics occasionally peeked in. But the essence of Clark's civilization was clearly High Visual Culture. His heroes were Michelangelo, da Vinci, Dürer, Constable, Turner, Delacroix.[1]

In fairness to Clark, his series was subtitled *A Personal View*. And he was not unaware of the implication – problematic already in 1969 – that 'the pre-Christian era and the East' were in some sense *un*civilized. Nevertheless, with the passage of four decades, it has become steadily harder to live with Clark's view, personal or otherwise (to say nothing of his now slightly grating *de haut en bas* manner). In this book I take a broader, more comparative view, and I aim to be more down and dirty than high and mighty. My idea of civilization is as much about sewage pipes as flying buttresses, if not more so, because without efficient public plumbing cities are death-traps, turning rivers and wells into havens for the bacterium *Vibrio cholerae*. I am, unapologetically, as interested in the price of a work of art as in its cultural value. To my mind, a civilization is much more than just the contents of a few first-rate art galleries. It is a highly complex human organization. Its paintings, statues and buildings may well be its most eye-catching achievements, but they are unintelligible without some understanding of the economic, social and political institutions which devised them, paid for them, executed them – and preserved them for our gaze.

'Civilisation' is a French word, first used by the French economist Anne-Robert-Jacques Turgot in 1752, and first published by Victor Riqueti, marquis de Mirabeau, father of the great revolutionary, four years later.[2] Samuel Johnson, as the first epigraph to this Introduction makes clear, would not accept the neologism, preferring 'civility'. If barbarism had an antonym for Johnson, it was the polite (though sometimes also downright rude) urban life he enjoyed so much in London. A civilization, as the etymology of the word suggests, revolves around its cities, and in many ways it is cities that are the heroes of this book.[3] But a city's laws (civil or otherwise) are as important as its walls; its constitution and customs – its inhabitants' manners (civil or otherwise) – as important as its palaces.[4] Civilization is as much about scientists' laboratories as it is about artists' garrets. It is as much about forms of land tenure as it is about landscapes. The success of a civilization is measured not just in its aesthetic achievements but also, and surely more importantly, in the duration and quality of life of its citizens. And that quality of life has many dimensions, not all easily quantified. We may be able to estimate the per-capita income of people around the world in the fifteenth century, or their average life expectancy at birth. But what about their comfort? Cleanliness? Happiness? How many garments did they own? How many hours did they have to work? What food could they buy with their wages? Artworks by themselves can offer hints, but they cannot answer such questions.

Clearly, however, one city does not make a civilization. A civilization is the single largest unit of human organization, higher though more amorphous than even an empire. Civilizations are partly a practical response by human populations to their environments – the challenges of feeding, watering, sheltering and defending themselves – but they are also cultural in character; often, though not always, religious; often, though not always, communities of language.[5] They are few, but not far between. Carroll Quigley counted two dozen in the last ten millennia.[6] In the pre-modern world, Adda Bozeman saw just five: the West, India, China, Byzantium and Islam.[7] Matthew Melko made the total twelve, seven of which have vanished (Mesopotamian, Egyptian, Cretan, Classical, Byzantine, Middle American, Andean) and five of which still remain (Chinese, Japanese, Indian, Islamic, Western).[8] Shmuel Eisenstadt counted six by adding Jewish civilization to the club.[9] The interaction of these few civilizations with one another, as much as with their own environments, has been among the most important drivers of historical change.[10] The striking thing about these interactions is that authentic civilizations seem to remain true unto themselves for very long periods, despite outside influences. As Fernand Braudel put it: 'Civilization is in fact the longest story of all ... A civilization ... can persist through a series of economies or societies.'[11]

If, in the year 1411, you had been able to circumnavigate the globe, you would probably have been most impressed by the quality of life in Oriental civilizations. The Forbidden City was under construction in Ming Beijing, while work had begun on reopening and improving the Grand Canal; in the Near East, the Ottomans were closing in on Constantinople, which they would finally capture in 1453. The Byzantine Empire was breathing its last. The death of the warlord Timur (Tamerlane) in 1405 had removed the recurrent threat of murderous invading hordes from Central Asia – the antithesis of civilization. For the Yongle Emperor in China and the Ottoman Sultan Murad II, the future was bright.

By contrast, Western Europe in 1411 would have struck you as a miserable backwater, recuperating from the ravages of the Black Death – which had reduced population by as much as half as it swept eastwards between 1347 and 1351 – and still plagued by bad sanitation and seemingly incessant war. In England the leper king Henry IV was on the throne, having successfully overthrown and murdered the ill-starred Richard II. France was in the grip of internecine warfare between the followers of the Duke of Burgundy and those of the assassinated Duke of Orléans. The Anglo-French Hundred Years' War was just about to resume. The other quarrelsome kingdoms of Western Europe – Aragon, Castile, Navarre, Portugal and Scotland – would have seemed little better. A Muslim still ruled in Granada. The Scottish King, James I, was a prisoner in England, having been captured by English pirates. The most prosperous parts of Europe were in fact the North Italian city-states: Florence, Genoa, Pisa, Siena and Venice. As for fifteenth-century North America, it was an anarchic wilderness compared with the realms of the Aztecs, Mayas and Incas in Central and South America, with their towering temples and skyscraping roads. By the end of your world tour, the notion that the West might come to dominate the Rest for most of the next half-millennium would have come to seem wildly fanciful.

And yet it happened.

For some reason, beginning in the late fifteenth century, the little states of Western Europe, with their bastardized linguistic borrowings from Latin (and a little Greek), their religion derived from the teachings of a Jew from Nazareth and their intellectual debts to Oriental mathematics, astronomy and technology, produced a civilization capable not only of conquering the great Oriental empires and subjugating

Africa, the Americas and Australasia, but also of converting peoples all over the world to the Western way of life – a conversion achieved ultimately more by the word than by the sword.

There are those who dispute that, claiming that all civilizations are in some sense equal, and that the West cannot claim superiority over, say, the East of Eurasia.[12] But such relativism is demonstrably absurd. No previous civilization had ever achieved such dominance as the West achieved over the Rest.[13] In 1500 the future imperial powers of Europe accounted for about 10 per cent of the world's land surface and at most 16 per cent of its population. By 1913, eleven Western empires* controlled nearly three-fifths of all territory and population and more than three-quarters (a staggering 79 per cent) of global economic output.[14] Average life expectancy in England was nearly twice what it was in India. Higher living standards in the West were also reflected in a better diet, even for agricultural labourers, and taller stature, even for ordinary soldiers and convicts.[15] Civilization, as we have seen, is about cities. By this measure, too, the West had come out on top. In 1500, as far as we can work out, the biggest city in the world was Beijing, with a population of between 600,000 and 700,000. Of the ten largest cities in the world by that time only one – Paris – was European, and its population numbered fewer than 200,000. London had perhaps 50,000 inhabitants. Urbanization rates were also higher in North Africa and South America than in Europe. Yet by 1900 there had been an astonishing reversal. Only one of the world's ten largest cities at that time was Asian and that was Tokyo. With a population of around 6.5 million, London was the global megalopolis.[16] Nor did Western dominance end with the decline and fall of the European empires. The rise of the United States saw the gap between West and East widen still further. By 1990 the average American was seventy-three times richer than the average Chinese.[17]

Moreover, it became clear in the second half of the twentieth century that the only way to close that yawning gap in income was for Eastern societies to follow Japan's example in adopting some (though

---

* The eleven were Austria, Belgium, France, Germany, Italy, Netherlands, Portugal, Spain, Russia, the United Kingdom and the United States. Of these only France, Portugal and Spain existed in 1500 in anything resembling their early twentieth-century form. For Russia's claim to be considered a part of the West, see below.

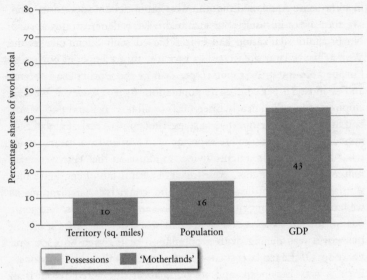

Western Future Empires, 1500

Possessions | 'Motherlands'

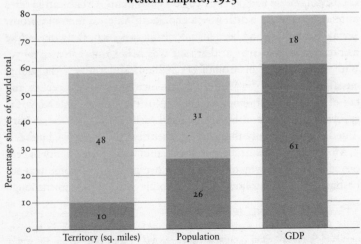

Western Empires, 1913

not all) of the West's institutions and modes of operation. As a result, Western civilization became a kind of template for the way the rest of the world aspired to organize itself. Prior to 1945, of course, there was a variety of developmental models – or operating systems, to draw a metaphor from computing – that could be adopted by non-Western societies. But the most attractive were all of European origin: liberal capitalism, national socialism, Soviet communism. The Second World War killed the second in Europe, though it lived on under assumed names in many developing countries. The collapse of the Soviet empire between 1989 and 1991 killed the third.

To be sure, there has been much talk in the wake of the global financial crisis about alternative Asian economic models. But not even the most ardent cultural relativist is recommending a return to the institutions of the Ming dynasty or the Mughals. The current debate between the proponents of free markets and those of state intervention is, at root, a debate between identifiably Western schools of thought: the followers of Adam Smith and those of John Maynard Keynes, with a few die-hard devotees of Karl Marx still plugging away. The birthplaces of all three speak for themselves: Kirkcaldy, Cambridge, Trier. In practice, most of the world is now integrated into a Western economic system in which, as Smith recommended, the market sets most of the prices and determines the flow of trade and division of labour, but government plays a role closer to the one envisaged by Keynes, intervening to try to smooth the business cycle and reduce income inequality.

As for non-economic institutions, there is no debate worth having. All over the world, universities are converging on Western norms. The same is true of the way medical science is organized, from rarefied research all the way through to front-line healthcare. Most people now accept the great scientific truths revealed by Newton, Darwin and Einstein and, even if they do not, they still reach eagerly for the products of Western pharmacology at the first symptom of influenza or bronchitis. Only a few societies continue to resist the encroachment of Western patterns of marketing and consumption, as well as the Western lifestyle itself. More and more human beings eat a Western diet, wear Western clothes and live in Western housing. Even the peculiarly Western way of work – five or six days a week from 9 until 5, with two or three weeks of holiday – is becoming a kind of universal standard. Meanwhile, the religion that Western missionaries sought to export to the rest of the world is followed by a third of mankind – as well as making remarkable gains in the world's most populous country. Even the atheism pioneered in the West is making impressive headway.

With every passing year, more and more human beings shop like us, study like us, stay healthy (or unhealthy) like us and pray (or don't pray) like us. Burgers, Bunsen burners, Band-Aids, baseball caps and Bibles: you cannot easily get away from them, wherever you may go. Only in the realm of political institutions does there remain significant global diversity, with a wide range of governments around the world resisting the idea of the rule of law, with its protection of individual rights, as the foundation for meaningful representative government. It is as much as a political ideology as a religion that a militant Islam seeks to resist the advance of the late twentieth-century Western norms of gender equality and sexual freedom.[18]

So it is not 'Eurocentrism' or (anti-)'Orientalism' to say that the rise of Western civilization is the single most important historical phenomenon of the second half of the second millennium after Christ. It is a statement of the obvious. The challenge is to explain how it happened. What was it about the civilization of Western Europe after the fifteenth century that allowed it to trump the outwardly superior empires of the Orient? Clearly, it was something more than the beauty of the Sistine Chapel.

The facile, if not tautological, answer to the question is that the West dominated the Rest because of imperialism.[19] There are still many people today who can work themselves up into a state of high moral indignation over the misdeeds of the European empires. Misdeeds there certainly were, and they are not absent from these pages. It is also clear that different forms of colonization – settlement versus extraction – had very different long-term impacts.[20] But empire is not a historically sufficient explanation of Western predominance. There were empires long before the imperialism denounced by the Marxist-Leninists. Indeed, the sixteenth century saw a number of Asian empires increase significantly in their power and extent. Meanwhile, after the failure of Charles V's project of a grand Habsburg empire stretching from Spain through the Low Countries to Germany, Europe grew more fragmented than ever. The Reformation unleashed more than a century of European wars of religion.

A sixteenth-century traveller could hardly have failed to notice the contrast. In addition to covering Anatolia, Egypt, Arabia, Mesopotamia and Yemen, the Ottoman Empire under Suleiman the Magnificent (1520–66) extended into the Balkans and Hungary, menacing the gates of Vienna in 1529. Further east, the Safavid Empire under Abbas I (1587–1629) stretched all the way from Isfahan and Tabriz to Kandahar, while Northern India from Delhi to Bengal was ruled by the mighty Mughal Emperor Akbar (1556–1605). Ming China, too, seemed serene and secure behind the Great Wall. Few European visitors to the court of the Wanli Emperor (1572–1620) can have anticipated the fall of his dynasty less than three decades after his death. Writing from Istanbul in the late 1550s, the Flemish diplomat Ogier Ghiselin de Busbecq – the man who transplanted tulips from Turkey to the Netherlands – nervously compared Europe's fractured state with the 'vast wealth' of the Ottoman Empire.

True, the sixteenth century was a time of hectic European activity overseas. But to the great Oriental empires the Portuguese and Dutch seafarers seemed the very opposite of bearers of civilization; they were merely the latest barbarians to menace the Middle Kingdom, if anything more loathsome – and certainly more malodorous – than the pirates of Japan. And what else attracted Europeans to Asia but the superior quality of Indian textiles and Chinese porcelain?

As late as 1683, an Ottoman army could march to the gates of Vienna – the capital of the Habsburg Empire – and demand that the city's population surrender and convert to Islam. It was only after the raising of the siege that Christendom could begin slowly rolling back Ottoman power in Central and Eastern Europe through the Balkans towards the Bosphorus, and it took many years before any European empire could match the achievements of Oriental imperialism. The 'great divergence' between the West and the Rest was even slower to materialize elsewhere. The material gap between North and South America was not firmly established until well into the nineteenth century, and most of Africa was not subjugated by Europeans beyond a few coastal strips until the early twentieth.

If Western ascendancy cannot therefore be explained in the tired old terms of imperialism, was it simply – as some scholars maintain – a matter of good luck? Was it the geography or the climate of the western end of Eurasia that made the great divergence happen? Were the Europeans just fortunate to stumble across the islands of the Caribbean, so ideally suited to the cultivation of calorie-rich sugar? Did the New World provide Europe with 'ghost acres' that China lacked? And was it just sod's law that made China's coal deposits harder to mine and transport than Europe's?[21] Or was China in some sense a victim of its own success – stuck in a 'high-level equilibrium trap' by the ability of its cultivators to provide a vast number of people with just enough calories to live?[22] Can it really be that England became the first industrial nation mainly because bad sanitation and disease kept life exceptionally short for the majority of people, giving the rich and enterprising minority a better chance to pass on their genes?[23]

The immortal English lexicographer Samuel Johnson rejected all such contingent explanations for Western ascendancy. In his *History of Rasselas: Prince of Abissinia*, published in 1759, he has Rasselas ask:

> By what means . . . are the Europeans thus powerful? or why, since they can so easily visit Asia and Africa for trade or conquest, cannot the Asiaticks and Africans invade their coasts, plant colonies in their ports, and give laws to their natural princes? The same wind that carries them back would bring us thither.*

To which the philosopher Imlac replies:

> They are more powerful, Sir, than we, because they are wiser; knowledge will always predominate over ignorance, as man governs the other animals. But why their knowledge is more than ours, I know not what reason can be given, but the unsearchable will of the Supreme Being.[24]

Knowledge is indeed power if it provides superior ways of sailing ships, digging up minerals, firing guns and curing sickness. But is it in

---

* This question was indeed being posed in non-Western empires in the eighteenth century. In 1731 the Ottoman writer İbrahim Müteferrika asked: 'Why do Christian nations, which were so weak in the past compared with Muslim nations, begin to dominate so many lands in modern times and even defeat the once victorious Ottoman armies?'

fact the case that Europeans were more knowledgeable than other people? Perhaps by 1759 they were; scientific innovation for around two and a half centuries after 1650 was almost exclusively Western in origin.[25] But in 1500? As we shall see, Chinese technology, Indian mathematics and Arab astronomy had been far ahead for centuries.

Was it therefore a more nebulous cultural difference that equipped Europeans to leap ahead of their Oriental counterparts? That was the argument made by the German sociologist Max Weber. It comes in many variants – medieval English individualism, humanism and the Protestant ethic – and it has been sought everywhere from the wills of English farmers to the account books of Mediterranean merchants and the rules of etiquette of royal courts. In *The Wealth and Poverty of Nations*, David Landes made the cultural case by arguing that Western Europe led the world in developing autonomous intellectual inquiry, the scientific method of verification and the rationalization of research and its diffusion. Yet even he allowed that something more was required for that mode of operation to flourish: financial intermediaries and good government.[26] The key, it becomes ever more apparent, lies with institutions.

Institutions are, of course, in some sense the products of culture. But, because they formalize a set of norms, institutions are often the things that keep a culture honest, determining how far it is conducive to good behaviour rather than bad. To illustrate the point, the twentieth century ran a series of experiments, imposing quite different institutions on two sets of Germans (in West and East), two sets of Koreans (in North and South) and two sets of Chinese (inside and outside the People's Republic). The results were very striking and the lesson crystal clear. If you take the same people, with more or less the same culture, and impose communist institutions on one group and capitalist institutions on another, almost immediately there will be a divergence in the way they behave.

Many historians today would agree that there were few really profound differences between the eastern and western ends of Eurasia in the 1500s. Both regions were early adopters of agriculture, market-based exchange and urban-centred state structures.[27] But there was one crucial institutional difference. In China a monolithic empire had been consolidated, while Europe remained politically fragmented. In *Guns,*

Germs and Steel, Jared Diamond explained why Eurasia had advanced ahead of the rest of the world.[28] But not until his essay 'How to Get Rich' (1999) did he offer an answer to the question of why one end of Eurasia forged so far ahead of the other. The answer was that, in the plains of Eastern Eurasia, monolithic Oriental empires stifled innovation, while in mountainous, river-divided Western Eurasia, multiple monarchies and city-states engaged in creative competition and communication.[29]

It is an appealing answer. And yet it cannot be a sufficient one. Look only at the two series of engravings entitled *Miseries of War*, published by the Lorraine artist Jacques Callot in the 1630s as if to warn the rest of the world of the dangers of religious conflict. The competition between and within Europe's petty states in the first half of the seventeenth century was disastrous, depopulating large tracts of Central Europe as well as plunging the British Isles into more than a century of recurrent, debilitating strife. Political fragmentation often has that effect. If you doubt it, ask the inhabitants of the former Yugoslavia. Competition is certainly a part of the story of Western ascendancy, as we shall see in Chapter 1 – but only a part.

In this book I want to show that what distinguished the West from the Rest – the mainsprings of global power – were six identifiably novel complexes of institutions and associated ideas and behaviours. For the sake of simplicity, I summarize them under six headings:

1. Competition
2. Science
3. Property rights
4. Medicine
5. The consumer society
6. The work ethic

To use the language of today's computerized, synchronized world, these were the six killer applications – the killer apps – that allowed a minority of mankind originating on the western edge of Eurasia to dominate the world for the better part of 500 years.

Now, before you indignantly write to me objecting that I have missed out some crucial aspect of Western ascendancy, such as capitalism or freedom or democracy (or for that matter guns, germs and steel), please read the following brief definitions:

1. Competition – a decentralization of both political and economic life, which created the launch-pad for both nation-states and capitalism
2. Science – a way of studying, understanding and ultimately changing the natural world, which gave the West (among other things) a major military advantage over the Rest
3. Property rights – the rule of law as a means of protecting private owners and peacefully resolving disputes between them, which formed the basis for the most stable form of representative government
4. Medicine – a branch of science that allowed a major improvement in health and life expectancy, beginning in Western societies, but also in their colonies
5. The consumer society – a mode of material living in which the production and purchase of clothing and other consumer goods play a central economic role, and without which the Industrial Revolution would have been unsustainable
6. The work ethic – a moral framework and mode of activity derivable from (among other sources) Protestant Christianity, which provides the glue for the dynamic and potentially unstable society created by apps 1 to 5

Make no mistake: this is not another self-satisfied version of 'The Triumph of the West'.[30] I want to show that it was not just Western superiority that led to the conquest and colonization of so much of the rest of the world; it was also the fortuitous weakness of the West's rivals. In the 1640s, for example, a combination of fiscal and monetary crisis, climate change and epidemic disease unleashed rebellion and the final crisis of the Ming dynasty. This had nothing to do with the West. Likewise, the political and military decline of the Ottoman Empire was internally driven more than it was externally imposed. North American political institutions flourished as South America's festered; but Simón Bolívar's failure to create a United States of Latin America was not the gringo's fault.

The critical point is that the differential between the West and the

Rest was institutional. Western Europe overtook China partly because in the West there was more competition in both the political and the economic spheres. Austria, Prussia and latterly even Russia became more effective administratively and militarily because the network that produced the Scientific Revolution arose in the Christian but not in the Muslim world. The reason North America's ex-colonies did so much better than South America's was because British settlers established a completely different system of property rights and political representation in the North from those built by Spaniards and Portuguese in the South. (The North was an 'open access order', rather than a closed one run in the interests of rent-seeking, exclusive elites.)[31] European empires were able to penetrate Africa not just because they had the Maxim gun; they also devised vaccines against tropical diseases to which Africans were just as vulnerable.

In the same way, the earlier industrialization of the West reflected institutional advantages: the possibility of a mass consumer society existed in the British Isles well before the advent and spread of steam power or the factory system. Even after industrial technology was almost universally available, the differential between the West and the Rest persisted; indeed, it grew wider. With wholly standardized cotton-spinning and weaving machinery, the European or North American worker was still able to work more productively, and his capitalist employer to accumulate wealth more rapidly, than their Oriental counterparts.[32] Investment in public health and public education paid big dividends; where there was none, people stayed poor.[33] This book is about all these differences – why they existed and why they mattered so much.

Thus far I have used words like 'West' and 'Western' more or less casually. But what exactly – or where – do I mean by 'Western civilization'? Post-war White Anglo-Saxon Protestant males used more or less instinctively to locate the West (also known as 'the free world') in a relatively narrow corridor extending (certainly) from London to Lexington, Massachusetts, and (possibly) from Strasbourg to San Francisco. In 1945, fresh from the battlefields, the West's first language was English, followed by halting French. With the success of European integration in the 1950s and 1960s, the Western club grew larger. Few would now dispute that the Low Countries, France, Germany, Italy,

Portugal, Scandinavia and Spain all belong to the West, while Greece is an *ex officio* member, despite its later allegiance to Orthodox Christianity, thanks to our enduring debt to ancient Hellenic philosophy and the Greeks' more recent debts to the European Union.

But what about the rest of the Southern and Eastern Mediterranean, encompassing not just the Balkans north of the Peloponnese, but also North Africa and Anatolia? What about Egypt and Mesopotamia, the seedbeds of the very first civilizations? Is South America – colonized by Europeans as surely as was North America, and geographically in the same hemisphere – part of the West? And what of Russia? Is European Russia truly Occidental, but Russia beyond the Urals in some sense part of the Orient? Throughout the Cold War, the Soviet Union and its satellites were referred to as 'the Eastern bloc'. But there is surely a case for saying that the Soviet Union was as much a product of Western civilization as the United States. Its core ideology had much the same Victorian provenance as nationalism, anti-slavery and women's suffrage – it was born and bred in the old circular Reading Room of the British Library. And its geographical extent was no less the product of European expansion and colonization than the settlement of the Americas. In Central Asia, as in South America, Europeans ruled over non-Europeans. In that sense, what happened in 1991 was simply the death of the last European empire. Yet the most influential recent definition of Western civilization, by Samuel Huntington, excludes not just Russia but all countries with a religious tradition of Orthodoxy. Huntington's West consists only of Western and Central Europe (excluding the Orthodox East), North America (excluding Mexico) and Australasia. Greece, Israel, Romania and Ukraine do not make the cut; nor do the Caribbean islands, despite the fact that many are as Western as Florida.[34]

'The West', then, is much more than just a geographical expression. It is a set of norms, behaviours and institutions with borders that are blurred in the extreme. The implications of that are worth pondering. Might it in fact be possible for an Asian society to become Western if it embraces Western norms of dressing and doing business, as Japan did from the Meiji era, and as much of the rest of Asia now seems to be doing? It was once fashionable to insist that the capitalist 'world-system' imposed a permanent division of labour between the

Western core and the Rest's periphery.[35] But what if the whole world eventually ends up being Westernized, in appearance and lifestyle at least? Or could it be that the other civilizations are, as Huntington famously argued, more resilient – particularly 'Sinic' civilization, meaning Greater China,* and Islam, with its 'bloody borders and innards'?[36] How far is their adoption of Western modes of operation merely a superficial modernization without any cultural depth? These are questions that will be addressed below.

Another puzzle about Western civilization is that disunity appears to be one of its defining characteristics. In the early 2000s many American commentators complained about the 'widening Atlantic' – the breakdown of those common values that bound the United States together with its West European allies during the Cold War.[37] If it has become slightly clearer than it was when Henry Kissinger was secretary of state whom an American statesman should call when he wants to speak to Europe, it has become harder to say who picks up the phone on behalf of Western civilization. Yet the current division between America and 'Old Europe' is mild and amicable compared with the great schisms of the past, over religion, over ideology – and even over the meaning of civilization itself. During the First World War, the Germans claimed to be fighting the war for a higher *Kultur* and against tawdry, materialistic Anglo-French *civilisation* (the distinction was drawn by Thomas Mann and Sigmund Freud, among others). But this distinction was hard to reconcile with the burning of the Leuven University library and the summary executions of Belgian civilians in the first phase of the war. British propagandists retorted by defining the Germans as 'Huns' – barbarians beyond the Pale of civilization – and named the war itself 'The Great War for Civilization' on their Victory medal.[38] Is it any more meaningful to talk today about 'the West' as a unitary civilization than it was in 1918?

Finally, it is worth remembering that Western civilization has declined and fallen once before. The Roman ruins scattered all over Europe, North Africa and the Near East serve as potent reminders of

* It is an idiosyncratic notion that one of the world's most venerable civilizations should have a name that no one but a political theorist has ever heard of. In his original 1993 essay, Huntington used 'Confucian'.

that. The first version of the West – Western Civilization 1.0 – arose in the so-called Fertile Crescent stretching from the Nile Valley to the confluence of the Euphrates and the Tigris, and reached its twin peaks with Athenian democracy and the Roman Empire.[39] Key elements of our civilization today – not only democracy but also athletics, arithmetic, civil law, geometry, the classical style of architecture and a substantial proportion of the words in modern English – had their origins in the ancient West. In its heyday, the Roman Empire was a startlingly sophisticated system. Grain, manufactures and coins circulated in an economy that stretched from the north of England to the upper reaches of the Nile, scholarship flourished, there was law, medicine and even shopping malls like Trajan's Forum in Rome. But that version of Western civilization declined and then fell with dramatic speed in the fifth century AD, undone by barbarian invasions and internal divisions. In the space of a generation, the vast imperial metropolis of Rome fell into disrepair, the aqueducts broken, the splendid market places deserted. The knowledge of the classical West would have been lost altogether, but for the librarians of Byzantium,[40] the monks of Ireland[41] and the popes and priests of the Roman Catholic Church – not forgetting the Abbasid caliphs.[42] Without their stewardship, the civilization of the West could not have been reborn as it was in the Italy of the Renaissance.

Is decline and fall the looming fate of Western Civilization 2.0? In demographic terms, the population of Western societies has long represented a minority of the world's inhabitants, but today it is clearly a dwindling one. Once so dominant, the economies of the United States and Europe are now facing the real prospect of being overtaken by China within twenty or even ten years, with Brazil and India not so very far behind. Western 'hard power' seems to be struggling in the Greater Middle East, from Iraq to Afghanistan, just as the 'Washington Consensus' on free-market economic policy disintegrates. The financial crisis that began in 2007 also seems to indicate a fundamental flaw at the heart of the consumer society, with its emphasis on debt-propelled retail therapy. The Protestant ethic of thrift that once seemed so central to the Western project has all but vanished. Meanwhile, Western elites are beset by almost millenarian fears of a coming environmental apocalypse.

What is more, Western civilization appears to have lost confidence in itself. Beginning with Stanford in 1963, a succession of major universities have ceased to offer the classic 'Western Civ.' history course to their undergraduates. In schools, too, the grand narrative of Western ascent has fallen out of fashion. Thanks to an educationalists' fad that elevated 'historical skills' above knowledge in the name of 'New History' – combined with the unintended consequences of the curriculum-reform process – too many British schoolchildren leave secondary school knowing only unconnected fragments of Western history: Henry VIII and Hitler, with a small dose of Martin Luther King, Jr. A survey of first-year History undergraduates at one leading British university revealed that only 34 per cent knew who was the English monarch at the time of the Armada, 31 per cent knew the location of the Boer War, 16 per cent knew who commanded the British forces at Waterloo (more than twice that proportion thought it was Nelson rather than Wellington) and 11 per cent could name a single nineteenth-century British prime minister.[43] In a similar poll of English children aged between eleven and eighteen, 17 per cent thought Oliver Cromwell fought at the Battle of Hastings and 25 per cent put the First World War in the wrong century.[44] Throughout the English-speaking world, moreover, the argument has gained ground that it is other cultures we should study, not our own. The musical sampler sent into outer space with the *Voyager* spacecraft in 1977 featured twenty-seven tracks, only ten of them from Western composers, including not only Bach, Mozart and Beethoven but also Louis Armstrong, Chuck Berry and Blind Willie Johnson. A history of the world 'in 100 objects', published by the Director of the British Museum in 2010, included no more than thirty products of Western civilization.[45]

Yet any history of the world's civilizations that underplays the degree of their gradual subordination to the West after 1500 is missing the essential point – the thing most in need of explanation. The rise of the West is, quite simply, the pre-eminent historical phenomenon of the second half of the second millennium after Christ. It is the story at the very heart of modern history. It is perhaps the most challenging riddle historians have to solve. And we should solve it not merely to satisfy our curiosity. For it is only by identifying the true causes of Western ascendancy that we can hope to estimate with any degree of accuracy the imminence of our decline and fall.

I

Competition

China seems to have been long stationary, and had probably long ago acquired that full complement of riches which is consistent with the nature of its laws and institutions. But this complement may be much inferior to what, with other laws and institutions, the nature of its soil, climate, and situation might admit of. A country which neglects or despises foreign commerce, and which admits the vessels of foreign nations into one or two of its ports only, cannot transact the same quantity of business which it might do with different laws and institutions . . . A more extensive foreign trade . . . could scarce fail to increase very much the manufactures of China, and to improve very much the productive powers of its manufacturing industry. By a more extensive navigation, the Chinese would naturally learn the art of using and constructing themselves all the different machines made use of in other countries, as well as the other improvements of art and industry which are practised in all the different parts of the world.

Adam Smith

Why are they small and yet strong? Why are we large and yet weak? . . . What we have to learn from the barbarians is only . . . solid ships and effective guns.

Feng Guifen

TWO RIVERS

The Forbidden City (Gugong) was built in the heart of Beijing by more than a million workers, using materials from all over the Chinese Empire. With nearly a thousand buildings arranged, constructed and decorated to symbolize the might of the Ming dynasty, the Forbidden City is not only a relic of what was once the greatest civilization in the world; it is also a reminder that no civilization lasts for ever. As late as 1776 Adam Smith could still refer to China as 'one of the richest, that is, one of the most fertile, best cultivated, most industrious, and most populous countries in the world ... a much richer country than any part of Europe'. Yet Smith also identified China as 'long stationary' or 'standing still'.[1] In this he was surely right. Within less than a century of the Forbidden City's construction between 1406 and 1420, the relative decline of the East may be said to have begun. The impoverished, strife-torn petty states of Western Europe embarked on half a millennium of almost unstoppable expansion. The great empires of the Orient meanwhile stagnated and latterly succumbed to Western dominance.

Why did China founder while Europe forged ahead? Smith's main answer was that the Chinese had failed to 'encourage foreign commerce', and had therefore missed out on the benefits of comparative advantage and the international division of labour. But other explanations were possible. Writing in the 1740s, Charles de Secondat, baron de Montesquieu, blamed the 'settled plan of tyranny', which he traced back to China's exceptionally large population, which in turn was due to the East Asian weather:

> I reason thus: Asia has properly no temperate zone, as the places situated in a very cold climate immediately touch upon those which are exceedingly hot, that is, Turkey, Persia, India, China, Korea, and Japan. In Europe, on the contrary, the temperate zone is very extensive ... it thence follows that each [country] resembles the country joining it; that there is no very extraordinary difference between them ... Hence it comes that in Asia, the strong nations are opposed to the weak; the warlike, brave, and active people touch immediately upon those who are indolent, effeminate, and timorous; the one must, therefore, conquer,

and the other be conquered. In Europe, on the contrary, strong nations are opposed to the strong; and those who join each other have nearly the same courage. This is the grand reason of the weakness of Asia, and of the strength of Europe; of the liberty of Europe, and of the slavery of Asia: a cause that I do not recollect ever to have seen remarked.[2]

Later European writers believed that it was Western technology that trumped the East – in particular, the technology that went on to produce the Industrial Revolution. That was certainly how it appeared to the Earl Macartney after his distinctly disappointing mission to the Chinese imperial court in 1793 (see below). Another argument, popular in the twentieth century, was that Confucian philosophy inhibited innovation. Yet these contemporary explanations for Oriental under-achievement were mistaken. The first of the six distinct killer applications that the West had but the East lacked was not commercial, nor climatic, nor technological, nor philosophical. It was, as Smith discerned, above all institutional.

If, in the year 1420, you had taken two trips along two rivers – the Thames and the Yangzi – you would have been struck by the contrast.

The Yangzi was part of a vast waterway complex that linked Nanjing to Beijing, more than 500 miles to the north, and Hangzhou to the south. At the core of this system was the Grand Canal, which at its maximum extent stretched for more than a thousand miles. Dating back as far as the seventh century BC, with pound locks introduced as early as the tenth century AD and exquisite bridges like the multi-arched Precious Belt, the Canal was substantially restored and improved in the reign of the Ming Emperor Yongle (1402–24). By the time his chief engineer Bai Ying had finished damming and diverting the flow of the Yellow River, it was possible for nearly 12,000 grain barges to sail up and down the Canal every year.[3] Nearly 50,000 men were employed in maintaining it. In the West, of course, the grandest of grand canals will always be Venice's. But when the intrepid Venetian traveller Marco Polo had visited China in the 1270s, even he had been impressed by the volume of traffic on the Yangzi:

> The multitude of vessels that invest this great river is so great that no one who should read or hear would believe it. The quantity of merchandise

carried up and down is past all belief. In fact it is so big, that it seems to be a sea rather than a river.

China's Grand Canal not only served as the principal artery of internal trade. It also enabled the imperial government to smooth the price of grain through the five state granaries, which bought when grain was cheap and sold when it was dear.[4]

Nanjing was probably the largest city in the world in 1420, with a population of between half a million and a million. For centuries it had been a thriving centre of the silk and cotton industries. Under the Yongle Emperor it also became a centre of learning. The name Yongle means 'perpetual happiness'; perpetual motion would perhaps have been a better description. The greatest of the Ming emperors did nothing by halves. The compendium of Chinese learning he commissioned took the labour of more than 2,000 scholars to complete and filled more than 11,000 volumes. It was surpassed as the world's largest encyclopaedia only in 2007, after a reign of almost exactly 600 years, by Wikipedia.

But Yongle was not content with Nanjing. Shortly after his accession, he had resolved to build a new and more spectacular capital to the north: Beijing. By 1420, when the Forbidden City was completed, Ming China had an incontrovertible claim to be the most advanced civilization in the world.

By comparison with the Yangzi, the Thames in the early fifteenth century was a veritable backwater. True, London was a busy port, the main hub for England's trade with the continent. The city's most famous Lord Mayor, Richard Whittington, was a leading cloth merchant who had made his fortune from England's growing exports of wool. And the English capital's shipbuilding industry was boosted by the need to transport men and supplies for England's recurrent campaigns against the French. In Shadwell and Ratcliffe, the ships could be hauled up on to mud berths to be refitted. And there was, of course, the Tower of London, more forbidding than forbidden.

But a visitor from China would scarcely have been impressed by all this. The Tower itself was a crude construction compared with the multiple halls of the Forbidden City. London Bridge was an ungainly bazaar on stilts compared with the Precious Belt Bridge. And primitive navigation techniques confined English sailors to narrow stretches of water – the Thames and the Channel – where they could remain within sight of familiar banks and coastlines. Nothing could have been more unimaginable, to Englishmen and Chinese alike, than the idea of ships from London sailing up the Yangzi.

By comparison with Nanjing, the London to which Henry V returned in 1421 after his triumphs over the French – the most famous of them at Agincourt – was barely a town. Its old, patched-up city walls extended about 3 miles – again, a fraction the size of Nanjing's. It had taken the founder of the Ming dynasty more than twenty years to build the wall around his capital and it extended for as many miles, with gates so large that a single one could house 3,000 soldiers. And it was built to last. Much of it still stands today, whereas scarcely anything remains of London's medieval wall.

By fifteenth-century standards, Ming China was a relatively pleasant place to live. The rigidly feudal order established at the start of the Ming era was being loosened by burgeoning internal trade.[5] The visitor to Suzhou today can still see the architectural fruits of that prosperity in the shady canals and elegant walkways of the old town centre. Urban life in England was very different. The Black Death – the bubonic plague caused by the flea-borne bacterium *Yersinia pestis*, which reached England in 1349 – had reduced London's population to around 40,000, less than a tenth the size of Nanjing's. Besides the plague, typhus, dysentery and smallpox were also rife. And, even in the absence of epidemics, poor sanitation made London a death-trap. Without any kind of sewage system, the streets stank to high heaven, whereas human excrement was systematically collected in Chinese cities and used as fertilizer in outlying paddy fields. In the days when Dick Whittington was lord mayor – four times between 1397 and his death in 1423 – the streets of London were paved with something altogether less appealing than gold.

Schoolchildren used to be brought up to think of Henry V as one of the heroic figures of English history, the antithesis of his predecessor but one, the effete Richard II. Sad to relate, their kingdom was very far from the 'sceptr'd isle' of Shakespeare's *Richard II* – more of a septic isle. The playwright fondly called it 'this other Eden, demi-paradise, / This fortress built by Nature for herself / Against infection . . .' But English life expectancy at birth was on average a miserable thirty-seven years between 1540 and 1800; the figure for London was in the twenties. Roughly one in five English children died in the first year of life; in London the figure was nearly one in three. Henry V himself became king at the age of twenty-six and was dead from dysentery at the age of thirty-five – a reminder that most history until relatively recently was made by quite young, short-lived people.

Violence was endemic. War with France was almost a permanent condition. When not fighting the French, the English fought the Welsh, the Scots and the Irish. When not fighting the Celts, they fought one another in a succession of wars for control of the crown. Henry V's father had come to the throne by violence; his son Henry VI lost it by similar means with the outbreak of the Wars of the Roses, which saw four kings lose their thrones and forty adult peers die in battle or on the scaffold. Between 1330 and 1479 a quarter of deaths in the English aristocracy were violent. And ordinary homicide was commonplace. Data from the fourteenth century suggest an annual homicide rate in Oxford of above a hundred per 100,000 inhabitants. London was somewhat safer with a rate of around fifty per 100,000. The worst murder rates in the world today are in South Africa (sixty-nine per 100,000), Colombia (fifty-three) and Jamaica (thirty-four). Even Detroit at its worst in the 1980s had a rate of just forty-five per 100,000.[6]

English life in this period truly was, as the political theorist Thomas Hobbes later observed (of what he called 'the state of nature'), 'solitary, poor, nasty, brutish and short'. Even for a prosperous Norfolk family like the Pastons, there could be little security. John Paston's wife Margaret was ejected bodily from her lodgings when she sought to uphold the family's rightful claim to the manor of Gresham, occupied by the previous owner's heir. Caister Castle had been left to the Pastons by Sir John Fastolf, but it was besieged by the Duke of Norfolk shortly after John Paston's death and held for seventeen long years.[7] And England was among the more prosperous and less violent countries in Europe. Life was even nastier, more brutal and shorter in France – and it got steadily worse the further east you went in Europe. Even in the early eighteenth century the average Frenchman had a daily caloric intake of 1,660, barely above the minimum required to sustain human life and about half the average in the West today. The average pre-revolutionary Frenchman stood just 5 feet 4¾ inches tall.[8] And in all the continental countries for which we have data for the medieval period, homicide rates were higher than in England, with Italy – a land as famous for its assassins as for its artists – consistently the worst.

It is sometimes argued that Western Europe's very nastiness was a kind of hidden advantage. Because high mortality rates were especially common among the poor, perhaps they somehow helped the rich to get richer. Certainly, one consequence of the Black Death was to give European per-capita income a boost; those who survived could earn higher wages because labour was so scarce. It is also true that the children of the rich in England were a good deal more likely to survive into adulthood than those of the poor.[9] Yet it seems unlikely that these quirks of European demography explain the great divergence of West and East. There are countries in the world today where life is almost as wretched as it was in medieval England, where pestilence, hunger, war and murder ensure average life expectancy stays pitifully low, where only the rich live long. Afghanistan, Haiti and Somalia show little sign of benefiting from these conditions. As we shall see, Europe leapt forward to prosperity and power despite death, not because of it.

Modern scholars and readers need to be reminded what death used to be like. *The Triumph of Death*, the visionary masterwork of the Flemish artist Pieter Bruegel the Elder (*c.* 1525–69), is not of course a work of realism, but Bruegel certainly did not have to rely entirely on his imagination to depict a scene of stomach-wrenching death and destruction. In a land ruled by an army of skeletons, a king lies dying, his treasure of no avail, while a dog gnaws on a nearby corpse. In the background we see two hanged men on gibbets, four men broken on wheels and another about to be beheaded. Armies clash, houses burn, ships sink. In the foreground, men and women, young and old, soldiers and civilians are all driven pell-mell into a narrow, square tunnel. No one is spared. Even the troubadour singing to his mistress is surely doomed. The artist himself died in his early forties, a younger man than this author.

A century later the Italian artist Salvator Rosa painted perhaps the most moving of all *memento mori*, entitled simply *L'umana fragilità* ('Human Frailty'). It was inspired by the plague that had swept his native Naples in 1655, claiming the life of his infant son, Rosalvo, as well as carrying off his brother, his sister, her husband and five of their children. Grinning hideously, the angel of death looms from the darkness behind Rosa's wife to claim their son, even as he makes his first attempt to write. The mood of the heartbroken artist is immortally summed up in just eight Latin words inscribed on the canvas:

> Conceptio culpa
> Nasci pena
> Labor vita
> Necesse mori

'Conception is sin, birth is pain, life is toil, death is inevitable.' What more succinct description could be devised of life in the Europe of that time?

THE EUNUCH AND THE UNICORN

How can we understand the pre-eminence of the East? For a start, Asian agriculture was considerably more productive than European. In East Asia an acre of land was enough to support a family, such was the efficiency of rice cultivation, whereas in England the average figure was closer to 20 acres. This helps explain why East Asia was already more populous than Western Europe. The more sophisticated Oriental system of rice cultivation could feed many more mouths. No doubt the Ming poet Zhou Shixiu saw the countryside through rose-tinted spectacles; still, the picture here is of a contented rural populace:

Humble doorways loom by the dark path, a crooked lane goes way down to the inlet. Here ten families . . . have been living side by side for generations. The smoke from their fires intermingles wherever you look; so too, in their routines, the people are cooperative. One man's son heads the house on the west, while another's daughter is the western neighbour's wife. A cold autumn wind blows at the soil god's shrine; piglets and rice-beer are sacrificed to the Ancestor of the Fields, to whom the old shaman burns paper money, while boys pound on a bronze drum. Mist drapes the sugar cane garden in silence, and drizzling rain falls on the taro fields, as the people come home after the rites, spread mats, and chat, half drunk . . .[10]

But such scenes of bucolic equipoise tell only part of the story. Later generations of Westerners tended to think of imperial China as a static society, allergic to innovation. In *Confucianism and Taoism* (1915) the German sociologist Max Weber defined Confucian rationalism as meaning 'rational adjustment to the world', as opposed to the Western concept of 'rational mastery of the world'. This was a view largely endorsed by the Chinese philosopher Feng Youlan in his *History of Chinese Philosophy* (1934), as well as by the Cambridge scholar Joseph Needham's multi-volume history of *Science and Civilization in China*. Such cultural explanations – always attractive to those, like Feng and Needham, who sympathized with the Maoist regime after 1949 – are hard to square with the evidence that, long before the Ming era, Chinese civilization had consistently sought to master the world through technological innovation.

We do not know for certain who designed the first water clock. It may have been the Egyptians, the Babylonians or the Chinese. But in 1086 Su Song added a gear escapement to create the world's first mechanical clock, an intricate 40-foot-tall contraption that not only told the time but also charted the movements of the sun, moon and planets. Marco Polo saw a bell tower operated by such a clock when he visited Dadu in northern China, not long after the tower's construction in 1272. Nothing remotely as accurate existed in England until a century later, when the first astronomical clocks were built for cathedrals in Norwich, St Alban's and Salisbury.

The printing press with movable type is traditionally credited to fifteenth-century Germany. In reality it was invented in eleventh-century China. Paper too originated in China long before it was introduced in the West. So did paper money, wallpaper and toilet paper.[11]

It is often asserted that the English agricultural pioneer Jethro Tull discovered the seed drill in 1701. In fact it was invented in China 2,000 years before his time. The Rotherham plough which, with its curved iron mouldboard, was a key tool in the eighteenth-century English Agricultural Revolution, was another innovation anticipated by the Chinese.[12] Wang Zhen's 1313 *Treatise on Agriculture* was full of implements then unknown in the West.[13] The Industrial Revolution was also prefigured in China. The first blast furnace for smelting iron ore was not built in Coalbrookdale in 1709 but in China before 200 BC. The oldest iron suspension bridge in the world is not British but Chinese; dating from as early as AD 65, remains of it can still be seen near Ching-tung in Yunnan province.[14] Even as late as 1788 British iron-production levels were still lower than those achieved in China in 1078. It was the Chinese who first revolutionized textile production with innovations like the spinning wheel and the silk reeling frame, imported to Italy in the thirteenth century.[15] And it is far from true that the Chinese used their most famous invention, gunpowder, solely for fireworks. Jiao Yu and Liu Ji's book *Huolongjing*, published in the late fourteenth century, describes land and sea mines, rockets and hollow cannonballs filled with explosives.

Other Chinese innovations include chemical insecticide, the fishing reel, matches, the magnetic compass, playing cards, the toothbrush and the wheelbarrow. Everyone knows that golf was invented in Scotland. Yet the Dongxuan Records from the Song dynasty (960–1279) describe a game called *chuiwan*. It was played with ten clubs, including a *cuanbang*, *pubang* and *shaobang*, which are roughly analogous to our driver, two-wood and three-wood. The clubs were inlaid with jade and gold, suggesting that golf, then as now, was a game for the well-off.

And that was not all. As a new century dawned in 1400, China was poised to achieve another technological breakthrough, one that had the potential to make the Yongle Emperor the master not just of the Middle Kingdom, but of the world itself – literally 'All under heaven'.

In Nanjing today you can see a full-size replica of the treasure ship of Admiral Zheng He, the most famous sailor in Chinese history. It is 400 feet long – nearly five times the size of the *Santa María*, in which Christopher Columbus crossed the Atlantic in 1492. And this was only part of a fleet of more than 300 huge ocean-going junks. With multiple masts and separate buoyancy chambers to prevent them from sinking in the event of a hole below the waterline, these ships were far larger than anything being built in fifteenth-century Europe. With a combined crew of 28,000, Zheng He's navy was bigger than anything seen in the West until the First World War.

Their master and commander was an extraordinary man. At the age of eleven, he had been captured on the field of battle by the founder of the Ming dynasty, Zhu Yuanzhang. As was customary, the captive was castrated. He was then assigned as a servant to the Emperor's fourth son, Zhu Di, the man who would seize and ascend the imperial throne as Yongle. In return for Zheng He's loyal service, Yongle entrusted him with a task that entailed exploring the world's oceans.

In a series of six epic voyages between 1405 and 1424, Zheng He's fleet ranged astoundingly far and wide.* The Admiral sailed to Thailand, Sumatra, Java and the once-great port of Calicut (today's Kozhikode in Kerala); to Temasek (later Singapore), Malacca and Ceylon; to Cuttack in Orissa; to Hormuz, Aden and up the Red Sea to Jeddah.[16] Nominally, these voyages were a search for Yongle's predecessor, who had mysteriously disappeared, as well as for the imperial seal that had vanished with him. (Was Yongle trying to atone for killing his way to the throne, or to cover up for the fact that he had done so?) But to find the lost emperor was not their real motive.

Before his final voyage, Zheng He was ordered 'on imperial duty to Hormuz and other countries, with ships of different sizes numbering sixty-one ... and [to carry] coloured silks ... [and] buy hemp-silk'. His officers were also instructed to 'buy porcelain, iron cauldrons, gifts and ammunition, paper, oil, wax, etc.'.[17] This might seem to suggest a commercial rationale, and certainly the Chinese had goods coveted by Indian Ocean merchants (porcelain, silk and musk), as well as commodities they wished to bring back to China (peppers, pearls, precious stones, ivory and supposedly medicinal rhinoceros horns).[18] In reality, however, the Emperor was not primarily concerned with trade as Adam Smith later understood it. In the words of

---

* There was a seventh voyage in 1430–33. It has been claimed by Gavin Menzies that Chinese ships rounded the Cape of Good Hope, sailed up the west coast of Africa to the Cape Verde Islands, crossed the Atlantic and then continued as far as Tierra del Fuego and the coast of Australia; and that one of Zheng He's admirals may have reached Greenland, returning to China along the north coast of Siberia and through the Bering Strait. The evidence for these claims is at best circumstantial and at worst non-existent.

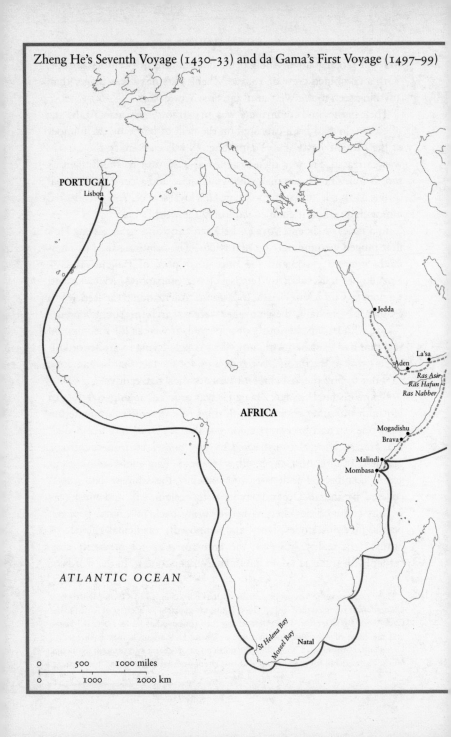

Zheng He's Seventh Voyage (1430–33) and da Gama's First Voyage (1497–99)

PORTUGAL
Lisbon

Jedda

La'sa
Aden

Ras Asir
Ras Hafun
Ras Nabber

AFRICA

Mogadishu
Brava

Malindi
Mombasa

ATLANTIC OCEAN

St Helena Bay
Mossel Bay   Natal

0   500   1000 miles
0   1000   2000 km

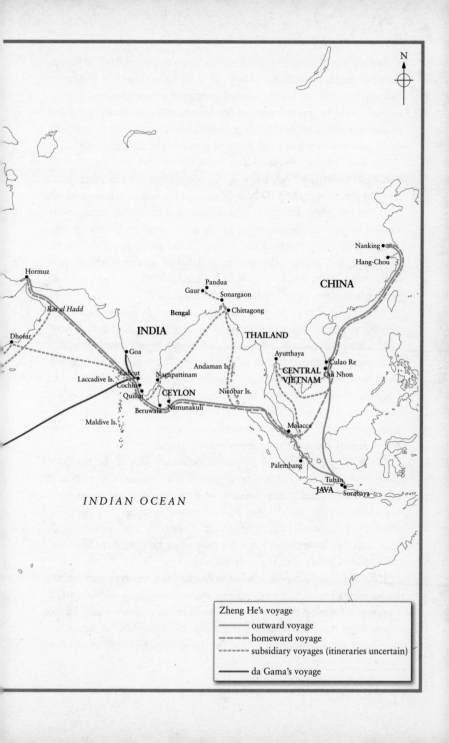

a contemporary inscription, the fleet was 'to go to the [barbarians'] countries and confer presents on them so as to transform them by displaying our power . . .'. What Yongle wanted in return for these 'presents' was for foreign rulers to pay tribute to him the way China's immediate Asian neighbours did, and thereby to acknowledge his supremacy. And who could refuse to kowtow to an emperor possessed of so mighty a fleet?[19]

On three of the voyages, ships from Zheng He's fleet reached the east coast of Africa. They did not stay long. Envoys from some thirty African rulers were invited aboard to acknowledge the 'cosmic ascendancy' of the Ming Emperor. The Sultan of Malindi (in present-day Kenya) sent a delegation with exotic gifts, among them a giraffe. Yongle personally received the animal at the gateway of the imperial palace in Nanjing. The giraffe was hailed as the mythical *qilin* (unicorn) – 'a symbol of perfect virtue, perfect government and perfect harmony in the empire and the universe'.[20]

But then, in 1424, this harmony was shattered. Yongle died – and China's overseas ambitions were buried with him. Zheng He's voyages were immediately suspended, and only briefly revived with a final Indian Ocean expedition in 1432–3. The *haijin* decree definitively banned oceanic voyages. From 1500, anyone in China found building a ship with more than two masts was liable to the death penalty; in 1551 it became a crime even to go to sea in such a ship.[21] The records of Zheng He's journeys were destroyed. Zheng He himself died and was almost certainly buried at sea.

What lay behind this momentous decision? Was it the result of fiscal problems and political wrangles at the imperial court? Was it because the costs of war in Annam (modern-day Vietnam) were proving unexpectedly high?[22] Or was it simply because of Confucian scholars' suspicion of the 'odd things' Zheng He had brought back with him, not least the giraffe? We may never be sure. But the consequences of China's turn inwards seem clear.

Like the Apollo moon missions, Zheng He's voyages had been a formidable demonstration of wealth and technological sophistication. Landing a Chinese eunuch on the East African coast in 1416 was in many ways an achievement comparable with landing an American astronaut on the moon in 1969. But by abruptly cancelling oceanic exploration, Yongle's successors ensured that the economic benefits of this achievement were negligible.

The same could not be said for the voyages that were about to be undertaken by a very different sailor from a diminutive European kingdom at the other end of the Eurasian landmass.

THE SPICE RACE

It was in the Castelo de São Jorge, high in the hills above the wind-swept harbour of Lisbon, that the newly crowned Portuguese King Manuel put Vasco da Gama in command of four small ships with a big mission. All four vessels could quite easily have fitted inside Zheng He's treasure ship. Their combined crews were just 170 men. But their mission – 'to make discoveries and go in search of spices' – had the potential to tilt the whole world westwards.

The spices in question were the cinnamon, cloves, mace and nut-meg which Europeans could not grow for themselves but which they craved to enhance the taste of their food. For centuries the spice route had run from the Indian Ocean up the Red Sea, or overland through Arabia and Anatolia. By the middle of the fifteenth century its lucra-tive final leg leading into Europe was tightly controlled by the Turks and the Venetians. The Portuguese realized that if they could find an alternative route, down the west coast of Africa and round the Cape of Good Hope to the Indian Ocean, then this business could be theirs. Another Portuguese mariner, Bartolomeu Dias, had rounded the Cape in 1488, but had been forced by his crew to turn back. Nine years later, it was up to da Gama to go all the way.

King Manuel's orders tell us something crucially important about the way Western civilization expanded overseas. As we shall see, the West had more than one advantage over the Rest. But the one that really started the ball rolling was surely the fierce competition that drove the Age of Exploration. For Europeans, sailing round Africa was not about exacting symbolic tribute for some high and mighty potentate back home. It was about getting ahead of their rivals, both economically and politically. If da Gama succeeded, then Lisbon trumped Venice. Maritime exploration, in short, was fifteenth-century Europe's space race. Or, rather, its spice race.

Da Gama set sail on 8 July 1497. When he and his fellow Portuguese sailors rounded the Cape of Good Hope at the southernmost tip of Africa four months later, they did not ask themselves what exotic animals they should bring back for their King. They wanted to know if they had finally succeeded where others had failed – in finding a new spice route. They wanted trade, not tribute.

In April 1498, fully eighty-two years after Zheng He had landed there, da Gama arrived at Malindi. The Chinese had left little behind aside from some porcelain and DNA – that of twenty Chinese sailors who are said to have been shipwrecked near the island of Pate, to have swum ashore and stayed, marrying African wives and introducing the locals to Chinese styles of basket-weaving and silk production.[23] The Portuguese, by contrast, immediately saw Malindi's potential as a trading post. Da Gama was especially excited to encounter Indian merchants there and it was almost certainly with assistance from one of them that he was able to catch the monsoon winds to Calicut.

This eagerness to trade was far from being the only difference between the Portuguese and the Chinese. There was a streak of ruthlessness – indeed, of downright brutality – about the men from Lisbon that Zheng He only rarely evinced. When the King of Calicut looked askance at the goods the Portuguese had brought with them from Lisbon, da Gama seized sixteen fishermen as hostages. On his second voyage to India, at the head of fifteen ships, he bombarded Calicut and horribly mutilated the crews of captured vessels. On another occasion, he is said to have locked up the passengers aboard a ship bound for Mecca and set it ablaze.

The Portuguese engaged in exemplary violence because they knew that their opening of a new spice route round the Cape would meet resistance. They evidently believed in getting their retaliation in first. As Afonso de Albuquerque, the second Governor of Portuguese India, proudly reported to his royal master in 1513: 'At the rumour of our coming the [native] ships all vanished and even the birds ceased to skim over the water.' Against some foes, to be sure, cannons and cutlasses were ineffective. Half of the men on da Gama's first expedition did not survive the voyage, not least because their captain attempted to sail back to Africa against the monsoon wind. Only two of the original four ships made it back to Lisbon. Da Gama himself died of malaria during a third trip to India in 1524; his remains were returned to Europe and are now housed in a fine tomb in the Jerónimos Monastery (now the church of Santa Maria de Belém in Lisbon). But other Portuguese explorers sailed on, past India, all the way to China. Once, the Chinese had been able to regard the distant barbarians of Europe with indifference, if not contempt. But now the spice race had brought the barbarians to the gates of the Middle Kingdom itself. And it must be remembered that, though the Portuguese had precious few goods the Chinese wanted, they did bring silver, for which Ming China had an immense demand as coins took the place of paper money and labour service as the principal means of payment.

In 1557 the Portuguese were ceded Macau, a peninsula on the Pearl River delta. Among the first things they did was to erect a gate – the Porta do Cerco – bearing the inscription: 'Dread our greatness and respect our virtue.' By 1586 Macau was an important enough trading outpost to be recognized as a city: Cidade do Nome de Deus na China (City of the Name of God in China). It was the first of many such European commercial enclaves in China. Luís da Camões, author of *The Lusiads*, the epic poem of Portuguese maritime expansion, lived in Macau for a time, after being exiled from Lisbon for assault. How was it, he marvelled, that a kingdom as small as Portugal – with a population less than 1 per cent of China's – could aspire to dominate the trade of Asia's vastly more populous empires? And yet on his countrymen sailed, establishing an amazing network of trading posts that stretched like a global necklace from Lisbon, round the coast of Africa, Arabia and India, through the Straits of Malacca, to the spice islands themselves and then on still further, beyond even Macau. 'Were there more worlds still to discover,' as da Camões wrote of his countrymen, 'they would find them too!'[24]

The benefits of overseas expansion were not lost on Portugal's European rivals. Along with Portugal, Spain had been first off the mark, seizing the initiative in the New World (see Chapter 3) and also establishing an Asian outpost in the Philippines, whence the Spaniards were able to ship immense quantities of Mexican silver to China.[25] For decades after the Treaty of Tordesillas (1494) had split the world between them, the two Iberian powers could regard their imperial achievements with sublime self-confidence. But the Spaniards' rebellious and commercially adept Dutch subjects came to appreciate the potential of the new spice route; indeed, by the mid-1600s they had overtaken the Portuguese in terms of both number of ships and tonnage sailing round the Cape. The French also entered the lists.

And what of the English, whose territorial ambitions had once extended no further than France and whose one novel economic idea in the Middle Ages had been selling wool to the Flemish? How could they possibly sit on the sidelines with news coming in that their arch-foes the Spaniards and French were making their fortunes overseas? Sure enough, it was not long before the English joined in the race for overseas commerce. In 1496 John Cabot made his first attempt to cross the Atlantic from Bristol. In 1553 Hugh Willoughby and Richard Chancellor set off from Deptford to seek a 'North-east Passage' to India. Willoughby froze to death in the attempt, but Chancellor managed to get to Archangel and then made his way overland to the court of Ivan the Terrible in Moscow. On his return to London, Chancellor lost no time in setting up the Muscovy Company to develop trade with Russia (its full name was 'The Mystery and Company of Merchant Adventurers for the Discovery of Regions, Dominions, Islands, and Places unknown'). Similar projects proliferated with enthusiastic royal support, not only across the Atlantic but also along the spice route. By the middle of the seventeenth century England's trade was flourishing from Belfast to Boston, from Bengal to the Bahamas.

The world was being carved up in a frenzy of cut-throat competition. But the question still remains: why did the Europeans seem to have so much more commercial fervour than the Chinese? Why was Vasco da Gama so clearly hungry for money – hungry enough to kill for it?

You can find the answer by looking at maps of medieval Europe, which show literally hundreds of competing states, ranging from the kingdoms of the western seaboard to the many city-states that lay between the Baltic and the Adriatic, from Lübeck to Venice. There were roughly a thousand polities in fourteenth-century Europe; and still around 500 more or less independent units 200 years later. Why was this? The simplest answer is geography. China had three great rivers, the Yellow, the Yangzi and the Pearl, all flowing from west to east.[26] Europe had multiple rivers flowing in multiple directions, not to mention a host of mountain ranges like the Alps and the Pyrenees, to say nothing of the dense forests and marshes of Germany and Poland. It may just have been easier for marauding Mongols to access China; Europe was less readily penetrable by a horde on horseback – and therefore had less need of unity. We cannot be sure exactly why the Central Asian threat receded from Europe after Timur. Perhaps Russian defences just got better. Perhaps the Mongol horses preferred steppe grass.

True, as we have seen, conflict could be devastating in Europe – think only of the mayhem caused by the Thirty Years' War in mid-seventeenth-century Germany. Woe betide those who lived at the frontiers between the dozen or so bigger European states, which were at war on average more than two-thirds of the time between 1550 and 1650. In all the years from 1500 to 1799, Spain was at war with foreign enemies 81 per cent of the time, England 53 per cent and France 52 per cent. But this constant fighting had three unintended benefits. First, it encouraged innovation in military technology. On land, fortifications had to grow stronger as cannon grew more powerful and manoeuvrable. The fate of the ruined 'robber baron's' castle on the Tannenberg above Seeheim in southern Germany served as a warning: in 1399 it became the first European fortification to be destroyed using explosives.

At sea, meanwhile, ships stayed small for good reasons. Compared with the Mediterranean galley, the design of which had scarcely changed since Roman times, the late fifteenth-century Portuguese caravel, with its square-rig sails and two masts, struck an ideal balance between speed and firepower. It was much easier to turn and much harder to hit than one of Zheng He's giant junks. In 1501 the French device of putting rows of cannon in special bays along both sides of a ship turned European 'men of war' into floating fortresses.[27] If it could somehow have come to a naval encounter between Zheng He and Vasco da Gama, it is possible that the Portuguese would have sent the lumbering Chinese hulks to the bottom, just as they made short work of the smaller but nimbler Arab dhows in the Indian Ocean – though at Tamao in 1521 a Ming fleet did sink a Portuguese caravel.

The second benefit of Europe's almost unremitting warfare was that the rival states grew progressively better at raising the revenue to pay for their campaigns. Measured in terms of grams of silver per head, the rulers of England and France were able to collect far more in taxation than their Chinese counterpart throughout the period from 1520 to 1630.[28] Beginning in thirteenth-century Italy, Europeans also began to experiment with unprecedented methods of government borrowing, planting the seeds of modern bond markets. Public debt was an institution wholly unknown in Ming China and only introduced under European influence in the late nineteenth century. Another fiscal innovation of world-changing significance was the Dutch idea of granting monopoly trading rights to joint-stock companies in return for a share of their profits and an understanding that the companies would act as naval subcontractors against rival powers. The Dutch East India Company, founded in 1602, and its eponymous English imitator were the first true capitalist corporations, with their equity capital divided into tradable shares paying cash dividends at the discretion of their directors. Nothing resembling these astoundingly dynamic institutions emerged in the Orient. And, though they increased royal revenue, they also diminished royal prerogatives by creating new and enduring stakeholders in the early-modern state: bankers, bond-holders and company directors.

Above all, generations of internecine conflict ensured that no one European monarch ever grew strong enough to be able to prohibit overseas exploration. Even when the Turks advanced into Eastern Europe, as they did repeatedly in the sixteenth and seventeenth centuries, there was no pan-European emperor to order the Portuguese to suspend their maritime explorations and focus on the enemy to the east.[29] On the contrary, the European monarchs all encouraged commerce, conquest and colonization as part of their competition with one another.

Religious war was the bane of European life for more than a century after the Lutheran Reformation swept through Germany (see Chapter 2). But the bloody battles between Protestants and Roman Catholics, as well as the periodic and localized persecution of Jews, also had beneficial side-effects. In 1492 the Jews were expelled from Castile and Aragon as religious heretics. Initially, many of them sought refuge in the Ottoman Empire, but a Jewish community was established in Venice after 1509. In 1566, with the revolt of the Dutch against Spanish rule and the establishment of the United Provinces as a Protestant republic, Amsterdam became another haven of tolerance. When the Protestant Huguenots were expelled from France in 1685, they were able to resettle in England, Holland and Switzerland.[30] And, of course, religious fervour provided another incentive to expand overseas. The Portuguese Prince Henrique the Navigator encouraged his sailors to explore the African coast partly in the hope that they might find the mythical kingdom of the lost Christian saint Prester John, and that he might then lend Europe a hand against the Turks. In addition to insisting on exemption from Indian customs duties, Vasco da Gama brazenly demanded that the King of Calicut expel all Muslims from his realm and waged a campaign of targeted piracy against Muslim shipping bound for Mecca.

In short, the political fragmentation that characterized Europe precluded the creation of anything remotely resembling the Chinese Empire. It also propelled Europeans to seek opportunities – economic, geopolitical and religious – in distant lands. You might say it was a case of divide and rule – except that, paradoxically, it was by being divided themselves that Europeans were able to rule the world. In Europe small was beautiful because it meant competition – and competition not just between states, but also within states.

Officially, Henry V was king of England, Wales and indeed France, to which he laid claim. But on the ground in rural England real power was in the hands of the great nobility, the descendants of the men who had imposed Magna Carta on King John, as well as thousands of gentry landowners and innumerable corporate bodies, clerical and lay. The Church was not under royal control until the reign of Henry VIII. Towns were often self-governing. And, crucially, the most important commercial centre in the country was almost completely autonomous. Europe was not only made up of states; it was also made up of estates: aristocrats, clergymen and townsfolk.

The City of London Corporation can trace its origin and structure back as far as the twelfth century. Remarkably, in other words, the Lord Mayor, the sheriffs, the aldermen, Common Council, liverymen and freemen have all been around for more than 800 years. The Corporation is one of the earliest examples of an autonomous commercial institution – in some ways the forerunner of the corporations we know today, in other ways the forerunner of democracy itself.

As early as the 1130s, Henry I granted Londoners the right to choose as their own sheriff and justice 'whom they will of themselves', and to administer their judicial and financial affairs without interference from the Crown or other authorities.[31] In 1191, while Richard I was crusading in the Holy Land, the right to elect a mayor was also granted, a right confirmed by King John in 1215.[32] As a result, the City was never in awe of the Crown. With the support of the City's freemen, Mayor Thomas fitz Thomas supported Simon de Montfort's revolt against Henry III in 1263–5. In 1319 it was the turn of Edward II to confront the City as the mercers (cloth dealers) sought to reduce the privileges of foreign merchants. When the Crown resisted, the 'London mob' supported Roger Mortimer's deposition of the King. In the reign of Edward III, the tide turned against the City; Italian and Hanseatic merchants established themselves in London, not least by providing the Crown with loans on generous terms, a practice which continued during Richard II's minority.[33] But the Londoners continued to challenge royal authority, showing little enthusiasm for the Crown's cause during either the Peasants' Revolt (1381) or the challenge to Richard's rule by the Lords Appellant. In 1392 the King revoked London's privileges and liberties, but five years later a generous 'gift' of £10,000 – negotiated by Mayor Whittington – secured their restoration. Loans and gifts to the Crown became the key to urban autonomy. The wealthier the City became, the more such leverage it had. Whittington lent Henry IV at least £24,000 and his son Henry V around £7,500.[34]

Not only did the City compete with the Crown for power. There was competition even within the City. The livery companies can all trace their origins back to the medieval period: the weavers to 1130, the bakers to 1155, the fishmongers to 1272, the goldsmiths, merchant taylors and skinners to 1327, the drapers to 1364, the mercers to 1384 and the grocers to 1428. These guilds or 'misteries' exerted considerable power over their particular sectors of the economy, but they had political power too. Edward III acknowledged this when he declared himself to be 'a brother' of the Linen-Armourers' (later Merchant Taylors') Guild. By 1607 the Merchant Taylors could count as past and present honorary members seven kings and a queen, seventeen princes and dukes, nine countesses, duchesses and baronesses, over 200 earls, lords and other gentlemen and an archbishop. The 'great twelve' companies – in order of precedence: mercers, grocers, drapers, fishmongers, goldsmiths, skinners, merchant taylors, haberdashers, salters, ironmongers, vintners and clothworkers – are a reminder of the power that London's craftsmen and merchants were once able to wield, even if their role today is largely ceremonial. In their competitive heyday they were as likely to fight as to dine with one another.[35]

Among other things, this multi-level competition, between states and within states – even within cities – helps to explain the rapid spread and advancing technology of the mechanical clock in Europe. Already in the 1330s Richard of Wallingford had installed a remarkably sophisticated mechanical clock in the wall of the south transept of St Albans Abbey, which showed the motion of the moon, of the tides and of certain celestial bodies. With their distinctive hourly bells (hence the name: clock, *clokke*, *Glocke*, *cloche*), the mechanical clock and the spring-driven clock that supplanted it in the fifteenth century were not only more accurate than Chinese waterclocks. They were also intended to be disseminated, rather than monopolized by the Emperor's astronomers. Thus, if one town's cathedral installed a fine new dial in its tower, its nearest rival soon felt obliged to follow suit. If Protestant watchmakers were unwelcome in France after 1685, the Swiss gladly took them in. And, as with military technology, competition bred progress as craftsmen tinkered to make small but cumulative improvements to the accuracy and elegance of the product. By the time the Jesuit missionary Matteo Ricci brought European clocks to China in the late sixteenth century, they were so much superior to their Oriental counterparts that they were greeted with dismay.[36] In 1602, at the request of the Wanli Emperor, Ricci produced a beautiful rice-paper map of the world, which depicted China at the centre of the earth. He must have known, however, that in terms of technology China was now drifting to the global periphery.

Because of the greater precision it permitted in measurement and in the co-ordination of action, the rise of the clock and later the portable watch went (it might be said) hand in hand with the rise of Europe and the spread of Western civilization. With every individual timepiece, a little bit more time ran out for the age of Oriental pre-eminence.

By comparison with the patchwork quilt of Europe, East Asia was – in political terms, at least – a vast monochrome blanket. The Middle Kingdom's principal competitors were the predatory Mongols to the north and the piratical Japanese to the east. Since the time of Qin Shihuangdi – often referred to as the 'First Emperor' of China (221–210 BC) – the threat from the north had been the bigger one – the one that necessitated the spectacular investment in imperial defence we know today as the Great Wall. Nothing remotely like it was constructed in Europe from the time of Hadrian to the time of Erich Honecker. Comparable in scale was the network of canals and ditches that irrigated China's arable land, which the Marxist Sinologist Karl Wittfogel saw as the most important products of a 'hydraulic-bureaucratic' Oriental despotism.

The Forbidden City in Beijing is another monument to monolithic Chinese power. To get a sense of its immense size and distinctive ethos, the visitor should walk through the Gate of Supreme Harmony to the Hall of Supreme Harmony, which contains the Dragon Throne itself, then to the Hall of Central Harmony, the emperor's private room, and then to the Hall of Preserving Harmony, the site of the final stage of the imperial civil service examination (see below). Harmony (和), it seems clear, was inextricably bound up with the idea of undivided imperial authority.[37]

Like the Great Wall, the Forbidden City simply had no counterpart in the fifteenth-century West, least of all in London, where power was subdivided between the Crown, the Lords Temporal and Spiritual and the Commons, as well as the Corporation of the City of London and the livery companies. Each had their palaces and halls, but they were all very small by Oriental standards. In the same way, while medieval European kingdoms were run by a combination of hereditary land-owners and clergymen, selected (and often ruthlessly discarded) on the basis of royal favour, China was ruled from the top down by a

Confucian bureaucracy, recruited on the basis of perhaps the most demanding examination system in all history. Those who aspired to a career in the imperial service had to submit to three stages of gruelling tests conducted in specially built exam centres, like the one that can still be seen in Nanjing today – a huge walled compound containing thousands of tiny cells little larger than the lavatory on a train:

> These tiny brick compartments [a European traveller wrote] were about 1.1 metres deep, 1 metre wide and 1.7 metres high. They possessed two stone ledges, one servicing as a table, the other as a seat. During the two days an examination lasted the candidates were observed by soldiers stationed in the lookout tower . . . The only movement allowed was the passage of servants replenishing food and water supplies, or removing human waste. When a candidate became tired, he could lay out his bedding and take a cramped rest. But a bright light in the neighbouring cell would probably compel him to take up his brush again . . . some candidates went completely insane under the pressure.[38]

No doubt after three days and two nights in a shoebox, it was the most able – and certainly the most driven – candidates who passed the examination. But with its strong emphasis on the Four Books and Five Classics of Confucianism, with their bewildering 431,286 characters to be memorized, and the rigidly stylized eight-legged essay introduced in 1487, it was an exam that rewarded conformity and caution.[39] It was fiercely competitive, no doubt, but it was not the kind of competition that promotes innovation, much less the appetite for change. The written language at the heart of Chinese civilization was designed for the production of a conservative elite and the exclusion of the masses from their activities. The contrast could scarcely be greater with the competing vernaculars of Europe – Italian, French and Castilian as well as Portuguese and English – usable for elite literature but readily accessible to a wider public with relatively simple and easily scalable education.[40]

As Confucius himself said: 'A common man marvels at uncommon things. A wise man marvels at the commonplace.' But there was too much that was commonplace in the way Ming China worked, and too little that was new.

THE MEDIOCRE KINGDOM

Civilizations are complex things. For centuries they can flourish in a sweet spot of power and prosperity. But then, often quite suddenly, they can tip over the edge into chaos.

The Ming dynasty in China had been born in 1368, when the war-lord Yuanzhang renamed himself Hongwu, meaning 'vast military power'. For most of the next three centuries, as we have seen, Ming China was the world's most sophisticated civilization by almost any measure. But then, in middle of the seventeenth century, the wheels came flying off. This is not to exaggerate its early stability. Yongle had, after all, succeeded his father Hongwu only after a period of civil war and the deposition of the rightful successor, his eldest brother's son. But the mid-seventeenth-century crisis was unquestionably a bigger disruption. Political factionalism was exacerbated by a fiscal crisis as the falling purchasing power of silver eroded the real value of tax revenues.[41] Harsh weather, famine and epidemic disease opened the door to rebellion within and incursions from without.[42] In 1644 Beijing itself fell to the rebel leader Li Zicheng. The last Ming Emperor hanged himself out of shame. This dramatic transition from Confucian equipoise to anarchy took little more than a decade.

The results of the Ming collapse were devastating. Between 1580 and 1650 conflict and epidemics reduced the Chinese population by between 35 and 40 per cent. What had gone wrong? The answer is that turning inwards was fatal, especially for a complex and densely populated society like China's. The Ming system had created a high-level equilibrium – impressive outwardly, but fragile inwardly. The countryside could sustain a remarkably large number of people, but only on the basis of an essentially static social order that literally ceased to innovate. It was a kind of trap. And when the least little thing went wrong, the trap snapped shut. There were no external resources to draw on. True, a considerable body of scholarship has sought to represent Ming China as a prosperous society, with considerable internal trade and a vibrant market for luxury goods.[43] The most recent Chinese research, however, shows that per-capita income stagnated in the Ming era and the capital stock actually shrank.[44]

UK/China per capita GDP Ratio, 1000–2008

Year

By contrast, as England's population accelerated in the late seventeenth century, overseas expansion played a vital role in propelling the country out of the trap identified by Thomas Malthus. Transatlantic trade brought an influx of new nutrients like potatoes and sugar – an acre of sugar cane yielded the same amount of energy as 12 acres of wheat[45] – as well as plentiful cod and herring. Colonization allowed the emigration of surplus population. Over time, the effect was to raise productivity, incomes, nutrition and even height.

Consider the fate of another island people, situated much like the English on an archipelago off the Eurasian coast. While the English aggressively turned outwards, laying the foundations of what can justly be called 'Anglobalization', the Japanese took the opposite path, with the Tokugawa shogunate's policy of strict seclusion (*sakoku*) after 1640. All forms of contact with the outside world were proscribed. As a result, Japan missed out entirely on the benefits associated with a rapidly rising level of global trade and migration. The results were striking. By the late eighteenth century, more than 28 per cent of the English farmworker's diet consisted of animal products; his Japanese counterpart lived on a monotonous intake, 95 per cent cereals, mostly rice. This nutritional divergence explains the marked gap in stature that developed after 1600. The average height of English convicts in the eighteenth century was 5 feet 7 inches. The average height of Japanese soldiers in the same period was just 5 feet 2½ inches.[46] When East met West by that time, they could no longer look one another straight in the eye.

In other words, long before the Industrial Revolution, little England was pulling ahead of the great civilizations of the Orient because of the material advantages of commerce and colonization. The Chinese and Japanese route – turning away from foreign trade and intensifying rice cultivation – meant that with population growth, incomes fell, and so did nutrition, height and productivity. When crops failed or their cultivation was disrupted, the results were catastrophic. The English were luckier in their drugs, too: long habituated to alcohol, they were roused from inebriation in the seventeenth century by American tobacco, Arabian coffee and Chinese tea. They got the stimulation of the coffee house, part café, part stock exchange, part chat-room;[47] the Chinese ended up with the lethargy of the opium den, their pipes filled by none other than the British East India Company.[48]

Not all European commentators recognized, as Adam Smith did, China's 'stationary state'. In 1697 the German philosopher and mathematician Gottfried Leibniz announced: 'I shall have to post a notice on my door: Bureau of Information for Chinese Knowledge.' In his book *The Latest News from China*, he suggested that 'Chinese missionaries should be sent to us to teach the aims and practice of natural theology, as we send missionaries to them to instruct them in revealed religion.' 'One need not be obsessed with the merits of the Chinese,' declared the French *philosophe* Voltaire in 1764, 'to recognize ... that their empire is in truth the best that the world has ever seen.' Two years later the Physiocrat François Quesnay published *The Despotism of China*, which praised the primacy of agriculture in Chinese economic policy.

Yet those on the other side of the Channel who concerned themselves more with commerce and industry – and who were also less inclined to idealize China as a way of obliquely criticizing their own

government – discerned the reality of Chinese stagnation. In 1793 the
1st Earl Macartney led an expedition to the Qianlong Emperor, in a
vain effort to persuade the Chinese to reopen their empire to trade.
Though Macartney pointedly declined to kowtow, he brought with
him ample tribute: a German-made planetarium, 'the largest and most
perfect glass lens that perhaps was ever fabricated', as well as tele-
scopes, theodolites, air-pumps, electrical machines and 'an extensive
apparatus for assisting to explain and illustrate the principles of science'. Yet the ancient Emperor (he was in his eighties) and his minions
were unimpressed by these marvels of Western civilization:

> it was presently discovered that the taste [for the sciences], if it ever
> existed, was now completely worn out ... [All] were ... lost and
> thrown away on the ignorant Chinese ... who immediately after the
> departure of the embassador [sic] are said to have piled them up in
> lumber rooms of Yuen-min-yuen [the Old Summer Palace]. Not more
> successful were the various specimens of elegance and art displayed in
> the choicest examples of British manufactures. The impression which
> the contemplation of such articles seemed to make on the minds of the
> courtiers was that alone of jealousy ... Such conduct may probably be
> ascribed to a kind of state policy, which discourages the introduction of
> novelties ...

The Emperor subsequently addressed a dismissive edict to King
George III: 'There is nothing we lack,' he declared. 'We have never set
much store on strange or ingenious objects, nor do we need any more
of your country's manufactures.'[49]

Macartney's abortive opening to China perfectly symbolized the
shift of global power from East to West that had taken place since
1500. The Middle Kingdom, once the mother of inventions, was now
the mediocre kingdom, wilfully hostile to other people's innovations.
That ingenious Chinese creation, the clock, had come home, but in its
modified and improved European form, with ever more accurate
mechanisms composed of springs and cogs. Today there is an entire
room in the Forbidden City given over to a vast imperial collection of
timekeeping machines. Unlike the dismissive Qianlong Emperor, his
predecessors had obsessively collected clocks. Nearly all were made in
Europe, or by European craftsmen based in China.

The West's ascendancy was confirmed in June 1842, when Royal Naval gunboats sailed up the Yangzi to the Grand Canal in retaliation for the destruction of opium stocks by a zealous Chinese official. China had to pay an indemnity of 21 million silver dollars, open five ports to British trade and cede the island of Hong Kong. It was ironic but appropriate that this first of the so-called 'Unequal Treaties' was signed in Nanjing, at the Jinghai Temple – originally built in honour of Admiral Zheng He and Tianfei, the Goddess of the Sea, who had watched over him and his fleet more than four centuries before.

They are building ships again in China – vast ships capable of circum-navigating the globe, leaving with containers full of Chinese manufactures and bringing back the raw materials necessary to feed the country's insatiably growing industrial economy. When I visited the biggest shipyard in Shanghai in June 2010, I was staggered by the sheer size of the vessels under construction. The scene made the Glasgow docks of my boyhood pale into insignificance. In the factories of Wenzhou, workers churn out suits by the hundred thousand and plastic pens by the million. And the waters of the Yangzi are constantly churned by countless barges piled high with coal, cement and ore. Competition, companies, markets, trade – these are things that China once turned its back on. Not any more. Today, Admiral Zheng He, the personifica-tion of Chinese expansionism and for so long forgotten, is a hero in China. In the words of the greatest economic reformer of the post-Mao era, Deng Xiaoping:

> No country that wishes to become developed today can pursue closed-door policies. We have tasted this bitter experience and our ancestors have tasted it. In the early Ming Dynasty in the reign of Yongle when Zheng He sailed the Western Ocean, our country was open. After Yon-gle died the dynasty went into decline. China was invaded. Counting from the middle of the Ming Dynasty to the Opium Wars, through 300 years of isolation China was made poor, and became backward and mired in darkness and ignorance. No open door is not an option.

It is a plausible reading of history (and one remarkably close to Adam Smith's).

Thirty years ago, if you had predicted that within half a century

China's would be the world's biggest economy, you would have been dismissed as a fantasist. But if back in 1420 you had predicted that Western Europe would one day be producing more than the whole of Asia, and that within 500 years the average Briton would be nine times richer than the average Chinese, you would have been regarded as no more realistic. Such was the dynamic effect of competition in Western Europe – and the retarding effect of political monopoly in East Asia.

2

Science

I feigned a mighty interest in science; and, by dint of pretending, soon became really attached to it. I ceased to be a man of affairs ... I resolved to leave my native land, and my withdrawal from court supplied a plausible excuse. I waited on the king; I emphasized the great desire I had to acquaint myself with the sciences of the West, and hinted that my travels might even be of service to him.

Montesquieu

It would be of some use to explain how the sandy country of Brandenburg came to wield such power that greater efforts have been marshalled against it than were ever mustered against Louis XIV.

Voltaire

THE SIEGE

Since the eruption of Islam from the Arabian deserts in the seventh century, there have been repeated clashes between West and East. The followers of Muhammad waged jihad against the followers of Jesus Christ, and the Christians returned the compliment with crusades to the Holy Land – nine in all between 1095 and 1272 – and the reconquest of Spain and Portugal. For most of the past 300 years, give or take the odd temporary setback, the West has consistently won this clash of civilizations. One of the main reasons for this has been the superiority of Western science. This advantage, however, did not always exist.[1]

It was not only religious fervour that enabled the successors of the Prophet Muhammad to establish a caliphate which, by the middle of the eighth century, extended from Spain, right across North Africa, through its Arabian heartland, north through Syria and into the Caucasus, then eastwards across Persia and into Afghanistan – all the way from Toledo to Kabul. The Abbasid caliphate was at the cutting edge of science. In the Bayt al-Hikma (House of Wisdom) founded in ninth-century Baghdad by Caliph Harun al-Rashid, Greek texts by Aristotle and other authors were translated into Arabic. The caliphate also produced what some regard as the first true hospitals, such as the *bimaristan* established at Damascus by Caliph al-Waleed bin Abdel Malek in 707, which was designed to cure rather than merely house the sick. It was home to what some regard as the first true institution of higher education, the University of Al-Karaouine founded in Fez in 859. Building on Greek and especially Indian foundations, Muslim mathematicians established algebra (from the Arabic *al-jabr*, meaning 'restoration') as a discipline distinct from arithmetic and geometry. The first algebraic textbook was *The Compendious Book on Calculation by Completion and Balancing* (*Hisab al-Jabr W'al-Musqabalah*), written in Arabic by the Persian scholar Muhammad ibn Mūsā al-Khwārizmī in around 820. The first truly experimental scientist was a Muslim: Abū 'Alī al-Ḥasan ibn al-Ḥasan ibn al-Haytham (965–c. 1039), whose seven-volume *Book of Optics* overthrew a host of ancient misconceptions, notably the idea that we are able to see objects because our eyes emit light. It was Ibn al-Haytham who first appreciated why a projectile was more likely to penetrate a wall if it struck it at right angles, who first discerned that the stars were not solid bodies, and who built the first camera obscura – the pinhole camera that is still used today to introduce schoolchildren to the science of optics. His studies were carried forward by the work of the late thirteenth-century Persian scholar Kamal al-Din al-Farisi on rainbows.[2] The West owes a debt to the medieval Muslim world, for both its custodianship of classical wisdom and its generation of new knowledge in cartography, medicine and philosophy as well as in mathematics and optics. The English thinker Roger Bacon acknowledged it: 'Philosophy is drawn from the Muslims.'[3]

So how did the Muslim world come to fall behind the West in the realm of science? And how exactly did a scientific revolution help Western civilization take over the world, militarily as well as academically? To answer those questions, we must travel back more than three centuries, to the last time an Islamic empire seriously menaced the security of the West.

The year was 1683 and once again – just as had happened in 1529 – an Ottoman army was at the gates of Vienna. At its head was Kara Mustafa Köprülü, Grand Vizier to Sultan Mehmed IV.

An Anatolian dynasty established in the ruins of the Byzantine Empire, the Ottomans had been the standard bearers of Islam since their conquest of Constantinople in 1453. Their empire did not have the great eastward sweep of the Abbasid caliphate,* but it had succeeded in spreading Islam into hitherto Christian territory – not only the old Byzantine realms on either side of the Black Sea Straits, but also Bulgaria, Serbia and Hungary. Belgrade had fallen to the Ottomans in 1521, Buda in 1541. Ottoman naval power had also brought Rhodes to its knees (1522). Vienna might have survived (as did Malta) but, having also extended Ottoman rule from Baghdad to Basra, from Van in the Caucasus to Aden at the mouth of the Red Sea, and along the Barbary Coast from Algiers to Tripoli, Suleiman the Magnificent (1520–66) could legitimately claim: 'I am the Sultan of Sultans, the Sovereign of Sovereigns, the distributor of crowns to the monarchs of the globe, the shadow of God upon Earth . . .'† The mosque in Istan-

---

* Crucially, the Ottoman claim to the caliphate was rejected and resisted by the Shi'a Muslims of Persia and by the less doctrinaire Mughals in India.
† Suleiman's full title was: 'His Imperial Majesty The Sultan Süleyman I, Sovereign of the Imperial House of Osman, Sultan of Sultans, Khan of Khans, Commander of the Faithful and Successor of the Prophet of the Lord of the Universe, Protector of the Holy Cities of Mecca, Medina and Jerusalem, Emperor of The Three Cities of Constantinople, Adrianople and Bursa, and of the Cities of Damascus and Cairo, of all Armenia, of the Magris, of Barka, of Kairuan, of Aleppo, of Arabic Iraq and of Ajim, of Basra, of El Hasa, of Dilen, of Raka, of Mosul, of Parthia, of Diyarbakır, of Cilicia, of the Vilayets of Erzurum, of Sivas, of Adana, of Karaman, of Van, of Barbary, of

bul that bears his name is an enduring vindication of his claim to greatness. Less well known is the fact that Suleiman also built a medical school (the Dâruttib or Süleymaniye Tıp Medresesi).[4] A law-maker and a gifted poet, Suleiman combined religious power, political power and economic power (including the setting of prices). In his eyes, the mighty Holy Roman Emperor Charles V was merely 'the King of Vienna',[5] and Portugal's merchant adventurers were no better than pirates. With Suleiman on the throne, it was far from inconceivable that the Ottomans would rise to the Portuguese challenge in the Indian Ocean and defeat it.[6]

To the late sixteenth-century envoy Ogier Ghiselin de Busbecq, the contrast between the Habsburg and Ottoman empires was alarming in the extreme:

> It makes me shudder to think of what the result of a struggle between such different systems must be; one of us must prevail and the other be destroyed, at any rate we cannot both exist in safety. On their side is the vast wealth of their empire, unimpaired resources, experience and practice in arms, a veteran soldiery, an uninterrupted series of victories, readiness to endure hardships, union, order, discipline, thrift and watchfulness. On ours are found an empty exchequer, luxurious habits, exhausted resources, broken spirits, a raw and insubordinate soldiery, and greedy quarrels; there is no regard for discipline, license runs riot, the men indulge in drunkenness and debauchery, and worst of all, the enemy are accustomed to victory, we to defeat. Can we doubt what the result must be?[7]

The seventeenth century saw further Ottoman gains: Crete was conquered in 1669. The Sultan's reach extended even into the Western Ukraine. As a naval power, too, the Ottomans remained formidable.[8] The events of 1683 were therefore long dreaded in the West. In vain did

Abyssinia, of Tunisia, of Tripoli, of Damascus, of Cyprus, of Rhodes, of Candia, of the Vilayet of the Morea, of the Marmara Sea, the Black Sea and also its coasts, of Anatolia, of Rumelia, Baghdad, Kurdistan, Greece, Turkistan, Tatary, Circassia, of the two regions of Kabarda, of Georgia, of the plain of Kypshak, of the whole country of the Tatars, of Kefa and of all the neighbouring countries, of Bosnia and its dependencies, of the City and Fort of Belgrade, of the Vilayet of Serbia, with all the castles, forts and cities, of all Albania, of all Iflak and Bogdania . . .'

Holy Roman Emperor Leopold I* cling to the peace that had been signed at Vasvár in 1664.[9] In vain did he tell himself that Louis XIV was the more serious threat.

In the summer of 1682 the Sultan made his first move, acknowledging the Magyar rebel Imre Thököly as king of Hungary in return for his recognition of Ottoman suzerainty (overlordship). In the course of the following winter an immense force was assembled at Adrianople and then deployed to Belgrade. By June 1683 the Turks had entered Habsburg territory. By the beginning of July they had taken Győr. In Vienna, meanwhile, Leopold dithered. The city's defences were woefully inadequate and the City Guard had been decimated by a recent outbreak of plague. The rusty Habsburg forces under Charles of Lorraine seemed unable to halt the Ottoman advance. False hope was furnished by Leopold's envoy in Istanbul, who assured him that the Turkish force was 'mediocre'.[10]

On 13 July 1683 this supposedly mediocre force – a 60,000-strong Ottoman army of Janissaries and *sipahi* cavalry, supported by 80,000 Balkan auxiliaries and a force of fearsome Tatars – reached the gates of Vienna. In overall command was Grand Vizier Kara Mustafa Köprülü, whose nickname Kara – 'the black' – referred as much to his character as to his complexion. This was a man who, after capturing a Polish city in 1674, had flayed his prisoners alive. Having pitched his camp 450 paces from the city walls, Kara Mustafa presented the defenders with a choice:

---

* Leopold embodied both the Habsburg family's capacity for acquiring territory by marriage rather than war and its attendant difficulties arising from inbreeding. He was christened Leopold Ignaz Joseph Balthasar Felician von Habsburg, and his full titulature when he was elected holy Roman emperor was 'Leopold I, by the grace of God elected Holy Roman Emperor, forever August, King of Germany, King of Hungary, King of Bohemia, Dalmatia, Croatia, Slavonia, Rama, Serbia, Galicia, Lodomeria, Cumania, Bulgaria, Archduke of Austria, Duke of Burgundy, Brabant, Styria, Carinthia, Carniola, Margrave of Moravia, Duke of Luxemburg, of Upper and Lower Silesia, of Württemberg and Teck, Prince of Swabia, Count of Habsburg, Tyrol, Kyburg and Goritia, Landgrave of Alsace, Marquis of the Holy Roman Empire, Burgovia, the Enns, the Higher and Lower Lusace, Lord of the Marquisate of Slavonia [and] of Port Naon and Salines'. Afflicted with an especially pronounced lower jaw (the notorious 'Habsburg lip'), Leopold married three times: first the Spanish Margarita Teresa, who was both his niece and first cousin, then the Tyrolean Archduchess Claudia Felicitas and finally Princess Eleanore of Neuburg. He had sixteen children in all, only four of whom outlived him.

Accept Islam, and live in peace under the Sultan! Or deliver up the fortress, and live in peace under the Sultan as Christians; and if any man prefer, let him depart peaceably, taking his goods with him! But if you insist [on resisting], then death or spoliation or slavery shall be the fate of you all![11]

As the Muslim conquerors of Byzantium confronted the Christian heirs of Rome, bells rang out across Central Europe, summoning the faithful to pray for divine intercession. The graffiti on the walls of St Stephen's Cathedral give a flavour of the mood in Vienna: 'Muhammad, you dog, go home!' That, however, was the limit of Leopold's defiance. Though the idea of flight affronted his 'sense of dignity', he was persuaded to slip away to safety.

The Ottoman encampment was itself a statement of self-confidence. Kara Mustafa had a garden planted in front of his own palatial tent.[12] The message was clear: the Turks had time to starve the Viennese into surrender if necessary. Strange and threatening music swept from the camp across the city walls as the Ottomans beat their immense *kös* drums. The noise also served to cover the sounds of shovels as the Turks dug tunnels and covered trenches. The detonation of a huge mine on 25 July successfully breached the city palisades, the first line of defence. Another massive explosion cleared a way to the Austrians' entrenchment at the ravelin, a triangular free-standing outer fortification. On 4 September the Turks nearly overwhelmed the defenders of the central fort itself.

But then, fatally, Kara Mustafa hesitated. Autumn was in the air. His lines of communication back to Ottoman territory were overextended. His men were now running short of supplies. And he was uncertain what his next move should be if he actually succeeded in capturing Vienna. The Turk's hesitation gave Leopold vital time to assemble a relief force. Before the Ottoman invasion he had signed a treaty of mutual defence with the Kingdom of Poland, so it was the newly elected Polish King Jan III Sobieski who led the 60,000-strong Polish–German army towards Vienna. Sobieski was past his prime, but intent on glory. It was in fact a motley force he led: Poles, Bavarians, Franconians and Saxons, as well as Habsburg troops. And it made slow progress towards Vienna, not least because its leader's grasp of Austrian geography was quite shaky. But finally, in the early hours of 12 September 1683, the counter-attack began with a burst of rocket fire. The Ottoman forces were divided, some still frantically trying to break into the city, others fighting a rearguard action against the advancing Polish infantry. Kara Mustafa had done too little to defend the approach routes. At 5 p.m. Sobieski launched his cavalry in a massive full-tilt charge from the Kahlenberg, the hill that overlooks Vienna, towards the Ottoman encampment. As one Turkish eyewitness put it, the Polish hussars looked 'like a flood of black pitch coming down the mountain, consuming everything it touched'. The final phase of the battle was ferocious but swiftly decided. Sobieski entered Kara Mustafa's tent to find it empty. The siege of Vienna was over.

Hailed by the defending Viennese as their saviour, Sobieski was exultant, modifying Caesar's famous words to: 'We came, we saw, God conquered.' Captured Ottoman cannon were melted down to make a new bell for St Stephen's that was decorated with six embossed Turkish heads. The retreating Kara Mustafa paid the ultimate price for his failure. At Esztergom the Turks suffered such a severe thrashing that the Sultan ordered his immediate execution. He was strangled in the time-honoured Ottoman fashion, with a silken cord.

A host of legends sprang up in the wake of Vienna's relief: that the crescents on the Turkish flags inspired the croissant,* that abandoned Ottoman coffee was used to found the first Viennese café and to make the first cappuccino, and that the captured Turkish percussion instruments (cymbals, triangles and bass drums) were adopted by the Austrian regimental bands. The event's true historical significance was far greater. For the Ottoman Empire, this second failure to take Vienna marked the beginning of the end – a moment of imperial overstretch with disastrous long-term consequences. In battle after battle, culminating in Prince Eugene of Savoy's crushing victory at Zenta in 1697, the Ottomans were driven from nearly all the European lands conquered by Suleiman the

---

* The story may have originated with Alfred Gottschalk, author of the first edition of the *Larousse Gastronomique* (1938). At first he attributed the croissant to the siege of Budapest in 1686, when a baker supposedly alerted the authorities to the sound of Turkish tunnelling. In a later publication Gottschalk changed the setting to Vienna in 1683.

Magnificent. The Treaty of Karlowitz, under which the Sultan renounced all claims to Hungary and Transylvania, was a humiliation.[13]

The raising of the siege of Vienna was not only a turning point in the centuries-old struggle between Christianity and Islam. It was also a pivotal moment in the rise of the West. In the field of battle, it is true, the two sides had seemed quite evenly matched in 1683. Indeed, in many respects there was little to choose between them. Tatars fought on both sides. Christian troops from Turkish-controlled Moldavia and Wallachia were obliged to support the Ottomans. The many paintings and engravings of the campaign make it clear that the differences between the two armies were sartorial more than technological or tactical. But the timing of the siege was significant. For the late seventeenth century was a time of accelerating change in Europe in two crucial fields: natural philosophy (as science was then known) and political theory. The years after 1683 saw profound changes in the way the Western mind conceived of both nature and government. In 1687 Isaac Newton published his *Principia*. Three years later, his friend John Locke published his *Second Treatise of Government*. If one thing came to differentiate the West from the East it was the widely differing degrees to which such new and profound knowledge was systematically pursued and applied.

The long Ottoman retreat after 1683 was not economically determined. Istanbul was not a poorer city than its near neighbours in Central Europe, nor was the Ottoman Empire slower than many parts of Europe to embrace global commerce and, later, industrialization.[14] The explanation for the decline of imperial China proposed in the previous chapter does not apply here; there was no shortage of economic competition and autonomous corporate entities like guilds in the Ottoman lands.[15] There was also ample competition between Ottomans, Safavids and Mughals. Nor should Ottoman decline be understood simply as a consequence of growing Western military superiority.[16] On closer inspection, that superiority was itself based on improvements in the application of science to warfare and of rationality to government. In the fifteenth century, as we saw earlier, political and economic competition had given the West a crucial advantage over China. By the eighteenth century, its edge over the Orient was a matter as much of brainpower as of firepower.

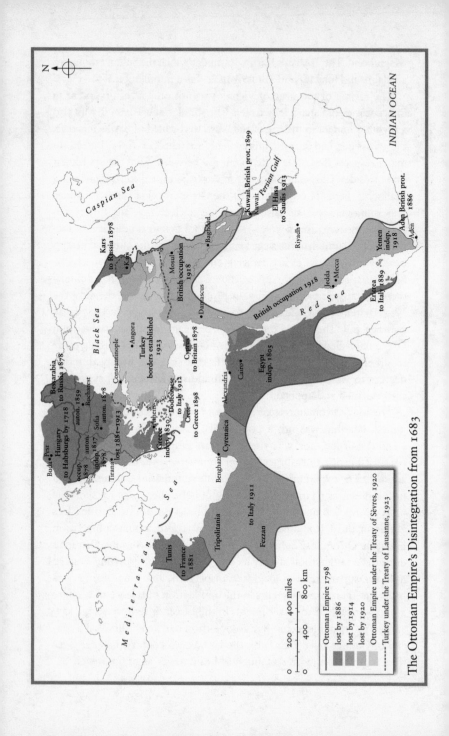

The Ottoman Empire's Disintegration from 1683

Map labels:

N

INDIAN OCEAN

Caspian Sea

Kuwait British prot. 1899
Kuwait Persian Gulf
El Hasa to Saudis 1913
Aden British prot.
Adan 1886
Aden

Kars to Russia 1878
Kars
Baghdad
Riyadh
British occupation 1918
Mosul
Damascus
Yemen indep. 1918

Black Sea
Angora
Turkey borders established 1923
Constantinople
Cyprus to Britain 1878
Cairo
Alexandria
Egypt indsp. 1805
Jedda
Mecca
British occupation 1918
Red Sea
Eritrea to Italy 1889

Bessarabia to Russia 1878
Hungary to Habsburgs by 1718
Buda Pest
occup. 1859
Bucharest
autonom. 1859
Sofia autonom. 1878
indep. 1817 autonom. 1878
Tirana lost 1881–1913
Greece indep. 1830
Dodecanese to Italy 1912
Crete to Greece 1898
Cyrenaica
Benghazi

Tunis to France 1881
Tripolitania to Italy 1911
Fezzan

Mediterranean Sea

Scale:
0   200   400 miles
0   400   800 km

Legend:
— Ottoman Empire 1798
lost by 1886
lost by 1914
lost by 1920
Ottoman Empire under the Treaty of Sèvres, 1920
‑‑‑‑ Turkey under the Treaty of Lausanne, 1923

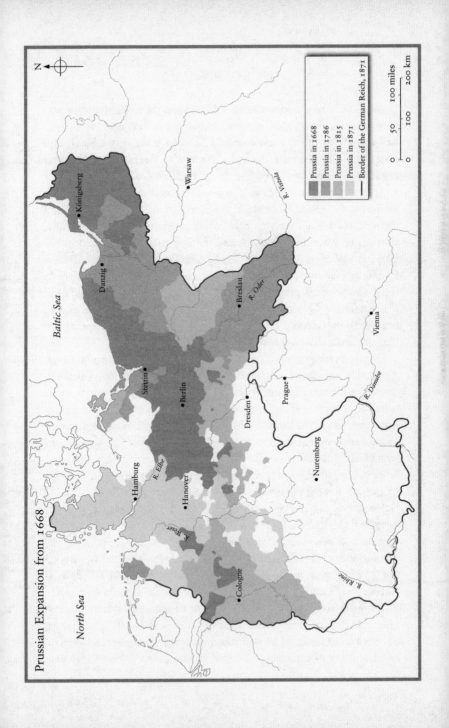

Prussian Expansion from 1668

Legend:
- Prussia in 1668
- Prussia in 1786
- Prussia in 1815
- Prussia in 1871
- Border of the German Reich, 1871

Scale:
0   50   100 miles
0   100   200 km

North Sea
Baltic Sea

Königsberg
Danzig
Breslau
R. Oder
Stettin
Berlin
Warsaw
R. Vistula
Hamburg
R. Elbe
Hanover
R. Weser
Dresden
Prague
Nuremberg
Cologne
R. Rhine
R. Danube
Vienna

MICROGRAPHIA

Europe's path to the Scientific Revolution and the Enlightenment was very far from straight and narrow; rather, it was long and tortuous. It had its origins in the fundamental Christian tenet that Church and state should be separate. 'Render therefore to Caesar the things that are Caesar's; and unto God the things that are God's' (Matthew 22: 21) is an injunction radically different from that in the Koran, which insists on the indivisibility of God's law as revealed to the Prophet and the unity of any power structure based on Islam. It was Christ's distinction between the temporal and the spiritual, adumbrated in the fifth century by St Augustine's *City of God* (as opposed to the Roman Empire's 'City of Man'), that enabled successive European rulers to resist the political pretensions of the papacy in Rome; indeed, until the reassertion of papal power over the investiture (appointment) of the clergy by Gregory VII (1073–85), it was the secular authorities that threatened to turn the Pope into a puppet.

Europe before 1500 was a vale of tears, but not of ignorance. Much classical learning was rediscovered in the Renaissance, often thanks to contact with the Muslim world. There were important innovations too. The twelfth century saw the birth of polyphony, a revolutionary breakthrough in the history of Western music. The central importance of the experimental method was proposed by Robert Grosseteste and seconded by Roger Bacon in the thirteenth century. In around 1413 Filippo Brunelleschi invented linear perspective in painting. The first true novel was the anonymous *La vida de Lazarillo de Tormes* (1500). But a more decisive breakthrough than the Renaissance was the advent of the Reformation and the ensuing fragmentation of Western Christianity after 1517. This was in large measure because of the revolutionary role of the printing press, surely the single most important technological innovation of the period before the Industrial Revolution. As we have seen, the Chinese can claim to have invented printing with a press (see Chapter 1). But Gutenberg's system of movable metal type was more flexible and scalable than anything developed in China. As he said, 'the wondrous agreement, proportion and harmony of punches and types' allowed for the very rapid production of pamphlets and books. It was far too powerful a technology to be monopolized (as Gutenberg hoped it could be). Within just a few years of his initial breakthrough in Mainz, presses had been established by imitators – notably the Englishman William Caxton – in Cologne (1464), Basel (1466), Rome (1467), Venice (1469), Nuremberg, Utrecht, Paris (1470), Florence, Milan, Naples (1471), Augsburg (1472), Budapest, Lyon, Valencia (1473), Kraków, Bruges (1474), Lübeck, Breslau (1475), Westminster, Rostock (1476), Geneva, Palermo, Messina (1478), London (1480), Antwerp, Leipzig (1481), Odense (1482) and Stockholm (1483).[17] Already by 1500 there were over 200 printing shops in Germany alone. In 1518 a total of 150 printed works were published in German, rising to 260 in 1519, to 570 in 1520 and to 990 by 1524.

No author benefited from this explosion of publication more than Martin Luther, not least because he saw the potential of writing in the vernacular rather than in Latin. Beginning modestly with the introduction to an edition of the *Theologia Deutsch* and the Seven Penitential Psalms, he and the Wittenberg printer Johann Grunenberg soon flooded the German market with religious tracts critical of the practices of the Roman Catholic Church. Luther's most famous broadside, the Ninety-Five Theses against the Church's sale of indulgences (as a form of penance for sin), was initially not published but nailed to the door of the Wittenberg Castle Church. But it was not long before multiple copies of the theses appeared in print.[18] Luther's message was that 'faith alone without works justifies, sets free, and saves' and that all men were 'priests for ever ... worthy to appear before God, to pray for others, and to teach one another mutually the things which are of God'.[19] This notion of an autodidact 'priesthood of all believers' was radical in itself. But it was the printing press that made it viable, unlike Jan Hus's earlier challenge to Papal power, which had been ruthlessly crushed like all medieval heresies. Within just a few years, Luther's pamphlets were available throughout Germany, despite the 1521 Edict of Worms ordering their burning. Of the thirty sermons and other writings Luther published between March 1517 and the summer of 1520, about 370 editions were printed. If the average size of an edition was a thousand copies, then around a third of a million copies of his works were in circulation by the latter date.

Between 1521 and 1545, Luther alone was responsible for half of all pro-Reformation publications.[20]

Because of its emphasis on individual reading of scripture and 'mutual teaching', the new medium truly was the message of the Reformation. As with so many other aspects of Western ascendancy, however, commercial competition played a part. Luther himself complained that his publishers were 'sordid mercenaries' who cared more 'for their profits than for the public'.[21] In fact, the economic benefits of the printing press were spread throughout society. In the course of the sixteenth century, towns with printers grew much more rapidly than those without printers.[22]

Crucially, the printing press spread teaching other than Luther's. The New Testament itself was first printed in English in 1526 in Matthew Tyndale's translation, permitting literate laymen to read the scriptures for themselves. Religious conservatives might denounce that 'villainous Engine', the printing press, and look back nostalgically to 'an happy time when all Learning was in Manuscript, and some little Officer ... did keep the Keys of the Library'.[23] But those days were gone for ever. As Henry VIII's minister Thomas More was quick to grasp, even those who opposed the Reformation had no option but to join battle in print. The only way of limiting the spread throughout Scotland and England of the Calvinists' Geneva Bible (1560) was for King James VI and I to commission an alternative 'authorized' version, the third and most successful attempt to produce an official English translation.* Also unlocked and spread by the printing press were the works of ancient philosophers, notably Aristotle, whose *De anima* was published in modern translation in 1509, as well as pre-Reformation humanists like Nicolaus Marschalk and George Sibutus. Already by 1500 more than a thousand scientific and mathematical works had appeared in print, among them Lucretius' *De natura rerum*, which had been rediscovered in 1417, Celsus' *De re medica*, a Roman compilation of Greek medical

---

* The Authorized Version (as the King James Bible of 1611 came to be known) stands alongside the plays of William Shakespeare among the greatest works of English literature. The team of forty-seven scholars who produced it were let down by the royal printers only once. The 1631 edition – known as 'the Wicked Bible' – omitted the word 'not' from the commandment 'Thou shalt not commit adultery.'

science, and Latin versions of the works of Archimedes.[24] Italian print-ers played an especially important role in disseminating commercially useful arithmetical and accounting techniques in works like *Treviso Arithmetic* (1478) and Luca Pacioli's *Summa de arithmetica, geometria, proportioni et proportionalita* (1494).

Perhaps most remarkably, at a time when anti-Turkish pamphlets were almost as popular as anti-Popish tracts in Germany,[25] the Koran was translated into Latin and published in Basel by the printer Johan-nes Oporinus. When, in 1542, the Basel city council banned the translation and seized the available copies, Luther himself wrote in Oporinus' defence:

> It has struck me that one is able to do nothing more grievous to Muham-
> mad or the Turks, nor more to bring them to harm (more than with all
> weaponry) than to bring their Koran to Christians in the light of day,
> that they may see therein, how entirely cursed, abominable, and desper-
> ate a book it is, full of lies, fables and abominations that the Turks con-
> ceal and gloss over ... to honour Christ, to do good for Christians, to
> harm the Turks, to vex the devil, set this book free and don't withhold
> it ... One must open sores and wounds in order to heal them.[26]

Three editions were duly published in 1543, followed by a further edition seven years later. Nothing could better illustrate the opening of the European mind that followed the Reformation.

Of course, not everything that is published adds to the sum of human knowledge. Much of what came off the printing presses in the sixteenth and seventeenth centuries was distinctly destructive, like the twenty-nine editions of *Malleus maleficarum* that appeared between 1487 and 1669, legitimizing the persecution of witches, a pan-European mania that killed between 12,000 and 45,000 people, mostly women.[27] To the audiences who watched Christopher Marlowe's *Doctor Faus-tus*, first performed in 1592, the idea that a German scholar might sell his soul to Satan in return for twenty-four years of boundless power and pleasure was entirely credible:

> By him I'll be great emperor of the world,
> And make a bridge through the moving air,
> To pass the ocean with a band of men;

I'll join the hills that bind the Afric shore,
And make that country continent to Spain,
And both contributory to my crown:
The Emperor shall not live but by my leave ...

Yet, just seventy years later, Robert Hooke could publish his *Micrographia* (1665), a triumphant celebration of scientific empiricism:

> *By the means of* Telescopes, *there is nothing so* far distant *but may be represented to our view; and by the help of* Microscopes, *there is nothing so* small, *as to escape our inquiry; hence there is a new visible World discovered to the understanding. By this means the Heavens are open'd, and a vast number of new Stars, and new Motions, and new Productions appear in them, to which all the ancient Astronomers were utterly Strangers. By this the Earth it self, which lyes so neer us, under our feet, shews quite a new thing to us ... We may perhaps be inabled to discern all the secret workings of Nature. What may not be therefore expected from it if thoroughly prosecuted?* Talking *and* contention of Arguments *would soon be turn'd into* labours; *all the fine* dreams *of* Opinions, *and* universal metaphysical natures, *which the luxury of subtil Brains has devis'd, would quickly vanish, and give place to* solid Histories, Experiments *and* Works. *And as at first, mankind fell by* tasting *of the forbidden Tree of Knowledge, so we, their Posterity, may be in part* restor'd *by the same way, not only by* beholding *and* contemplating, *but by* tasting *too those fruits of Natural knowledge, that were never yet forbidden. From hence the World may be assisted with* variety *of* Inventions, *new* matter for Sciences *may be* collected, *the* old improv'd, *and their* rust rubb'd away ...

Hooke's use of the term 'cell' for a microscopic unit of organic matter was one of a host of conceptual breakthroughs, crowded together astonishingly in both time and space, that fundamentally redefined humanity's understanding of the natural world.

The Scientific Revolution may be said to have begun with almost simultaneous advances in the study of planetary motion and blood circulation. But Hooke's microscope took science to a new frontier by revealing what had hitherto been invisible to the human eye. *Micrographia* was a manifesto for the new empiricism, a world away from Faustus' sorcery. However, the new science was about more than just accurate observation. Beginning with Galileo, it was about systematic experimentation and the identification of mathematical relationships. The possibilities of mathematics were in turn expanded when Isaac Newton and Gottfried Leibniz introduced, respectively, infinitesimal and differential calculus. Finally, the Scientific Revolution was also a revolution in philosophy as René Descartes and Baruch Spinoza overthrew traditional theories about both perception and reason. Without exaggeration, this cascade of intellectual innovation may be said to have given birth to modern anatomy, astronomy, biology, chemistry, geology, geometry, mathematics, mechanics and physics. Its character is best illustrated by a list of just the most important twenty-nine breakthroughs of the period from 1530 to 1789.*

1530 Paracelsus pioneers the application of chemistry to physiology and pathology

1543 Nicolaus Copernicus' *De revolutionibus orbium coelestium* states the heliocentric theory of the solar system
Andreas Vesalius' *De humani corporis fabrica* supplants Galen's anatomical textbook

1546 Agricola's *De natura fossilium* classifies minerals and introduces the term 'fossil'

1572 Tycho Brahe records the first European observation of a supernova

1589 Galileo's tests of falling bodies (published in *De motu*) revolutionize the experimental method

1600 William Gilbert's *De magnete, magnetisque corporibus* describes the magnetic properties of the earth and electricity

1604 Galileo discovers that a free-falling body increases its distance as the square of the time

1608 Hans Lippershey and Zacharias Jansen independently invent the telescope

* Of the world's most important scientific breakthroughs – 369 events that are mentioned in literally all reference works on the history of science – an astonishingly high proportion (38 per cent) happened between the beginning of the Reformation and the beginning of the French Revolution. The role of freedom of thought, both religious and political, is a key variable in Charles Murray's remarkable but neglected theory of human accomplishment. Murray also identifies the positive contributions of urbanization and, perhaps paradoxically, military conflict. As we shall see, the relationship between warfare and scientific progress was very close indeed.

1609 Galileo conducts the first telescopic observations of the night sky

1610 Galileo discovers four of Jupiter's moons and infers that the earth is not at the centre of the universe

1614 John Napier's *Mirifici logarithmorum canonis descriptio* introduces logarithms

1628 William Harvey writes *Exercitatio anatomica de motu cordis et sanguinis in animalibus*, accurately describing the circulation of blood

1637 René Descartes' 'La Géométrie', an appendix to his *Discours de la méthode*, founds analytic geometry

1638 Galileo's *Discorsi e dimonstrazioni matematiche* founds modern mechanics

1640 Pierre de Fermat founds number theory

1654 Fermat and Blaise Pascal found probability theory

1661 Robert Boyle's *Skeptical Chymist* defines elements and chemical analysis

1662 Boyle states Boyle's Law that the volume occupied by a fixed mass of gas in a container is inversely proportional to the pressure it exerts

1669 Isaac Newton's *De analysi per aequationes numero terminorum infinitas* presents the first systematic account of the calculus, independently developed by Gottfried Leibniz

1676 Antoni van Leeuwenhoek discovers micro-organisms

1687 Newton's *Philosophiae naturalis principia mathematica* states the law of universal gravitation and the laws of motion

1735 Carolus Linnaeus' *Systema naturae* introduces systematic classification of genera and species of organisms

1738 Daniel Bernoulli's *Hydrodynamica* states Bernoulli's Principle and founds the mathematical study of fluid flow and the kinetic theory of gases

1746 Jean-Etienne Guettard prepares the first true geological maps

1755 Joseph Black identifies carbon dioxide

1775 Antoine Lavoisier accurately describes combustion

1785 James Hutton's 'Concerning the System of the Earth' states the uniformitarian view of the earth's development

1789 Lavoisier's *Traité élémentaire de chimie* states the law of conservation of matter

1. Petty warring kingdoms: England and France clash yet again in the Hundred Years' War

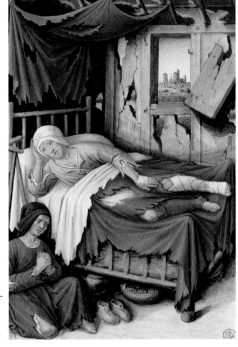

2. *The Four Conditions of Society: Poverty* by Jean Bourdichon, *c.* 1500

3. *The Triumph of Death* by Peter Bruegel the Elder, *c.* 1562

4. The Yongle Emperor

5. Su Song's water clock in the Forbidden City, Beijing

6. A game of Chinese golf (*chuiwan*)

7. The *qilin*: the Sultan of Malindi's tribute to the Middle Kingdom

8. The culture of conformity: the Chinese civil service examination in the reign of the Jen Tsung Emperor

9. The victor of the spice race: Vasco da Gama's tomb, monastery of St Jerome, Lisbon

10. Earl Macartney vainly seeks to arouse the Xianlong Emperor's interest in Western civilization: a cartoon by James Gillray

11. Jan Sobieski's men raise the Ottoman siege of Vienna

12. Prisoner of
the harem: Sultan
Osman III

13. The
Ottoman envoy
Ahmed Resmî
Effendi's arrival
in Berlin, 1763

14. The original manuscript of Frederick the Great's *Anti-Machiavel*, with annotations by Voltaire

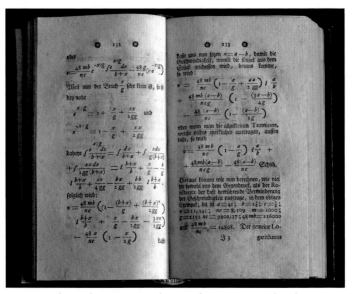

15. Pages from the German edition of Benjamin Robins's *New Principles of Gunnery*

By the mid-1600s this kind of scientific knowledge was spreading as rapidly as had the doctrine of the Protestant Reformers a century before. The printing press and increasingly reliable postal services combined to create an extraordinary network, small by modern standards, but more powerful than anything previously achieved by a community of scholars. There was of course a great deal of intellectual resistance, as is always the case when the paradigm – the conceptual framework itself – shifts.[28] Indeed, some of this resistance came from within. Newton himself dabbled in alchemy. Hooke all but killed himself with quack remedies for indigestion. It was by no means easy for such men to reconcile the new science with Christian doctrine, which few were ready to renounce.[29] But it remains undeniable that this was an intellectual revolution even more transformative than the religious revolution that preceded and unintentionally begat it. The ground rules of scientific research – including the dissemination of findings and the assigning of credit to the first into print – were laid. 'Your first letter [paper] baptised me in the Newtonian religion,' wrote the young French philosopher and wit François-Marie Arouet (better known by his pen-name Voltaire) to Pierre-Louis Moreau de Maupertuis following the publication of the latter's *Discourse on the Different Figures of the Planets* in 1732, 'and your second gave me confirmation. I thank you for your sacraments.'[30] This was irony; yet it also acknowledged the revelatory nature of the new science.

Those who decry 'Eurocentrism' as if it were some distasteful prejudice have a problem: the Scientific Revolution was, by any scientific measure, wholly Eurocentric. An astonishingly high proportion of the key figures – around 80 per cent – originated in a hexagon bounded by Glasgow, Copenhagen, Kraków, Naples, Marseille and Plymouth, and nearly all the rest were born within a hundred miles of that area.[31] In marked contrast, Ottoman scientific progress was non-existent in this same period. The best explanation for this divergence was the unlimited sovereignty of religion in the Muslim world. Towards the end of the eleventh century, influential Islamic clerics began to argue that the study of Greek philosophy was incompatible with the teachings of the Koran.[32] Indeed, it was blasphemous to suggest that man might be able to discern the divine mode of operation, which God might in any case vary at will. In the words of Abu Hamid al-Ghazali, author of *The Incoherence of the Philosophers*, 'It is rare that someone becomes absorbed in this [foreign] science without renouncing religion and letting go the reins of piety within him.'[33] Under clerical influence, the study of ancient philosophy was curtailed, books burned and so-called freethinkers persecuted; increasingly, the madrasas became focused exclusively on theology at a time when European universities were broadening the scope of their scholarship.[34] Printing, too, was resisted in the Muslim world. For the Ottomans, script was sacred: there was a religious reverence for the pen, a preference for the art of calligraphy over the business of printing. 'Scholar's ink', it was said, 'is holier than martyr's blood.'[35] In 1515 a decree of Sultan Selim I had threatened with death anyone found using the printing press.[36] This failure to reconcile Islam with scientific progress was to prove disastrous. Having once provided European scholars with ideas and inspiration, Muslim scientists were now cut off from the latest research. If the Scientific Revolution was generated by a network, then the Ottoman Empire was effectively offline. The only Western book translated into a Middle Eastern language until the late eighteenth century was a medical book on the treatment of syphilis.[37]

Nothing better illustrates this divergence than the fate of the observatory built in Istanbul in the 1570s for the renowned polymath Takiyüddīn al-Rāsid (Taqi al-Din). Born in Syria in 1521 and educated in Damascus and Cairo, Takiyüddīn was a gifted scientist, the author of numerous treatises on astronomy, mathematics and optics. He designed his own highly accurate astronomical clocks and even experimented with steam power. In the mid-1570s, as chief astronomer to the Sultan, he successfully lobbied for the construction of an observatory. By all accounts the Darü'r-Rasadü'l-Cedid (House of the New Observations) was a sophisticated facility, on a par with the Dane Tycho Brahe's more famous observatory, Uraniborg. But on 11 September 1577 the sighting of a comet over Istanbul prompted demands for astrological interpretation. Unwisely, according to some accounts, Takiyüddīn interpreted it as a harbinger of a coming Ottoman military victory. But Sheikh ul-Islam Kadizade, the most senior cleric of the time, persuaded the Sultan that Takiyüddīn's prying into secrets of the heavens was as blasphemous as the planetary tables of the Samarkand astronomer Ulugh Beg, who had supposedly been beheaded for similar temerity. In January 1580, barely five years after its completion, the Sultan ordered the demolition of Takiyüddīn's observatory.[38] There would not be another observatory in Istanbul until 1868. By such methods, the Muslim clergy effectively snuffed out the chance of Ottoman scientific advance – at the very moment that the Christian Churches of Europe were relaxing their grip on free inquiry. European advances were dismissed in Istanbul as mere 'vanities'.[39] The legacy of Islam's once celebrated House of Wisdom vanished in a cloud of piety. As late as the early nineteenth century, Hüseyin Rıfkı Tamani, the head teacher at the Mühendishane-i Cedide, could still be heard explaining to students: 'The universe in appearance is a sphere and its centre is the Earth . . . The Sun and Moon rotate around the globe and move about the signs of the zodiac.'[40]

By the second half of the seventeenth century, while the heirs of Osman slumbered, rulers all across Europe were actively promoting science, largely regardless of clerical qualms. In July 1662, two years after its initial foundation at Gresham College, the Royal Society of London for Improving Natural Knowledge received its royal charter from King Charles II. The aim was to found an institution 'for the promoting of physico-mathematical experimental learning'. Significantly, in the words of the Society's first historian, the founders:

> freely admitted Men of different Religions, Countries, and Profession of Life. This they were oblig'd to do, or else they would come far short of the largeness of their own Declarations. For they openly profess, not to lay the Foundation of an English, Scotch, Irish, Popish or Protestant Philosophy; but a Philosophy of Mankind . . . By their naturalizing Men of all Countries, they have laid the beginnings of many great advantages for the future. For by this means, they will be able to settle a constant Intelligence, throughout all civil Nations; and make the Royal Society the general Banck and Free-port of the World.[41]

Four years later, the Académie Royale des Sciences was set up in Paris, initially as a pioneering centre for cartography.[42] These became the models for similar institutions all over Europe. Among the Royal Society's founders was Christopher Wren – architect, mathematician, scientist and astronomer. When, in 1675, Charles II commissioned Wren to design his Royal Observatory in Greenwich, he certainly did not expect him to predict the outcomes of battles. Real science, the King well understood, was in the national interest.

What made the Royal Society so important was not so much royal patronage as the fact that it was part of a new kind of scientific community, which allowed ideas to be shared and problems to be addressed collectively through a process of open competition. The classic example is the law of gravity, which Newton could not have formulated without the earlier efforts of Hooke. In effect, the Society – of which Newton became president in 1703 – was a hub in the new scientific network. This is not to suggest that modern science was or is wholly collaborative. Then, as now, individual scientists were actuated by ambition as much as by altruism. But because of the imperative to publish new findings, scientific knowledge could grow cumulatively – albeit sometimes acrimoniously. Newton and Hooke quarrelled bitterly over who had first identified the inverse-square law of gravity or the true nature of light.[43] Newton had an equally nasty argument with Leibniz, who dismissed gravity as having 'an occult quality'.[44] There was indeed an important intellectual fault-line here, between the metaphysical thought of the continent and the empirical practice of the British Isles. It was always more likely that the latter, with its distinctive culture of experimental tinkering and patient observation, would produce the technological advances without which there could have been no Industrial Revolution (see Chapter 5).[45] The line that led from Newton's laws to Thomas Newcomen's steam engine – first used to drain the Whitehaven collieries in 1715 – was remarkably short and straight, though Newcomen was but a humble Dartmouth iron-monger.[46] It is not accidental that three of the world's most important technological innovations – James Watt's improved steam engine (1764), John Harrison's longitude-finding chronometer (1761) and Richard Arkwright's water frame (1769) – were invented in the same country, in the same decade.

When Newton died in March 1727 his body lay in state for four days at Westminster Abbey, before a funeral service in which his coffin was borne by two dukes, three earls and the Lord Chancellor. The service was watched by Voltaire, who was astonished at the veneration accorded to a scientist of low birth. 'I have seen', the famous *philosophe* wrote on his return to France, 'a professor of mathematics, only because he was great in his vocation, buried like a king who had done well by his subjects.' In the West, science and government had gone into partnership. And no monarch would better exemplify the benefits of that partnership than Voltaire's friend Frederick the Great of Prussia.

OSMAN AND FRITZ

Seventy years after the siege of Vienna, two men personified the widening gap between Western civilization and its Muslim rival in the Near East. In Istanbul Sultan Osman III presided indolently over a decadent Ottoman Empire, while in Potsdam Frederick the Great enacted reforms that made the Kingdom of Prussia a byword for military efficiency and administrative rationality.

Viewed from afar, the Ottoman Empire still seemed as impressive an autocracy as it had been in the days of Suleiman the Magnificent. In truth, from the mid-seventeenth century onwards, the empire was afflicted by acute structural problems. There was a severe fiscal crisis as expenditure ran ahead of tax revenue, and a monetary crisis as inflation, imported from the New World and worsened by debasement of the coinage, drove up prices (as also happened in Europe).[47] Under the vizierate of Mehmed Köprülü, his son Ahmed and his ill-fated foster-son Kara Mustafa, it was a constant struggle to cover the expenses of the Sultan's huge court, to restrain the Janissaries, the once celibate Ottoman infantry who had become a kind of hereditary caste and a law unto themselves, and to control the more remote imperial provinces. Corruption was rife. Centrifugal forces were strengthening. The power of the landowning class, the *sipahi*, was in decline. Insurgents like the *celali* in Anatolia were challenging central authority. There was religious conflict, too, between orthodox clerics like Kadizade, who attributed all Ottoman reverses to deviations from the word of the Prophet,[48] and Sufi mystics like Sivasi Efendi.[49] The Ottoman bureaucracy had formerly been staffed by slaves (under the system of *devşirme*), often taken as captives from Christian communities in the Balkans. But now selection and promotion seemed to depend more on bribery and favouritism than on aptitude; the rate of churn became absurdly high as people jostled for the perquisites of office.[50] The deterioration in administrative standards can be traced today in Ottoman government records. The census of 1458 is a meticulous document, for example. By 1694 the equivalent records had become hopelessly sloppy, with abbreviations and crossings out.[51] Ottoman officials were well aware of the deterioration, but the only remedy they could recommend was a return to the good old days of Suleiman the Magnificent.[52]

But perhaps the most serious problem was the decline in the quality of the sultans themselves. Turnover at the top was high; there were nine sultans between 1566, when Suleiman the Magnificent died, and 1648, when Mehmed IV succeeded to the throne. Of these, five were deposed and two assassinated. Polygamy meant that Ottoman sultans did not have the difficulties of Christian monarchs like Henry VIII, whose struggle to produce a male heir required no fewer than six wives, two of whom he executed, two of whom he divorced. In Istanbul, it was being one of the sultan's usually numerous sons that was dangerous. Only one of them could succeed as sultan and, until 1607, the others were invariably strangled as an insurance against challenges to the succession. This was hardly a recipe for filial love. The fate of Suleiman's talented eldest son, Mustafa, was not entirely untypical. He was murdered in his father's own tent as a result of successful intrigues by the Sultan's second wife, his stepmother, on behalf of her own sons. Another son, Bayezid, was also strangled. At the accession of Mehmed III in 1597 nineteen of his brothers were put to death. After 1607 this practice was abandoned in favour of the rule of primogeniture. Henceforth, the younger sons were merely confined to the harem – literally 'the forbidden' – inhabited by the sultan's wives, concubines and offspring.[53]

To describe the atmosphere in the harem as unhealthy would be an understatement. Osman III became sultan at the age of fifty-seven, having spent the previous fifty-one years effectively as a prisoner in the harem. By the time he emerged, almost wholly ignorant of the realm he was supposed to rule, he had developed such a loathing for women that he took to wearing iron-soled shoes. On hearing his clunking footsteps, the ladies of the harem were expected to scurry out of sight. Half a century of dodging concubines was hardly the best preparation for power. Royal life was very different in the lands that lay to the north of the Balkans.

'The ruler is the first person of the state,' wrote Frederick the Great in 1752, in the first of two Political Testaments written for posterity. 'He is paid well so that he can maintain the dignity of his office. But he is required in return to work effectively for the well-being of the state.'[54] Very similar sentiments had been expressed a century earlier by his great-grandfather the Elector Frederick William, whose achievement it was to turn the Mark of Brandenburg from a war-ravaged waste-land into the core of the most tightly run state in Central Europe, its finances based on the efficient administration of the extensive royal domain, its social order based on a landowning class that loyally served atop horses or behind desks, its security based on a well-drilled peasant army. By the time his son was acknowledged as 'King in Prus-sia' in 1701, Frederick William's realm was the closest approximation in existence to the ideal absolute monarchy recommended by the English political theorist Thomas Hobbes as the antidote to anarchy. It was a young and lean Leviathan.

The contrast with the Ottoman system was exemplified by Freder-ick the Great's favourite royal residence at Potsdam. Designed by the King himself, it was more a villa than a palace and though he called it Sanssouci – 'Carefree' – its royal master was anything but free of care. 'I can have no interests', he declared, 'which are not equally those of my people. If the two are incompatible, the preference is always to be given to the welfare and advantage of the country.'

The simple design of Sanssouci served as an example to the entire Prussian bureaucracy. Strict self-discipline, iron routine and snow-white incorruptibility were to be their watchwords. Frederick maintained only a small retinue of staff at Sanssouci: six running footmen, five regular footmen and two pages, but no valet owing to the simplicity of his ward-robe, almost invariably a threadbare military uniform, stained with snuff. In Frederick's opinion, regal robes had no practical purpose, and a crown was merely 'a hat that let the rain in'.[55] In comparison with his counterpart in the Topkapı Palace, he lived like a monk. Instead of a harem, he had a wife (Elisabeth Christine of Brunswick) whom he detested. 'Madam has grown fatter,' was how he greeted her after one of many lengthy separations.[56] The contrast is there in the written record too. The minutes of the Prussian Royal Cabinet – page after page of crisply recorded royal decisions – are the antithesis of eighteenth-century Ottoman documents.

The poet Lord Byron once wrote to a friend: 'In England, the vices in fashion are whoring and drinking, in Turkey sodomy and smoking, we prefer a girl and bottle, they a pipe and pathic [catamite] . . .' Ironically, Frederick the Great, the pioneer of enlightened absolutism, might well have been happier in the Ottoman court as a young man. A highly sensitive and probably homosexual intellectual, he endured an austere, and at times sadistic, schooling under the direction of his irascible, parade-loving father, Frederick William I.

While Frederick William unwound with boorish drinking companions at his 'Tobacco Ministry', his son sought solace in history, music and philosophy. To his martinet of a father, he was 'an effeminate boy, who is without a single manly inclination, who cannot ride nor shoot, and who, into the bargain, is dirty in his person, never has his hair cut, and curls it like an idiot'.[57] When Frederick was caught attempting to flee Prussia, his father had him imprisoned in Küstrin Castle and forced him to watch the beheading of the friend who had helped plan the escape, Hans Hermann von Katte. His friend's body and severed head were left lying on the ground outside the Crown Prince's cell.[58] He remained in captivity at Küstrin for two years.

Yet Frederick could not afford to repudiate his father's passion for the Prussian army. As colonel of the Goltz Regiment (following his release from prison), he sought to hone his military skills. These were to prove indispensable as he strove to compensate for Prussia's vulnerable geographical position, stretched as it was almost diagonally across Central Europe. In the course of his reign, Frederick increased the size of the army he inherited from 80,000 to 195,000 men, making it Europe's third largest. Indeed, with one soldier for every twenty-nine subjects, Prussia was in relative terms the most militarized country in the world by the end of Frederick's reign in 1786.[59] And, unlike his father, Frederick was prepared to deploy his army beyond the parade ground in pursuit of new territory. Within months of his accession in 1740, he stunned the continent by invading and seizing the wealthy province of

Silesia from Austria. The sensitive aesthete who had once struggled to remain in the saddle and who preferred the sound of the flute to the click of heels had emerged as an artist in the exercise of power: *der alte Fritz*.

How can one explain this transformation? One clue lies in Frederick's early work of political philosophy, *The Anti-Machiavel*, one of a number of royal refutations of the Florentine Niccolò Machiavelli's notoriously cynical user's manual for rulers, *The Prince*. In his version, Frederick defends the right of a monarch to wage preventive war 'when the excessive greatness of the greatest powers of Europe seems about to overflow its banks and engulf the world', in other words to maintain the balance of power, 'that wise equilibrium by which the superior force of some sovereigns is counterbalanced by the united forces of other powers': 'It is . . . better to engage in an offensive war when one is free to opt between the olive branch and the laurel wreath than to wait until those desperate times when a declaration of war can only momentarily postpone slavery and ruin.'[60] Frederick later described neighbouring Poland as 'an artichoke, ready to be consumed leaf by leaf' – and consumed it duly was when the country was partitioned between Austria, Prussia and Russia.[61] Frederick's seizure of Silesia was thus no spur-of-the-moment affair. Prussia's expansion was to be like a mirror image of Ottoman contraction: the achievement of a new kind of power based on ruthless rationalism.

Frederick William I had hoarded money, squeezing every penny out of his extensive Crown lands, and bequeathing his heir a chest of 8 million thalers. His son was determined to put his treasure to use, not only to enlarge his domain but also to give it a capital worthy of a first-ranking kingdom. One of the first grand edifices in what he intended to be a splendid forum in the heart of Berlin was the State Opera. Next to it he built the magnificent St Hedwig's Cathedral. In the eyes of the incurious modern tourist, these are little different from the opera houses and cathedrals to be seen in other European capitals. But they repay closer scrutiny. Unusually in northern Europe, the Berlin State Opera House was never connected to a royal palace. It existed not for the monarch's personal pleasure but for the enjoyment of a wider public. Frederick's cathedral, too, was unusual, as it was a Catholic church in a Lutheran city – built by an agnostic king, not grudgingly at the margins, but at the heart of the city's grandest square. The portico of the cathedral is consciously modelled on the Pantheon – the temple to all the gods – of ancient Rome.[62] It remains as a monument to Frederick the Great's religious tolerance.

The liberalism of the decrees issued at Frederick's accession is startling even today: not only complete religious toleration but also unrestricted press freedom and openness to immigrants. In 1700 almost one in every five Berliners was, in fact, a French Huguenot, living in a French 'colony'. There were also Salzburg Protestants, Waldensians, Mennonites, Scottish Presbyterians, Jews, Catholics and avowed religious sceptics. 'Here everyone can seek salvation in the manner that seems best to him,' declared Frederick, including even Muslims.[63] True, Jews and Christians were tolerated in the Ottoman Empire, in the sense that they could live there. But their status was closer to that of the Jews in medieval Europe – confined to specified areas and occupations, and taxed at higher rates.[64]

Invigorated by the combination of freedom and foreigners, Prussia experienced a cultural boom marked by the founding of new reading societies, discussion groups, bookshops, journals and scientific societies. Though he himself professed to despise the language, preferring to write in French and speak German only to his horse, Frederick's reign saw a surge of new publications in German. It was under his rule that Immanuel Kant emerged as perhaps the greatest philosopher of the eighteenth century, his *Critique of Pure Reason* (1781) probing the very nature and limitations of human rationality itself. Living and working throughout his life at the Albertina University at Königsberg, Kant was an even more austere figure than his king, taking his daily walk so punctually that locals set their watches by him. It mattered not one whit to Frederick that the great thinker was the grandson of a Scottish saddle-maker. What mattered was the quality of his mind rather than his birth. Nor did it bother Frederick that one of Kant's intellectual near-equals, Moses Mendelssohn, was a Jew. Christianity, the King remarked sardonically, was 'stuffed with miracles, contradictions and absurdities, was spawned in the fevered imaginations of the Orientals and then spread to our Europe, where some fanatics espoused it, some intriguers pretended to be convinced by it and some imbeciles actually believed it'.[65]

Here was the very essence of that movement we know as the

Enlightenment, which was in many – though not all – ways an extension of the Scientific Revolution. The differences were twofold. First, the circle of *philosophes* was wider. What was happening in Prussia was happening all over Europe: publishers of books, magazines and newspapers were supplying an enlarged market, thanks to a significant improvement in literacy rates. In France the proportion of men able to sign their own name – a good enough proxy for literacy – rose from 29 per cent in the 1680s to 47 per cent in the 1780s, though the rates for women (from 14 per cent to 27 per cent) remained markedly lower. In Paris by 1789 male literacy was around 90 per cent, female literacy 80 per cent. Competition between Protestant and Catholic institutions as well as increased state provision, high rates of urbanization and improved transportation – all these things together made Europeans better able to read. Nor was the Enlightenment transmitted purely through reading. The public sphere of the eighteenth century also consisted of subscription concerts (like Wolfgang Amadeus Mozart's in Vienna in 1784), new public theatres and art exhibitions, to say nothing of a complex web of cultural societies and fraternities like the Freemasonic Lodges that proliferated at this time. 'I write as a citizen of the world,' enthused the German poet and playwright Friedrich Schiller in 1784:

> The public now is everything to me – my preoccupation, my sovereign and my friend. Henceforth I belong to it alone. I wish to place myself before this tribunal and no other. It is the only thing I fear and respect. A feeling of greatness comes over me with the idea that the only fetter I wear is the verdict of the world – and that the only throne I shall appeal to is the human soul.[66]

Second, the principal concern of Enlightenment thinkers was not natural but social science, what the Scottish philosopher David Hume called the 'science of man'. How scientific the Enlightenment actually was is debatable. Especially in France, empiricism was at a discount. The seventeenth-century scientists had been interested in discovering how the natural world actually was. The eighteenth-century *philosophes* were more concerned to propose how human society might or ought to be. We have already encountered Montesquieu asserting the role of climate in shaping China's political culture, Quesnay admiring the primacy of agriculture in Chinese economic policy and Smith arguing that China's stagnation was due to insufficient foreign trade. Not one of these men had been to China. John Locke and Claude Adrien Helvétius concurred that the human mind was like a blank slate, to be formed by education and experience. But neither had the slightest experimental evidence for this view. This, and much else, was the result of reflection, and a great deal of reading.

Where the Enlightenment scored easy points was in pitting reason against the superstitions associated with religious faith or metaphysics. In heaping scorn on Christianity, Frederick the Great was putting very bluntly what Voltaire, David Hume, Edward Gibbon and others suggested more subtly in their philosophical or historical writings. The Enlightenment was always most effective when it was being ironical – in Gibbon's breathtaking chapter on early Christianity (volume I, chapter 15 of his *Decline and Fall of the Roman Empire*) or in *Candide*, Voltaire's devastating mockery of Leibniz's claim that 'all is for the best in the best of all possible worlds'.*

Yet perhaps the greatest achievement of the era was Smith's analysis of the interlocking institutions of civil society (*The Theory of Moral Sentiments*) and the market economy (*The Wealth of Nations*). Significantly, by comparison with much else that was written in the period, both works were firmly rooted in observation of the Scottish bourgeois world Smith inhabited all his life. But where Smith's 'Invisible Hand' of the market manifestly had to be embedded in a web of customary practice and mutual trust, the more radical Francophone *philosophes* sought to challenge not just established religious institutions but also established political institutions. The Swiss Jean-Jacques Rousseau's *Social Contract* (1762) cast doubt on the legitimacy of any political system not based on 'the general will'. Nicolas de Caritat, marquis de Condorcet, questioned the legitimacy of unfree labour in his *Reflections on Negro Slavery* (1781). And if a Prussian king could deride the Christian faith, what was to stop Parisian hacks from heaping opprobrium on their own monarch and his queen? The Enlightenment had a very long tail,

---

* In their travels, Candide, Cunégonde and the Leibnizian Dr Pangloss and Cacambo suffer or witness flogging, war, syphilis, shipwreck, hanging, an earthquake, enslavement, bestiality, illness and death by firing squad.

stretching down from the rarefied heights of Kant's Königsberg to the insalubrious depths of the Parisian gutter, home of such so-called *libelles* as *Le Gazetier Cuirassé*, edited by Charles Théveneau de Morande. Even Voltaire was appalled by the *Gazetier*'s scurrilous attacks on the government, calling it 'one of those satanic works where everyone from the monarch to the last citizen is insulted with furor'.[67]

The irony of the Enlightenment's half-intended revolutionary consequence was that it was itself a highly aristocratic affair. Among its leading lights were the baron de Montesquieu, the marquis de Mirabeau, the marquis de Condorcet and the arch-atheist baron d'Holbach. The lower-born *philosophes* all depended more or less on royal or aristocratic patronage: Voltaire on the marquise de Châtelet, Smith on the Duke of Buccleuch, Friedrich Schiller on the Duke of Württemberg, Denis Diderot on Catherine the Great.

Like other European monarchs, Frederick the Great did more than merely give intellectuals freedom from religious and other constraints. His patronage extended far beyond offering Voltaire a roof over his head at Sanssouci. In June 1740 – impressed by Maupertuis' vindication of Newton's hypothesis that the earth was an oblate sphere, somewhat flattened at the two poles – Frederick invited the Frenchman to come to Berlin and help found a Prussian equivalent of the Royal Society. This project suffered a setback when Maupertuis was ignominiously taken prisoner by the Austrians during the first Silesian War, but the project survived.[68] In January 1744 Frederick created the Prussian Academy of Science and Belles-Lettres, amalgamating an earlier Royal Academy of Science and a non-governmental Literary Society established the year before, and persuaded Maupertuis to return to Berlin as its president – 'the finest conquest I have ever made in my life', as the King put it to Voltaire.[69]

Frederick was without doubt a serious thinker in his own right. In its insistence on the monarch's function as a public servant, his *Anti-Machiavel* is a remarkably revolutionary document:

> the true wisdom of sovereigns is to do good and to be the most accomplished at it in their states ... it is not enough for them to perform brilliant actions and satisfy their ambition and glory, but ... they must

prefer the happiness of the human race ... Great princes have always forgotten themselves for the common good ... A sovereign pushed into war by his fiery ambition should be made to see all of the ghastly consequences for his subjects – the taxes which crush the people of a country, the levies which carry away its youth, the contagious diseases of which so many soldiers die miserably, the murderous sieges, the even more cruel battles, the maimed deprived of their sole means of subsistence, and the orphans from whom the enemy has wrested their very flesh and blood ... They sacrifice to their impetuous passions the well being of an infinity of men whom they are duty bound to protect ... The sovereigns who regard their people as their slaves risk their lives without pity and see them die without regret, but the princes who consider men as their equals and in certain regards as their masters [*comme leurs egaux et à quelques egards ... comme leurs maitres*], are economists with their blood and misers with their lives.[70]

Frederick's musical compositions, too, had real merit – notably the serene Flute Sonata in C major, which is no mere pastiche of Johann Sebastian Bach. His other political writings were far from the work of a dilettante. Yet there was an important difference between the Enlightenment as he conceived it and the earlier Scientific Revolution. The Royal Society had been the hub of a remarkably open intellectual network. By contrast, the Prussian Academy was intended to be a top-down hierarchy, modelled on the absolutist monarchy itself. 'Just as it would have been impossible for Newton to delineate his system of attraction if he had collaborated with Leibniz or Descartes,' noted Frederick in his *Political Testament* (1752), 'so it is impossible for a political system to be made and sustained if it does not emerge from a single head.'[71] There was only so much of this kind of thing that the free spirit Voltaire could stand. When Maupertuis abused his position of quasi-royal authority to exalt his own principle of least action, Voltaire wrote the cruelly satirical *Diatribe du Docteur Akakia, médecin du Pape*. This was precisely the kind of insubordinate behaviour Frederick could not stand. He ordered copies of the *Diatribe* to be destroyed and made it clear that Voltaire was no longer a welcome guest in Berlin.[72]

Others were more inclined to submit. An astronomer before he became a philosopher, Kant had first come to public attention in 1754 when he won a Prussian Academy prize for his work on the effect of surface friction in slowing the earth's rotation. The philosopher showed his gratitude in a remarkable passage in his seminal essay, 'What is Enlightenment?', which called on all men to 'Dare to reason!' (*Sapere aude!*), but not to disobey their royal master:

> Only one who is himself enlightened ... and has a numerous and well-disciplined army to assure public peace, can say: 'Argue as much as you will, and about what you will, only obey!' A republic could not dare say such a thing ... A greater degree of civil freedom appears advantageous to the freedom of mind of the people, and yet it places inescapable limitations upon it. A lower degree of civil freedom, on the contrary, provides the mind with room for each man to extend himself to his full capacity.[73]

Prussia's Enlightenment, in short, was about free thought, not free action. Moreover, this free thought was primarily designed to enhance the power of the state. Just as immigrants contributed to Prussia's economy, which allowed more tax to be raised, which allowed a bigger army to be maintained, which allowed more territory to be conquered, so too could academic research make a strategic contribution. For the new knowledge could do more than illuminate the natural world, demystifying the movements of heavenly bodies. It also had the potential to determine the rise and fall of earthly powers.

Today, Potsdam is just another dowdy suburb of Berlin, dusty in summer, dreary in winter, its skyline marred by ugly apartment blocks that bear the hallmarks of East German 'real existing socialism'. In Frederick the Great's time, however, most of the inhabitants of Potsdam were soldiers and almost all the buildings in Potsdam had some sort of military connection or purpose. Today's film museum was originally built as an orangery but then turned into cavalry stables. Take a walk through the centre of town and you pass the Military Orphanage, the Parade Ground and the former Riding School. At the junction of Lindenstrasse and Charlottenstrasse, bristling with military ornamentation, is the former Guardhouse. Even the houses were built with an extra storey on top as lodgings for soldiers.

Potsdam was Prussia in caricature as well as in miniature.

Military Labour Productivity in the French Army:
Rate of Successful Fire per Infantryman, 1600–1750

Approximate date	Rate of successful fire per handgun (shots per minute)	Handguns per infantryman	Rate of successful fire per infantryman (shots per minute)	Assumptions
1600 (1620 for handguns per infantryman)	0.50	0.40	0.20	1 shot per minute with matchlock; 0.50 misfire rate
1700	0.67	1.00	0.67	1 shot per minute with flintlock, 0.33 misfire rate: bayonets have led to replacement of pikemen
1750	2.00	1.00	2.00	3 shots per minute with flintlock, ramrod and paper cartridge, 0.33 misfire rate

Frederick's adjutant Georg Heinrich von Berenhorst once observed, only half in jest: 'The Prussian monarchy is not a country which has an army, but an army which has a country in which – as it were – it is just stationed.'[74] The army ceased to be merely an instrument of dynastic power; it became an integral part of Prussian society. Land-owners were expected to serve as army officers and able-bodied peasants took the places of foreign mercenaries in the ranks. Prussia was the army – and the army was Prussia. By the end of Frederick's reign over 3 per cent of the Prussian population were under arms, more than double the proportion in France and Austria.

A focus on drill and discipline was widely regarded as the key to Prussian military success. In this respect Frederick was the true successor to Maurice of Nassau and the Swedish King Gustavus Adolphus, the masters of seventeenth-century warfare. The blue-clad Prussian infantry marched like clockwork soldiers at ninety paces a minute, slowing to seventy as they neared the enemy.[75] The Battle of Leuthen was fought in December 1757, when the very existence of Prussia was threatened by an alliance of three great powers: France, Austria and

Russia. True to form, the Prussian infantry surprised the long Austrian line, attacking on its southern flank and rolling it up. But then, as the Austrians tried to regroup, they encountered something far more lethal even than a swiftly marching foe: artillery. For deadly accurate firepower was as crucial to Prussia's rise as the legendary 'cadaver-like obedience' of the infantry.[76]

In his early years, Frederick had dismissed artillery as a 'pit of expense'.[77] But he came to appreciate its value. 'We are now fighting against something more than men,' he argued. 'We must get it into our heads that the kind of war we shall be waging from now on will be a question of artillery duels . . .'[78] At Leuthen the Prussians had sixty-three field guns and eight howitzers as well as ten 12-pound guns known as *Brummer* – 'growlers' – because of their ominous rumbling report. The mobile horse-artillery batteries Frederick created soon became a European standard.[79] Their rapid and concentrated deployment on an unprecedented scale would be the key to Napoleon Bonaparte's later victories.

Weapons like these exemplified the application of scientific knowledge to the realm of military power. It was a process of competition, innovation and advance that quickly opened a yawning gap between the West and the Rest. Yet its heroes remain largely unsung.

Benjamin Robins was born with nothing but brains. Without the means to attend university, he taught himself mathematics and earned his crust as a private tutor. Already elected a member of the Royal Society at the age of twenty-one, he was employed as an artillery officer and military engineer by the East India Company. In the early 1740s Robins applied Newtonian physics to the problem of artillery, using differential equations to provide the first true description of the impact of air resistance on the trajectories of high-speed projectiles (a problem that Galileo had not been able to solve). In *New Principles of Gunnery*, published in England in 1742, Robins used a combination of his own careful observations, Boyle's Law and the thirty-ninth proposition of book I of Newton's *Principia* (which analyses the movement of a body under the influence of centripetal forces) to calculate the velocity of a projectile as it left the muzzle of a gun. Then, using his own ballistics pendulum, he demonstrated the effect of air resistance, which could be as much as 120 times the weight of the projectile itself, completely distorting the parabolic trajectory proposed by Galileo. Robins was also the first scientist to show how the rotation of a flying musket ball caused it to veer off the intended line of fire. His paper 'Of the Nature and Advantage of a Rifled Barrel Piece', which he read before the Royal Society in 1747 – the year he was awarded the Society's Copley Medal – recommended that bullets should be egg-shaped and gun barrels rifled. The paper's conclusion showed how well Robins appreciated the strategic as well as the scientific importance of his work:

> whatever state shall thoroughly comprehend the nature and advantages of rifled barrel pieces, and, having facilitated and completed their construction, shall introduce into their armies their general use with a dexterity in the management of them; they will by this means acquire a superiority, which will almost equal any thing, that has been done at any time by the particular excellence of any one kind of arms.[80]

For the more accurate and effective artillery became, the less valuable were sophisticated fortifications; the less lethal were even the best-drilled regular infantry regiments.

It took Frederick the Great just three years to commission a German translation of Robins's *New Principles of Gunnery*. The translator Leonard Euler, himself a superb mathematician, improved on the original by adding a comprehensive appendix of tables determining the velocity, range, maximum altitude and flight time for a projectile fired at a given muzzle velocity and elevation angle.[81] A French translation followed in 1751. There were of course other military innovators at this time – notably Austria's Prince Joseph Wenzel von Liechtenstein and France's General Gribeauval – but to Robins belongs the credit for the eighteenth-century ballistics revolution. The killer application of science had given the West a truly lethal weapon: accurate artillery. It was rather a surprising achievement for a man born, as Robins was, a Quaker.

The Robinsian revolution in ballistics was something from which the Ottomans were of course excluded, just as they had missed out on the more general Newtonian laws of motion. In the sixteenth century Ottoman arms from the Imperial State Cannon Foundry were more than a match for European artillery.[82] In the seventeenth, that began to change. As early as 1664, Raimondo Montecuccoli, the Habsburg master strategist who routed the Ottoman army at St Gotthard, observed: 'This enormous artillery [of the Turks] produces great damage when it hits, but it is awkward to move and it requires too much time to reload and sight . . . Our artillery is more handy to move and more efficient and here resides our advantage over the cannon of the Turks.'[83] For the next two centuries that gap only widened as the Western powers honed their knowledge and weaponry at institutions like the Woolwich Academy of Engineering and Artillery, founded in 1741. When Sir John Duckworth's squadron forced the Dardanelles in 1807, the Turks were still employing ancient cannon that hurled huge stone balls in the general direction of the attacking ships.

TANZIMAT TOURS

Montesquieu's epistolary novel *Persian Letters* imagines two Muslims embarking on a voyage of discovery to France via Turkey. 'I have marked with astonishment the weakness of the empire of the Osmanli,' writes Usbek on his journey westwards. 'These barbarians have abandoned all the arts, even that of war. While the nations of Europe become more refined every day, these people remain in a state of primitive ignorance; and rarely think of employing new inventions in war, until they have been used against them a thousand times.'[84]

Such expeditions to investigate the reasons for the West's manifestly growing military superiority did in fact happen. When Yirmisekiz Çelebi Mehmed was sent to Paris in 1721 he was instructed 'to visit the fortresses, factories and works of French civilization generally and report on those which might be applicable'. He wrote back glowingly about French military schools and training grounds.

The Ottomans knew by this time that they had to learn from the West. In 1732 İbrahim Müteferrika, an Ottoman official born a Christian in Transylvania, presented Sultan Mahmud I with his *Rational Bases for the Politics of Nations*, which posed the question that has haunted Muslims ever since: 'Why do Christian nations which were so weak in the past compared with Muslim nations begin to dominate so many lands in modern times and even defeat the once victorious

Ottoman armies?' Müteferrika's answer ranged widely. He referred to the parliamentary system in England and Holland, to Christian expansion in America and the Far East and even mentioned that, while the Ottoman Empire was subject to sharia law (*sheriat*), Europeans had 'laws and rules invented by reason'. But it was above all the military gap that had to be closed:

> Let Muslims act with foresight and become intimately acquainted with new European methods, organization, strategy, tactics and warfare . . . All the wise men of the world agree that the people of Turkey excel all other peoples in their nature of accepting rule and order. If they learn the new military sciences and are able to apply them, no enemy can ever withstand this state.[85]

The message was clear: the Ottoman Empire had to embrace both the Scientific Revolution and the Enlightenment if it was to be credible as a great power. It is no coincidence that it was Müteferrika who finally introduced the printing press to the Ottoman Empire in 1727 and, a year later, published the first book to use movable Arabic type, the Van Kulu dictionary. In 1732 he published a compilation of several English and Latin works as *Fuyuzat-ı miknatisiye* ('The Enlightenment of Magnetism').[86]

On 2 December 1757 the Ottoman civil servant and diplomat Ahmed Resmî Efendi left Istanbul for Vienna to announce the accession of a new sultan: Mustafa III. This was to be a very different Ottoman expedition from the one led by Kara Mustafa in 1683. Resmî was accompanied not by an army but by more than one hundred military and civilian officials; his mission was not to besiege the Habsburg capital but to learn from it. After a stay of 153 days he wrote a detailed – and enthusiastic – report of over 245 manuscript folios.[87] In 1763 he was sent on another diplomatic mission, to Berlin. If anything, he was even more impressed by Prussia than by Austria. Though a trifle disconcerted by Frederick's outfit ('dusty with daily use'), he applauded the King's dedication to the business of government, his lack of religious prejudice and the abundant evidence of Prussian economic development.[88]

Earlier accounts of Europe by Ottoman envoys had dripped with derision. Indeed, a chronic superiority complex had been another obstacle to Ottoman reform. Resmî's enthusiastic accounts marked a dramatic – and painful – shift. Not everyone in Istanbul was receptive, however. Resmî's implicit and explicit criticisms of the Ottoman systems of civil and military service were probably the reason this gifted official never became grand vizier. To describe the superiority of European governments was one thing. To implement reforms of the Ottoman system was quite another.

Western experts were invited to Istanbul to advise the Sultan. Claude Alexandre, comte de Bonneval oversaw reform of the Ottoman Corps of Miners and Artillery Transport as well as the Corps of Bombardiers. A French officer of Hungarian origin, Baron François de Tott, was brought in to oversee the construction of new, effective defences for the Ottoman capital. As he boated along the Bosphorus, de Tott realized with amazement that many of the fortifications were not merely outdated but also wrongly located, so that any enemy ships would be completely out of range even of modern guns. In his memoirs he described them as 'more like the ruins of a siege than preparations for a defence'. He set up the Sür'at Topçulari Ocaği, modelled on the French Corps de Diligents, and the Hendesehane (Military Academy), where a Scotsman, Campbell Mustafa, instructed the cadets in mathematics. De Tott also built a new foundry for the manufacture of cannon and encouraged the creation of mobile artillery units.[89]

Time and again, however, attempts at change fell foul of political opposition, not least that of the Janissaries, who in 1807 succeeded in dismantling altogether the New Order Army (Nizam-ı Cedid) instituted under the direction of another French expert, General Albert Dubayet. By now the Ottoman army appeared to be run primarily for the enrichment and convenience of its officers. Increasingly vulnerable in battle, it was no longer even effective at suppressing internal revolts.[90] It was not until the Tanzimat (Reorganization) era – the reigns of the reforming sultans Mahmud II and Abdülmecid I – that a sultan was prepared to confront such opposition head on.

On 11 June 1826, on a large parade ground near the main Janissary barracks, 200 soldiers were put through their paces wearing new European-style uniforms. Two days later some 20,000 Janissaries gathered to protest, shouting: 'We do not want the military exercises of the infidels!' They symbolically overturned their *pilav* cauldrons and threatened to march on the Topkapı Palace. Mahmud II seized his moment. Either the Janissaries would be massacred, he declared, or cats would walk over the ruins of Istanbul. He had prepared well, ensuring the loyalty of key army units like the artillery corps. When their guns were turned against the Janissary barracks, the forces of reaction were thrown into disarray. Hundreds were killed. On 17 June the Janissaries were abolished.[91]

It was not only the army's uniforms that were Europeanized. Soldiers also had to march to a brand new beat, following the appointment as instructor general of the imperial Ottoman music of Giuseppe Donizetti, brother of the more famous Gaetano Donizetti, the composer of *Lucia di Lammermoor*. Donizetti wrote two distinctly Italianate national anthems for his employer as well as overseeing the creation of a European-style military band, which he taught to play Rossini overtures. Gone were the war drums that had once struck the fear of Allah into the defenders of Vienna. As the French journal *Le Ménestrel* reported in December 1836:

> In Istanbul, the ancient Turkish music has died in agony. Sultan Mahmoud loves Italian music and has introduced it to his armies ... He particularly loves the piano, so much so that he ordered many instruments from Vienna for his ladies. I do not know how they are going to learn to play, since no one has so far succeeded in going anywhere near them.[92]

The most enduring symbol of the era of reform was built by Sultan Abdülmecid I. Constructed between 1843 and 1856, the Dolmabahçe Palace has no fewer than 285 rooms, forty-four halls, sixty-eight toilets and six hammams (Turkish baths). Fourteen tons of gold leaf were used to gild the palace ceilings, from which hung a grand total of thirty-six chandeliers. At the top of the dazzling Crystal Staircase, the palace's biggest room, the Muayede (Ceremonial) Hall, boasts an immense one-piece carpet measuring 1,300 square feet and a chandelier that weighs over 4 tons. It looks rather like a cross between Grand Central Station and a stage set at the Paris Opéra.

All that remained was to implement, after a lag of roughly 200 years, the Scientific Revolution. A government report published in 1838 confirmed the new importance of Western knowledge: 'Religious knowledge serves salvation in the world to come, but science serves the perfection of man in this world.' However, it was not until 1851 that an Assembly of Knowledge (Encümen-i Daniş) was established on the model of the Académie Française (members were expected to be 'well versed in learning and science, having a perfect knowledge of one of the European languages'), followed ten years later by an Ottoman Scientific Society (Cemiyet-i İlmiye-i Osmaniye).[93] At the same time, with the creation of something like an industrial park west of Istanbul, there was a concerted effort to build factories capable of manufacturing modern uniforms and weaponry. It seemed that the Ottomans were at last sincerely opening to the West.[94] The Orientalist James Redhouse, who was first employed as a teacher at the Ottoman Naval Engineering School after jumping ship at the age of seventeen, toiled for decades to translate English works into Turkish and to compile dictionaries, grammars and phrasebooks that would make European knowledge more accessible to Ottoman readers, as well as improving Western understanding of the disreputable Turk. In 1878 Ahmed Midhat founded the *Interpreter of Truth* newspaper, in which he serialized many of his own works, including *Avrupa'da Bir Cevelan* ('A Tour of Europe, 1889'), which described his experiences at the Exposition Universelle in Paris and in particular his impressions of the Palace of Machines.[95]

Yet, despite sincere efforts by grand viziers like Reshid Pasha, Fuad and Ali Pasha and Midhat Pasha, none of these changes was accompanied by the kind of reform of the Ottoman system of administration that might have provided a solid foundation to support this fine façade.[96] New armies, new uniforms, new anthems and new palaces were all very well. But without an effective system of taxation to finance them, a rising share of the cost was met by borrowing in Paris and London. And the more revenue that had to be spent on interest payments to European bond-holders, the less there was to finance defence of the now crumbling empire. Driven from Greece in the 1820s, and losing large chunks of Balkan territory in 1878, the Ottoman Empire appeared to be in terminal decline, its currency debased by the issue of crude (and easily forged) paper notes known as *kaime*,[97] a rising share of its revenues consumed by interest payments to European creditors,[98] its periphery menaced by a combination of Slavic nationalism and great-power machination. The attempt to introduce a constitution to limit the Sultan's power ended with the exile of Midhat Pasha and the reimposition of absolute rule by Abdul Hamid II.

In one corner of the Dolmabahçe Palace's many vast halls stands the most extraordinary clock, which is also a thermometer, a barometer and a calendar. It was a gift from the Khedive of Egypt to the Sultan. It even has an inscription in Arabic: 'May your every minute be worth an hour and your every hour, a hundred years.' It looks like a masterpiece of Oriental technology – except for one small detail: it was made in Austria, by Wilhelm Kirsch. As Kirsch's clock perfectly illustrates, the mere importation of Western technology was no substitute for a home-grown Ottoman modernization. The Turks needed not just a new palace, but a new constitution, a new alphabet – in fact a new state. The fact that they finally got all these things was largely due to the efforts of one man. His name was Kemal Atatürk. His ambition was to be Turkey's Frederick the Great.

FROM ISTANBUL TO JERUSALEM

I have serious reason to believe that the planet from which the little prince came is the asteroid known as B-612. This asteroid has only once been seen through the telescope. That was by a Turkish astronomer, in 1909. On making his discovery, the astronomer had presented it to the International Astronomical Congress, in a great demonstration. But he was in Turkish costume, and so nobody would believe what he said ... Fortunately, however, for the reputation of Asteroid B-612, a Turkish dictator made a law that his subjects, under pain of death, should change to European costume. So in 1920 the astronomer gave his demonstration all over again, dressed with impressive style and elegance. And this time everybody accepted his report.

In Antoine de Saint-Exupéry's story, *The Little Prince*, the modernization of Turkey was gently mocked. To be sure, the Turks changed their mode of dress after the First World War, increasingly conforming to Western norms, just as the Japanese had after their Meiji Restoration (see Chapter 5). But how profound a change did this represent? In particular, was the new Turkey really capable of playing in the same scientific league as the Western powers?

Mustafa Kemal was not born to power in the way that Frederick the Great had been in Prussia. A hard-drinking womanizer, Kemal was a beneficiary of the late nineteenth-century overhaul of the Ottoman army overseen by Colmar Freiherr von der Goltz (Goltz Pasha) in the 1880s and early 1890s. Goltz was the personification of the Prussia created by Frederick the Great: born in East Prussia, the son of a mediocre soldier and farmer, he rose to the rank of field marshal with a combination of bravery and brains. Kemal learned the German way of warfare and turned theory into practice at Gallipoli in 1915, where he played a key role in the successful Turkish defence against the British invasion force. After the war, with the Ottoman Empire disintegrating and a Greek army marching into Anatolia, it was Kemal who organized the decisive counter-attack and proclaimed himself the father – Atatürk – of a new Turkish republic. Though he moved the capital from Istanbul to Ankara in the heart of Anatolia, there was no question in Atatürk's mind that the state he had forged should face westwards. For centuries, he argued, Turks had 'walked from the East in the direction of the West'.[99] 'Can one name a single nation', he asked the French writer Maurice Pernot, 'that has not turned to the West in its quest for civilization?'[100]

A key part of Atatürk's reorientation of Turkey was the radical alphabet reform he personally introduced. Not only was Arabic script symbolic of the dominance of Islam; it was also poorly suited to the sounds of the Turkish language and therefore far from easy for the bulk of the population to read or write. Atatürk made his move in Gülhane Park, once a garden of the Topkapı Palace, on an August evening in 1928. Addressing a large invited audience, he asked for someone who could read Turkish to recite from a paper in his hand. When the volunteer looked in obvious bafflement at what was written on the sheet, Atatürk told the crowd: 'This young man is puzzled because he does not know the true Turkish alphabet.' He then handed it to a colleague who read aloud:

Our rich and harmonious language will now be able to display itself with new Turkish letters. We must free ourselves from these incomprehensible signs that for centuries have held our minds in an iron vice . . . You must learn the new Turkish letters quickly . . . Regard it as a patriotic and national duty . . . For a nation to consist of ten or twenty per cent of literates and eighty or ninety per cent of illiterates is shameful . . . We shall repair these errors . . . Our nation will show, with its script and with its mind, that its place is with the civilized world.[101]

The Westernization of the alphabet was only part of a wider cultural revolution designed by Atatürk to propel Turkey into the twentieth century. Modes of dress were Westernized for both men and women; the fez and turban were replaced by the Western hat, the wearing of the veil discouraged. The Western calendar was adopted, including the Christian numbering of years. But the single most important thing Atatürk did was to establish the new Turkey as a secular state quite separate from all religious authority. The caliphate was abolished in March 1924; a month later religious courts were shut down and sharia law replaced by a civil code based on Switzerland's. In Atatürk's eyes, nothing had done more to retard the advance of the Ottoman Empire than religious interference in the realm of science. In 1932, after consulting Albert Malche of the University of Geneva, he replaced the old Darülfünun (Abode of Sciences), which had been firmly in the hands of the imams, with a Western-style University of Istanbul, subsequently opening its doors to around a hundred German academics fleeing the National Socialist regime because they were Jews or on the political left. 'For everything in the world – for civilization, for life, for success,' he declared in words inscribed on the main building of Ankara University, 'the truest guide is knowledge and science. To seek a guide other than knowledge and science is [a mark of] heedlessness, ignorance and aberration.'[102]

In breaking up the Ottoman Empire and propelling its Turkish core towards secularism, the First World War struck a blow – admittedly an unintended one – for the values of the Scientific Revolution and the Enlightenment. To ensure victory, however, the British sought to mobilize internal enemies against the Sultan, among them the Arabs and the Jews. To the Arabs the British promised independent kingdoms. To the Jews they promised a new 'national home for the Jewish people' in Palestine. These promises, as we know, proved to be incompatible.

Though holy to all three monotheistic religions, Jerusalem today sometimes seems like the modern equivalent of Vienna in 1683 – a fortified city on the frontier of Western civilization. Founded in May 1948 as a Jewish state, by Jews but not exclusively for Jews, the State of Israel regards itself as a Western outpost. But it is a beleaguered one. Israel, which claims Jerusalem as its capital,* is menaced on all sides by Muslim forces that threaten its very existence: Hamas in the occupied territories of Gaza (which it now controls) and the West Bank, Hezbollah in neighbouring Lebanon, Iran to the east, not forgetting Saudi Arabia. In Egypt and Syria Israelis see Islamists making inroads against secular governments. Even traditionally friendly Turkey is now clearly moving in the direction of Islamism and anti-Zionism, not to mention a neo-Ottoman foreign policy. As a result, many people in Israel feel as threatened as the Viennese did in 1683. The key question is how far science can continue to be the killer application that gives a Western society like Israel an advantage over its enemies.

To an extent that is truly remarkable for such a small country, Israel is at the cutting edge of scientific and technological innovation. Between 1980 and 2000 the number of patents registered in Israel was 7,652 compared with 367 for all the Arab countries combined. In

---

* Jerusalem was temporarily seized by Arab forces in 1948 after heavy fighting that saw the expulsion of the Jewish community and the destruction of the city's old synagogues. However, by the time of the January 1949 ceasefire, Israel had staked a claim to the new city (West Jerusalem) and the old Jewish quarter. Transjordan claimed East Jerusalem, along with the West Bank of the Jordan. For nearly two decades the city was divided in two, much as Berlin was between 1961 and 1989, though without international recognition for the arrangement. But then, in the Six Day War of 1967, East Jerusalem was 'liberated' by the Israel Defence Forces, again in defiance of the UN. Under Mayor Teddy Kollek, large parts of Arab Jerusalem were destroyed, including the Maghribi Quarter. The policy of building Jewish settlements in East Jerusalem was also designed to make Israeli control permanent. Yet recurrent bouts of violence, notably the youth-led Arab *intifadas*, have tended to restore the division of the city, while persuading many Israelis that a return to the pre-1967 borders must be part of an enduring peace settlement. Nevertheless, Israeli law still asserts that 'Jerusalem, completed and unified, is the capital of Israel'. Since 1988, meanwhile, the Palestinians have claimed the city (which they call al-Quds al-Sharif) as their capital. At the time of writing, any compromise on the issue is hard to imagine.

2008 alone Israeli inventors applied to register 9,591 new patents. The equivalent figure for Iran was fifty and for all majority Muslim countries in the world 5,657.[103] Israel has more scientists and engineers per capita than any other country and produces more scientific papers per capita. As a share of gross domestic product its civilian research and development expenditure is the highest in the world.[104] The German-Jewish banker Siegmund Warburg was not wrong when, at the time of the Six Day War, he compared Israel with eighteenth-century Prussia. (Warburg was especially impressed by the Weizmann Institute of Science in Rehovoth, a research centre established in 1933 by Chaim Weizmann, the distinguished chemist who had gone on to become the first president of Israel.)[105] A sandbox surrounded by foes, each country needed science to ensure its strategic survival. Today, nothing illustrates better the nexus between science and security than the police surveillance control room in the heart of Jerusalem. Literally every crowded street in the old city has its own closed-circuit television camera, allowing the police to monitor, record and where necessary thwart suspected terrorists.

Yet today that scientific gap finally shows signs of closing. Although it is an Islamic republic, Iran hosts two annual science festivals – the International Kharazmi Festival in Basic Science and the Annual Razi Medical Sciences Research Festival – designed to encourage high-level research in both theoretical and applied fields. The Iranian government recently committed 150 billion rials (roughly $17.5 million) to build a new observatory as part of a major investment in astronomy and astrophysics. Surprisingly, given the strictness of the regime's application of sharia law, around 70 per cent of its Science and Engineering students are now women. From Tehran to Riyadh to the private, Saudi-financed Muslim girls' school I visited last year in West London, the taboo against educating women is receding. That is in itself a welcome development. What is much less welcome is the use to which Iran is putting its newfound scientific literacy.

On 11 April 2006 the Iranian President Mahmoud Ahmadinejad announced that Iran had successfully enriched uranium. Ever since, despite the threat of economic sanctions, Iran has been closing in on its long-cherished dream of being a nuclear power. Ostensibly, this is a programme designed to produce nuclear energy. In reality, it is an open secret that Mahmoud Ahmadinejad aspires to own a nuclear weapon. This would not make Iran the first Islamic nuclear power, however. Thanks to the pioneering work of the unscrupulous Dr A. Q. Khan, Pakistan has for years been the principal locomotive of nuclear-arms proliferation. At the time of writing, it is far from clear that Israel alone has a viable military answer to the threat of a nuclear-armed Iran.

Today, then, more than three centuries after the siege of Vienna, the key question is how far the West is still capable of maintaining the scientific lead on which, among many other things, its military superiority has for so long been based. Or perhaps the question could be phrased differently. Can a non-Western power really hope to benefit from downloading Western scientific knowledge, if it continues to reject that other key part of the West's winning formula: the third institutional innovation of private property rights, the rule of law and truly representative government?

3

Property

Freedom is . . . a Liberty to dispose, and order, as he lists, his Person, Actions, Possessions, and his whole Property, within the Allowance of those Laws under which he is; and therein not to be subject to the arbitrary Will of another . . . The great and *chief end* therefore, of Men's uniting into Commonwealths . . . is *the preservation of their Property*.

John Locke

We are the vile offspring of the predatory Spaniards who came to America to bleed her white and to breed with their victims. Later the illegitimate offspring of these unions joined with the offspring of slaves transported from Africa. With such racial mixture and such a moral record, can we afford to place laws above leaders and principles above men?

Simón Bolívar

NEW WORLDS

It was a new world. But it was to be the West's world. It would be Europeans that reached out across the Atlantic Ocean to take possession of a vast landmass that, prior to Martin Waldseemüller's *Universalis cosmographia* of 1507, simply did not appear on maps: America – named after the explorer Amerigo Vespucci.* It was Europe's monarchies – above all

---

* He might equally well have called the continent 'Columbia', but Vespucci's 1504 book *Mundus novus* ('New World') had stolen some of Columbus' thunder.

Spain and England – who, vying for souls, gold and land, were willing to cross oceans and conquer whole continents. To many historians, the discovery of the Americas (broadly defined to include the Caribbean) is *the* paramount reason for the ascendancy of the West. Without the New World, it has been asserted, 'Western Europe would have remained a small, backward region of Eurasia, dependent on the East for transfusions of technology, transmissions of culture, and transfers of wealth.'[1] Without American 'ghost acres' and the African slaves who worked them, there could have been no 'European Miracle', no Industrial Revolution.[2] In view of the advances already achieved in Western Europe both economically and scientifically prior to large-scale development of the New World, these claims seem overblown. The real significance of the conquest and colonization of the Americas is that it was one of history's biggest natural experiments: take two Western cultures, export them and impose them on a wide range of different peoples and lands – the British in the North, the Spanish and Portuguese in the South. Then see which does better.

It was no contest. Looking at the world today, four centuries on, no one could possibly doubt that the dominant force in Western civilization is the United States of America. Until very recently, Latin America has lagged far behind Anglo-America. How and why did that happen? You might think it was because the northern soil was more fertile or had more gold and oil beneath it, or because the weather was better, or because the rivers were more propitiously located – or just because Europe was geographically closer. But these were not the keys to North American success. Nor can it be claimed that the Spanish Empire – or the Portuguese – was afflicted with the defects of the great Oriental empires. Unlike the Chinese, the Spaniards were early participants in the global trade boom after 1500. Unlike the Ottomans, they were early participants in the Scientific Revolution.[3] Instead, it was an idea that made the crucial difference between British and Iberian America – an idea about the way people should govern themselves. Some people make the mistake of calling that idea 'democracy' and imagining that any country can adopt it merely by holding elections. In reality, democracy was the capstone of an edifice that had as its foundation the rule of law – to be precise, the sanctity of individual freedom and the security of private property rights, ensured by representative, constitutional government.

'There are few words which are used more loosely than the word "Civilization",' declared the greatest of all Anglo-Americans, at a time when civilization as he understood it stood in mortal danger. 'What does it mean?' His answer is as perfect a definition of the political difference between the West and the Rest as has ever been formulated:

> It means a society based upon the opinion of civilians. It means that violence, the rule of warriors and despotic chiefs, the conditions of camps and warfare, of riot and tyranny, give place to parliaments where laws are made, and independent courts of justice in which over long periods those laws are maintained. That is Civilization – and in its soil grow continually freedom, comfort and culture. When Civilization reigns in any country, a wider and less harassed life is afforded to the masses of the people. The traditions of the past are cherished and the inheritance bequeathed to us by former wise or valiant men becomes a rich estate to be enjoyed and used by all.
>
> The central principle of Civilization is the subordination of the ruling class to the settled customs of the people and to their will as expressed in the Constitution . . .[4]

Thus Winston Churchill, son of an English aristocrat and an American heiress, in 1938. But where did that peculiarly Anglo-American definition of civilization – of freedom and peace based on the rule of law and constitutional government – spring from? And why did it fail to take root in America south of the Rio Grande?

Our story begins with two ships. On one, landing in northern Ecuador in 1532, were fewer than 200 Spaniards accompanying the man who already claimed the title 'Governor of Peru'. Their ambition was to conquer the Inca Empire for the King of Spain and to secure a large share of its reputed wealth of precious metal for themselves. The other ship, the *Carolina*, reached the New World 138 years later, in 1670, at an island off the coast of what today is South Carolina. Among those on board were servants whose modest ambition was to find a better life than the grinding poverty they had left behind in England.

The two ships symbolized this tale of two Americas. On one, conquistadors; on the other indentured servants. One group dreamt of instant plunder – of mountains of Mayan gold, there for the taking. The others knew that they had years of toil ahead of them, but also that they would be rewarded with one of the world's most attractive assets – prime North American land – plus a share in the process of law-making. Real estate plus representation: that was the North American dream.

Yet at the outset it was not the poor English migrants in the North but the conquistadors in the South who seemed better placed. The Spaniards, after all, had got there first. During the sixteenth century, the work of colonizing the Americas was left almost entirely to the people of the Iberian peninsula. While Englishmen still hankered after conquering Calais, mighty native American empires were being subjugated by Spanish adventurers. In Mexico the bloodthirsty Aztecs were laid low by Hernán Cortés between 1519 and 1521. And in Peru, just over a decade later, the lofty Andean empire of the Incas was laid low by Francisco Pizarro.

Pizarro had no illusions about the relationship between the risks and rewards of conquest. It took two expeditions in 1524 and 1526 even to locate the Inca Empire. In the course of the second, when some of his less tenacious brethren were faltering, Pizarro spelt out that relationship by drawing a line in the sand:

> Comrades and friends, *there* lies the part that represents death, hardship, hunger, nakedness, rains and abandonment; this side represents comfort. Here you return to Panama to be poor; there you may go forward to Peru to be rich. Choose which best becomes you as good Spaniards.[5]

His third expedition, which set sail from Panama in 1530, consisted of 180 men, among them a core of brothers and intimates from his home town of Trujillo. By the time they reached the Peruvian Highlands, Pizarro had just sixty horsemen and ninety footsoldiers at his command. The audacity of what they did remains astonishing even after the passage of half a millennium. The population of the empire they intended to subjugate was somewhere between 5 and 10 million.

On the conquistadors' side, however, was an invisible ally: the European diseases to which South Americans had no resistance – smallpox, influenza, measles and typhus. At the same time, the Spaniards' horses, guns and crossbows were weapons far superior to anything in the Inca armoury; they gave the invaders a terrifying extra-terrestrial aspect. And the Incas themselves were divided. Since the death of the Inca Huayna Capac, his sons Atahualpa and Huascar had been battling for the succession, while subject tribes scented a chance to throw off the Inca yoke. The Battle of Cajamarca (14 November 1532) was thus scarcely a battle at all. As Pizarro's brother Hernando described it, Atahualpa walked into a trap when he accepted the Spaniards' invitation to dinner:

> When Atahualpa had advanced to the centre of an open space, he stopped, and a Dominican friar, who was with the Governor [Pizarro], came forward to tell him, on the part of the Governor, that he waited for him in his lodging, and that he was sent to speak with him. The friar then told Atahualpa that he was a priest, and that he was sent there to teach the things of the faith if they should desire to be Christians. He showed Atahualpa a book which he carried in his hands [the Bible], and told him that that book contained the things of God. Atahualpa asked for the book, and threw it on the ground, saying: 'I will not leave this place until you have restored all that you have taken in my land. I know well who you are and what you have come for.' Then he rose up in his litter and addressed his men, and there were murmurs among them and calls to those who were armed. The friar went to the Governor and reported what was being done and that no time was to be lost. The Governor sent to me; and I had arranged with the captain of the artillery that, when a sign was given, he should discharge his pieces, and that, on hearing the reports, all the troops should come forth at once. This was done, and as the Indians were unarmed they were defeated without danger to any Christian.[6]

In the words of the sixteenth-century Andean chronicler Waman Poma, the Spaniards killed the panic-stricken Indians 'like ants'.[7]

Peru was not conquered in a single battle. There were Inca revolts led by Manco Cápac in 1535 and again, on a much larger scale, between 1536 and 1539. Nor were the Indians slow to adopt European ways of warfare. They proved to be tenacious guerrilla fighters. At the same time, the Spaniards quarrelled enough among themselves to jeopardize their dominance – to the extent that fraternal strife claimed Pizarro's own life in 1541. It was not until the execution of Túpac Amaru more than thirty years later, in September 1572, that Inca resistance was irreparably broken.

Among the Spaniards was a young captain from Segovia named Jerónimo de Aliaga. To de Aliaga, Peru was as weird as it was wonderful. He marvelled at the scale and sophistication of Inca architecture, not least the huge northern wall of the Sacsayhuamán fortress at their capital, Cuzco, with its perfectly interlocking 200-ton stones. Much of what the Spaniards later built at Cuzco they erected on top of Inca walls and foundations, recognizing their extraordinary, earthquake-resistant quality.[8] Today we can get a better sense of the pre-Conquest grandeur of the Inca achievement at Machu Picchu – the legendary 'lost city of the Incas', which seems to float amid the clouds of the Andes, a city the Spaniards never found and so never despoiled and rebuilt. High above the Urubamba River, Machu Picchu was probably constructed in the mid-fifteenth century. Despite its seemingly impractical location, clinging to steep mountainsides more than 8,000 feet above sea-level, it was clearly a self-sufficient settlement, with running spring water and terraces for the cultivation of crops and the grazing of livestock. Wholly unknown to the Western world until 1911, when it was found by the American academic and explorer Hiram Bingham,[9] it serves as a warning that no civilization, no matter how mighty it may appear to itself, is indestructible. We still do not know what purpose the city served. Nor do we know exactly when and why the Incas abandoned it. One strong possibility is that epidemic disease arrived there from Hispaniola (the island which is today divided between the Dominican Republic and Haiti) ahead of the conquistadors, killing the population and leaving Machu Picchu a ghost town.

The pretext for the initial Spanish assault at Cajamarca was that the Incas refused to convert to Christianity. But it was not God but gold that really interested Pizarro. The captured Atahualpa's vain attempt to secure his freedom by filling his cell once with gold and twice with silver merely aroused the conquistadors' appetite for precious metal. The 13,420 pounds of 22-carat gold and 26,000 pounds of pure silver that were duly piled up made every man in the expedition rich at a stroke. But there was more – much more.[10] The Spaniards had also found gold in Hispaniola and vast deposits of silver at

Zacatecas in Central Mexico. Now they found the *cerro rico* ('rich mountain') at Potosí, a silver mine without equal in the world. Everywhere the Spaniards looked in Peru, it seemed, there was specie. As Pizarro's chief accountant, Jerónimo de Aliaga was well placed to grasp the full extent of this newfound wealth. Prior to 1550, gold worth around 10 million pesos was taken from Peru, about half of it plundered, the rest mined.[11] Over time, the output of the silver mines rose steadily, from around 50 tonnes a year in the early 1500s to over 900 tonnes by 1780.[12] In all, between 1500 and 1800, precious metal worth roughly £109 billion at today's prices was shipped from the New World to Europe or via the Pacific to Asia, a large part of it from the mines of Peru. Men like de Aliaga became very rich indeed. He was able to build himself a magnificent townhouse in the new Peruvian capital of Lima, with an inner courtyard that stands on the site of an Inca temple. The house has been occupied by his descendants ever since; the present occupant, Gonzalo de Aliaga, is unabashedly proud of his conquistador ancestor.

The Spaniards appeared to be laying the foundation for an entirely new and spectacular civilization, to be run from a few splendid cities by a tiny, wealthy Spanish-born elite. And those cities grew rapidly. Mexico City had 100,000 inhabitants in 1692, at a time when Boston had barely 6,000. Twenty-five Spanish American universities were founded, like the one at Santo Domingo, which predates Harvard by nearly a century.[13] The sciences of cartography and metallurgy flourished.[14] The Spaniards learned to enjoy at least some of the staples of Meso-American cuisine: chillies, peanuts, potatoes and turkeys (all later adopted by North Americans).[15] Hundreds of lavishly adorned churches were built, and some of the most imposing cathedrals in the world, like the magnificent one at Cuzco designed by the architect Francisco Becerra and completed in 1669 by the Flemish Jesuit Juan Bautista Egidiano. Franciscans as well as Jesuits flocked to South America in their thousands to convert what remained of the indigenous population. But while the Church was influential, ultimate power resided with the Spanish Crown. And, crucially, the Crown owned all the land. The story of property-ownership in North America would be altogether different.

LAND OF THE FREE

In 1670 a penniless young English couple stepped off the first ship to land on the shores of Carolina, after a harrowing transatlantic journey. Like her travelling companion Abraham Smith, Millicent How had signed herself into service with a standard deed of indenture made in September 1669:

> Know all men that I Millicent How of London Spinster the day of the date hereof doe firmly by these pnts [points] bind and oblige my selfe as a faithfull & obedient Servant in all things whatsoever, to serve and dwell with Capt. Joseph West of the sd City of London Merchant, in the plantation, or province of Carolina.[16]

Between 65 and 80 per cent of all the Britons who came to the Chesapeake in the course of the seventeenth century did so on this basis.[17] That was by no means exceptional. Fully three-quarters of all European migrants to British America over the entire colonial period came as indentured servants.[18]

This was a very different migration from the one experienced by Jerónimo de Aliaga. The Spaniards had literally found mountains of silver in Mexico and Peru. All there seemed to be on the shores of Carolina was a bone-yard of bleached tree-trunks. This was no El Dorado. Instead, settlers in North America had to plant corn to eat and tobacco to trade.[19] For many years Britain's American colonies remained a patchwork of farms and villages, with a few towns and virtually no true cities. And here the natives, though less numerous, were not so easily subjugated. Even in 1670 you could still have been forgiven for thinking that Jerónimo de Aliaga's America was the land of the future, while Millicent How's was destined to remain an obscure Ruritania.

What if it had been the other way round? What if de Aliaga had ended up in a Spanish Carolina and How and Smith had ended up in a British Peru? 'If [England's] Henry VII had been willing to sponsor Columbus's first voyage,' the historian J. H. Elliott once half-playfully reflected,

> and if an expeditionary force of [Englishmen] had conquered Mexico for Henry VIII, it is possible to imagine a ... massive increase in the

wealth of the English crown as growing quantities of American silver flowed into the royal coffers; the development of a coherent imperial strategy to exploit the resources of the New World; the creation of an imperial bureaucracy to govern the settler societies and their subjugated populations; the declining influence of parliament in the national life, and the establishment of an absolutist English monarchy financed by the silver of America.[20]

In other words, it is not at all self-evident that the British colonies would have turned out as they did if they had been established in South rather than North America.

What if New England had been in Mexico and New Spain in Massachusetts? If it is possible to imagine England, rather than Castile, seduced into absolutism by the silver of the Peruvian mines, is it equally possible to imagine Castile, rather than England, planting the seeds of republican virtue at higher latitudes? Might the *cortes* – the nearest thing early-modern Spain had to a parliament – have built up enough power to establish the first constitutional monarchy in Western Europe? And might the Estados Unidos have emerged from a crisis of Hispanic rather than British imperial authority, speaking Spanish from its very inception? Such a role reversal is not so implausible. The United Provinces, after all, emerged from the Dutch Revolt against Spanish rule. Perhaps it was mere contingency – the absence or presence of New World gold and silver – that sent England along the high road to parliamentarism and Spain down the primrose path to absolutism. With an additional source of revenue outside the control of parliament, Charles I might have maintained his 'Personal Rule' and avoided the fateful confrontation that produced the British Civil War. His Puritan opponents in the House of Commons were elderly men by 1640. A few more years would have seen their challenge fade.[21] Nor was there any certainty that Britain would be steered a second time away from absolutism by the Dutch invasion and coup that installed William of Orange as king.[22] The chain of events that led from the financial travails of James I to the deposition of James II might easily have been broken on many occasions. No narrative is more tendentious than the Whig interpretation of English history, with its assumption that the Glorious Revolution of 1688 was a divinely ordained compromise between monarch and legislature. Even after 1688 the dominance of the Whig aristocrats who were the real beneficiaries of the Stuarts' ouster was still periodically vulnerable to Jacobite counter-coups, which enjoyed considerable support on the Celtic periphery.

The crux of the matter is the relative importance in the historical process of, on the one hand, initial resource endowments in the colonized territories of the New World and, on the other hand, the institutional blueprints the colonizers brought with them from Europe. If initial conditions were determining, then it did not much matter if Englishmen or Spaniards turned up in Peru; the result would have been much the same, because Englishmen would have been just as tempted to plunder the Incas and just as likely to succumb to the 'resource curse' of cheap gold and silver.[23] Presumably, too, Spanish settlers might have been more innovative had they found themselves goldless in the Chesapeake Bay. But if you believe that the key variable was the institutions the settlers brought with them, then quite different alternatives suggest themselves.

British colonization generally produced better economic results than Spanish or Portuguese, wherever it was tried. There is no perfect test for this proposition, since no two colonies were exactly alike, but Arizona is richer than Mexico and Hong Kong is richer than Manila. So perhaps British colonization of Mexico and Peru would have had better long-run results than Spanish, ultimately producing some kind of United States of Central and South America. And perhaps Spanish colonization of North America would have left that region both relatively impoverished and divided into quarrelsome republics: multiple nation-states like Colombia rather than a single District of Columbia as the seat of a federal government, and undying enmity between Wisconsin and Minnesota, rather than between Colombia and Venezuela.

England was already different from Spain in 1670, long before the advent of industrialization. Violence as measured by the homicide rate had been declining steadily since the 1300s. With the Glorious Revolution of 1688, an era of intermittent civil war had come to an end, though hard battles remained to be fought to impose order on the Celtic periphery, especially Northern Scotland and Southern Ireland. Beginning in around 1640, the English birth rate rose steadily from around twenty-six per 1,000 to a peak of forty per 1,000 in the early 1800s. Yet the Malthusian trap did not close, as it had in the past and continued to do elsewhere. Real wages moved upwards. Rents trended downwards. And literacy rose markedly.[24] A crucial change was the availability of an exit option for those willing to risk a transatlantic voyage. As early as the 1640s net emigration exceeded 100,000, and it ranged between 30,000 and 70,000 in every decade until the 1790s.[25] Those who feared that these adventurous types were being lost to the land of their birth failed to see the reciprocal benefits of transatlantic migration as trade between the American colonies and Europe flourished. The exported labour was simply more productive in land-rich, labour-poor America. The emigrants' departure also indirectly benefited their more risk-averse kinsmen who stayed behind by raising slightly the price of their work.

Those, like Millicent How and Abraham Smith, who left England for America after around 1670 took little with them. Even the price of their passage was paid by, in effect, a mortgage on their future labour. But they carried in their minds a number of ideas that had profound implications for the American future. The first was the idea of property rights* as they had evolved in the common law courts (and the Court of Chancery) since the twelfth century.[26] The second idea was that of militant Protestantism (though it is important not to forget that Quakers, Catholics and Jews also played their part in settling the eastern seaboard).[27] The third idea was that taxation depended for its legitimacy on parliamentary approval; the Crown was granted 'supply' in return for consenting to the redress of grievances through legislation. These had been the core issues of Britain's Civil War.

Antagonism to the uniformity of Anglican worship to which Archbishop William Laud had aspired, combined with hostility to Charles I's fiscal innovations, had given the mid-seventeenth-century crisis a distinctive character in the British Isles. As early as 1628, in the Petition of Right, the King's parliamentary critics had demanded that 'No man hereafter be compelled to make or yield any gift, loan, benevolence, tax

---

* Specifically, the presumptive right of the male heir to inherit his father's land, the distinction in terms of alienability between fee simple and fee tail, the distinction in terms of security of tenure between freehold and copyhold, the use of trespass and ejectment to determine title and the legitimacy of the 'use' and the 'trust' as a way of evading feudal dues or other impositions.

or such like charge without common consent by act of parliament.' When a botched attempt to impose Laud's Book of Common Prayer on Presbyterian Scotland ended in war, Charles was forced back to parliament, cap in hand. But rather than accept what became the Long Parliament's violations of his royal prerogative, Charles raised the royal standard in August 1642, plunging the country into war. He lost and paid the price with his head on 30 January 1649. Regicide was followed by Republic (the Commonwealth), which in turn was followed – much as foreseen in classical political theory – by Tyranny, in the form of Oliver Cromwell as lord protector. With Cromwell's death, the monarchy was restored, but the old issues soon resurfaced. Charles II and his brother were both suspected, with good reason, of Roman Catholic leanings, and of yearning to reduce the power of parliament. The deposition of James II in 1688 was a Dutch coup by parliamentary invitation; the Declaration of Rights emphatically ended the argument about fiscal power: 'Levying money for or to the use of the Crown by pretence of prerogative, without grant of Parliament, for longer time, or in other manner than the same is or shall be granted, is illegal.' By ending the threat of arbitrary taxation and by putting the government's revenue, expenditure and borrowing under the supervision of a body in which property-owners were disproportionately represented, the Glorious Revolution laid a solid foundation for the subsequent development of what might be called the British 'maritime–fiscal complex'.[28] Even if the Stuarts had been restored to power in 1714 or 1745 it is doubtful that they would have undone this.

Yet the more profound change that happened in seventeenth-century England had to do with the very nature of politics itself. The argument was between two Oxford men – one educated at Magdalen Hall, the other at Christ Church – both of whom were beneficiaries of aristocratic patronage – the Earl of Devonshire in the former case, the Earl of Shaftesbury in the latter – and both of whom derived inspiration from time spent abroad – in, respectively, France and the Netherlands. For Thomas Hobbes, writing in his *Leviathan* (1651), the lesson of the first half of the seventeenth century was clear: 'During the time men live without a common power to keep them all in awe, they are in . . . a war . . . of every man against every man.'[29] Men are held to perform their duties only by 'fear', Hobbes argued, and therefore power must be delegated to a strong sovereign with responsibility for defence, education, legislation and justice. The crucial point was Hobbes's belief that the sovereign must be secure against any challenge from below. He could not be bound by any 'covenant' (constitution), could not be 'divisible' and could not 'justly be put to death'.[30] This was not (as is sometimes thought) a justification of royal absolutism; on the contrary, with its dark view of man's imperfectibility and its pragmatic arguments for a strong sovereign, *Leviathan* severed Hobbes's ties to the then exiled Stuarts. For Hobbes made it clear that his sovereign could be either a monarch or a parliament ('one man, or an assembly of men').[31] His conception was thus very far removed from the divine-right absolutism of a Stuart loyalist like Sir Robert Filmer, the author of *Patriarcha*.

John Locke's first *Treatise of Government* (1690) was a rebuttal of Filmer, but his second *Treatise* offered a more searching and original challenge to Hobbes. Far from a strong sovereign's being the solution to a natural state of war, Locke argued, the true state of nature is harmonious; it is the would-be absolutist, in seeking to 'take away *Freedom*', who is at war with society.[32] People do not choose to be governed purely out of fear. As 'a Society of Rational Creatures', they enter into 'a Community for their mutual good'. In a commonwealth constituted on this basis, Locke suggested, power is merely delegated by 'Civil Society' to a 'Legislative', whose majority decisions are based on the implicit consent of all citizens. In contradistinction to Hobbes's belief that the sovereign must be unitary and indivisible, Locke explicitly favoured separating the 'Executive' and what he called the 'Federative' branches from the Legislative, though he saw the Legislative as the dominant institution, with the responsibility for appointing judges as well as for making laws. Even more striking is the difference between Hobbes's theory of liberty and Locke's. According to the former, 'the liberty of a subject, lieth ... only in those things, which ... the sovereign hath praetermitted [that is, explicitly conceded]' – in cases of 'the silence of the law', the presumption must be in favour of the sovereign. Locke saw the matter quite differently:

> *Where there is no Law, there is no Freedom* ... The *Legislative* ... is *bound to dispense Justice* ... *by promulgated standing Laws, and*

known Authoris'd Judges ... designed *for* no other end ultimately but *the good of the People.*[33]

Freedom in Locke's view was something quite distinctive. It was a man's 'Liberty to dispose, and order, as he lists, his Person, Actions, Possessions, and his whole Property, within the Allowance of those Laws under which he is; and therein not to be subject to the arbitrary Will of another . . .'[34] Here was the heart of the matter: 'The great and *chief end* therefore, of Men's uniting into Commonwealths ... is *the preservation of their Property.*'[35] And the Legislative may not 'take from any Man any part of his *Property* without his own consent', meaning a consent of the majority of representatives to taxation. This had truly revolutionary implications, as Locke well knew, writing as he was so soon after the events of 1688:

> the Legislative being only a Fiduciary Power to act for certain ends, there remains still *in the People a Supream Power* to remove or *alter the Legislative*, when they find the *Legislative* act contrary to the trust reposed in them.[36]

Though only one American edition of the *Two Treatises* appeared before 1776 – and an imperfect edition at that – Locke's ideas would have a seminal influence on the development of both society and politics in North America. By contrast, Latin America's politics after independence would end up oscillating between Hobbes's anarchic state of nature and a crude caricature of his authoritarian sovereign.

The New World represented a vast addition of territory to the West European monarchies. The key question that faced the new settlers in the Americas – Spaniards in the south, Britons in the north – was how to allocate all this new land. Their answers to this question would ultimately determine the future leadership of Western civilization. They could scarcely have been more different.

When the captain of the first ship to arrive in the Carolinas stepped on to the beach he brought with him an institutional template for the New World – one that had the issue of land at its heart. 'The Fundamental Constitutions of Carolina' were drawn up in March 1669 by none other than Locke, in his capacity as secretary to one of Carolina's eight 'Lords Proprietor', the Earl of Shaftesbury. The document is remarkable as much for the things the colonists did not adopt as for what they did adopt. Obedient to his aristocratic patron, who was anxious to 'avoid erecting a numerous democracy', Locke outlined a scheme that would have established a hereditary aristocracy and a hierarchical society in the Americas, complete with a supreme lord palatine, landgraves, baronies and all kinds of oddities like caziques and leet-men, as well as strict limits on the alienation and subdivision of land from their large estates. He also sought to ban professional lawyers, arguing that 'it shall be a base and vile thing to plead for money or reward'. And, to his considerable discomfiture, he was forced by his noble patron to include an article (number 96) naming the Church of England as the established Church of Carolina.[37] The colonists wisely ignored most of this, but they did retain one of Locke's key assumptions – that there should be a link between political representation and property-ownership. Article 4 specified that three-fifths of the land was to be divided 'amongst the people'. Articles 71 and 72 declared that there would be a parliament, meeting biennially, and that:

> No man shall be chosen a member of parliament who has less than five hundred acres of freehold within the precinct for which he is chosen; nor shall any have a vote in choosing the said member that hath less than fifty acres of freehold within the said precinct.

Much therefore hinged on how the land in Carolina would be divided up.

For a time it was feared that the first fleet of settlers sent to Carolina had been lost at sea. When it was discovered that they had in fact arrived safely, what became known as the Barbados Proclamation was drawn up to regulate the distribution of land. The important thing was that there was a guaranteed minimum: 'To every freeman that shall arrive there to plant and inhabit before the 25 March 1672 one hundred akers of land to him and his heires for ever . . .'. But what if there were insufficient freemen to take advantage of this offer? The obvious answer was that when the indentured servants had served out their time – usually five or six years – they too should be given land.

Life in England had been hard for Millicent How and Abraham Smith. The Atlantic crossing had been fraught with peril and they were doubtless aware that significant numbers of immigrants to the North American colonies did not survive the first year or two of 'seasoning'. But here was an incentive to run those risks. In England property rights were secure, but property was held in a few hands. (In 1436 between 6,000 and 10,000 families of nobles and gentry had owned around 45 per cent of the land; the Church 20 per cent; the Crown 5 per cent.) But in America even the lowest of the low had the chance to get a first foot on the property ladder. This was the essence of the headright system, also introduced in Virginia, Maryland, New Jersey and Pennsylvania. It was a system that made perfect sense in colonies where land was plentiful and labour in short supply.[38] As Locke observed in his 'Considerations of the Consequences of the Lowering of Interests': 'Most nations in the civilized parts of the world are more or less rich or poor, proportionably to the paucity or plenty of their people and not the sterility or fruitfulness of their lands.' Rival empires – like the Spanish and Dutch – did not make 'any improvement by planting; what they do in the East Indies being only by war, trade, and building of fortified towns and castles upon the seacoast, to secure the sole commerce of the places and with the people whom they conquer, not by clearing, breaking up of the ground, and planting, as the English have done'.[39] Not only was this active planting of land an economically superior form of imperialism. It also legitimized the expropriation of land from indigenous hunter-gatherers. In Locke's words: 'As much land as a man tills, plants, improves, cultivates and can use the product of, so much is his property. He by his labour does, as it were, inclose it from the Common.'[40] Indian hunting grounds were, by this definition of private property, *terra nullius* – ownerless land, ripe for development. This was a charter for expropriation.

Every land transaction since the arrival of the first settlers is recorded in the North Charleston Conveyancing Office, including all the small plots granted to the men and women who had fulfilled the terms of their deed of indenture. Millicent How and Abraham Smith were duly given, respectively, 100 acres and 270 acres of land, to keep or sell as they saw fit. They had indeed arrived – not only economically but also politically. For Locke had made it clear in his 'Fundamental Constitutions' that in Carolina it would be landowners who held political power. If you were a man like Abraham Smith – although not a woman like Millicent How – and owned 50 or more acres of land, then you could vote as well as sit on a jury. With 500 acres you could become a member of the Carolina assembly or a judge. And, crucially, as a voter, a juryman or a member of parliament, you had one and only one vote, regardless of whether you owned the minimum number of acres or a hundred times that amount.

This property-owners' democracy had a homespun start. The first elected representatives of Carolina originally met upstairs at number 13, Church Street, a modest Charleston house. Yet institutions like this were to be the launching pad for a revolution in government. The English Crown had laid the foundations of its American empire simply by granting rights to trading companies. Though governors were royally appointed, there was an assumption that the colonists should have their own representative assemblies, which followed logically from their origins as chartered companies. And indeed, they wasted little time in establishing such bodies. The Virginia assembly met for the first time as early as 1619. By 1640 eight such assemblies existed in the British colonies, including Massachusetts Bay, Maryland, Connecticut, Plymouth and New Haven as well as Barbados.[41] No such institutions existed in Latin America.

The key, in short, was social mobility – the fact that a man like Abraham Smith could arrive in a wilderness with literally nothing and yet within just a few years become both a property-owner and a voter. In seven out of thirteen future American states on the eve of the American Revolution, the right to vote was a function of landownership or the payment of a property tax – rules that remained in force in some cases well into the 1850s.

In the Spanish colonies to the south, land had been allocated in a diametrically different way.

In a *cedula* (decree) dated 11 August 1534, Francisco Pizarro granted Jerónimo de Aliaga and another conquistador named Sebastián de Torres a vast domain – an *encomienda* – called Ruringuaylas, in the beautiful valley of Callejón de Huaylas in the Peruvian Andes. The valley was fertile, the mountains full of precious ore. The question facing de Aliaga was how to exploit these resources. The answer was quite unlike the one devised by John Locke for North America.

At first it was not land that was being given to de Aliaga and de Torres; technically, it was just the labour of the 6,000 or so Indians who lived here. Unlike in British colonies like Carolina, where acres were widely distributed, in Spanish America it was the right to exploit the indigenous people that was granted to a tiny elite. Previously, they had worked for the Inca Emperor under the *mita* system. Now their lot was to work for the Spaniards. It was essentially a tribute system – and tribute took the form of toil. The Indians were de Aliaga's to direct as he pleased, whether to plough the land or to dig gold and silver out of the mountains. This system changed only slightly with the introduction in 1542 of the *repartimiento de labor*, which imposed royal control over the allocation of native labour in response to reports of abuse by the *encomenderos*. (De Torres was in fact murdered by some of his Indian workers because of his cruelty.) *Encomiendas* were not granted in perpetuity to a man and his heirs; under Castilian law, the land on which they stood remained the property of the Crown; they were not even supposed to be fenced. Only slowly did they evolve into hereditary haciendas.[42] But the ultimate result was that the conquistador class became the idle rich of America. The majority of people were left with only tiny plots of land. Even among Spanish immigrants, the *encomenderos* were a minority, perhaps as few as 5 per cent of the Hispanic population in Peru.[43] Because, despite the depredations of disease, indigenous labour remained relatively abundant – population density in 1700 in the three leading Spanish colonies was several times greater than in the British mainland colonies – the Spaniards felt no need to import indentured labour from Europe on a large scale. Indeed, from the early sixteenth century the Spanish government went out of its way to restrict migration to its American colonies.[44] Under Spanish rule, as a result, there was none of the upward mobility that characterized British America.

Spanish rule also meant Roman Catholicism, which was not all bad – it was the Dominican missionary Fray Pedro de Córdoba who first exposed the appalling abuse of the indigenous peoples under the *encomienda* system – but was fundamentally a monopoly of another sort. North America, on the other hand, became home to numerous Protestant sects; dissent and diversity were among the organizing principles of British settlement. This had its shadow side (the Salem witchcraft trials spring to mind), but the clear benefit was the creation of a society of merchants and farmers committed to religious as well as political freedom. In article 97 of his 'Fundamental Constitutions of Carolina', John Locke made clear the extent of the British commitment to religious toleration:

> Since the natives of that place, who will be concerned in our plantation, are utterly strangers to Christianity, whose idolatry, ignorance, or mistake gives us no right to expel or use them ill; and those who remove from other parts to plant there will unavoidably be of different opinions concerning matters of religion, the liberty whereof they will expect to have allowed them, and it will not be reasonable for us, on this account, to keep them out; that civil peace may be maintained amidst diversity of opinions, and our agreement and compact with all men may be duly and faithfully observed; the violation whereof, upon what presence soever, cannot be without great offence to Almighty God, and great scandal to the true religion which we profess; and also that Jews, heathens, and other dissenters from the purity of Christian religion may not be scared and kept at a distance from it, but, by having an opportunity of acquainting themselves with the truth and reasonableness of its doctrines, and the peaceableness and inoffensiveness of its professors, may, by good usage and persuasion, and all those convincing methods of gentleness and meekness, suitable to the rules and design of the gospel, be won over to embrace and unfeignedly receive the truth; therefore, *any seven or more persons agreeing in any religion, shall constitute a church* or profession, to which they shall give some name, to distinguish it from others [emphasis added].

It took remarkable self-confidence, after so many years of bitter religious conflict in Europe, to envisage a society in which just seven people could legitimately start a new church. These profound differences between the civil societies of colonial North and South America would have enduring consequences when the time came for them to govern themselves independently.

AMERICAN REVOLUTIONS

In 1775, despite all the profound economic and social differences that had developed between them, both North and South America were still composed of colonies ruled by distant kings. That, however, was about to change.

On 2 July 1776 a large crowd gathered on the steps of the old trading exchange in Charleston to hear South Carolina's government declare the colony's independence from Britain. It was the first to do so. Some forty years later Spanish rule was ended in Latin America. Yet while one revolution cemented the democratic rights of property-owners, and brought into being a federal republic that within a hundred years was the world's wealthiest country, the South American revolutions consigned all of America south of the Rio Grande to two centuries of division, instability and underdevelopment. Why was that?

Both the Spanish and the British empires experienced crises in the late eighteenth century. The increased regulation of transatlantic trade by the imperial authorities and the high cost of the Seven Years' War (1756–63) paved the way for colonial revolts. Those that broke out in Britain's American colonies in the 1770s had their counterparts in Spain's: Túpac Amaru II's Andean Rebellion of 1780–83 and the Comunero Revolt in New Granada (present-day Colombia) in 1781. But when independence was claimed by thirteen of Britain's North American colonies, it was the reaction of a self-consciously libertarian society of merchants and farmers against what they saw as an over-extension of imperial authority. It was not only the hoary old question of taxation and representation that caused what can legitimately be seen as a sequel to the British Civil War of the 1640s.[45] Significantly, land played a vitally important part in the American Revolution. The British government's attempt to limit further settlement to the west of the Appalachians struck at the heart of the colonists' expansionist vision of the future[46] – a vision of manifest larceny that was especially dear to property speculators like George Washington.* When the government in London struck deals with the Indian tribes during the Seven Years' War, Washington assumed they were mere wartime expedients. He was appalled when the Indians were effectively confirmed in their lands by the royal proclamation of 1763:

> I can never look upon that Proclamation in any other light (but this I say between ourselves) than as a temporary expedient to quiet the minds of the Indians [he wrote to his future partner William Crawford in 1767]. It must fall, of course, in a few years, especially when those Indians consent to our occupying the lands. Any person ... who neglects the present opportunity of hunting out good lands, and in some measure marking and distinguishing them for his own, in order to keep others from settling them, will never regain it. If you will be at the trouble of seeking out the lands, I will take upon me the part of securing them, as soon as there is a possibility of doing it and will, moreover, be at all the cost and charges of surveying and patenting the same ... By this time it may be easy for you to discover that my plan is to secure a good deal of land. You will consequently come in for a handsome quantity ... [But] keep this whole matter a secret, or trust it only to those ... who can assist you in bringing it to bear by their discoveries of land.[47]

In 1768 Washington acquired 45,000 acres of present-day Mason, Putnam and Kanawha counties in what is now West Virginia; he was also a direct beneficiary of the subsequent forcible ejection of the Delaware, Shawnee and Mingo tribes from the land south of the Ohio River. But in his eyes the Quebec Act of 1774 made matters worse, by not only expanding what had been French Canada into present-day Illinois, Indiana, Michigan, Ohio, Wisconsin and parts of Minnesota, but also guaranteeing freedom of worship to Francophone Catholics.

---

* At the age of seventeen Washington was appointed as a county surveyor for the newly created frontier county of Culpeper. These skills stood him in good stead as an officer in the French and Indian War, as the colonists called the Seven Years' War. In 1752 Washington began his career as a land speculator when he bought 1,459 acres along Bullskin Creek in Frederick County, Virginia. After victory in the War of Independence, he and his fellow veterans fell upon the lands west of the Ohio River as the legitimate spoils of war.

Small wonder the rebellious New Englanders bracketed it, along with the four punitive measures passed following the Boston Tea Party, as one of the 'Intolerable Acts'.

War might have been averted by timely concessions from London on the headline issues of tax and representation. And the war might have gone the other way if the British generals Howe and Burgoyne had been better at their jobs. Perhaps more skilled diplomacy could have prevented the fateful isolation of Britain that culminated in the French victory – for that is what it was – at Yorktown in 1781. It is even possible to imagine the thirteen colonies subsequently falling apart instead of coming together. The economic problems of the war and post-war period were severe: inflation close to 400 per cent per annum at its peak in 1779, then a slump that halved per-capita income between 1774 and 1790, a mountain of debt equivalent to 62 per cent of gross national product in 1790, states imposing tariffs on each other and – worst of all – Massachusetts farmers like Daniel Shays driven to open revolt when their property was confiscated to pay for tax arrears and private debts. Had the revolution not progressed beyond the Articles of Confederation, then perhaps the fate of North America would have been more like that of South America – a story of fragmentation rather than unification. It took the constitution of 1787, the most impressive piece of political institution-building in all history, to establish a viable federal structure for the new republic, creating not only a Lockean quartet of powers – executive, bicameral legislature and supreme court – but also a single market, a single trade policy, a single currency, a single army and (significantly) a single law of bankruptcy for people whose debts exceeded their property – not forgetting an amendment, the Fourth, protecting the individual against 'unreasonable searches and seizures'.

At root, it was all about property. And in these terms Washington was one of those hard-nosed men who did well out of the War of Independence. His will, executed in 1800, lists a total of 52,194 acres of land in Virginia, Pennsylvania, Maryland, New York, Kentucky and the Ohio Valley, as well as lots in the Virginian cities of Alexandria, Winchester, Bath (now Berkeley Springs, West Virginia) and the newly founded city that bore his name. Nothing could better illustrate the tightness of the nexus between land and liberty in the early history

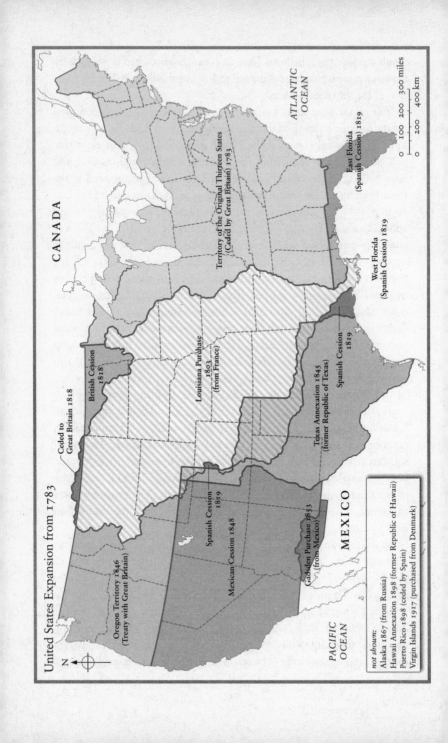

United States Expansion from 1783

CANADA

ATLANTIC OCEAN

Ceded to Great Britain 1818

British Cession 1818

Oregon Territory 1846 (Treaty with Great Britain)

Louisiana Purchase 1803 (from France)

Territory of the Original Thirteen States (Ceded by Great Britain) 1783

East Florida (Spanish Cession) 1819

West Florida (Spanish Cession) 1819

Spanish Cession 1819

Texas Annexation 1845 (former Republic of Texas)

Spanish Cession 1819

Mexican Cession 1848

Gadsden Purchase 1853 (from Mexico)

MEXICO

PACIFIC OCEAN

N

0   100   200   300 miles
0   200   400 km

not shown:
Alaska 1867 (from Russia)
Hawaii Annexation 1898 (former Republic of Hawaii)
Puerto Rico 1898 (ceded by Spain)
Virgin Islands 1917 (purchased from Denmark)

of the United States. In South America the Indians worked the land. In North America they lost it.

The South American Washington should have been Simón Bolívar. He too overthrew an empire – Spain's. But he failed to create a United States of South America. The American Revolution not only achieved unity for the former British colonies (though of course the Canadian and Caribbean colonies remained faithful to the empire, as did many American Loyalists who chose to leave the fledgling republic).[48] Independence also set the United States on the road to as yet unsurpassed prosperity and power. Yet independence from Spain left South America with an enduring legacy of conflict, poverty and inequality. Why did capitalism and democracy fail to thrive in Latin America? Why, when I once asked a colleague at Harvard if he thought Latin America belonged to the West, was he unsure? Why, in short, was Bolívar not the Latin Washington?

Born in July 1783, the son of a wealthy Venezuelan cacao planter, an orphan before he was ten and a soldier by the age of fourteen, Bolívar studied in both Spain and France, spending time in Paris in 1804 after all foreigners – including Latin American creoles – had been expelled from Madrid in response to a food shortage. He returned to Venezuela in 1807, as inspired by the Napoleonic phase of the French Revolution (see Chapter 4) as he was disgusted with Spanish rule. Bolívar was already dreaming of analogous changes in his native land. But when revolution came to South America, it was not a premeditated plan so much as a chaotic response to the sudden vacuum of power that followed Napoleon's assault on Spain in 1808. Two years later, Bolívar was sent to London to seek British support in the event of a French attack on Spain's American colonies. He did not get it, but he did meet and befriend Francisco Miranda, the veteran campaigner for Venezuelan independence. On their return home in July 1811, they proclaimed the First Venezuelan Republic.

The republic ended in failure. The constitution of 1811 explicitly confined the right to vote to property-owners but, as we shall see, that excluded a much larger proportion of the population than equivalent rules in North America. The result was that the propertyless, including large numbers of freed slaves (*pardos*), rallied to the royalist cause.[49] After the royalists had secured Puerto Cabello, Bolívar became disillusioned with Miranda and betrayed him to the Spaniards. Fleeing to New Granada, Bolívar then sought to rally the creoles there behind a second bid for independence.

Having proclaimed a Second Republic with himself in the role of dictator, Bolívar waged a so-called *campaña admirable* that drove the royalists from Mérida, Bogotá, Caracas and Trujillo and won him the epithet *el Libertador*. His Decree of War to the Death in 1813 illustrates the increasing viciousness of the conflict: 'Any Spaniard who does not, by every active and effective means, work against tyranny in behalf of this just cause, will be considered an enemy and punished; as a traitor to the nation, he will inevitably be shot by a firing squad.'[50] Prisoners were routinely killed – 800 at a time, on one occasion. Bolívar drew the line only when one of his confederates, nicknamed *el Diablo*, sent him the head of an elderly Spaniard. Yet, despite this resort to terror, non-whites continued to defect to the royalists. A devastating earthquake that struck Caracas in March 1812, killing around 10,000 people, seemed to vindicate the Church's condemnation of the independence movement.* Characteristically, Bolívar was defiant, declaring: 'If nature opposes us we will fight against her and force her to obey us.'[51] His biggest problem was not nature, however, but José Tomás Boves, a renegade Spaniard whose ragtag army of *llaneros* – Indians, fugitive slaves and deserters, interested more in plunder than in freedom – proved impossible to subdue.[52] A succession of military reverses at their hands forced Bolívar to flee once again, this time to Jamaica. A brief sojourn on Haiti only added to his conviction that the liberation of Venezuela's slaves must now become a part of his strategy. Only by making the cause of independence appealing to blacks as well as to white creoles could he hope to succeed.[53] He now directed his appeals to all South Americans, including *gente de color* ('people of colour').[54]

It worked – for a time, at least. Enticed by the offer of political representation, many *pardos* enlisted in Bolívar's army. The symbol of their aspirations became Manuel Carlos Piar, the son of a Spanish merchant and a half-Dutch, half-African mulatta from Curaçao. For

---

* However, some clergy did support the independence movement, particularly in New Granada, where there was considerable dissatisfaction with Spain's taxation of the South American Church. Against these dissident priests the royalists unleashed the Inquisition of Cartagena.

a casta (a person of mixed race) like Piar to attain the rank of general-in-chief seemed to prove that Bolívar was sincere in his claim to be the liberator of all South Americans, regardless of colour. Meanwhile, Spanish support for the reassertion of royal authority was waning. In 1820 there was huge mutiny in Cadiz among the 14,000 men about to be sent across the Atlantic to 'recolonize America'.[55] This was a bitter blow to Pablo Morillo, the royalist commander, whose thankless task it was to shore up Spain's crumbling imperium.

The tide was turning in Bolívar's favour. But there were many battles still to fight. To bolster still further the forces at his disposal, Bolívar now looked abroad for assistance.[56] Improbably, he found it in Britain.

Brown, MacGregor and even Ferguson – to say nothing of O'Connor, O'Leary and Robertson – are rather incongruous names to find engraved prominently on the grandiose monument to the founding fathers of Venezuela in the heart of Caracas. But these were just a few of the British and Irish soldiers who fought and in many cases died for the cause of Latin American freedom between 1810 and 1825.

In all, around 7,000 British and Irish volunteers signed up to help liberate South America from Spanish rule. Some were veterans of the Napoleonic Wars who had no appetite for the peace that followed Waterloo. But the majority (two-thirds of the total) were military novices. A few were doubtless inspired by the loftier cause that Bolívar now embodied: a free and united South America. Liberation was in the air after 1815 and other idealists, most famously Byron, went to help the Greeks wrest back their independence from the Ottomans. But the majority of those who sailed to Venezuela were, like the earlier British migrants to North America, attracted mainly by promises of land – the *haberes militares* promised as the reward for military service. Among them was a young captain from Manchester named Thomas Ferrier, who soon found himself in command of Bolívar's British Legion.

Ferrier's first view of the new Bolívarian America was a town called Angostura (the home of the bitters)* on the inhospitable banks of the

---

* Angostura bitters were in fact invented by a German in Bolívar's service, by the name of Dr Johann Gottlieb Benjamin Siegert, who first produced the alcoholic concentrate from a still-secret recipe in 1824. A Pisco Sour without a few drops of Siegert's concoction is not worthy of the name.

Orinoco River, where Bolívar had established his base. For four years, he and his men fought in a succession of battles from the Atlantic coast to the Pacific. In August 1819, after the Battle of Boyacá, they helped take Tunja and Bogotá, where Bolívar proclaimed the Republic of Colombia.[57] They then turned north to Venezuela. Finally, on 24 June 1821, they reached Carabobo, south of Puerto Cabello. This was to be the decisive battle of Bolívar's Venezuelan campaign. Around 6,500 republicans faced 5,000 royalists loyal to Spain. If Bolívar's troops could win the day, the road eastward to Caracas would lie open.

Bolívar ordered 600 men under Ferrier's command to outflank the Spaniards, who were dug in on a hill that commanded the battlefield. They were able to approach undetected along some well-hidden gullies. But as soon as they were spotted, the Spaniards opened fire with at least two cannon and 3,000 muskets. In the sweltering heat, Ferrier vainly waited for Bolívar to send reinforcements. Finally the order was given to advance. The bayonet charge that followed was one of the greatest military feats ever seen on the battlefields of South America. One account describes it as 'a task that required not only heroic courage, but herculean endurance and bull-dog determination to keep on while the last spark of life and strength was left'. By the time the enemy position had been taken, Ferrier lay fatally wounded. An ecstatic Bolívar called the British soldiers 'Salvadores de mi Patria!' – 'Saviours of my country'.

Bolívar was now master of what he called 'Gran Colombia', encompassing New Granada, Venezuela and Quito (modern Ecuador). José de San Martín, the liberator of Argentina and Chile, had yielded political leadership to him. By April 1825, his men had driven the last Spanish forces from Peru; Upper Peru was renamed 'Bolivia' in his honour. The next step was to create an Andean Confederation of Gran Colombia, Peru and Bolivia.

Why did Bolívar's Gran Colombia fail to establish itself as the core of a United States of Latin America? The superficial answer lies in his determination to centralize power and the resistance of the regional *caudillos* (warlords) who had stepped into the vacuum left by the Spanish collapse.[58] But this is to miss three deeper difficulties.[59]

The first is that the South Americans had virtually no experience of democratic decision-making, of the sort that had been normal in North American colonial assemblies from the outset. Indeed, because power had been so concentrated in the hands of the Spanish-born *peninsulares*, the creoles had little experience of any kind of administrative responsibility. As Bolívar put it in 1815:

> We are . . . neither Indian nor European, but a species midway between the legitimate proprietors of this country and the Spanish usurpers . . . We were cut off and, as it were, removed from the world in relation to the science of government and administration of the state. We were never viceroys or governors, save in the rarest of instances; seldom archbishops and bishops; diplomats never; as military men, only subordinates; as nobles, without royal privileges. In brief, we were neither magistrates nor financiers and seldom merchants.[60]

He was dismayed by the factional infighting he witnessed in the creole assemblies of New Granada.[61] In his Cartagena Manifesto of 1812, he poured scorn on 'the . . . fatal . . . system of tolerance . . . a system long condemned as weak and inadequate by every man of common sense' and on the 'criminal clemency' of the 'benevolent visionaries, who, creating fantastic republics in their imaginations, have sought to attain political perfection, assuming the perfectibility of the human race'. He also denounced the First Venezuelan Republic's experiment with federalism, which 'by authorizing self-government, disrupts social contracts and reduces nations to anarchy'.[62] By the time of his second period of exile in Jamaica, he had become convinced that 'institutions which are wholly representative are not suited to our character, customs, and present knowledge'.[63] Two years before the Battle of Carabobo, he addressed the newly formed Congress in Angostura in a similar vein:

> Although that nation was cradled in liberty, raised on freedom, and maintained by liberty alone . . . it is a marvel . . . that so weak and complicated a government as the federal system has managed to govern them in the difficult and trying circumstances of their past . . .

In his view, the United States constitution would require 'a republic of saints' to work.[64] Such a system could not possibly succeed in South America:

> Regardless of the effectiveness of this form of government with respect to North America, I must say that it has never for a moment entered my

mind to compare the position and character of two states as dissimilar as the English American and the Spanish American.

So Bolívar's dream turned out to be not democracy but dictatorship, not federalism but the centralization of authority, 'because', as he had put it in the Cartagena Manifesto, 'our fellow-citizens are not yet able to exercise their rights themselves in the fullest measure, because they lack the political virtues that characterize true republicans'.[65] Under the constitution he devised – which, among other peculiarities, featured a tricameral legislature – Bolívar was to be dictator for life, with the right to nominate his successor. 'I am convinced to the very marrow of my bones', he declared, 'that America can only be ruled by an able despotism ... [We cannot] afford to place laws above leaders and principles above men.'[66] His Organic Decree of Dictatorship of 1828 made clear that there would be no property-owning democracy in a Bolívarian South America, and no rule of law.

The second problem had to do with the unequal distribution of property itself. After all, Bolívar's own family had five large estates, covering more than 120,000 acres. In post-independence Venezuela, nearly all the land was owned by a creole elite of just 10,000 people – 1.1 per cent of the population. The contrast with the United States is especially striking in this regard. After the North American Revolution, it became even easier for new settlers to acquire land, whether as a result of government credits (under various acts from 1787 to 1804) or of laws like the General Pre-emption Act of 1841, which granted legal title to squatters, and the Homestead Act of 1861, which essentially made smallholder-sized plots of land free in frontier areas. Nothing of this sort was done in Latin America because of the opposition of groups with an interest in preserving large estates in the countryside and cheap labour in crowded coastal cities. In Mexico between 1878 and 1908, for example, more than a tenth of the entire national territory was transferred in large plots to land-development companies. In 1910 – on the eve of the Mexican Revolution – only 2.4 per cent of household heads in rural areas owned any land at all. Ownership rates in Argentina were higher – ranging from 10 per cent in the province of La Pampa to 35 per cent in Chubut – but nowhere close to those in North America. The rural property-ownership rate in the United States in 1900 was just under 75 per cent.[67]

It should be emphasized that this was not an exclusively US phenomenon. The rate of rural property-ownership was even higher for Canada – 87 per cent – and similar results were achieved in Australia, New Zealand and even parts of British Africa, confirming that the idea of widely dispersed (white) landownership was specifically British rather than American in character. To this day, this remains one of the biggest differences between North and South America. In Peru as recently as 1958, 2 per cent of landowners controlled 69 per cent of all arable land; 83 per cent held just 6 per cent, consisting of plots of 12 acres or less. So the British volunteers who came to fight for Bolívar in the hope of a share in the *haberes militares* ended up being disappointed. Of the 7,000 who set off for Venezuela, only 500 ended up staying. Three thousand died in battle or from disease, and the rest went home to Britain.[68]

The third – and closely related – difficulty was that the degree of racial heterogeneity and division was much higher in South America. Creoles like Bolívar hated *peninsulares* with extraordinary bitterness, far worse than the enmity between 'patriots' and 'redcoats' even in Massachusetts. But the feelings of the *pardos* and slaves towards the creoles were not much more friendly. Bolívar's bid for black support was not based on heartfelt belief in racial equality; it was a matter of political expediency. When he suspected Piar of planning to rally his fellow castas against the whites, he had him arrested and tried for desertion, insubordination and conspiring against the government. On 15 October 1817 Piar was executed by a firing squad against the wall of the cathedral at Angostura, the shots audible in Bolívar's nearby office.[69] Nor was Bolívar remotely interested in extending political rights to the indigenous population. The constitutional requirement that all voters be literate effectively excluded them from the political nation.

To understand why racial divisions were more complex in South America than in North America, it is vital to appreciate the profound differences that had emerged by the time of Bolívar. In 1650 the American Indians had accounted for around 80 per cent of the population in both North America and South America, including also Brazil. By 1825, however, the proportions were radically different. In Spanish America indigenous peoples still accounted for 59 per cent of

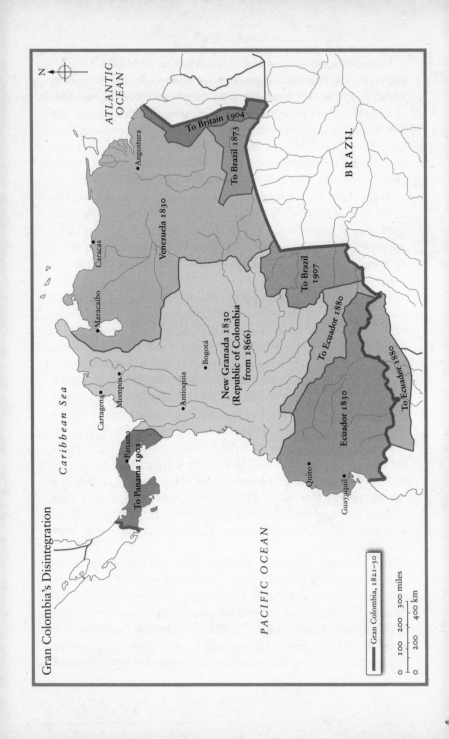

Gran Colombia's Disintegration

ATLANTIC
OCEAN

To Britain 1904

To Brazil 1873

Caribbean Sea

• Angostura

Venezuela 1830

To Brazil
1907

• Caracas

• Maracaibo

New Granada 1830
(Republic of Colombia
from 1866)

• Bogotá

To Ecuador 1880

• Cartagena
• Mompos
• Antioquia

To Ecuador 1880

BRAZIL

• Panama 1903

Ecuador 1830

To Panama 1903

• Quito

• Guayaquil

PACIFIC OCEAN

N

0   100   200   300 miles
0   200   400 km

Gran Colombia, 1821–30

the population. In Brazil, however, the figure was down to 21 per cent, while in North America it was below 4 per cent. In the United States and Canada massive migration from Europe was already under way, while the expropriation of the Indian peoples and their displacement to 'reservations' of marginal land was relatively easily achieved by military force. In Spanish America the Indians were not only more numerous but were also, in the absence of comparably large immigration, the indispensable labour force for the *encomienda* system. Moreover, as we shall see, the institution of African slavery had quite different demographic impacts in the various regions of European settlement.[70]

In the end, then, Bolívar's vision of South American unity proved impossible to realize. After revolts in New Granada, Venezuela and Quito, the proposed Andean Confederation was rejected and Gran Colombia itself disintegrated when Venezuela and Quito seceded. The victor was Bolívar's former confederate, the caudillo José Antonio Páez, who had thrust himself forward as the proponent of a narrow Venezuelan nation-state.[71] A month before his death from tuberculosis in December 1830, having resigned his posts of president and captain-general, Bolívar wrote a last despairing letter:

> . . . I have ruled for twenty years, and from these I have derived only a few certainties: (1) [South] America is ungovernable, for us; (2) Those who serve a revolution plough the sea; (3) The only thing one can do in America is to emigrate; (4) This country will fall inevitably into the hands of the unbridled masses and then pass almost imperceptibly into the hands of petty tyrants, of all colours and races; (5) Once we have been devoured by every crime and extinguished by utter ferocity, the Europeans will not even regard us as worth conquering; (6) If it were possible for any part of the world to revert to primitive chaos, it would be America in her final hour.[72]

It was a painfully accurate forecast of the next century and a half of Latin American history. The newly independent states began their lives without a tradition of representative government, with a profoundly unequal distribution of land and with racial cleavages that closely approximated to that economic inequality. The result was a cycle of revolution and counter-revolution, coup and counter-coup, as the propertyless struggled for just a few acres more, while the creole elites clung to their haciendas. Time and again, democratic experiments failed because, at the first sign that they might be expropriated, the wealthy elites turned to a uniformed *caudillo* to restore the status quo by violence. This was not a recipe for rapid economic growth.

It is not by chance that today's President of Venezuela, 'El Comandante' Hugo Chávez, styles himself the modern Bolívar – and indeed so venerates the Liberator that in 2010 he opened Bolívar's tomb to commune with his spirit (under the television arc lights). An ex-soldier with a fondness for political theatre, Chávez loves to hold forth about his 'Bolívarian revolution'. All over Caracas today you can see Bolívar's elongated, elegantly whiskered face on posters and murals, often side by side with Chávez's coarser, chubbier features. The reality of Chávez's regime, however, is that it is a sham democracy, in which the police and media are used as weapons against political opponents and the revenues from the country's plentiful oil fields are used to buy support from the populace in the form of subsidized import prices, handouts and bribes. Private property rights, so central to the legal and political order of the United States, are routinely violated. Chávez nationalizes businesses more or less at will, from cement manufacturers to television stations to banks. And, like so many tinpot dictators in Latin American history, he makes a mockery of the rule of law by changing the constitution to suit himself – first in 1999, shortly after his first election victory; most recently in 2009, when he abolished term-limits to ensure his own indefinite re-election.

Nothing better exemplifies the contrast between the two American revolutions than this: the one constitution of the United States, amendable but inviolable, and the twenty-six constitutions of Venezuela, all more or less disposable. Only the Dominican Republic has had more constitutions since independence (thirty-two); Haiti and Ecuador are in third and fourth positions with, respectively, twenty-four and twenty.[73] Unlike in the United States, where the constitution was designed to underpin 'a government of laws not of men', in Latin America constitutions are used as instruments to subvert the rule of law itself.

Yet before we celebrate the long-run success of the British model of colonization in North America, we need to acknowledge that in one peculiar respect it was in no way superior to Latin America. Especially after the American Revolution, the racial division between white and black hardened. The US constitution, for all its many virtues, institutionalized that division by accepting the legitimacy of slavery – the original sin of the new republic. On the steps of the Old Exchange in Charleston, where the Declaration of Independence was read, they continued to sell slaves until 1808, thanks to article 1, section 9, of the constitution, which permitted the slave trade to continue for another twenty years. And South Carolina's representation in Congress was determined according to the rule that a slave – 'other persons' in the language of the constitution – should be counted as three-fifths of a free man.

How, then, are we to resolve this paradox at the heart of Western civilization – that the most successful revolution ever made in the name of liberty was a revolution made in considerable measure by the owners of slaves, at a time when the movement for the abolition of slavery was already well under way on both sides of the Atlantic?

THE FATE OF THE GULLAHS

Here is another story, about two ships bringing a very different kind of immigrant to the Americas. Both left from the little island of Gorée, off the coast of Senegal. One was bound for Bahia in northern Brazil, the other for Charleston, South Carolina. Both carried African slaves – just a tiny fraction of the 8 million who crossed the Atlantic between 1450 and 1820. Nearly two-thirds of migrants to the Americas between 1500 and 1760 were slaves, increasing from a fifth prior to 1580 and peaking at just under three-quarters between 1700 and 1760.[74]

At first sight, slavery was one of the few institutions that North and South America had in common. The Southern tobacco farm and the Brazilian *engenho* alike came to rely on imported African slaves, once it became clear that they were cheaper and could be worked harder than indentured Europeans in the North and native Americans in the South. From the King of Dahomey down, the African sellers of slaves made no distinction; they were as happy to serve British slave-buyers as Portuguese, or for that matter their traditional Arab clients. A trans-Saharan slave trade dated back to the second century AD, after all. The Portuguese found fully functional slave markets when they arrived in Benin in 1500.[75] From the vantage point of a captive African held in the slave house at Gorée, it seemed to make little difference whether he was loaded on to the ship bound for North or South America. The probability of his dying in transit (roughly one in six, since we know that 16 per cent did not survive the ordeal) was about the same.

Nevertheless, there were important differences between the forms of slavery that evolved in the New World. Slavery had been an integral part of the Mediterranean economy since ancient times and had revived in the era of the Crusades, whereas in England it had essentially died out. The status of villeinage had ceased to feature in the common law at a time when the Portuguese were opening a new sea route from the West African slave markets to the Mediterranean and establishing the first Atlantic sugar plantations, first in the Madeiras (1455) and then on São Tomé in the Gulf of Guinea (1500).[76] The first African slaves arrived in Brazil as early as 1538; there were none in the future United States before 1619, when 350 arrived at Jamestown, having been taken as booty from a Spanish ship bound for Veracruz.[77] There were no sugar plantations in North America; and these – the *engenhos* of Bahia and Pernambuco – were undoubtedly the places where working conditions for slaves were harshest, because of the peculiarly labour-intensive characteristics of pre-industrial sugar cultivation.* The goldmines of southern Brazil (such as Minas Gerais) were not much better, nor the coffee plantations of the early nineteenth century. Many more Africans were shipped to Brazil than to the southern United States. Indeed, Brazil swiftly outstripped the Caribbean as the world's principal centre of sugar production, producing nearly 16,000 tons a year as early as 1600. (It was only later that production in Santo Domingo and Cuba reached comparable levels.)[78] Although the economy diversified over time from sugar production to mining, coffee growing and basic manufacturing, slaves

---

* Every stage of the process – cutting, carting, milling, boiling and drying – was physically demanding, and there could be no delay between them.

continued to be imported in preference to free migrants, and slavery was the normal form of labour in almost every economic sector.[79] So important was slavery to Brazil that by 1825 people of African origin or descent accounted for 56 per cent of the population, compared with 22 per cent in Spanish America and 17 per cent in North America. Long after the abolition of the slave trade and slavery itself in the English-speaking world, the Brazilians continued with both, importing more than a million new slaves between 1808 and 1888, despite an Anglo-Brazilian treaty of 1826 that was supposed to end the trade. By the 1850s, when British naval interventions began seriously to disrupt the transatlantic traffic, the Brazilian slave population was double what it had been in 1793.

The lot of slaves in pre-revolutionary Latin America was not wholly wretched. Royal and religious authority could and did intervene to mitigate the condition of the slaves, just as it could limit other private property rights. The Roman Catholic presumption was that slavery was at best a necessary evil; it could not alter the fact that Africans had souls. Slaves on Latin American plantations could more easily secure manumission than those on Virginian tobacco farms. In Bahia slaves themselves purchased half of all manumissions.[80] By 1872 three-quarters of blacks and mulattos in Brazil were free.[81] In Cuba and Mexico a slave could even have his price declared and buy his freedom in instalments.[82] Brazilian slaves were also said to enjoy more days off (thirty-five saints' days as well as every Sunday) than their counterparts in the British West Indies.[83] Beginning in Brazil, it became the norm in Latin America for slaves to have their own plots of land.

Not too rosy a picture should be painted, to be sure. When exports were booming, some Brazilian sugar plantations operated twenty hours a day, seven days a week, and slaves were quite literally worked to death. It was a Brazilian plantation-owner who declared that 'when he bought a slave, it was with the intention of using him for a year, longer than which few could survive, but that he got enough work out of him not only to repay this initial investment, but even to show a good profit'.[84] As in the Caribbean, planters lived in constant fear of slave revolts and relied on exemplary brutality to maintain discipline. A common punishment on some Brazilian plantations was the *novenas*, a flogging over nine consecutive nights, during which the victim's wounds were rubbed with salt and urine.[85] In eighteenth-century Minas Gerais it was not unknown for the severed heads of fugitive slaves to be displayed at the roadside. Small wonder average life expectancy for a Brazilian slave was just twenty-three as late as the 1850s; a slave had to last only five years for his owner to earn twice his initial investment.[86] On the other hand, Brazilian slaves at least enjoyed the right to marry, which was denied to slaves under British (and Dutch) law. And the tendency of both the Portuguese and the Spanish slave codes was to become less draconian over time.

In North America slave-owners felt empowered to treat all their 'chattels' as they saw fit, regardless of whether they were human beings or plots of land. As the population of slaves grew – reaching a peak of nearly a third of the British American population by 1760 – the authorities drew an ever sharper distinction between white indentured labourers, whose period of servitude was usually set at five or six years, and black slaves, who were obliged to serve for their whole lives. Legislation enacted in Maryland in 1663 was unambiguous: 'All Negroes or other slaves in the province . . . shall serve *durante vitae*; and all children born of any Negro or other slave shall be slaves as their fathers were.'[87] And North American slavery became stricter over time. A Virginian law of 1669 declared it no felony if a master killed his slave. A South Carolina law of 1726 explicitly stated that slaves were 'chattels' (later 'chattels personal'). Corporal punishment was not only sanctioned but codified.[88] It reached the point that fugitive slaves from Carolina began to cross the border into Spanish Florida, where the Governor allowed them to establish an autonomous settlement, provided they converted to Catholicism.[89] This was a remarkable development, given that – as we have seen – chattel slavery had died out in England centuries before, illustrating how European institutions were perfectly capable of mutating on American soil. A Virginian magistrate neatly captured the tension at the heart of the 'peculiar institution' when he declared: 'Slaves are not only property, but they are rational beings, and entitled to the humanity of the Court, when it can be exercised *without invading the rights of property*.'[90] Slave-traders laid themselves open to attack by abolitionists only when they overstepped a very elevated threshold, as the captain of the Liverpool ship the *Zong* did when, in 1782, he threw 133 slaves overboard, alive and chained, because of a shortage of water on board. Significantly, he was first prosecuted for insurance fraud before Olaudah Equiano alerted the abolitionist Granville Sharp to the real nature of the crime that had been committed.[91]

An especially striking difference between North and South was the North American taboo against racial interbreeding – 'miscegenation', as it was once known. Latin America accepted from early on the reality of interracial unions, classifying their various products (mestizos, the offspring of Spanish men and Indian women; mulattos, born of unions of creoles and blacks; and zambos, the children of Indians and blacks) in increasingly elaborate hierarchies. Pizarro himself had taken an Inca wife, Inés Huayllas Yupanqui, who bore him a daughter Doña Francisca.[92] By 1811 these various 'half-breeds' – the English term was intended to be pejorative – constituted more than a third of the population of Spanish America, a share equal to the indigenous population, and more than creoles of pure Hispanic origin, who accounted for less than a fifth. In eighteenth-century Brazil mulattos accounted for just 6 per cent of the predominantly African plantation workforce, but a fifth of the more skilled artisanal and managerial positions; they were the subaltern class of the Portuguese Empire.

In the United States, by contrast, elaborate efforts were made to prohibit (or at least deny the legitimacy of) such unions. This was partly a practical consequence of another difference. When the British emigrated to America, they often took their womenfolk with them. When Spanish and Portuguese men crossed the Atlantic, they generally travelled alone. For example, of the 15,000 names recorded in the 'Catálogo de Pasajeros a Indias', a list of Spanish passengers who embarked for the New World between 1509 and 1559, only 10 per cent were female. The results were not difficult to foresee. Scientists led by Andrés Ruiz-Linares have studied individual mitochondrial DNA samples from thirteen Latin American mestizo populations in seven countries from Chile to Mexico. The results show clearly that, right across Latin America, European men took indigenous and African women as mates, not the other way round.[93] Case studies of places like Medellín in Colombia – where the population is often regarded as 'purely' Hispanic – support this finding. In one sample, Y-chromosome lineages (inherited from the father) were found to be around 94 per cent European, 5 per cent African and just 1 per cent Amerindian, whereas mitochondrial DNA lineages (inherited from the mother) were 90 per cent Amerindian, 8 per cent African and 2 per cent European.[94]

It was not that miscegenation did not happen in North America. It did. Thomas Jefferson is only the most famous American to have fathered children by one of his slaves. There were approximately 60,000 mulattos in British America by the end of the colonial era. Today between a fifth and a quarter of the DNA of most African-Americans in the United States can be traced back to Europeans. But the model that took root in the colonial period was essentially binary. An individual with even a 'drop' of African-American blood – in Virginia, a single black grandparent – was categorized as black no matter how pale her skin or Caucasian her physiognomy. Interracial marriage was treated as a punishable offence in Virginia from as early

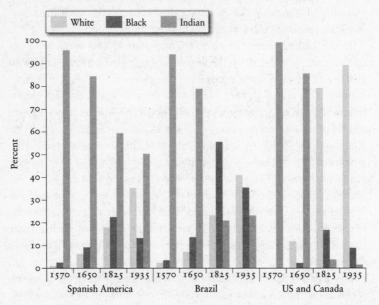

The Racial Structure of the New World, 1570–1935

NOTE: Data on mixed-race populations unavailable.

as 1630 and was legally prohibited in 1662; the colony of Maryland had passed similar legislation a year earlier. Such laws were enacted by five other North American colonies. In the century after the foundation of the United States, no fewer than thirty-eight states banned interracial marriages. As late as 1915, twenty-eight states retained such statutes; ten of them had gone so far as to make the prohibition on miscegenation constitutional. There was even an attempt, in December 1912, to amend the US constitution so as to prohibit miscegenation 'for ever'.[95]

It made a big difference, then, where African slaves went. Those bound for Latin America ended up in something of a racial melting pot where a male slave had a reasonable chance of gaining his freedom if he survived the first few years of hard labour and a female slave had a non-trivial probability of producing a child of mixed race. Those consigned to the United States entered a society where the distinction between white and black was much more strictly defined and upheld.

As we have seen, it was John Locke who had made private property the foundation of political life in Carolina. But it was not only landed property he had in mind. In article 110 of his 'Fundamental Constitutions', he had stated clearly: 'Every freeman of Carolina shall have absolute power and authority over his negro slaves, of what opinion or religion soever.' For Locke, the ownership of human beings was as much a part of the colonial project as the ownership of land. And these human beings would be neither landowners nor voters. Subsequent law-makers strove to maintain this distinction. Section X of the South Carolina Slave Code of 1740 authorized a white person to detain and examine any slave found outside a house or plantation who was not accompanied by a white person. Section XXXVI prohibited slaves from leaving their plantation, especially on Saturday nights, Sundays and holidays. Slaves who violated the law could be subjected to a 'moderate whipping'. Section XLV prohibited white persons from teaching slaves to read and write.

The profound effects of such laws are discernible in parts of the United States even today. The Gullah Coast stretches from Sandy Island, South Carolina, to Amelia Island, Florida. People here have their own distinctive patois, cuisine and musical style.[96] Some anthropologists believe that 'Gullah' is a corruption of 'Angola', where the inhabitants' ancestors may have come from. It is possible. Beginning in the mid-seventeenth century, a very high proportion of all the slaves transported to the Americas – perhaps as many as 44 per cent – came from the part of Africa contemporaries called Angola (the modern country plus the region between the Cameroons and the north bank of the Congo River).[97] A third of the slaves who passed through Charleston were from Angola.[98] Most of these were taken from the Mbundu people of the Ndongo kingdom, whose ruler, the *ngola*, gives the modern country its name. They ended up scattered all over the Americas, from Brazil to the Bahamas to the Carolinas.

That there are still discernible echoes of Angola in South Carolina – including traces of the Kimbundu language – is in itself significant. The people living here are directly descended from Angolan slaves and not much has happened to dilute their gene pool. The survival of Gullah culture testifies to the remarkable endurance of the colour line in states like South Carolina. By contrast, Angolans who were sent to South America had a significantly better chance of escaping from the prison of enslavement – sometimes literally, in the case of the fugitives from Pernambuco who founded their own independent colony of Quilombo, also known as Little Angola, in Palmares, deep in the jungle of the north-east Brazilian state of Alagoas. At its height, this little kingdom had a population of more than 10,000 and an elected chief, the 'Ganga Zumba'. Established in the early 1600s, it was not conquered by Portuguese forces until 1694. The fate of 'Gullah' Jack Pritchard, an Angolan slave who planned to launch an uprising against the *buckra* (whites) in Charleston in 1822, was very different. He was hanged. Ironically, the Land of the Free looked like being, for around a fifth of its population, the Land of the Permanently Unfree. North of the Rio Grande, slavery had become hereditary.

In the end, of course, the anomaly of slavery in a supposedly free society could be resolved only by war between the pro-slavery states of the South and the anti-slavery states of the North. Only British naval intervention on the side of the Confederacy could have defeated the upholders of the Union and that was never very likely. Yet, although the Civil War ended slavery, many Americans continued to believe for more than a century that they owed their prosperity to the dividing line between white and black. As early as the 1820s, Edward Everett could write in the *North American Review*:

> We have no concern with South America; we have no sympathy, we can have no well founded political sympathy with them. *We are sprung from different stocks* ... Not all the treaties we could make, nor the commissioners we could send out, nor the money we could lend them, would transform their ... Bolivars into Washingtons.[99]

To a later generation of white supremacists, segregation was the key reason why the United States had prospered, while the 'mongrel' peoples of Latin America were mired in poverty (not to mention, in some cases, communism).

With the rallying cry 'Segregation now! Segregation tomorrow! Segregation forever!' Alabama Governor George Wallace put racial separateness at the heart of the American success story as recently as 1963, in his inaugural gubernatorial address:

> This nation was never meant to be a unit of one ... but a united of the many ... that is the exact reason our freedom loving forefathers established the states, so as to divide the rights and powers among the states, insuring that no central power could gain master government control ...
>
> And so it was meant in our racial lives ... each race within its own framework has the freedom to teach ... to instruct ... to develop ... to ask for and receive deserved help from others of separate racial stations. This is the great freedom of our American founding fathers ... but if we amalgamate into the one unit as advocated by the communist philosophers ... then the enrichment of our lives ... the freedom for our development ... is gone forever. We become, therefore, a mongrel unit of one under a single all powerful government ... and we stand for everything ... and for nothing.

Such arguments were far from unappealing at the time: 10 million voters (13.5 per cent of the total) voted for Wallace and his American Independent Party when he ran for the presidency in 1968.

Yet the idea that the success of the United States was contingent on racial segregation was nonsense. It was quite wrong to believe, as Wallace did, that the United States was more prosperous and stable than Venezuela or Brazil because of anti-miscegenation laws and the whole range of colour bars that kept white and black Americans apart in neighbourhoods, hospitals, schools, colleges, workplaces, parks, swimming pools, restaurants and even cemeteries. On the contrary, North America was better off than South America purely and simply because the British model of widely distributed private property rights and democracy worked better than the Spanish model of concentrated wealth and authoritarianism. Far from being indispensable to its success, slavery and segregation were handicaps to American development, their legacy still painfully apparent in the social problems – teenage pregnancy, educational underachievement, drug abuse and disproportionate incarceration – that now bedevil so many African-American communities.

Today, a man with an African father and a white mother – a man who would have been called a casta in Simón Bolívar's day – is the President of the United States, having defeated a decorated war hero of classic Scotch-Irish origin even in the state of Virginia. That is something that would have seemed a fantastically remote possibility as recently as thirty years ago, when I first visited the American South. It is easy to forget that, as late as 1967, sixteen states still had laws prohibiting racial intermarriage. It was only with the Supreme Court judgment in the aptly named *Loving* v. *Virginia* that legal prohibitions on interracial marriage were ruled unconstitutional throughout the United States. Even then, Tennessee did not formally repeal the relevant article of its constitution until March 1978 and Mississippi put off doing so until December 1987. American racial attitudes have changed profoundly since that time. A whole time-honoured complex of words and thoughts can no longer publicly be uttered.

At the same time, the people in the streets of many North American cities increasingly resemble those in South America. Continuing migration from Latin America, especially Mexico, means that in forty years' time non-Hispanic whites will probably be a minority of the US population.[100] By that time the country may be practically if not legally bilingual. And American society is also becoming racially blended as never before. The US census distinguishes between four 'racial' categories: 'black', 'white', 'Native American' and 'Asian or Pacific

Islander'. On this basis, one in every twenty children in the United States is of mixed origin, in that their parents do not both belong to the same racial category. The number of such mixed-race couples quadrupled between 1990 and 2000, to roughly 1.5 million. Seen in this light, Barack Obama's election in 2008 appears far less surprising.

Meanwhile, one of the most dynamic economies in the world is that of multi-coloured Brazil. The key to success in Brazil – still among the world's most unequal societies – has been long-overdue reform to give a rising share of the population a chance to own property and make money. After more than a century of over-reliance on protectionism, import substitution and other forms of state intervention, most of Latin America – with the sorry exception of Venezuela – has achieved higher growth since the 1980s with a combination of privatization, foreign investment and export orientation.[101] The days when the region's economies veered between hyperinflation and debt default appear to be receding into the past. In 1950 South America's gross domestic product was less than a fifth of US GDP. Today it is approaching a third.

Five hundred years since the process of conquest and colonization began, in other words, the yawning divide between Anglo-America and Latin America finally seems to be closing. Throughout the Western hemisphere, a single American civilization is finally emerging – a kind of belated fulfilment of Bolívar's original pan-American dream.

This, however, is to anticipate a great deal. For the high tide of theories of racial distinction was not in fact in the nineteenth century but in the first half of the twentieth. To appreciate why it was that race became such a preoccupation of the West's interaction with other civilizations, we must now turn to Africa itself, which was to become the focal point of European imperial expansion in the period. In the speech with which this chapter began, Churchill – whose own imperial career had started in the Sudan and South Africa – asked a question that was in many ways central to the lives of an entire generation of empire-builders: 'Why should not the same principles which have shaped the free, ordered, tolerant civilization of the British Isles and British Empire be found serviceable in the organization of this anxious world?' Civilization as he understood it had successfully taken root in North America – as successfully in those parts that remained under

British rule as in the United States. It had flourished in the arid wilderness of Australia. Why not in Africa, too?

In America four European powers had tried their hands at planting their civilizations in foreign soil (five if we count the Dutch in Guiana and 'New Amsterdam', six if we count the Swedes in Saint-Barthélemy, seven including the Danes in the Virgin Islands, and eight with the Russian settlements in Alaska and California), with widely varying degrees of success. In the race to do the same in Africa, there were to be even more competitors. And Britain's biggest rival in this race turned out to be the country it had so successfully eclipsed in America: France.

4

Medicine

Let us first consider what state of things is described by the word 'civilization'. Its true test lies in the fact that people living in it make bodily welfare the object of life ... The people of Europe today live in better-built houses than they did a hundred years ago ... Formerly, they wore skins, and used spears as their weapons. Now, they wear long trousers, and ... instead of spears, they carry with them revolvers ... Formerly, in Europe, people ploughed their lands mainly by manual labour. Now, one man can plough a vast tract by means of steam engines and can thus amass great wealth ... Formerly, men travelled in wagons. Now, they fly through the air in trains at the rate of four hundred and more miles per day ... Formerly, when people wanted to fight with one another, they measured between them their bodily strength; now it is possible to take away thousands of lives by one man working behind a gun from a hill ... There are now diseases of which people never dreamt before, and an army of doctors is engaged in finding out their cures, and so hospitals have increased. This is a test of civilization ... What more need I say? ...

This civilization is such that one has only to be patient and it will be self-destroyed. According to the teaching of Muhammad this would be considered a Satanic Civilization. Hinduism calls it the Black Age ... It must be shunned.

Mahatma Gandhi

It is a people which by its sons (Robespierre, Descartes, etc.) has done much for humanity. I do not have the right to wish it evil.

Senegalese student

BURKE'S PROPHECY

From the middle of the nineteenth century until the middle of the twentieth, the West ruled over the Rest. This was the age not just of empires but of imperialism, a theory of overseas expansion that justified the formal and informal domination of non-Western peoples on both self-interested and altruistic grounds. Empire meant 'living space' for surplus population. It meant secure export markets that a rival power could not enclose behind tariffs. It meant higher returns on investment than were available at home.[1] Empire could also have a political function, sublimating the social conflicts of the industrial age in a gung-ho mood of patriotic pride, or generating placatory pay-offs for powerful interest groups. But it also meant the spread of civilization, a term used with increasing frequency to describe the whole complex of distinctly Western institutions we have already encountered in the preceding chapters: the market economy, the Scientific Revolution, the nexus of private property rights and representative government. It also meant the spread of Christianity, for in the process of empire-building missionaries were nearly as important as merchants and military men (see Chapter 6).

Of all the Western empires, by far the biggest was Britain's. From Grant Land, the northernmost extremity of Canada, to the sweltering shores of Georgetown, Guiana, and on to Graham Land in the Antarctic; down the Nile to Nyanza, across the Zambezi to the Cape; from the Persian Gulf across all of India to the Bay of Bengal, and on to Burma and Borneo; from Singapore to Sydney – immense swathes of the map of the world, including countless tiny islands, turned the bright-pink hue that a Scotsman's skin acquires under the tropical sun. By the eve of the First World War, the British Empire covered roughly a quarter of the world's land surface and embraced around the same proportion of humanity. It also exerted an unrivalled control over the world's sea-lanes and international telegraph network. Yet Britain was far from being the sole imperialist power. Despite the horrendous cost in human life of the Revolutionary and Napoleonic Wars, the French resumed imperial expansion within fifteen years of their defeat at Waterloo. Combining old sugar-producing islands like

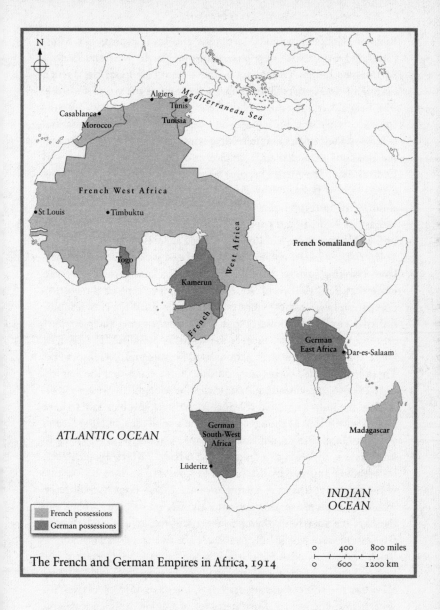

The French and German Empires in Africa, 1914

Réunion, Guadeloupe and Martinique and trading posts like Saint-Louis and Gorée with new possessions in North, West and Central Africa, the Indian Ocean, Indo-China and Polynesia, the French Empire by 1913 covered just under 9 per cent of the world's surface. The Belgians, the Germans and the Italians also acquired overseas colonies, while the Portuguese and Spaniards retained substantial chunks of their earlier empires. Meanwhile, over land rather than sea, the Russians extended their empire into the Caucasus, Siberia and Central Asia. The Austrians, too, acquired new territory; after being driven out of Germany by Prussia in 1866, the Habsburgs turned southwards into the Balkans. Even former colonies became colonizers, as the United States seized Puerto Rico and the Philippines, as well as Hawaii and a handful of smaller Pacific islands.

By 1913 Western empires dominated the world. Eleven motherlands covering just 10 per cent of the world's land surface governed more than half the world. An estimated 57 per cent of the world's population lived in these empires, which accounted for close to four-fifths of global economic output. Even at the time, their conduct aroused bitter criticism. Indeed, the word 'imperialism' is a term of abuse that caught on with nationalists, liberals and socialists alike. These critics rained coruscating ridicule on the claim that the empires were exporting civilization. Asked what he thought of Western civilization, the Indian nationalist leader Mahatma Gandhi is said to have replied wittily that he thought it would be a good idea. In *Hind Swaraj* ('Indian Home Rule'), published in 1908, Gandhi went so far as to call Western civilization 'a disease' and 'a bane'.[2] Mark Twain, America's leading anti-imperialist, preferred irony. 'To such as believe', he wrote in 1897, 'that the quaint product called French civilization would be an improvement upon the civilization of New Guinea and the like, the snatching of Madagascar and the laying on of French civilization there will be fully justified.'[3] The Bolshevik leader Vladimir Ilyich Lenin was also being ironic when he called imperialism 'the highest stage of capitalism', the result of monopolistic banks struggling 'for the sources of raw materials, for the export of capital, for spheres of influence, i.e., for spheres for profitable deals, concessions, monopoly profits and so on'. In fact he regarded imperialism as 'parasitic', 'decaying' and 'moribund capitalism'.[4] These are views of the age of empire still shared by many people today. Moreover, it is a truth almost universally acknowledged in the schools and colleges of the Western world that imperialism is the root cause of nearly every modern problem, from conflict in the Middle East to poverty in sub-Saharan Africa – a convenient alibi for rapacious dictators like Zimbabwe's Robert Mugabe.

Yet it is becoming less and less easy to blame the contemporary plight of the 'bottom billion' – the people living in the world's poorest countries – on the colonialism of the past.[5] There were and remain serious environmental and geographical obstacles to Africa's economic development. Independent rulers, with few exceptions, did not perform better than colonial rulers before or after independence; most did much worse. And today, an altogether different Western civilizing mission – the mission of the governmental and non-governmental aid agencies – has clearly achieved much less than was once hoped, despite the transfer of immense sums in the form of aid.[6] For all the best efforts of Ivy League economists and Irish rock stars, Africa remains the poor relation of the continents, reliant either on Western alms or on the extraction of its raw materials. There are, it is true, glimmers of improvement, not least the effects of cheap mobile telephony, which (for example) is providing Africans for the first time with efficient and low-cost banking services. There is also a real possibility that clean water could be made far more widely available than it currently is.* Nevertheless the barriers to growth remain daunting, not least the abysmal governance that plagues so many African states, symbolized by the grotesque statue that now towers over Dakar, representing a gigantic Senegalese couple in the worst socialist-realist style. (It was built by a North Korean state enterprise.) The advent of China as a major investor in Africa is doing little to address that problem. On the contrary, the Chinese are happy to trade infrastructure investment for access to Africa's mineral wealth, regardless of whether they are doing business with military dictators, corrupt kleptocrats or senile autocrats

---

* Dean Kamen's simple but effective water-purifier could quite easily be distributed through the soft-drink company Coca-Cola's unrivalled network of production facilities and sales outlets, which extends throughout the developing world. Considering the staggering number of lives lost each year to contaminated drinking water, this would surely lay to rest for ever the pejorative term 'coca-colonization'.

(or all three). Just when Western government and non-government agencies are at least beginning to demand improvements in African governance as conditions for aid, they find themselves undercut by a nascent Chinese empire.

This coincidence of foreign altruism and foreign exploitation is nothing new in African history. In the nineteenth century, as we have seen, Europeans came to Africa with a mixed bag of motives. Some were in it for the money, others for the glory. Some came to invest, others to rob. Some came to uplift souls, others to put down roots. Nearly all, however, were certain – as certain as today's aid agencies – that the benefits of Western civilization could and should be conferred on the 'Dark Continent'.* Before we rush to condemn the Western empires as evil and exploitative – capable only of behaviour that was the very reverse of civilized – we need to understand that there was more than a little substance to their claim that they were on a civilizing mission.

Take the case of the West's most remarkable killer application – the one that, far from being a killer, had the power to double human life expectancy: modern medicine. The ascetic holy man Gandhi was scornful of Western civilization's 'army of doctors'. In an interview in London in 1931 he cited the 'conquest of disease' as one of the purely 'material' yardsticks by which Western civilization measured progress.[7] To the countless millions of people whose lives have been lengthened by Western medicine, however, the choice between spiritual purity and staying alive was not difficult to make. Average global life expectancy at birth in around 1800 was just 28.5 years. Two centuries later, in 2001, it had more than doubled to 66.6 years. The improvement was not confined to the imperial metropoles. Those historians who habitually confuse famines or civil wars with genocides and gulags, in a wilful attempt to represent colonial officials as morally equivalent to Nazis or Stalinists, would do well to ponder the measurable impact of Western medicine on life expectancy in the colonial and post-colonial world.

* The phrase alluded both to the skin colour of the continent's inhabitants and to their relative economic backwardness (like the 'Dark Ages'). Today Africa is still the Dark Continent in the sense that, viewed at night from space, there is comparatively little man-made light to be seen, apart from in the extreme north and south.

Life Expectancy at Birth: England, the United States, India and China, 1725–1990

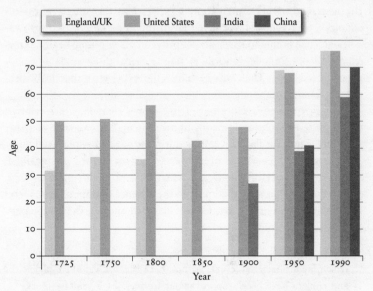

The timing of the 'health transition' – the beginning of sustained improvements in life expectancy – is quite clear. In Western Europe it came between the 1770s and the 1890s, beginning first in Denmark, with Spain bringing up the rear. By the eve of the First World War typhoid and cholera had effectively been eliminated in Europe as a result of improvements in public health and sanitation, while diphtheria and tetanus were controlled by vaccine. In the twenty-three modern Asian countries for which data are available, with one exception, the health transition came between the 1890s and the 1950s. In Africa it came between the 1920s and the 1950s, with just two exceptions out of forty-three countries. In nearly all Asian and African countries, then, life expectancy began to improve *before* the end of European colonial rule. Indeed, the rate of improvement in Africa has declined since independence, especially but not exclusively because of the HIV-AIDS epidemic. It is also noteworthy that Latin American countries did not fare any better, despite enjoying political independence from the early 1800s.[8] The timing of the improvement in life expectancy is especially striking as much of it predated the introduction of antibiotics (not least streptomycin as a cure for tuberculosis), the insecticide DDT and vaccines other than the simple ones for smallpox and yellow fever invented in the imperial era (see below). The evidence points to sustained improvements in public health along a broad front, reducing mortality due to faecal disease, malaria and even tuberculosis. That was certainly the experience of one British colony, Jamaica, and the story was probably similar in others like Ceylon, Egypt, Kenya, Rhodesia, Trinidad and Uganda, which experienced more or less simultaneous improvements.[9] As we shall see, the same holds true for France's colonies. It turns out that Africa's uniquely life-threatening repertoire of tropical diseases elicited a sustained effort on the part of the West's scientists and health officials that would not have been forthcoming in the absence of imperialism. Here the Irish playwright and wit George Bernard Shaw provides the perfect answer to Gandhi:

> For a century past civilization has been cleaning away the conditions which favour bacterial fevers. Typhus, once rife, has vanished: plague and cholera have been stopped at our frontiers by a sanitary blockade ... The dangers of infection and the way to avoid it are better understood than they used to be ... Nowadays the troubles of consumptive patients are greatly increased by the growing disposition to treat them as lepers ... But the scare of infection, though it sets even doctors talking as if the only really scientific thing to do with a fever patient is to throw him into the nearest ditch and pump carbolic acid on him from a safe distance until he is ready to be cremated on the spot, has led to much greater care and cleanliness. And the net result has been a series of victories over disease.[10]

These victories were not confined to the imperialists but also benefited their colonial subjects.

The twist in the tale is that even the medical science of the late nineteenth and early twentieth centuries had its dark side. The fight against pathogens coincided with a pseudo-scientific fight against the illusory threat of racial degeneration. Finally, in 1914, a war between the rival Western empires, billed as 'the great war for civilization', would reveal that Africa was not, after all, the world's darkest continent.

Most empires proclaim their own irenic intention to bring civilization to backward countries. But few in history were fonder of the phrase 'civilizing mission' than the French. To understand why, it is necessary first to appreciate the profound difference between the French and American revolutions. The first man to understand this difference was the Whig parliamentarian Edmund Burke, the greatest political thinker to emerge from the Pale of Protestant Settlement in Southern Ireland. Burke had supported the American Revolution, sympathizing strongly with the colonists' argument that they were being taxed without representation, and correctly discerning that Lord North's ministry was bungling the original crisis over taxation in Massachusetts. Burke's reaction to the outbreak of revolution in France was diametrically opposite. 'Am [I] seriously to felicitate a madman', he wrote in his *Reflections on the Revolution in France*, 'who has escaped from the protecting restraint and wholesome darkness of his cell, on his restoration to the enjoyment of light and liberty? Am I to congratulate a highwayman and murderer who has broke prison upon the recovery of his natural rights?'[11] Burke divined the French Revolution's violent character at an amazingly early stage. Those words were published on 1 November 1790.

The political chain reaction that began in 1789 was the result of a chronic fiscal crisis that had been rendered acute by French intervention in the American Revolution. Since the traumatic financial crisis of 1719–20 – the Mississippi Bubble – the French fiscal system had lagged woefully behind the English. There was no central note-issuing bank. There was no liquid bond market where government debt could be bought and sold. The tax system had in large measure been privatized. Instead of selling bonds, the French Crown sold offices, creating a bloated public payroll of parasites. A succession of able ministers – Charles de Calonne, Loménie de Brienne and Jacques Necker – tried and failed to reform the system. The easy way out of the mess would have been for Louis XVI to default on the monarchy's debts, which took a bewildering variety of different forms and cost almost twice what the British government was paying on its standardized bonds.[12] Instead, the King sought consensus. An Assembly of Notables went nowhere. The lawyers of the *parlements* only made trouble. Finally, in August 1788, Louis was persuaded to summon the Estates General, a body that had not met since 1614. He should have foreseen that a seventeenth-century institution would give him a seventeenth-century crisis.

At first the French Revolution was the British Civil War, with only the Puritanism lost in translation. The summoning of the Estates General gave malcontents within the aristocracy an opportunity to vent their spleen, with the comte de Mirabeau and marquis de Lafayette in the vanguard. As in England, the lower house developed a will of its own. On 17 June 1789 the Third Estate (Commons) proclaimed itself a 'National Assembly'. Three days later, in the famous Tennis Court Oath, its members swore not to be dissolved until France had a new constitution. Thus far it was the Long Parliament in French. But when it came to devising the new ground rules of French political life, the revolutionaries adopted some recognizably American language. At first glance, the Declaration of the Rights of Man and of the Citizen of 27 August 1789 would have raised few eyebrows in Philadelphia:

2. The natural and imprescriptible rights of man . . . are liberty, property, security, and resistance to oppression . . .

10. No one shall be disquieted on account of his opinions, including his religious views . . .

17. Since property is an inviolable and sacred right, no one shall be deprived thereof . . .[13]

So why, beginning with a searing speech on 1 February 1790, did Edmund Burke react so violently against this revolution? Here he is in full flow:

The French [have] rebel[led] against a mild and lawful monarch with more fury, outrage, and insult than ever any people has been known to rise against the most illegal usurper or the most sanguinary tyrant. Their resistance was made to concession . . . their blow was aimed at a hand holding out graces, favours, and immunities . . . They have found their punishment in their success: laws overturned; tribunals subverted; industry without vigour; commerce expiring; the revenue unpaid, yet the people impoverished; a church pillaged, and a state not relieved; civil and military anarchy made the constitution of the kingdom; everything human and divine sacrificed to the idol of public credit, and national bankruptcy the consequence; and, to crown all, the paper securities of new, precarious, tottering power ... held out as a currency for the support of an empire.[14]

If Burke had written those words in 1793, there would be no great mystery. But to have foreseen the true character of the French Revolution within a year of its outbreak was extraordinary. What had he spotted? The answer is Rousseau.

Jean-Jacques Rousseau's book *The Social Contract* (1762) was among the most dangerous books Western civilization ever produced. Man, Rousseau argued, is a 'noble savage' who is reluctant to submit to authority. The only legitimate authority to which he can submit is the sovereignty of 'the People' and the 'General Will'. According to Rousseau, that General Will must be supreme. Magistrates and legislators must bow down before it. There can be no 'sectional associations'. There can be no Christianity, which after all implies a separation of powers (the spiritual from the temporal). Freedom is a good thing, no doubt. But for Rousseau virtue is more important. The General Will should be virtue in action.[15] Turning back to the Declaration of the Rights of Man and of the Citizen, the modern reader can begin to see what appalled Burke:

6. Law is the expression of the general will ...
10. No one shall be disquieted on account of his opinions, including his religious views, *provided their manifestation does not disturb the public order established by law* ...
17. Since property is an inviolable and sacred right, no one shall be deprived thereof *except where public necessity, legally determined, shall clearly demand it* ... [emphasis added]

It was these caveats that Burke mistrusted. The primacy Rousseau gave to 'the public order' and 'public necessity' struck him as deeply sinister. The General Will was, to Burke's mind, a less reliable selector of a ruler than the hereditary principle, since rulers chosen that way were more likely to respect 'ancient liberties', which Burke preferred to the new, singular and abstract 'freedom'. The Third Estate, he argued, would inevitably be corrupted by power (and by the 'monied interest'), unlike an aristocracy, which enjoyed the independence that private wealth confers. Burke also grasped the significance of the expropriation of Church lands in November 1789 – one of the first truly revolutionary acts – and the dangers of printing paper money (the assignats) with nothing more than confiscated Church land as backing. The real social contract, he argued, was not Rousseau's pact between the noble savage and the General Will, but a 'partnership' between the present generation and future generations. With astonishing prescience, Burke warned against the utopianism of 'the professors': 'At the end of every vista', he wrote in the greatest prophecy of the era, 'you see nothing but the gallows.'* The assault on traditional institutions, he warned, would end in a 'mischievous and ignoble oligarchy' and, ultimately, military dictatorship.[16] In all of this, Burke was to be proved right.

The constitution of September 1791 upheld the inviolability of property rights, the inviolability of 'the King of the French', the inviolability of the right of association and the inviolability of the freedom of worship. Within two years all four had been violated, beginning with the Church's property rights. The right of free association followed with the abolition of the monastic orders, guilds and trade unions (though not of political factions, which flourished). And in August 1792 the King's privileged status was violated when he was arrested following the storming of the Tuileries. To be sure, Louis XVI brought it upon himself with the royal family's fatally botched flight to Varennes, a vain attempt to escape from Paris (disguised as the entourage of a Russian baroness) to the royalist citadel of Montmédy near the north-eastern border. With the election of a new and democratic National Convention in September 1792, the likelihood of a regicide increased still further. But the execution of Louis XVI on 21 January 1793 had very different consequences from the execution of Charles I. In the English Revolution, killing the King had been the finale of a civil war. In the French Revolution it was merely the overture, as power passed via the Jacobin Society of Friends of the

---

* Burke failed only to anticipate the Revolution's adoption of the guillotine as a characteristically rationalist solution to the problem of how most efficiently to terminate a human life.

Constitution to the Insurrectionary Commune and on to the National Convention's Committees of Surveillance and of Public Safety. Not for the last time in Western history, the revolutionaries armed themselves with a new religion to steel themselves for greater outrages. On 10 November 1793 the worship of God was prohibited and the cult of Reason instituted, the first political religion of the modern age, complete with icons, rites – and martyrs.

The French Revolution had in fact been violent from the outset.[17] The storming of the hated Bastille prison on 14 July 1789 was celebrated with the decapitations of the marquis de Launay (the governor of the Bastille) and Jacques de Flesselles (provost of the merchants of Paris). Just over a week later, the King's Secretary of State Joseph-François Foullon de Doué and his son-in-law Berthier de Sauvigny were also murdered. When the revolutionary mob attacked the royal family at Versailles the following October, around a hundred people were killed. Seventeen-ninety-one saw the Day of the Daggers and the massacre on the Champs de Mars. In September 1792 around 1,400 royalist prisoners were executed following counter-revolutionary demonstrations in Brittany, Vendée and Dauphiné. Yet something more was needed to produce the carnage of the Terror, the first demonstration in the modern age of the grim truth that revolutions devour their own children.

A generation of historians in thrall to the ideas of Karl Marx (see Chapter 5) sought the answer in class conflict, attributing the Revolution to bad harvests, the rising price of bread and the grievances of the sans-culottes, the nearest thing the *ancien régime* had to a proletariat. But Marxist interpretations foundered on the abundant evidence that the bourgeoisie did not wage class war on the aristocracy. Rather, it was an elite of 'notables', some bourgeois, some aristocrats, who together made the Revolution. A far subtler interpretation had already been offered by an aristocratic intellectual named Alexis de Tocqueville whose two major works, *Democracy in America* (1835) and *The Old Regime and the Revolution* (1856), offer an unrivalled answer to the question: why was France not America? There were, Tocqueville argues, five fundamental differences between the two societies, and therefore between the two revolutions they produced. First, France was increasingly centralized, whereas America was a naturally federal state, with a lively provincial associational life and civil society. Second, the French tended to elevate the general will above the letter of the law, a tendency resisted by America's powerful legal profession. Third, the French revolutionaries attacked religion and the Church that upheld it, whereas American sectarianism provided a bulwark against the pretensions of secular authorities. (Tocqueville was a religious sceptic but he grasped sooner than most the social value of religion.) Fourth, the French ceded too much power to irresponsible intellectuals, whereas in America practical men reigned supreme. Finally, and most important to Tocqueville, the French put equality above liberty. In sum, they chose Rousseau over Locke.

In chapter XIII of *Democracy in America*, Tocqueville hit the nail squarely on the head:

> The citizen of the United States is taught from his earliest infancy to rely upon his own exertions in order to resist the evils and the difficulties of life; he looks upon social authority with an eye of mistrust and anxiety, and he only claims its assistance when he is quite unable to shift without it ... In America the liberty of association for political purposes is unbounded ... There are no countries in which associations are more needed, to prevent the despotism of faction or the arbitrary power of a prince, than those which are democratically constituted.[18]

The comparative weakness of French civil society was therefore a large part of the reason why French republics tended to violate individual liberties and to degenerate into autocracies. But Tocqueville added a sixth point, almost as an afterthought:

> In France the passion for war is so intense that there is no undertaking so mad, or so injurious to the welfare of the State, that a man does not consider himself honoured in defending it, at the risk of his life.[19]

Here, surely, was the biggest difference between the two revolutions. Both had to wage war to survive. But the war the French revolutionaries had to fight was both larger and longer. This made all the difference.

From the moment in July 1791 when the Holy Roman Emperor

Leopold II called on his fellow monarchs to come to Louis XVI's aid – a call answered first by Frederick the Great's heir, Frederick William II – the French Revolution was obliged to fight for its life. The declarations of war on Austria (April 1792) and Britain, Holland and Spain (February 1793) unleashed a conflagration that was far larger and longer than the American War of Independence. According to the US Department of Defense, 4,435 Patriots lost their lives in defence of the United States up to and including the Battle of Yorktown; 6,188 were wounded. The figures for the War of 1812 were respectively 2,260 and 4,505.[20] British casualties were somewhat less. Even if a large proportion of the wounded perished and a significant number of soldiers and civilians succumbed to disease or hardship caused by war, this was still a small conflict. Some of the most celebrated battles – Brandywine or Yorktown itself – were mere skirmishes by European standards; total US combat deaths at the latter were just eighty-eight. The death toll for the French Revolutionary and Napoleonic Wars was vastly larger – by one estimate, total battlefield mortality on all sides between 1792 and 1815 was 3.5 million. A conservative calculation is that twenty times as many Frenchmen as Americans lost their lives in defending their revolution. And this does not include the victims of internal repression. An estimated 17,000 French men and women were executed after due process, between 12,000 and 40,000 went to the guillotine or gallows without a trial, and somewhere between 80,000 and 300,000 perished in the suppression of the royalist rebellion in the Vendée.[21] The French Revolution was also far more economically disruptive than the American. The Americans had inflation followed by stabilization; the French had hyperinflation, culminating in the complete collapse of the assignat paper currency. The entire male population was mobilized for war. Prices and wages were controlled. The market economy broke down.

It is against this background that the radicalization of the French Revolution – the fulfilment of Burke's prophecy – needs to be understood. From April 1793, when power became concentrated in the Committee of Public Safety, Paris was a madhouse. First the faction of the Jacobin Club known as the Girondists (their more extreme rivals were the Montagnards) were arrested and, on 31 October, executed. Then the followers of Georges-Jacques Danton followed them to the scaffold (6 April 1794). Finally, it was the turn of the dominant figure on the Committee of Public Safety, the high priest of Rousseau's cult of republican virtue, Maximilien Robespierre, who fittingly was made to face the falling blade. Throughout this *danse macabre*, the musical accompaniment of which was the still startlingly bloodthirsty Marseillaise,* the most deadly accusation to be levelled at an 'enemy of the people' was that of treason. Military setbacks propelled the paranoid turn. As Burke had foreseen, for he knew his classical political theory, such a democracy must inevitably be supplanted by an oligarchy and finally by the tyranny of a general. In the space of a decade, the Convention was replaced by the Directory (October 1795), the Directory by the First Consul (November 1799) and the title of first consul by that of emperor (December 1804). What had begun with Rousseau ended as a remake of the fall of the Roman Republic.

At the Battle of Austerlitz,† on 2 December 1805, some 73,200 French troops defeated 85,700 Russians and Austrians. These figures should be compared with the forces at Yorktown in 1781, where Washington's 17,600 men defeated Cornwallis's 8,300 Redcoats. The casualties inflicted by the later battle exceeded all the participants in the earlier battle by more than 12,000. At Austerlitz more than a third of the Russian army was killed, wounded or captured. Yet the weaponry used there was not significantly different from that used by Frederick the Great's army at Leuthen nearly half a century before. Mobile artillery inflicted most of the casualties. What was new was the scale of Napoleonic warfare, not the technology. By 1812 the French army numbered 700,000. In all, 1.3 million Frenchmen were conscripted between 1800 and that fateful year. Around 2 million men lost their lives in all the wars waged by Bonaparte; close to half of them were French – approximately one in five of all those born

---

* Composed by Claude-Joseph Rouget de Lisle in April 1792: 'Against us tyranny's / Bloody standard is raised / ... Can you hear in the fields / The howling of these fearsome soldiers? / They are coming into our midst / To cut the throats of our sons and consorts! / To arms, citizens, / Form in battalions, / March, march! / Let impure blood / Water our furrows! ... [Spare] not these bloody despots / ... All these tigers who pitilessly / Ripped out their mothers' wombs!'
† Now Slavkov in the Czech Republic, Austerlitz was the scene of the battle that prompted Napoleon to commission the Arc de Triomphe.

between 1790 and 1795. In more ways than one did this revolution devour its own children.

Was there something distinctive about American civil society that gave democracy a better chance than in France, as Tocqueville argued? Was the already centralized French state more likely to produce a Napoleon than the decentralized United States? We cannot be sure. But it is not unreasonable to ask how long the US constitution would have lasted if the United States had suffered the same military and economic strains that swept away the French constitution of 1791.

THE JUGGERNAUT OF WAR

The Revolution devoured not only its own children. Many of those who fought against it literally were children. Carl von Clausewitz was twelve years old, and already a lance corporal in the Prussian army, when he first saw action against the French. A true warrior-scholar, Clausewitz survived the shattering Prussian defeat at Jena in 1806, refused to fight with the French against the Russians in 1812, and also saw action at Ligny in 1815. It was he who, better than anyone (including Napoleon himself), understood the way the French Revolution had transformed the dark art of war. His posthumously published masterpiece *On War* (1832) remains the single most important work on the subject to have been produced by a Western author. Though in many ways a timeless work, *On War* is also the indispensable commentary on the Napoleonic era, for it explains *why* war had changed in its scale, and what that implied for its conduct.

'War', Clausewitz declares, '*is* ... *an act of force to compel our enemy to do our will* ... [It is] *not merely an act of policy but a true political instrument, a continuation of political intercourse, carried on with other means.*' These are perhaps his most famous – and also most mistranslated and misunderstood – words. But they are not his most important. Clausewitz's insight was that in the wake of the French Revolution a new passion had arrived on the field of battle. 'Even the most civilized of peoples', he noted, clearly alluding to the French, 'can be fired with passionate hatred for each other ...' After 1793 'war again became the business of the people', as opposed to the hobby of kings; it became a 'juggernaut' driven by the 'temper of a nation'. Clausewitz acknowledged Bonaparte's genius as the driver of this new military juggernaut. His 'audacity and luck' had 'cast the old accepted practices to the winds'. Under Napoleon, warfare had 'achieve[d] [the] state of absolute perfection'. Indeed, the Corsican upstart was nothing less than 'the God of War himself ... [whose] superiority has consistently led to the enemy's collapse'. Yet his exceptional generalship was less significant than the new popular spirit that propelled his army.

War, Clausewitz wrote, in what deserves to be his best-known formulation, was now 'a paradoxical trinity – composed of primordial violence, hatred and enmity, which are to be regarded as a blind natural force; of the play of chance and probability ... and of its element of subordination, as an instrument of policy, which makes it subject to reason alone'. True, the 'wish to annihilate the enemy's forces' is a very powerful urge – the 'first-born son' of this new war of the nations. But, Clausewitz warned, defence is always 'a stronger form of fighting than attack', for 'the force of an attack gradually diminishes ...' Even in defence there is an inherent difficulty: 'Everything in war is very simple, but the simplest thing is difficult ... a kind of friction ... lower[s] the general level of performance.' For these reasons, an effective commander must always remember four things. First, 'assess probabilities'.* Second, 'act with the utmost concentration'. Third, 'act with the utmost speed':

> The whole of military activity must therefore relate directly or indirectly to the engagement. The end for which the soldier is recruited, clothed, armed and trained ... *is simply that he should fight at the right place and the right time.*

Above all, however, the juggernaut must be kept under control. What Clausewitz calls 'absolute' war therefore '*requires* [the] *primacy of politics*' – in other words, the subordination of the means of warfare to the ends of foreign policy. That is the real message of *On War*.[22]

So what were Napoleon's policy aims? In some respects, it is true,

---

* At the Ecole Militaire in Paris, Napoleon had been examined by Pierre-Simon Laplace, one of the pioneers of the mathematics of probability.

they acquired a reactionary patina: contrast Jacques-Louis David's *Consecration of Napoleon I* (1804), swathed in imperial ermine in Notre Dame, with the romantic hero of the same artist's *Napoleon at the Saint-Bernard Pass* (1801), every inch the revolutionary *Zeitgeist* on horseback (in the philosopher Georg Wilhelm Friedrich Hegel's phrase). This was the metamorphosis so repellent to Ludwig van Beethoven, the musical spirit of the age, that he angrily scratched out the original title of his Third Symphony – 'Buonaparte' – and changed it to 'Sinfonia eroica'. Having crowned himself emperor in December 1804, Napoleon obliged the Austrian Emperor Francis II to renounce the title of holy Roman emperor and then married his daughter. With the Concordat of 1801, meanwhile, Napoleon made France's peace with the Pope, sweeping away the remnants of the Jacobin Cult of Reason.

Yet there was little else that was backward-looking about the empire Napoleon sought to build in Europe. It was truly revolutionary. Not only did he enlarge France to its 'natural frontiers' and shrink Prussia. He also created a new Swiss confederation; a new forty-state western German Confederation of the Rhine, stretching from the Baltic to the Alps; a new kingdom of (North) Italy; and a new Duchy of Warsaw. True, these new states were to be French vassals; he even installed his spendthrift youngest brother Jérôme as the titular ruler of the new Kingdom of Westphalia and his dandy of a brother-in-law, Joachim Murat, as the equivalent in Naples. True, too, the vanquished paid a heavy tribute to the French victors. Altogether between 1795 and 1804 the Dutch gave 229 million guilders to the French, more than a year's national income. Napoleon's campaigns of 1806–7 were not only self-financing, but covered at least a third of ordinary French government expenditure. And in Italy between 1805 and 1812 fully half of all the taxes raised went to the French treasury. Nevertheless, the European map as redrawn by Napoleon transformed the old patchwork of hereditary territories into a new grid of nation-states. Moreover, French rule was accompanied by a fundamental change to the legal order with the introduction of the new civil law code he had sponsored – a change that was later to have lasting and positive effects on the economies of the countries concerned. French rule swept away the various privileges that had protected the nobility, clergy, guilds and urban oligarchies and established the principle of equality before the law.[23] When Napoleon later said that he had 'wished to found a European system, a European Code of Laws, a European judiciary' so that 'there would be but one people in Europe', he was not entirely making it up.[24] Simply because his empire did not endure does not mean he lacked a political vision. For Napoleon, war was not an end in itself. It was, as Clausewitz understood, the armed pursuit of a policy.

It was not Bonaparte's goal that was at fault; it was the fact that sooner or later his enemies' forces were bound to outnumber his, even if their commanders could never match his skill. Ravaged not so much by the Russian winter as by the Russian strategy of deep retreat and attrition (not to mention rampant typhus), the Grande Armée succumbed to superior numbers – in particular superior numbers of horses – at Leipzig in 1813.[25] It was much the same story when the Prussians tipped the balance at Waterloo in 1815. Long before then, however, France had already lost the war at sea. At Aboukir Bay (the Battle of the Nile) in 1798, Sir Horatio Nelson won his ennoblement by craftily attacking the French fleet from both sides, dealing a death-blow to Napoleon's dream of conquering Egypt. Seven years later, at Trafalgar, Nelson's force of twenty-seven ships outmanoeuvred a larger Franco-Spanish flotilla by employing the 'Nelson touch' – the tactic of sailing at high speed through the enemy line, firing broadsides to the starboard side of one ship, the rear of another and then the second ship's port side.

The significance of Napoleon's defeat at sea was twofold. First, France was gradually cut off from its overseas possessions. Already in 1791 the hugely lucrative sugar colony of Saint-Domingue had exploded into revolution under the leadership of the freed slave François-Dominique Toussaint 'Louverture' (literally 'the opening') after the Legislative Assembly in Paris had extended the vote to free blacks and mulattos but not to slaves. The abolition of slavery by the National Convention in 1794 plunged the island into a bloody racial civil war that spilled over into neighbouring Spanish Santo Domingo and raged until Toussaint's arrest and deportation to France in 1802, and the restoration of slavery by Napoleon. Altogether, between 160,000 and 350,000 people lost their lives in the Haitian Revolution. A year later the French opted to sell the vast North American territory then known as Louisiana (not to be confused with the present-day state) to the United States at a bargain-basement price: 828,800 square miles for $15 million (less than 3 cents an acre). Secondly, and perhaps more importantly, France lost the financial war. Despite continued sales of former Church lands, the introduction of a new currency and the squeezing of Dutch and Italian taxpayers, Napoleon could not get the cost of borrowing down below 6 per cent. Between Trafalgar and Waterloo, the average yield on French government *rentes* was two full percentage points higher than that on British consols. It was a fateful spread.

Mercantilist that he was, Bonaparte sought to weaken Britain's economic position by banning trade between the continent and Britain. But British merchants were able quite quickly to switch to markets further overseas, secure in the Royal Navy's dominance of the principal sea-lanes. It is sometimes mistakenly assumed that Britain's earlier industrialization gave it an advantage over Napoleon. In fact it was commerce and finance that won the day, not iron and steam. Not only did trade hold up; crucially, Britain was able to run a current-account surplus in invisible earnings from shipping, insurance and overseas investment, plus the profits of empire (earnings from the slave trade and from the taxation of Indians by the East India Company). The UK's services surplus amounted to £14 million a year between 1808 and 1815, far outweighing the merchandise trade deficit over the same period. This enabled Britain to make massive transfers abroad – at peak equivalent to 4.4 per cent of national income per annum – in the form of pay to its armies and subsidies to its allies. Between 1793 and 1815, the total amount Britain gave France's continental foes was £65.8 million. The new spirit of the age, leaning against a pillar in the stock market, was a Frankfurt-born Jew named Nathan Rothschild – the *Finanzbonaparte* – who played a key role in furnishing the Duke of Wellington and his allies with the sinews of war.[26]

Napoleon had been defeated. France was now burdened with a huge reparations bill and the restored Bourbons in the form of the corpulent Louis XVIII. Yet neither the dream of revolution nor the dream of revolutionary empire died with Napoleon when he expired, almost certainly of stomach cancer, on the forlorn South Atlantic island of St Helena in 1821. The 1789 Revolution had given France a political script of unequalled drama. For the better part of the following century the temptation to re-enact the play was irresistible; it happened in 1830, in 1848 and again in 1871. The critical point is that, each time the barricades went up across the streets of central Paris, a shockwave – albeit one of diminishing magnitude – swept through Europe and the European empires. The red revolutionary promise of the Declaration of the Rights of Man could not simply be wrapped up in clerical black and forgotten, a point made with the utmost force in Stendhal's novel *The Red and the Black* (1830). Anyone, after all, could adopt both the terminology and the iconography of Revolution. The hastily armed civilians, the bare-chested warriors, the sprawling martyrs – these figures had long careers as clichés ahead of them.*

The revolutions of 1848 were even more widespread. People took to the streets in Berlin, Dresden, Hanover, Karlsruhe, Kassel, Munich, Stuttgart and Vienna, as well as in Milan, Naples, Turin and Venice. It was a revolution led by intellectuals disenchanted above all with the limits imposed on free expression by the royal regimes restored in 1815. Typically, the composer Richard Wagner and the Russian anarchist Mikhail Bakunin did their bit for the 'world conflagration' by plotting to write a blasphemous opera together.† Britain was one of the few West European countries spared, not least because 35,000 soldiers, 85,000 special constables, 1,200 military pensioners and 4,000 police were on hand to make sure the Chartists – proponents of universal suffrage – behaved themselves. As a result, 1848 in London was a matter of speeches in parks, not blood in the streets.

But the so-called Springtime of the Peoples was not confined to Europe. Like so many other Western ideas in the nineteenth century,

---

* Compare Eugène Delacroix's *Liberty Leads the People* (1830) with Egide, Baron Wappers's *Episode of the Belgian Revolution of 1830* (1835) and (among many twentieth-century examples) the Mexican Diego Rivera's *The Arsenal* (1928).

† Wagner had, according to his autobiography, 'conceive[d] the plan of a tragedy for the ideal stage of the future, entitled Jesus of Nazareth. Bakunin begged me to spare him any details; and when I sought to win him over to my project by a few verbal hints, he wished me luck, but insisted that I must at all costs make Jesus appear as a weak character. As for the music of the piece, he advised me, amid all the variations, to use only one set of phrases, namely: for the tenor, "Off with His head!"; for the soprano, "Hang Him!"; and for the basso continuo, "Fire! fire!"' The anecdote nicely captures the overheated spirit of 1848.

16. The city the Spaniards failed to find: Machu Picchu, Peru

17. Boneyard Beach, South Carolina

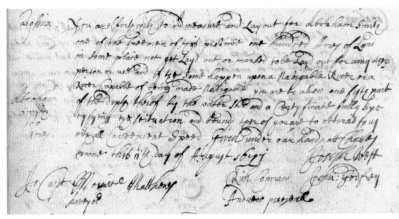

18. You do the work … Millicent How's indenture document

19. … you get the land: Abraham Smith's land grant

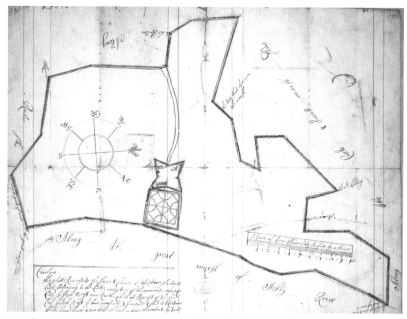

20. The American dream: a piece of Charleston

21. Conquistador: Jerónimo de Aliaga

22. The Washington who wasn't: Simón Bolívar as seen in present-day Caracas

23. The scars of slavery in the United States

24. The baguette as a legacy of empire: Saint-Louis, Senegal

25. The black sheep who beat the white sheep: Blaise Diagne, the first black member of the French National Assembly

26. Louis Faidherbe, Governor of Senegal, ponders his *mission civilisatrice*

27. Tirailleurs Sénégalais proudly show off their samples

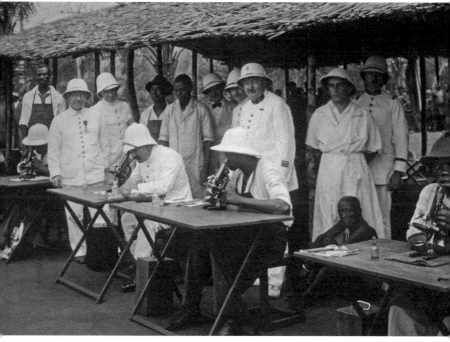

28. Médecins Sans Frontières, imperial style: French doctors brave the tropics

29. Three photographs of 'Bastard' women from the German racial theorist Eugen Fischer's study of the Rehoboth Basters

30. 'I didn't know what the war was really like': a Senegalese tirailleur on the Western Front

31. Lüderitz, Namibia

French-style revolution swiftly became a global phenomenon. Across the British Empire there was unrest – in Ceylon, Guiana, Jamaica, New South Wales, the Orange River Sovereignty, the Punjab and Van Diemen's Land.[27] Even more remarkable were the events in French West Africa. There, unlike in British colonies, radical political change had the backing of a revolutionary government in the metropolis.

All this serves to illuminate the most distinctive feature of French imperialism: its enduring revolutionary character. The British Empire was by instinct socially conservative; with every passing year its administrators grew fonder of local elites, more comfortable with indirect rule through tribal chiefs and ornamental maharajahs. But the French still cherished the hope that liberty, equality and fraternity – along with the *Code Napoléon* and canned food (another Napoleonic invention) – were commodities for universal export.[28]

France, like all the European empires, had based its overseas empire at least partly on slavery. But in 1848 France's new republican government declared that slavery would again be abolished throughout the French Empire, including in the West African colony of Senegal. The British had already done this in their empire fifteen years before. But abolition was only the first part of this revolution in French Africa. It was also announced that the newly freed slaves would get to vote – unlike the natives in British colonies. With the introduction of universal manhood suffrage throughout the French Empire, the almost entirely African and *métis* or mixed-race electorate (whites accounted for only 1 per cent of the total) voted in the elections of November 1848 and chose the first man of colour ever to sit in the French National Assembly.[29] Although the right to send a deputy to Paris was withdrawn from Senegal by the Emperor Napoleon III in 1852 and not restored until 1879, the practice continued of electing the councils of the *quatre communes* (Saint-Louis, Gorée, Rufisque and Dakar) on the basis of universal manhood suffrage.[30] The first multiracial democratic assembly in African history met in what was then the colonial capital of Saint-Louis.

Contemporaries recognized what a huge departure this was. 'The visitor to the Council', wrote one British traveller to Saint-Louis, 'will frequently witness a black president calling a European member to order for rowdiness . . . Black members have unmercifully criticised officials in Senegal. No British colony would tolerate the attacks which the natives make upon European officials in Senegal.'[31] For the British, empire was about hierarchy in the same way that society at home was about class. At the top was Victoria, the Queen and Empress. Every one of her 400 million subjects was arranged below her in an elaborate chain of status, all the way down to the lowliest punkah wallah in Calcutta. The French Empire was different.

To the revolutionaries of 1848, it seemed self-evident that colonial subjects should be transformed into Frenchmen with the maximum possible speed. In the jargon of the time, Africans were to be 'assimilated'. At the same time, intermarriage (*métissage*) between French officials and African women was positively encouraged.[32] This progressive imperialism was personified by Louis Faidherbe, an experienced soldier who became governor of Senegal in 1854. In Saint-Louis Faidherbe oversaw the building of new bridges, paved roads, schools, quays, a fresh water supply and the introduction of a regular ferry service on the river. 'Villages of Liberty' were founded throughout Senegal for emancipated slaves. In 1857 Faidherbe set up a Senegalese colonial army – the Tirailleurs Sénégalais – transforming the African soldier from indentured military labourer to fully fledged regular infantryman. A school was established for the sons of native chiefs.[33] Faidherbe himself married a fifteen-year-old Senegalese girl.

'Our intentions are pure and noble,' declared Faidherbe towards the end of his time as governor. 'Our cause is just.' Of course, his mission was more than to civilize. 'The aim', he declared in 1857, was 'to dominate the country at as low a cost as possible and through commerce [to] get the greatest advantages'.[34] He was under instructions to extend French influence inland and to achieve Senegal's *mise en valeur* (economic development) by challenging the indigenous African control of the trade in gum arabic, made from the sap of acacia trees, and peanuts. Faidherbe's strategy was to build a chain of French forts along the Senegal River, beginning at Médine below the Félou waterfall. This led inevitably to conflict with the predominant inland powers: the Trarza Moors in Waalo, the Cayor in the south and El Hadj Umar Tall, the Muslim ruler of middle Niger, who later established the Toucouleur Empire in neighbouring Mali.[35] Gradually and inexorably, however, these African rivals were forced to retreat. In 1857 French forces overthrew the Lebu Republic, turning the capital Ndakarou into the new colonial city of Dakar. The city centre today remains a monument to the French colonial vision, from the white Governor General's palais to the broad Avenue Faidherbe, from the boulangeries with their fresh, fragrant baguettes to the patisseries serving café au lait. To formalize the process of Gallicization, the entire country was divided up into arrondissements, cercles and cantons. By the time Faidherbe stepped down in 1865, a Frenchman could stroll around Saint-Louis and take real pride in his country's achievement. The former slave markets had become proud outposts of Gallic culture. The erstwhile victims of imperialism had been transformed into citizens with the right to vote and the duty to bear arms. As the journalist Gabriel Charmes put it:

> If in these immense regions where only fanaticism and brigandage reign today, [France] were to bring ... peace, commerce, tolerance, who could say this was a poor use of force? ... Having taught millions of men civilization and freedom would fill it with the pride that makes great peoples.[36]

Of course, the reality of French imperialism could not possibly live up to this exalted billing. The biggest challenge was to attract competent officials from France. Those volunteering to serve in West Africa, one of Faidherbe's successors suggested bluntly, were generally 'persons who if not compromised at home were at least incapable of making a livelihood' there: if not petty criminals then drunks and bankrupts.[37] As one settler put it in 1894, the colonies were 'the *refugium peccatorum* for all our misfits, the depository of the excrement of our political and social organism'. When a man left for the colonies, recalled the director of the Ecole Coloniale, his friends asked: 'What crime must he have committed? From what corpse is he fleeing?'[38] A number of colonial officials became notorious for their brutality towards the natives; one man, Emile Toqué, celebrated Bastille Day in 1903 by blowing up a prisoner with gunpowder.[39] Most colonial officials probably shared the view of at least one professor at the Ecole that their African subjects were all intellectually retarded. The *indigénat* code empowered them, if they saw fit, to jail fractious natives for up to fifteen days for forty-six different offences, most of which were not considered unlawful in France.[40] There was no mechanism of appeal. Forced labour (the *corvée*) was an integral part of the tax system in West Africa; that was how the Dakar–Niger railway was built. For a worker in a rubber plantation, the head tax in the French Congo was equivalent to as many as a hundred days of work a year. Hostages were taken when villages fell behind with their dues. Some officials – like the one in French Sudan who was charged with multiple murders, at least one rape, grievous bodily harm, miscarriages of justice and embezzlement – appear to have taken the novelist Joseph Conrad's Kurtz as a role model.[41] One man, named Brocard, decapitated on 'compassionate grounds' a prisoner who had gone blind as a result of the filthy conditions in his cell.[42] The culmination of such madness was the mission of Paul Voulet and Julien Chanoine to Lake Chad (1898–9), which left a trail of incinerated villages, hanged natives and even roasted children in its wake, until finally the African soldiers under their command mutinied and murdered both men.[43]

Nevertheless, the standard of French colonial administrators clearly improved, especially after the First World War, when the Ecole Coloniale attracted not only better students but also distinguished ethnologists like Maurice Delafosse and Henri Labouret. As the Ecole's director, the saintly Georges Hardy personified the *mission civilisatrice*. At the same time, the French made a real effort to attract and train native talent. Faidherbe made his thinking clear in a speech he gave while awarding the rank of second lieutenant to a soldier named Alioun Sall:

> This nomination . . . demonstrates that, even for loftier positions in our social hierarchy, colour is no longer a reason for exclusion . . . Only the most capable will succeed. Those who obstinately prefer ignorance to civilization will remain in the lowly ranks of society, as is the case in all the countries of the world.[44]

In 1886 the son of the king of Porto Novo (later Dahomey/Benin) joined a dozen Asian students at the Ecole Coloniale. Each year from 1889 until 1914 the 'native section' of the Ecole admitted around twenty non-French students.[45] It was clearly thanks to the French idea of a civilizing mission that a man like Blaise Diagne, born in a modest house in the old slave trading centre of Gorée in 1872, could join the colonial customs service and rise through its ranks. Such an ascent would have been much harder – indeed, almost inconceivable – in British Africa. In 1914 Diagne ended up as the first black African (of unmixed race) in the French National Assembly, no mean feat for the grandson of a Senegalese slave. Compared with the ethos of the other European empires of the time, there is no question that the French Empire was the most liberal in design. In the communes of Dakar the Wolof song that was sung to celebrate Diagne's victory succinctly summarized the new political situation: 'The black sheep [has beaten] the white sheep.'[46]

The supreme back-handed compliment to French imperialism was paid in 1922 by one 'Nguyen Ai Quoc', in a letter to the Governor General of another French colony on the other side of the world: Indo-China. 'Your Excellency,' began the author, whose real name was Nguyen Sinh Cung, and whose fluent French he owed to his time at the Hue *lycée*:

> We know very well that your affection for the natives; of the colonies in general, and the Annamese in particular is great. Under your procon-sulate the Annamese people have known true prosperity and real hap-piness, the happiness of seeing their country dotted all over with an increasing number of spirits and opium shops which, together with firing squads, prisons, 'democracy' and all the improved apparatus of modern civilization, are combining to make the Annamese the most advanced of the Asians and the happiest of mortals. These acts of benevolence save us the trouble of recalling all the others, such as enforced recruitment and loans, bloody repressions, the dethronement and exile of kings, profanation of sacred places, etc.[47]

It was not only French that the Governor's correspondent had learned at school. Under another pseudonym, 'Ho Chi Minh', he would later lead the movement for an independent Vietnam – pointedly citing the 1791 Declaration of the Rights of Man in his own declar-ation of Vietnamese independence, just as Vo Nguyen Giap, the victor of the decisive battle of Dien Bien Phu (and an alumnus of the same *lycée*), had learned the art of war by studying the campaigns of Napo-leon. Such was the inevitable fate of a civilizing mission that exported the revolutionary tradition along with boules and baguettes.[48] It was no accident that the presidents of the independent Ivory Coast, Niger, Dahomey and Mali were all graduates of the Ecole William Ponty – as was the Senegalese Prime Minister.[49]

And yet all of this – the whole French *mission civilisatrice* – was threatened with defeat by one lethal foe – disease – which made large tracts of sub-Saharan Africa almost uninhabitable for Europeans.[50] Life-spans a century and a half ago were short enough in the West. Life expectancy at birth in Britain in 1850 was still only forty, compared with seventy-five today. But in Africa the rates of infant mortality and premature death were appallingly high. Life expectancy in mid-nineteenth-century Senegal was probably in the low to mid-twenties.[51] So Africa was to be the ultimate testing ground for the fourth killer application of Western civilization: the power of modern medicine to prolong human life.

MÉDECINS SANS FRONTIÈRES

Not for nothing was West Africa known as the white man's grave-yard: all over Africa the European colonial project ran the risk of being snuffed out in its infancy. A good illustration of the risks Europeans ran in Africa is the monument on Gorée Island to the twenty-one French doctors who perished in a yellow-fever outbreak in 1878. Tropical diseases took a heavy toll on the French colonial civil service; between 1887 and 1912, a total of 135 out of 984 appointees (16 per cent) died in the colonies. On average, retired colonial officials expired seventeen years earlier than their counterparts in the metropolitan service. As late as 1929, nearly a third of the 16,000 Europeans living in French West Africa were hospitalized for an average of fourteen days a year.[52] Things were little better in British Africa. The mortality rate among British soldiers in Sierra Leone was the worst in the entire British Empire, thirty times higher than for soldiers who stayed at home. If death rates like these had persisted, the colonization of Africa by Europeans would surely have been abandoned.

Like all good colonial administrations, the French kept impeccable records. In the National Archives in Dakar you can still find every detail of every reported outbreak of every disease to strike French West Africa: yellow fever in Senegal, malaria in Guinea, leprosy in Ivory Coast. Health bulletins, health laws, health missions – health, it seemed, was an obsession for the French. And why not? A way had to be found to keep these diseases in check. As Sir Rubert William Boyce put it in 1910, whether or not there would be a European presence in the tropics boiled down to this: 'Mosquito or Man'. 'The future of imperialism', in the words of John L. Todd, 'lay with the microscope.'[53] But the key advances would not be made in the squeaky-clean laboratories of Western universities and pharmaceutical companies.

In September 1903 the satirical magazine *Punch* published an insomniac's ode to the students of tropical disease:

> Men of science, you that dare
> Beard the microbe in his lair
> Tracking through the jungly thickness
> Afric's germ of Sleeping Sickness
> Hear, oh hear, my parting plea
> Send *a microbe home to me*![54]

It was no fantasy to imagine the men of science tracking through the jungle. Researchers into tropical diseases set up laboratories in the most far-flung African colonies – the one established in Saint-Louis in 1896 was among the first. Animals kept there were injected with trial vaccines: eighty-two cats injected with dysentery, eleven dogs with tetanus. Other labs worked on cholera, malaria, rabies and smallpox. Such efforts had their roots in the pioneering work on germ theory by Louis Pasteur in the 1850s and 1860s.

Empire inspired a generation of European medical innovators. It was in Alexandria in 1884 that the German bacteriologist Robert Koch – who had already isolated the anthrax and tuberculosis bacilli – discovered *Vibrio cholerae*, the bacterium that transmits cholera, which only the previous year had killed Koch's French rival Louis Thuillier. It was after an outbreak in Hong Kong in 1894 that another Frenchman, Alexandre Yersin, identified the bacillus responsible for bubonic plague.[55] It was a doctor in the Indian Medical Service, Ronald Ross, who first fully explained the aetiology of malaria and the role of the anopheles mosquito in transmitting it; he himself suffered from the disease. It was three Dutch scientists based in Java, Christiaan Eijkman, Adolphe Vorderman and Gerrit Grijns, who worked out that beriberi was caused by a dietary deficiency in polished rice (the lack of vitamin B_1). It was an Italian, Aldo Castellani, whose research in Uganda identified the trypanosome protozoan in the tsetse fly that is responsible for sleeping sickness. And it was Jean Laigret's team of researchers at the Pasteur Institute in Dakar that first succeeded in isolating the yellow-fever virus and devising a vaccine that could be administered simply, without the need for sterilized needles and syringes, later improved to produce the so-called Dakar scratch vaccine (or Peltier-Durieux vaccine), which also offered protection against smallpox.[56] These and other breakthroughs, clustered in the period from the 1880s to the 1920s, proved to be crucial in keeping Europeans, and hence the colonial project, alive in the tropics. Africa and Asia had become giant laboratories for Western medicine.[57] And the more successful the research – the more remedies (like quinine, the anti-malarial properties of which were discovered in Peru) could be found – the further the Western empires could spread and, with them, the supreme benefit of longer human life.

Colonization in Africa was limited at first to coastal settlements. But with the advent of another Western breakthrough – the mechanization of mobility – it could spread inland. Railways like the one from Dakar to Bamako in Mali were vital to the Western imperial project. 'Civilization spreads and takes root along the paths of communication,' declared Charles de Freycinet, the French Minister for Public Works, in 1880. 'Africa, lying open before us, most particularly demands our attention.'[58] Following the creation in 1895 of the Federation of French West Africa (Afrique Occidentale Française), which stretched beyond Timbuktu into Niger and extended French rule to more than 10 million Africans, this became one of the leitmotifs of French rule. In the words of Ernest Roume, the Federation's first Governor:

> We wish to truly open up to civilization the immense regions that the foresight of our statesmen and the bravery of our soldiers and explorers have bequeathed to us ... The necessary condition for achieving

this goal is the creation of lines of penetration, a perfected means of transportation to make up for the absence of natural means of communication that has kept this country in poverty and barbarism . . . True economic activity cannot even be conceived without railroads. It is therefore our duty . . . as a civilized nation, to take those steps that nature itself imposes and which are the only effective ones . . . It is now everyone's conviction that no material or moral progress is possible in our African colonies without railroads.[59]

Railways helped impose European rule on the African hinterland. But they spread other things too: not only trade in peanuts and gum, but also Western medical knowledge. For without improvements in public health, the railways would end up spreading disease, increasing the danger of epidemics. This was to be Doctors without Borders, nineteenth-century style. The benefits were often overlooked by those, like Gandhi, who maintained that the European empires had no redeeming feature.

The overthrow of native power structures was followed by an attempt to overthrow native superstitions. Today, the village of Jajak is remarkable because it has no fewer than three traditional healers, one of them an elderly woman named Han Diop. People come from miles around to consult her and, as she told me when I visited Jajak in 2010, she can cure everything from asthma to love sickness with herbal remedies and a spot of prophecy. This kind of medicine has been practised by Africans for hundreds if not thousands of years. It is one reason that life expectancy in Africa still remains so much lower than in the West. Herbs and spells are singularly ineffective against most tropical diseases.

In 1897 the French colonial authorities banned witch doctors. Seven years later, they went further by drawing up plans for the first African national health service, the Assistance Médicale Indigène. Not only did the French extend their own public health system to the whole of French West Africa; in February 1905 Governor General Roume issued an order creating a free healthcare service for the indigenous population, something that did not exist in France. From now on, 'health posts' in the localities would make modern medicine available to all Africans under French rule.[60] Addressing the

National Assembly in 1884, the Prime Minister Jules Ferry had summed up a new mood:

> Gentlemen, we must speak more loudly and more honestly! We must say openly that indeed the higher races have a right over the lower races ... I repeat, that the superior races have a right because they have a duty. They have the duty to civilize the inferior races ... In the history of earlier centuries these duties, gentlemen, have often been misunderstood; and certainly when the Spanish soldiers and explorers introduced slavery into Central America, they did not fulfil their duty as men of a higher race ... But, in our time, I maintain that European nations acquit themselves with generosity, with grandeur, and with sincerity of this superior civilizing duty.[61]

This was very different from the indirect style of rule increasingly favoured in British Africa. In the words of Robert Delavignette, an experienced colonial administrator and director of the Ecole Coloniale:*

> The representative of the powers of the Republic in Dakar, a member of French Masonry and the Radical Socialist party, will on the spot, in Africa, be an authoritarian governor, and he will use autocratic methods of rule to lead the natives toward progress ... Many administrators wanted to treat the feudal lords [that is, native chiefs] in the same way we had treated them during the French Revolution. It was either break them or use them for our purposes. The British administrators had more sympathy for the feudal lords; it was aristocracy respecting aristocracy.[62]

In the eyes of William Ponty, Governor General of French West Africa between 1908 and 1915, traditional African institutions were the principal obstacle between their people and the civilization he was trying to spread. Tribal chiefs were, Ponty declared, 'nothing but parasites'. 'We did not take the feudal lords very seriously,' recalled a colonial official of the 1920s. 'We found them rather ridiculous. After the French Revolution we could not be expected to return to the Middle Ages.'[63] Delavignette took a similar view. In the revolutionary empire of which he dreamt, the heroes were the 'black peasants', the

* Pretentiously renamed the Ecole Nationale de la France d'Outre Mer in 1934.

title of his award-winning novel of 1931. In the words of the first Socialist Minister of Colonies, Marius Moutet, the aim of French policy was 'to consider the application to the overseas countries of the great principles of the Declaration of the Rights of Man and of the Citizen'.[64]

It is easy today to dismiss such aspirations as products of insufferable Gallic arrogance. But there is no question that here, as elsewhere, Western empire brought real, measurable progress. After the introduction of compulsory vaccination in 1904, smallpox was significantly reduced in Senegal. In only four years between 1925 and 1958 did the number of cases exceed 400 a year.[65] Malaria was also curbed by the systematic destruction of the mosquitoes' swampy breeding grounds and by the isolation of victims, as well as by the distribution of free quinine.[66] Yellow-fever epidemics, too, became less frequent in Senegal after the introduction of an effective vaccine.

The Scramble for Africa has become a byword for the ruthless carve-up of an entire continent by rapacious Europeans. Its bizarre climax was the Fashoda incident, when rival French and British expeditions converged on the Eastern Sudanese town of Fashoda (today Kodok) in the province of Bahr-el-Ghazal. The French, led by Major Jean-Baptiste Marchand, dreamt of a line from Dakar to Djibouti (then French Somaliland), linking the Niger to the Nile and creating an unbroken chain of French control from Senegal to the Red Sea coast. The British, led by Sir Herbert (later Lord) Kitchener, saw control of Sudan as the key to a comparable British line stretching north to south from Cairo to the Cape. The showdown came on 18 September 1898 at the point where these two lines intersected. Though the numbers of men were absurdly small – Marchand was accompanied by twelve French officers and 150 tirailleurs – and the bone of contention an utterly desolate quagmire of reeds, mud and dead fish, Fashoda brought Britain and France to the brink of war.[67]

Yet the Scramble for Africa was also a scramble for scientific knowledge, which was as collaborative as it was competitive, and which had undoubted benefits for natives as well as for Europeans. The bacteriologist, often risking his life to find cures for lethal afflictions, was another kind of imperial hero, as brave in his way as the soldier-explorer.

Now every European power with serious imperial ambitions had to have a tropical medicine institute: the Pasteur Institute in Paris, founded in 1887, was later matched by the London and Liverpool schools of tropical medicine (1899) and by the Hamburg-based Institute for Shipping and Tropical Illnesses (1901).

There were limits to what could be achieved, however. By 1914 there were still fewer than a hundred doctors available to staff the rural health posts in Senegal. Even as late as 1946 there were only 152 health posts in the whole of French West Africa. In the French Congo, the post at Stanley Pool (later Brazzaville) was supposed to serve 80,000 people with a yearly budget of just 200 francs. When the writer André Gide visited there in 1927 he was told that if 'the medical service is asked for medicines it generally sends, after an immense delay, nothing but iodine, sulphate of soda, and – boric acid!' This 'lamentable penury' allowed 'diseases that might easily be checked . . . to hold their own and even to gain ground'.[68] This was partly a matter of economic reality. France itself was still a very long way from having universal healthcare. The resources simply were not available to send doctors and vaccines into the isolated villages of inland Senegal or Congo. But it was also a matter of priorities. The Western research institutes were generally more concerned with the diseases that affected Europeans most severely – notably malaria and yellow fever – than with cholera and sleeping sickness, the biggest killers of Africans.

The original French civilizing mission had been based on the revolutionary idea of universal citizenship. But even as the French Empire expanded, that idea retreated. In theory, a West African *sujet* could still become a *citoyen*. In practice, few were considered eligible (for example, practising polygamy was considered a disqualification). As late as 1936, out of French West Africa's total population of 15 million, there were only 2,136 French citizens outside the four coastal communes.[69] Residential segregation became the norm (separating the European 'Plateau' from the African 'Medina' in Dakar, for example), on the ground that Africans were the bearers of infectious disease. Education, too, was restricted to a tiny elite of 'intermediaries'.[70] Once the French had aspired to racial assimilation.[71] Now medical science recommended separation. This accorded with the prevailing view that 'association' was a more realistic goal than assimilation because, as the colonial theorist Louis Vignon put it, of the 'opposition between the principles of 1789 and the conservatism of non-European populations'.[72]

The battle against tropical disease was not just fought in Petri dishes. It was fought in African towns and villages. When bubonic plague struck Senegal, the French authorities were ruthless in their response. The homes of the infected were torched; residents were forcibly removed and quarantined under armed guard; the dead were unceremoniously buried in creosote or lime in violation of Muslim traditions. This was a battle in which Africans felt themselves to be more victims than beneficiaries. In Dakar there were mass protests, riots and the first general strike in Senegalese history.[73]

The imperatives of medical science required harsh measures to contain the epidemic. Yet the science of the day also provided a spurious rationale for treating Africans brutally. They were not merely ignorant of medical science. According to the theory of eugenics, they were an inferior species. Nowhere did the pseudo-science of eugenics, the mutant half-brother of bacteriology, have a more pernicious influence than in the new and rapidly growing German Empire.

THE SKULLS OF SHARK ISLAND

As the twentieth century dawned, Germany was in the vanguard of Western civilization. It was German professors who won the lion's share of Nobel science prizes: 33 per cent of the total awarded between 1901 and 1910 and 29 per cent in the following decade. It was German universities that led the world in chemistry and biochemistry. Ambitious graduates flocked from all over Europe to Göttingen, Heidelberg and Tübingen to tremble before the titans of German *Wissenschaft*. After Pasteur, Robert Koch had emerged as the dominant force in bacteriology. Another German, Emil von Behring, was one of the developers of the tetanus and diphtheria antitoxins, for which he was awarded both the Nobel Prize and the Iron Cross. Two other German scientists, Fritz Schaudinn and Erich Hoffmann, identified the spirocheta pallida as the cause of syphilis, and a third, Paul Ehrlich, was one of the inventors of Salvarsan, the first effective treatment for the disease.

Yet there was a shadow side to this extraordinary scientific success. Lurking within the real science was a pseudo-science, which asserted that mankind was not a single more or less homogeneous species but was subdivided and ranked from an Aryan 'master race' down to a black race unworthy of the designation *Homo sapiens*. And where better to test these theories than in Germany's newly acquired African colonies? Africa was about to become another kind of laboratory – this time for racial biology.

Each European power had its own distinctive way of scrambling for Africa. The French, as we have seen, favoured railways and health centres. The British did more than just dig for gold and hunt for happy valleys; they also built mission schools. The Belgians turned the Congo into a vast slave state. The Portuguese did as little as possible. The Germans were the latecomers to the party. For them, colonizing Africa was a giant experiment to test, among other things, a racial theory. Earlier colonizing powers had, of course, been bolstered by a sense of innate superiority. According to the theory of 'social Darwinism', Africans were biologically inferior, an inconvenient obstacle to the development of Africa by more advanced white 'Aryans'. But no one turned that theory into colonial practice more ruthlessly than the Germans in South-West Africa, today's Namibia.

The Germans first laid claim to the bleak shores of South-West Africa in 1884. A year later Heinrich Ernst Göring – father of the more famous Hermann – was appointed Reich commissioner. By the time Theodor Leutwein was appointed the colony's first governor in 1893, German intentions were becoming clear: to expropriate the native Herero and Nama peoples and settle their land with German farmers. This was the policy that would be openly advocated by Paul von Rohrbach in his influential book *German Colonial Economics* (1907).[74] It was a project that at the time seemed as scientifically legitimate as the ongoing European campaign against tropical disease.

In 1851 Charles Darwin's half-cousin Francis Galton had come to this arid yet lovely country under the aegis of the Royal Geographical Society. On returning to London, Galton reported that he had seen 'enough of savage races to give me material to think about all the rest of my life'. Galton's observations of the Herero and Nama would later inform his thinking about human evolution. It was Galton's anthropometric work on human heredity that laid the foundation for the discipline he christened 'eugenics' – the use of selective breeding to improve the human gene pool.* Here was the ultimate solution to the problem of public health: a master-race of superhumans, bred to withstand the attacks of pathogens. The crucial point to note is that a hundred years ago work like Galton's was at the cutting edge of science. Racism was not some backward-looking reactionary ideology; the scientifically uneducated embraced it as enthusiastically as people today accept the theory of man-made global warming. It was only in the second half of the twentieth century that eugenics and the related concept of 'racial hygiene' were finally discredited with the realization that genetic differences between the races are relatively small, and the variations within races quite large.

A century ago hardly anyone in the West doubted that white men were superior to black. Hardly anyone white, that is. Racial theory justified flagrant inequality of the sort that would later be institutionalized in the American South as segregation and in South Africa as 'apartheid' – apartness. In German South-West Africa, blacks were forbidden to ride horses, had to salute whites, could not walk on the footpaths, could not own bicycles or go to libraries. In the colony's rudimentary courts of law, the word of one German was worth the word of seven Africans. Settlers got fined for crimes like murder and rape for which Africans were summarily hanged. As a missionary commented, 'the average German looks down upon the natives as being about on the same level as the higher primates (baboon being their favourite term for the natives) and treats them like animals.'[75] The British and the French had made a point of abolishing slavery in their colonies during the nineteenth century. The Germans did not.[76]

There was only one small problem. The Herero and Nama were not the childlike creatures of racial theory. The Herero were tough herdsmen, skilled at maintaining their cattle in the sparse pastureland

---

* Late in life, Galton wrote a novel, *Kantsaywhere*, which imagines a eugenicist utopia in which the individual's right to reproduce was contingent on examination performance and where 'the propagation of children by the Unfit is looked upon ... as a crime to the State'.

that lay between the Namib and Kalahari deserts. The Nama were raiders every bit as skilled as horsemen and marksmen as the Boers to the east.[77] Having seen the Dutch and British in action in South Africa, they knew full well what the Germans were up to. The economic position of the Herero had been severely weakened at the turn of the century by a devastating outbreak of rinderpest. As a result, the process of selling land to German settlers was already under way. There was also mounting tension between the Herero and German merchants, whose debt-collection methods were less than subtle.[78] But flagrant robbery the Herero were bound to resist, especially after a succession of egregious acts of violence, including the murder (and attempted rape) by a German settler of the daughter-in-law of one of their chiefs.[79]

It was the forgery by a young district chief lieutenant named Zürn of Herero elders' signatures on documents setting the boundaries of new native reservations that put the match to the powder keg.[80] On 12 January 1904, under the leadership of Samuel Maharero, the Herero rose in rebellion, killing every able-bodied German man they could find in the area around Okahandja, though pointedly sparing women and children. More than a hundred settlers were killed.[81] In response, the German Kaiser, William II, sent General Adrian Dietrich Lothar von Trotha with instructions to 'restore order . . . by all means necessary'. He chose the foulest means at his disposal.

German theorists of colonization already went further than their French or British counterparts when they spoke of the need for 'actual eradication' of 'bad, culturally inept and predatory [native] tribes'. Now Trotha resolved to put this theory into practice. He vowed to use 'absolute terrorism' to 'destroy the rebellious tribes by shedding rivers of blood'.[82] In a chilling decree addressed to the Herero, he spelled out in rudimentary Otjiherero what German racial theory meant in practice:

> I am the great General of the Germans. I am sending a word to you Hereros, you who are Hereros are no longer under the Germans [that is, are no longer German subjects] . . . You Hereros must now leave this land, it belongs to the Germans. If you do not do this I shall remove you with the *Groot Rohr* [big cannon]. A person in German land shall

be killed by the gun. I shall not catch women or the sick but I will chase them after their chiefs or I will kill them with the gun.

These are my words to the Herero people.

The great General of the mighty German Kaiser.

Trotha.[83]

The Battle of Hamakari near the Waterberg Plateau on 11 August 1904 was not a battle. It was a massacre. The Herero were concentrated in a large encampment, where, having seen off an earlier German force, they were awaiting peace negotiations. Instead, Trotha encircled them, unleashed a lethal bombardment and proceeded to mow men, women and children down with Maxim guns. As he seems to have intended, the survivors fled into the arid Omaheke desert and, in his words, 'their doom'. Waterholes on the edge of the desert were tightly guarded. In the words of an official report by the South-West African General Staff: 'The waterless Omaheke should finish what German guns had started: the extermination of the Herero people.' Trotha was equally explicit: 'I believe that the nation as such should be annihilated.'[84]

The Germans did not just rely on the desert. Herero who had not participated in the uprising were hunted down by 'Cleansing Patrols' of settler *Schutztruppen*, whose motto was 'clean out, hang up, shoot down till they are all gone'.[85] Those not killed on the spot, mostly women and children, were put in five concentration camps. They were later joined by the Nama clans who made the mistake of joining the anti-German revolt and the even bigger mistake of laying down their arms in return for assurances that their lives would be spared. These concentration camps differed from the ones set up by the British in South Africa during the Boer War. There, a guerrilla war was still raging and the intention was to disrupt the Boer supply lines; the appalling mortality rates were the unintended consequence of abysmal sanitation. In German South-West Africa the war was over and the concentration camps were intended to be death camps. The most notorious was on Shark Island, near Lüderitz.

The camp was located at the far end of the island to maximize its exposure to the wind. Denied adequate shelter, clothing and food, the prisoners were forced to build jetties, standing waist-deep in the ice-cold water. Those who faltered in their labours were mercilessly whipped by the *sjambok*-wielding guards. A missionary named August

Kuhlman visited the island in September 1905. He was horrified to see an exhausted woman fatally shot in the thigh and arm simply for crawling in search of water. Between September 1906 and March 1907, a total of 1,032 out of 1,795 prisoners on Shark Island died. The final mortality rate was close to 80 per cent. Before the uprising, the Herero had numbered 80,000; afterwards only 15,000 remained. There had been 20,000 Nama; fewer than 10,000 were left when a census was conducted in 1911. Only one in ten Nama prisoners survived the camps. With all Herero and Nama land now confiscated, under an imperial decree of December 1905, the number of German settlers trebled to nearly 15,000 by 1913. The surviving Herero and Nama were little better than slave labourers, liable to brutal corporal punishment for the most trivial insubordination.[86]

Nor did the sufferings of the native peoples of South-West Africa end there. As if obliterating the greater number of them were not sufficient, the Germans inflicted further trials on the Herero and Nama peoples in the name of 'race hygiene'. At least one doctor conducted lethal experiments on concentration-camp prisoners in South-West Africa. In 1906 as many as 778 autopsies were performed on prisoners for so called racial-biological research. After that, sample skulls were sent back to Germany for further research. Incredibly, female prisoners were forced to scrape the skulls clean with glass shards.[87]

Dr Eugen Fischer was one of many German scientists intensely interested in the voguish new field of race. Intrigued by what he heard about a mixed-race people in South-West Africa, the Rehoboth Basters, Fischer spent two months in the field measuring them from head to foot and scrutinizing their physiognomies. In 1913 he published his findings, trumpeting them as the first ever attempt to apply to humans the principles of genetic inheritance developed by the Austrian Gregor Mendel. 'The Bastards', as he called them, were racially superior to pure negroes but inferior to pure whites. There might therefore be a useful role for people of mixed race as colonial policemen or lower officials. But any further racial mixing should be avoided:

> We know this absolutely for sure: without exception, any European people . . . that has absorbed the blood of less valuable races – and only a zealot can deny that blacks, Hottentots and many others are less

valuable [than whites] – has paid for this absorption with its spiritual [and] cultural downfall.[88]

By this time there was already a complex of laws against miscegenation in German South-West Africa.

Not everyone in Germany subscribed to such views. German Socialists and Catholics raised their voices to protest at what was being done in Africa by their supposedly civilized country.[89] Even the theorist of colonial economics, Paul Rohrbach, condemned Trotha's genocidal policy, pointing out that South-West Africa simply could not function without African labour.[90] Yet the disturbing question remains. Was South-West Africa the testing site of future, much larger genocides?[91] Was it, as Conrad suggested in his novel *Heart of Darkness*, a case of Africa turning Europeans into savages, rather than Europeans civilizing Africa? Where was the real heart of darkness? In Africa? Or within the Europeans who treated it as a laboratory for a racial pseudo-science that ranks alongside the ideology of communism as the most lethal of all Western civilization's exports?[92]

Yet the cruelties inflicted on the Africans were to be avenged in a terrible way. For racial theory was too virulent an idea to be confined to the colonial periphery. As a new century dawned, it came home to Europe. Western civilization was about to encounter its most dangerous foe: itself.

The war that began in 1914 was not a war between a few quarrelling European states. It was a war between world empires. It was a war within Western civilization. And it was the first sign that the West carried within it the seeds of its own destruction. In this war, more than in any previous conflict, the West unleashed its killer applications against itself. The industrial economy supplied the means of mechanized destruction. And modern medicine, too, played its part in the bloody business of total war.

In no theatre were the problems of communication more severe than in Africa and, in the absence of extensive railways and reliable beasts of burden, there was only one solution: men. Over 2 million Africans served in the First World War, nearly all as carriers of supplies, weapons and wounded, and although they were far from the fields of Flanders, these forgotten auxiliaries had as hellish a time as the most exposed front-line troops in Europe. Not only were they underfed and overworked; once removed from their usual locales they were every bit as susceptible to disease as their white masters. Roughly a fifth of all Africans employed as carriers died, many of them the victims of the dysentery that ravaged all colonial armies in the field. In East Africa 3,156 whites in British service died in the line of duty; of these, fewer than a third were victims of enemy action. But if black troops and carriers are included, total losses were over 100,000.[93]

As we have seen, the familiar rationale of white rule in Africa was that it conferred the benefits of civilization. The war – which was fought in all Germany's African colonies (Togoland, the Cameroons and East Africa as well as South-West Africa) – made a mockery of that claim. 'Behind us we leave destroyed fields, ransacked magazines and, for the immediate future, starvation,' wrote Ludwig Deppe, a doctor in the German East African Army. 'We are no longer the agents of culture; our track is marked by death, plundering and evacuated villages, just like the progress of our own and enemy armies in the Thirty Years War.'[94]

For most of the First World War there was a stalemate. As the defenders, whom the French and British had somehow to drive from their entrenched positions on the Western Front, the Germans had the advantage in what amounted to the biggest siege in history. There was a similar impasse on the Trentino and Isonzo Fronts, where the Italians could not dislodge the Austro-Hungarians. The war in the East was much more mobile, but here too the Germans had the upper hand, despite the blunders of their Habsburg allies. Attempts to break the deadlock by opening new fronts – Gallipoli, Salonika, Mesopotamia – yielded miserable results. Nor did any wonder weapons materialize in the way that the atomic bomb later would; poison gas was widely used, horrible in its effects, but not decisive; submarines could disrupt Britain's import trade but not stop it. By the spring of 1917, as the war of attrition ground on, the outlook for France was darkening. Mutiny and revolution in Russia in February had given Germany the prospect of victory on the Eastern Front. The United States, though officially at war with Germany from 6 April, would not be able to play a significant military role on the Western Front for at least six months. And, after the staggering losses suffered at the Battle of Verdun (1916), the French government was deeply concerned about the shortage of men. The limitation of family size had begun earlier in France than elsewhere – perhaps because sex was better understood by French women and contraception more readily available to them – so there were significantly fewer young Frenchmen than Germans. Already by the end of March 1917, some 1.3 million Frenchmen had been killed or taken prisoner. In all, French wartime losses were nearly double those of the British. Roughly one in eight Frenchmen aged between fifteen and forty-nine lost their lives. The 'blood tax' – *l'impôt du sang* – was heavy indeed.

It is easy to forget that France lost two out of three wars against Germany between 1870 and 1940. In 1917 it seemed on the verge of losing the First World War too. Where should France turn for help? The answer was to Africa. Although, as we have seen, most of them were denied full French citizenship, France's African subjects were still regarded as eligible to bear arms in the defence of *la patrie*. Yet everywhere – in Senegal, French Congo, French Sudan, Dahomey and Ivory Coast – Africans declined to answer the call of the motherland. The collective mood was captured by the lament of one mother to a French officer: 'You have already taken all that I have, and now you are taking my only son.' Most felt that induction into the army amounted to a sentence of 'certain death'. The only man who seemed capable of resolving this situation was Blaise Diagne, the first African to have been elected to the French National Assembly. Now, was he willing to return to Senegal as a kind of glorified recruiting sergeant?

Diagne saw the chance to strike a bargain with Prime Minister Georges Clemenceau. He insisted that any African who came to fight should be given French citizenship. More hospitals and schools should be built in West Africa. Veteran tirailleurs should be exempt from taxation and receive decent pensions. Diagne cabled his colleagues in Dakar to discourage enlistment if the concessions he demanded were not forthcoming.[95]

In his maiden speech in the French National Assembly Diagne had said, 'If we can come here to legislate, we are French citizens, and if we are, we demand the right to serve [in the army] as all French citizens do.' It was an ingenious appeal to the tradition of the French Revolution, with its ideal of the nation in arms – everyone a citizen with the right to liberty, equality and fraternity, but also with the solemn duty to bear arms for the defence of the nation. Clemenceau was won over: 'Those who fall under fire fall neither as whites nor as blacks,' he declared. 'They fall as Frenchmen and for the same flag.'[96]

As an incentive to join up, the promise of French citizenship proved startlingly successful. At least 63,000 West Africans answered Diagne's call, more than twice the number the French had asked for. In all, 164,000 men from French West Africa and Equatorial Africa were combatants in Europe during the war, a substantial part of a half-million strong colonial force drawn from all over the French Empire. As one recruit, Ndematy Mbaye, recalled: 'He [Diagne] told us that France had entered a war with the Germans. And he said that "You are friends of the Frenchmen. So, when you are friends with someone – when someone has troubles – you have to help them. So, the Frenchmen have asked [you] to come to help them in the war."'[97] The majority of volunteers were enthusiastic – averring how 'glad' they were to serve, how 'happy' they were to fight, how 'proud' they felt to be in the army. Demba Mboup was among those eager to fight for France:

> I was very happy because I didn't know what the war was really like. So it was a kind of curiosity – to know what the war was about, and about being a soldier … So I was happy [thinking] I was going to discover new experiences. I didn't know.[98]

He was to find out soon enough.

His commanding officer General Charles Mangin thought he knew a thing or two about Africans. He had been a member of Marchand's Fashoda expedition. In 1910, as an ambitious young lieutenant colonel, he and a group of scientists had toured West Africa with orders to increase recruitment. Mangin was familiar with the latest racial science. His survey team, after examining recruits with the full range of pseudo-scientific methods, concluded that, thanks to their supposedly underdeveloped nervous systems, African soldiers would feel less fear and suffer less pain than their European counterparts. They would therefore be exceptionally steadfast under fire. In 1917 Mangin was able to put his theory to the test. Under his leadership, Mboup and his fellow tirailleurs were pitted against perhaps the best-trained soldiers the West has ever produced: the fighting machine that was the imperial German army.

BLACK SHAME

In April 1917 Demba Mboup and his comrades in the French Colonial Corps, part of General Charles Mangin's Sixth Army and General Denis Duchêne's Tenth Army, faced the heavily fortified positions of the Seventh German Army under General Hans von Boehn on the Chemin des Dames – the Ladies' Road, so called after its use by the two daughters of Louis XV in the eighteenth century. In March 1814 Napoleon's retreating soldiers had fought along the same road against the invading Austrian and Russian armies. It was the key to the German defensive position on the Western Front.

The French commander General Robert Nivelle was confident that he would be the man who achieved the long-awaited breakthrough on the Western Front. The French built 300 miles of new railway lines to supply the offensive with 872 trainloads of munitions. Altogether more than a million men were massed in readiness for the assault, stretched along a 25-mile front. Days of artillery barrages were supposed to soften up the Germans. Then, at 6 a.m. on 16 April, the colonial troops advanced up hills that had become mudslides in the rain and sleet. Mangin had placed the Senegalese in the first wave of the attack. But he almost certainly had an ulterior motive: to spare French lives. According to Lieutenant Colonel Debieuvre, commander of the 58th Regiment of Colonial Infantry, the Africans were 'finally and above all superb attack troops permitting the saving of the lives of whites, who behind them exploit their success and organize the positions they conquer'.[99]

From the German trenches, Captain Reinhold Eichacker watched in horror:

> The black Senegal negroes, France's cattle for the shambles. Hundreds of fighting eyes, fixed, threatening, deadly. And they came. First singly, at wide intervals. Feeling their way, like the arms of a horrible cuttlefish.

Eager, grasping, like the claws of a mighty monster. Thus they rushed closer, flickering and sometimes disappearing in their cloud. Strong, wild fellows, showing their grinning teeth like panthers. Horrible their unnaturally wide-opened, burning, bloodshot eyes.

On they came, a solid, rolling black wall, rising and falling, swaying and heaving, impenetrable, endless.

'Close range! Individual firing! Take careful aim!' My orders rang out sharp and clear.

The first blacks fell headlong in full course in our wire entanglements, turning somersaults like the clowns in a circus. Whole groups melted away. Dismembered bodies, sticky earth, shattered rocks, were mixed in wild disorder. The black cloud halted, wavered, closed its ranks and rolled nearer and nearer, irresistible, crushing, devastating!

A wall of lead and iron suddenly hurled itself upon the attackers and the entanglements just in front of our trenches. A deafening hammering and clattering, cracking and pounding, rattling and crackling, beat everything to earth in ear-splitting, nerve-racking clamor. Our machine guns had flanked the blacks!

Like an invisible hand they swept over the men and hurled them to earth, mangling and tearing them to pieces! Singly, in files, in rows and heaps, the blacks fell. Next to each other, behind each other, on top of each other.[100]

Eleven days before the battle, the Germans had in fact obtained detailed plans of the attack from a captured French NCO. They were well protected from the French bombardment by a complex of deep quarries known as the Dragon's Grotto, which they used as bomb shelters. And when the infantry advanced, the Germans were ready with state-of-the-art mobile machine guns. On the first day alone, the attacking forces suffered 40,000 casualties. By 10 May, one in five French soldiers had been either killed or wounded. For Demba Mboup, who was disabled by shrapnel, it was a revelation of the distinctly uncivilized reality of European life in time of total war. So disillusioned were the Africans that some of them joined in the massive mutiny that subsequently swept through the French ranks and forced the government to replace Nivelle. In August, 200 men of the 61st Battalion of the Tirailleurs Sénégalais – known as the Battalion Malafosse, after their commanding officer – refused to take up positions along the Chemin des Dames. As one of them succinctly put it: 'Battalion Malafosse has no good. No rest, always make war, always kill blacks.'[101] Several of the mutineers were court-martialled, and four sentenced to death, though none of the sentences was actually carried out.

Though Blaise Diagne protested about the wasteful use of his countrymen, he was soon back in Senegal in search of fresh recruits, this time armed with a guarantee that fighting meant not just citizenship but a Croix de Guerre. On 18 February 1918 Clemenceau defended the resumption of military recruitment before a group of senators, making clear exactly how the French saw the Senegalese:

> Although I have infinite respect for these brave blacks, I would much prefer to have ten blacks killed than a single Frenchman, because I think that enough Frenchmen have been killed and that it is necessary to sacrifice them as little as possible.[102]

In all more than 33,000 West Africans died in the war, one in five of those who joined up. The comparable figure for French soldiers was less than 17 per cent. By contrast, the mortality rate among British Indian troops was half that for soldiers from the United Kingdom.[103]

War is hell. When the bard of empire Rudyard Kipling visited a French section of the Western Front in 1915 – not long before his own son's death at the Battle of Loos – he encountered the reality of the great war for civilization:

> 'The same work. Always the same work!' [one] officer said. 'And you could walk from here to the sea or to Switzerland in that ditch – and you'll find the same work going on everywhere. It isn't war.'
>
> 'It's better than that,' said another. 'It's the eating-up of a people. They come and fill the trenches and they die, and they die; and they send more and *those* die. We do the same, of course, but – look!'
>
> He pointed to the large deliberate smoke-heads renewing themselves along that yellowed beach. 'That is the frontier of civilization. They have all civilization against them – those brutes yonder [meaning the Germans]. It's not the local victories of the old wars that we're after. It's the barbarian – all the barbarian [*sic*]. Now you've seen the whole thing in little.'[104]

Yet war can also be a driver of human progress. As we have seen, the impressive advances of the Scientific Revolution were helped not hindered by the incessant feuding of the European states. The same was true of the clash of empires between 1914 and 1918. The slaughter-house of the Western Front was like a vast and terrifying laboratory for medical science, producing significant advances in surgery, not to men-tion psychiatry. The skin graft and antiseptic irrigation of wounds were invented. The earliest blood transfusions were attempted. For the first time, all British soldiers were vaccinated against typhoid, and wounded soldiers were routinely given anti-tetanus shots.[105]

Not that these advances helped the tirailleurs, however. If they were not killed in the trenches, they died in enormous numbers from pneumonia. Why? According to French doctors, they had a racial pre-disposition to the disease.

Europeans had come to Africa claiming that they would civilize it. But even the French, with all their good intentions, failed to implant more than a very limited version of Western civilization there. Elsewhere, the challenges of inhospitable terrain and tribal resistance brought out the destructive worst in Europeans, most obviously but by no means uniquely in the German colonies. Methods of total warfare first tried out on the likes of the Herero were then imported back to Europe and combined to devastating effect with the next generation of industrialized weaponry. And in a final bitter twist, Africans were lured to Europe and sacrificed in one of the war's stupidest offensives.

The legacy of the war in Africa was as profound in Europe as it was in Africa. General Paul Emil von Lettow-Vorbeck, who had played his part in the genocide against the Herero, also led the campaign against British forces in East Africa. With the end of the war, Lettow-Vorbeck returned to Germany, but it was not long before he and his veterans saw action again. As their fatherland descended into revolution, they marched into Hamburg to snuff out the threat of a German soviet republic. Civil war raged not only in the big German cities but also along Germany's eastern frontier, where so-called Freikorps led by veterans like Franz Xavier Ritter von Epp and Hermann Ehrhardt waged war on the Bolsheviks and Slav nationalists as if they were

African tribes in all but the colour of their skins. For Epp and Ehrhardt this came naturally; both had been officers in the wars against the Herero and Nama.[106]

Although the racial theorist Eugen Fischer ended up on the losing side, the First World War proved surprisingly fruitful for his chosen field. As colonial troops found their way into German prisoner-of-war camps, they furnished racial science experts like Otto Reche with a convenient new supply of specimens.[107] Fischer's *Human Heredity and Race Hygiene*, co-authored with Erwin Baur and Fritz Lens and published in 1921, swiftly became a standard work in the rapidly expanding field of eugenics. Adolf Hitler read it while he was imprisoned after the failed Munich coup of 1923 and referred to it in *Mein Kampf*. For Hitler, few ideas were more horrific than that Senegalese soldiers stationed in the Rhineland after the war had impregnated German women. This was the notorious 'Black Shame' that produced the 'Rhineland Bastards' – fresh evidence of the conspiracy to pollute the blood of the Aryan race. Given that he was now director of the new Kaiser William Institute for Anthropology, Human Heredity and Eugenics, founded in Berlin in 1927, Fischer's influence was as far-reaching as it was malign. He later served as one of the scientists on the Gestapo's Special Commission Number Three, which planned and carried out the forced sterilization of the 'Rhineland Bastards'. Among his students was Josef Mengele, responsible for the notoriously inhuman experiments on prisoners at Auschwitz.[108]

For the many ex-colonial soldiers who joined the ranks of the Nazi Party – their old uniforms provided the SA with their first brown shirts – it was entirely natural that the theories born in the concentration camps of Africa should be carried over to the Nazi 'colonization' of Eastern Europe and the murderous racial policies that produced the Holocaust. It was no mere coincidence that the Reichsmarschall in charge of the Luftwaffe was the son of the Reichskommissar of South-West Africa. It was no coincidence that Hans Grimm, the author of *People without Space* (1926), had spent fourteen years in southern Africa. It was no coincidence that the man Hitler appointed as provincial governor of Posen in 1939, Viktor Böttcher, had been a civil servant in the German Cameroons. He was one of many Nazi functionaries who sought 'to perform now in the East of the Reich the constructive work they had once carried out in Africa'. The Nazis always intended to regard the territories they annexed in Eastern Europe 'from a colonial viewpoint', to be 'exploited economically with colonial methods'.[109]

The main difference that most struck contemporaries was that, in Eastern Europe, the colonized were the same colour as the colonizers. 'No nation belonging to the white race has ever before had such conditions forced upon it,' wrote Eugene Erdely, one of the earliest commentators on Nazi imperial rule. Yet the Nazis had no difficulty with that, thanks to the warped ingenuity of their own racial theories. To Heinrich Himmler, the SS chief, the Slavic peoples were all 'Mongol types' who had to be replaced with 'Aryans' in order to create a new 'blond province' in the East. To Hitler, Russians could easily be equated with 'Redskins'. If Auschwitz marked the culmination of state violence against racially defined alien populations, the war against the Herero and Nama was surely the first step in that direction.

Some empires are worse than others. It is a simple point that blanket critiques of imperialism nearly always overlook. To get a flavour of the French Empire's mode of operation in the inter-war era it is worth watching *La Croisière noire*, a documentary made in the 1920s by the Citroën car company. When Georges-Marie Haardt and Louis Audoin-Dubreuil set off in halftrack automobiles on the Expédition Citroën Centre-Afrique in October 1924, they were not just trying to sell more cars. This was a bid to publicize France's benign rule in Africa, extending even into 'l'inconnu de la forêt équatoriale'. A celebration of 'civilization's conquests', the film juxtaposes scenes of 'white sorcerers' amazing Africans with their technical prowess with glimpses of the 'strange little gnomes' (pygmies) in the forest. It ends with the *tricolore* flying proudly over the entire African continent, from Algiers to Dakar, from Brazzaville to Madagascar. It would not be hard to mock this classic expression of French imperial aspiration.[110] Yet that aspiration was not without its results. In Senegal, as we have seen, colonial rule was associated with a sustained improvement in life expectancy of around ten years, from thirty to forty.

The Timing and Pace of Health Transitions in the French Empire

	Senegal	Tunisia	Algeria	Vietnam	France
Beginning of transition	c. 1945	1935	c. 1940	c. 1930	c. 1795
Years gained per annum	0.63	0.68	0.70	0.67	0.25
Life expectancy at beginning	30.2	28.8	31.2	22.5	28.1
Life expectancy in 1960	39.6	45.8	45.2	42.6	69.4
Life expectancy in 2000	52.3	72.1	71.0	69.4	78.6
Passed 65 in year	–	c. 1985	1987	1987	1948

Algeria and Tunisia saw comparable improvements.[111] Better medical care – in particular reduced infant mortality and premature infertility – was the reason why populations in French Africa began to grow so rapidly after 1945.[112] In Indo-China it was the French who constructed 20,000 miles of road and 2,000 of railways, opened coal, tin and zinc mines and established rubber plantations.[113] In 1922 around 20,000 Vietnamese were granted French citizenship – still a tiny minority in a population of 3 million, but not a trivial number.[114] In French West Africa the franchise was extended to a million Africans in 1946 and a further 3 million five years later.[115] Sleeping sickness, which had been the scourge of Cameroon under German rule, was largely eradicated under French rule.[116]

By contrast, the Belgians ran the worst of all African empires in the Congo,[117] while the Third Reich deserves to be considered the worst of all the European empires – the *reductio ad absurdum* and *ad nauseam* of the nineteenth-century notion of the civilizing mission, because its actual effect on the territories it briefly controlled was to barbarize them. The aim, as Himmler conceived it in September 1942, was that 'the Germanic peoples' would grow in number from 83 million to 120 million and would resettle all the land Germany had conquered from Czechoslovakia, Poland and the Soviet Union. They would go forth and multiply in splendid new provinces with names like Ingermanland. Autobahns and high-speed railways would connect a 'string of pearls' – fortified German outposts – as far as the Don, the Volga and ultimately even the Urals. In Himmler's words, the German conquest of 'the East' would be 'the greatest piece of colonization which the world will ever have seen'.[118]

In reality, the Nazi Empire turned out to be the least successful piece of colonization ever seen. Launched in 1938, the campaign to expand beyond Germany's 1871 borders peaked in late 1942, by which time the empire encompassed around one-third of the European landmass and nearly half its inhabitants – 244 million people. Yet by October 1944, when the Red Army marched into East Prussia, it was gone, making it one of the shortest-lived empires in all history, as well as one of the worst. This fleeting duration is, of course, primarily to be explained in military terms. Once the Third Reich was embroiled in a war with not only the British Empire but also the Soviet Union and the United States, its empire was surely doomed. Yet there is a secondary, endogenous explanation for the Third Reich's failure as an empire.

From the point of view of simple demographics, there was in fact nothing implausible about the project of putting 80 million Germans in charge of the European continent. In theory, it should have been easier for Germany to rule Ukraine than it was for Britain to rule Uttar Pradesh. For one thing, Kiev was nearer to Berlin than Kanpur was to London. For another, the Germans were genuinely welcomed as liberators in many parts of Ukraine in 1941. And not only there. All over the Western Soviet Union there were ethnic minorities whom Stalin had treated with suspicion and violence in the 1930s. Most assumed that German rule would be an improvement on Russian rule. Yet the Germans wholly failed to exploit these advantages.

The 'arrogant and overbearing Reich Germans', strutting around in their snazzy uniforms, alienated even the ethnic Germans they were supposed to be freeing from foreign oppression. Worse, they took positive pride in starving the newly subject peoples. 'I will pump every last thing out of this country,' declared Reichskommissar Erich Koch, when put in charge of the Ukraine. 'I did not come here to spread bliss . . .' Göring boasted that he 'could not care less' if non-Germans were 'collapsing from hunger'.[119] A clear indication of what such inhumanity implied was the treatment meted out to Red Army prisoners of war in the wake of Operation Barbarossa. By February 1942 only 1.1 million were still alive of the 3.9 million originally captured. Herded together in barbed-wire stockades, they were simply left to the ravages of malnutrition and disease. Nor were the Nazis content to starve the conquered. They also relished inflicting violence on them, ranging from impromptu beatings (which could be administered either for failing to give the Hitler salute or for presumptuously giving it, according to taste) all the way to industrialized genocide. This was indeed Hereroland writ large.

A few Germans saw the folly of this. In the words of Gauleiter Alfred Frauenfeld in February 1944:

> The principle of ruthless brutality, the treatment of the country [Ukraine] according to points of view and methods used in past centuries against coloured slave peoples; and the fact, defying any sensible policy, that the contempt for that people was not only expressed in actions against individuals but also in words at every possible and impossible occasion . . . all this bears testimony to the complete lack of instinct with regard to the treatment of alien peoples, which in view of its consequences can only be called . . . disastrous.[120]

It was, as an official at the Ministry for the East put it, a 'masterpiece of wrong treatment . . . to have, within a year, chased into the woods and swamps, as partisans, a people which was absolutely pro-German and had jubilantly greeted us as their liberator'.[121]

Added to arrogance, callousness and brutality was downright ineptitude. As early as 1938 a Wehrmacht staff officer remarked on the 'crass extent' of 'the State's inability to govern' in the newly acquired Sudetenland. Alfred Rosenberg's Ministry for the East (Ost-Ministerium) was soon nicknamed the 'Ministry for Chaos' (Cha-Ost-Ministerium). The SS aspired to establish some kind of centralizing grip on the empire, but Himmler and his lackeys messed up even the resettlement of 800,000 ethnic Germans. Otto Ohlendorf – who, as a loyal *Einsatz-gruppe* commander, was responsible for the mass murder of tens of thousands of Soviet Jews – lamented that Himmler's speciality was 'organizing disorder'.[122] Yet ultimate responsibility for the dysfunctional character of the Nazi Empire lay not with Rosenberg or Himmler, but with their master. It was, after all, Hitler who was in charge of the Third Reich. (Of 650 major legislative orders issued during the war, all but 72 were decrees or orders issued in his name.) It was Hitler who argued, shortly after the invasion of the Soviet Union, that 'In view of the vast size of the conquered territories in the east, the forces available for establishing security in these areas will be sufficient only if, instead of punishing resistance by sentences in a court of law, the occupying forces spread such terror as to crush every will to resist among the population.' It was Hitler whose preferred method for pacifying occupied territory was 'shooting everyone who looked in any way suspicious'. In the eyes of Werner Best (one of those rare figures in the Third Reich with a semi-sane conception of imperial rule), Hitler was a latter-day Genghis Khan – a specialist in destruction, whose empire of barbarism could not hope to endure.[123]

In many ways, then, the Nazi Empire was the last, loathsome incarnation of a concept that by 1945 was obsolete. It had seemed plausible for centuries that the road to riches lay through the exploitation of foreign peoples and their land. Long before the word *Lebensraum* was coined, as we have seen, European empires had contended for new places to settle, new people to tax – and before them Asian, American and African empires. Yet in the course of the twentieth century it gradually became apparent that an industrial economy could get on perfectly well without colonies. Indeed, colonies might be something of a needless burden. Writing in 1942, the economist Helmut Schubert noted that Germany's real future was as 'a large industrial zone', dependent on 'a permanent and growing presence of foreign workers'. Germanization of the East was an impossibility; Easternization of Germany was far more likely as the shift of labour from agriculture to industry continued. The exigencies of the war economy vindicated this view. By the end of 1944 around 5 million foreigners had been conscripted to work in the factories and mines of the old Reich. By a rich irony, the dream of a racially pure imperium had turned Germany itself into a multi-ethnic state, albeit a slave state. The replacement of East European slaves with Turkish and Yugoslav 'guest workers' after the war did not change the economic argument. Modern Germany did not in fact need 'living space'. It needed living immigrants.

The French Empire was never so irredeemably barbaric as the Nazi Empire. If it had been, it would surely have been impossible to revive so much of it after the Second World War – and even to reaffirm the old assimilationist ambition by rebranding it as a 'French Union'. Even the ten years between the Brazzaville Conference of 1944 and the twin blows of defeat at Dien Bien Phu and revolt in Algeria exceeded the total duration of Hitler's extra-German imperium. Nevertheless, the world wars were the terrible nemesis that followed the hubris of the *mission civilisatrice*, as all the European empires applied the methods against one another that they had pioneered (albeit with varying degrees of cruelty) against Africans. Medical science, which had seemed like a universal saviour in the war against disease, ended up being perverted by racial prejudice and the pseudo-science of eugenics, turning even some doctors into killers. By 1945 'Western civilization' did indeed seem like a contradiction in terms, just as Gandhi had said. The rapid dissolution of the European empires in the post-war years appeared to be a just enough sentence, regardless of whether or not the majority of former colonies were ready for self-government.[124]

The great puzzle is that, somehow, out of this atrocious age of destruction, there emerged a new model of civilization centred around not colonization but consumption. By 1945, it was time for the West to lay down its arms and pick up its shopping bags – to take off its uniform and put on its blue jeans.

5

Consumption

What we must do is to transform our Empire and our people, make the empire like the countries of Europe and our people like the peoples of Europe.

Inoue Kaoru

Will the West, which takes its great invention, democracy, more seriously than the Word of God, come out against this coup that has brought an end to democracy in Kars? . . . Or are we to conclude that democracy, freedom and human rights don't matter, that all the West wants is for the rest of the world to imitate it like monkeys? Can the West endure any democracy achieved by enemies who in no way resemble them?

Orhan Pamuk

THE BIRTH OF THE CONSUMER SOCIETY

In 1909, inspired by a visit to Japan, the French-Jewish banker and philanthropist Albert Kahn* set out to create an album of colour photographs of people from every corner of the world. The aim, Kahn said, was 'To put into effect a sort of photographic inventory of the surface of the globe as inhabited and developed by Man at the begin-

---

* Kahn, a pupil of the philosopher Henri Bergson, was ruined by the Depression, bringing his grand photographic project to an end. A selection of the images can be viewed at http://www.albertkahn.co.uk/photos.html.

ning of the twentieth century.' Created with the newly invented autochrome process, the 72,000 photographs and 100 hours of film in Kahn's 'archives of the planet' show a dazzling variety of costumes and fashions from more than fifty different countries: dirt-poor peasants in the Gaeltacht, dishevelled conscripts in Bulgaria, forbidding chieftains in Arabia, stark-naked warriors in Dahomey, garlanded maharajas in India, come-hither priestesses in Indo-China and strangely stolid-looking cowboys in the Wild West.[1] In those days, to an extent that seems astonishing today, we were what we wore.

Today, a century later, Kahn's project would be more or less pointless, because these days most people around the world dress in much the same way: the same jeans, the same sneakers, the same T-shirts. There are just a very few places where people hold out against the giant sartorial blending machine. One of them is rural Peru. In the mountains of the Andes, the Quechua women still wear their brightly coloured dresses and shawls and their little felt hats, pinned at jaunty angles and decorated with their tribal insignia. Except that these are not traditional Quechua clothes at all. The dresses, shawls and hats are in fact of Andalusian origin and were imposed by the Spanish Viceroy Francisco de Toledo in 1572, in the wake of Túpac Amaru's defeat. Authentically traditional Andean female attire consisted of a tunic (the *anacu*), secured at the waist by a sash (the *chumpi*), over which was worn a mantle (the *lliclla*), which was fastened with a *tupu* pin. What Quechua women wear nowadays is a combination of these earlier garments with the clothes they were ordered to wear by their Spanish masters. The bowler hats popular among Bolivian women came later, when British workers arrived to build that country's first railways.[2] The current fashion among Andean men for American casual clothing is thus merely the latest chapter in a long history of sartorial Westernization.

What is it about our clothes that other people seem unable to resist? Is dressing like us about wanting to *be* like us? Clearly, this is about more than just clothes. It is about embracing an entire popular culture that extends through music and movies, to say nothing of soft drinks and fast food. That popular culture carries with it a subtle message. It is about freedom – the right to dress or drink or eat as you please (even if that turns out to be like everybody else). It is about democracy – because only those consumer products that people really like get made. And, of course, it is about capitalism – because corporations have to make a profit by selling the stuff. But clothing is at the heart of the process of Westernization for one very simple reason. That great economic transformation which historians long ago named the Industrial Revolution – that quantum leap in material standards of living for a rising share of humanity – had its origins in the manufacture of textiles. It was partly a miracle of mass production brought about by a wave of technological innovation, which had its origin in the earlier Scientific Revolution (see Chapter 2). But the Industrial Revolution would not have begun in Britain and spread to the rest of the West without the simultaneous development of a dynamic consumer society, characterized by an almost infinitely elastic demand for cheap clothes. The magic of industrialization, though it was something contemporary critics generally overlooked, was that the worker was at one and the same time a consumer. The 'wage slave' also went shopping; the lowliest proletarian had more than one shirt, and aspired to have more than two.

The consumer society is so all-pervasive today that it is easy to assume it has always existed. Yet in reality it is one of the more recent innovations that propelled the West ahead of the Rest. Its most striking characteristic is its seemingly irresistible appeal. Unlike modern medicine, which (as we saw in the previous chapter) was often imposed by force on Western colonies, the consumer society is a killer application the rest of the world has generally yearned to download. Even those social orders explicitly intended to be anti-capitalist – most obviously the various derivatives of the doctrine of Karl Marx – have been unable to exclude it. The result is one of the greatest paradoxes of modern history: that an economic system designed to offer infinite choice to the individual has ended up homogenizing humanity.

The Industrial Revolution is often misrepresented as if a broad range of technological innovations simultaneously transformed multiple economic activities. This was not the case. The first phase of industrialization was firmly concentrated on textiles. The archetypal factory was a cotton mill, like the Anchor Mill in Paisley, which still stands today as a monument to Scotland's industrial heyday.*

What exactly happened? One simple answer is that at some point in the nineteenth century British economic output per person, which had already begun to accelerate in the seventeenth century, took off like a rocket. Because of the extreme difficulty of retrospectively calculating anachronistic measures such as gross domestic product or national income, scholars differ about the precise timing. One authoritative estimate is that the average annual rate of growth of per-capita national income rose from below 0.2 per cent between 1760 and 1800 to 0.52 per cent between 1800 and 1830 and to 1.98 per cent between 1830 and 1870.[3] All these figures are miserably low by twenty-first-century standards. Nevertheless the effect was revolutionary. No such sustained acceleration in economic growth had happened before; nor did it stop. On the contrary, even faster growth meant that the average Briton in 1960 was nearly six times richer than his great-grandfather had been in 1860.[4] Especially striking was the speed with which the British labour force left agriculture for other sectors (not only manufacturing but also services). As early as 1850 little more than a fifth of the active population in Britain was engaged in farming, at a time when the figure was closer to 45 per cent even in the Low Countries. By 1880 fewer than one in seven Britons worked on the land; by 1910 it was one in eleven.[5] Aggregate growth figures mask the dramatic nature of this change. Though it was spread over decades, the Industrial Revolution was highly localized. In Gloucestershire, for example, it was barely visible. In Lancashire it was unmissable – though swathed in smog. The Highlands of Scotland were untouched; that was why the Victorians learned to love what had struck Dr Johnson's generation as merely a grim wasteland. Glasgow, by contrast, was transformed by trade and industry into the 'Second City' of the British Empire, its smokestacks out-reeking its famously malodorous rival Edinburgh.

The Industrial Revolution has been characterized as a 'wave of

---

* Clark's, the firm that built it (and provided Kenneth Clark with the means to be a gentleman scholar), was founded in 1812. The mill we know today was built in 1886 in a utilitarian style that Jeremy Bentham would have admired. It closed in 1968, having been rendered unprofitable, like most of the British textile industry, by Japanese competition.

gadgets'.[6] Certainly, it was technological innovation that explained much of the decisive increase in the productivity of land, labour and capital (the so-called factors of production). The second and third of these increased in quantity in the nineteenth century,* but it was the qualitative improvement that really mattered – the fact that total output exceeded the combined increments of workers and mills. In terms of supply, then, the Industrial Revolution was a hunt for efficiency. James Hargreaves's spinning jenny (1766), Richard Arkwright's water frame (1769), Samuel Crompton's mule (1779), Edmund Cartwright's steam-powered loom (1787) and Richard Roberts's self-acting mule (1830): these were all ways of making more thread or cloth per man-hour. The spinning jenny, for example, allowed a single worker simultaneously to spin cotton yarn with eight spindles. Thanks to these innovations, the unit price of British cotton manufactures declined by approximately 90 per cent between the mid-1790s and 1830.[7] The same applied to the other key breakthroughs in iron production and steam-power generation. James Neilson's blast furnace, patented in 1828, hugely improved the coke-smelting process invented by Abraham Darby in 1709. Iron output at Darby's Coalbrookdale furnace leapt from 81 tons a year in 1709 to 4,632 in 1850. Likewise, Thomas Newcomen's 1705 steam engine was of little practical use; but James Watt's addition of a separate condenser greatly improved it, and Richard Trevithick's high-pressure version was better still. Newcomen's engine had burned 45 pounds of coal to produce a single horsepower hour. A late nineteenth-century steam engine could do the same with less than 1 pound.[8] By 1870 Britain's steam engines together were generating 4 million horsepower, equivalent to the work of 40 million men. Feeding such a large human workforce would have required three times Britain's entire wheat

---

* The population of England surged by more than a third between the 1740s and the 1790s; by the 1860s it was more than three times larger. Average age at marriage fell from twenty-six to twenty-three, fewer women remained unmarried and there were more illegitimate births. Gregory Clark has argued that the tendency for the children of richer individuals to live longer than those of the poor explains the Industrial Revolution, since 'Middle-class values, and economic orientation, were most likely being spread through reproductive advantage ... Thrift, prudence, negotiation and hard work were imbuing themselves into communities that had been spendthrift, violent, impulsive and leisure loving' (Clark, *Farewell to Alms*, pp. 132, 166). But presumably rich French and Italian children also fared better than poor ones.

output.[9] None of this was as intellectually profound as the big scientific breakthroughs of the seventeenth century, though Boulton's and Watt's membership of the Birmingham Lunar Society, which also counted the pioneering chemist Joseph Priestley among its luminaries, shows how close the connections were between the two revolutions.[10] Rather, it was a cumulative, evolutionary process of improvement characterized by tinkering, sometimes carried out by men with minimal scientific education. The spirit of the age had got off its cavalry charger and was now to be found toiling in the workshop of Boulton & Watt's Soho Manufactory. Innovation, personified by the dour Watt, and entrepreneurship, personified by the ebullient Boulton: that was the quintessential partnership at the heart of the Industrial Revolution.

'I sell here, Sir,' Boulton told James Boswell in 1776, 'what all the world desires to have – POWER.'[11] But what for? The Industrial Revolution would have been pointless if it had consisted only of a massive increase in the quantity of cloth, iron and mechanical power that could be produced in a year. Equally important was the rapid development and spread of a consumer society that actually wanted more of these things.[12] If technological innovation spurred the supply side, the demand side of the Industrial Revolution was driven by the seemingly insatiable appetite human beings have for clothes. Nothing did more to stimulate that appetite than the large-scale import of Indian cloth by the East India Company, beginning in the seventeenth century. (Imports of Chinese porcelain had a similar effect on the demand for crockery.)[13] Housewives wanted these things and adjusted their behaviour and budgets accordingly.[14] Entrepreneurs sought to use new technology to imitate imported goods and then displace them.[15]

Cotton was indeed the king of the British economic miracle. The textile sector accounted for around a tenth of British national income, and cotton manufacturing achieved much the most rapid increases in efficiency. The factories of Manchester and the workshops of Oldham became the focal point of the transformation. The striking thing is that a very large share of British cotton production was not for domestic consumption. In the mid-1780s cotton exports were only around 6 per cent of total British exports. By the mid-1830s, the proportion had risen to 48 per cent, the bulk of it to continental Europe.[16] Historians used to argue about which came first in Britain, the technological wave or the consumer society. On the continent, there is no doubt. Europeans acquired a taste for cheap factory-made cloth well before they learned how to produce it themselves.

Why did Britain industrialize first? The consumer society was not significantly more advanced than in other North-west European states. The level and dissemination of scientific knowledge was not notably superior. There had been impressive advances in other sectors of the British economy during the eighteenth century, for example in agriculture, banking and commerce, but it is not immediately obvious why these would trigger a surge of productivity-enhancing investment in cotton, iron and steam production. It has been suggested that the explanation for Britain's early industrialization must lie in the realm of politics or of law. The common law, for example, is said to have encouraged the forming of corporations and offered creditors better protection than continental systems like those derived from Napoleon's civil law code.[17] Institutional advantages certainly helped Britain to pull ahead of other would-be empires in the seventeenth and especially the eighteenth century, as we have seen. But it not at all clear why the doctrine of the sovereignty of parliament or the evolution of the common law would have provided Boulton and Watt with stronger incentives than their unsung counterparts on the continent.

It is possible that eighteenth-century tariffs erected against Indian calicoes gave British manufacturers some advantage, just as similar protectionist policies would later nurture the infant industries of the United States against British competition.[18] David Ricardo's doctrine of comparative advantage* was not the sole reason why cotton exports from Britain soared in the first half of the nineteenth century. Aside from that, the case seems unconvincing that British (or, for that matter, American) political or legal institutions were more favourable

* Comparative advantage means one country's ability to produce a good or service with a lower opportunity cost/higher relative efficiency than another. Ricardo's famous example concerns the trade between England and Portugal. In Portugal it is possible to produce both wine and cloth more easily and cheaply than in England, but in England it is much harder and therefore more expensive to produce wine than cloth. Both sides therefore gain if Portugal focuses on producing wine, where its comparative advantage is greatest, leaving the English to produce only cloth. The Portuguese exchange their surplus wine for surplus English cloth. The former get more cloth than would be the case if they produced their own; the latter get cheaper wine. This theory,

to industrial development than Dutch, French or German.[19] In the eyes of contemporaries, the state of the British political and legal systems in the key decades of industrial take-off was the very reverse of favourable to fledgling industry. 'Old Corruption' was how the radical polemicist William Cobbett characterized the way parliament, the Crown and the City interacted. In *Bleak House* (1852–3) Charles Dickens portrayed the Court of Chancery as a grotesquely inefficient hindrance to the resolution of property disputes, while in *Little Dorrit* (1855–7) the target of his satire was the 'Circumlocution Office', a government department dedicated to obstructing economic progress. Joint-stock companies remained illegal until the 1720 Bubble Act was repealed in 1824, while debtors' prisons like the Marshalsea – so vividly depicted in *Little Dorrit* – continued to operate until the passage of the 1869 Bankruptcy Act. It is also worth remembering that much of the legislation passed by Victorian parliaments in connection with the textile industry was designed to limit the economic freedom of factory-owners, notably with respect to child labour.

Britain differed significantly from other North-west European countries in two ways that make the Industrial Revolution intelligible. The first was that labour was significantly dearer than on the continent – or indeed anywhere for which records exist. In the second half of the eighteenth century a Parisian worker's real wages (in terms of silver adjusted for consumer prices) were just over half a Londoner's. Real wages in Milan were 26 per cent of the London level.[20] Wages in China and South India were even lower, and not only because of the higher productivity of Asian rice cultivation relative to European wheat production.[21] The second reason was that coal in Britain was abundant, accessible and therefore significantly cheaper than on the other side of the English Channel. Between the 1820s and the 1860s, the annual out-

---

when applied to Ireland, had catastrophic results. Specialization in meat production for the English market led to an excessive dependence on the potato to feed the rural workforce and therefore acute vulnerability to the blight of that vegetable, *Phytophthora infestans*, which struck in the mid-1840s. True to Ricardian principles, the British government declined to send emergency food to alleviate the famine; a million people died, vindicating not Ricardo but Thomas Malthus, the author of the *Essay on the Principle of Population* (1798), which predicted such calamities. The surviving Irish were reduced to exporting themselves, mostly to America.

put of British coal mines quadrupled; the price per ton fell by a quarter. Together, these differentials explain why British entrepreneurs were so much more motivated to pursue technological innovation than their continental counterparts. It made better sense in Britain than anywhere else to replace expensive men with machines fuelled by cheap coal.

Like the French Revolution before it, the British Industrial Revolution spread across Europe. But this was a peaceful conquest.[22] The great innovators were largely unable to protect what would now be called their intellectual property rights. With remarkable speed, the new technology was therefore copied and replicated on the continent and across the Atlantic. The first true cotton mill, Richard Arkwright's at Cromford in Derbyshire, was built in 1771. Within seven years a copy appeared in France. It took just three years for the French to copy Watt's 1775 steam engine. By 1784 there were German versions of both, thanks in large measure to industrial espionage. The Americans, who had the advantage of being able to grow their own cotton as well as mine their own coal, were a little slower: the first cotton mill appeared in Bass River, Massachusetts, in 1788, the first steam engine in 1803.[23] The Belgians, Dutch and Swiss were not far behind. The pattern was similar after the first steam locomotives began pulling carriages on the Stockton and Darlington Railway in 1825, though that innovation took a mere five years to cross the Atlantic, compared with twelve years to reach Germany and twenty-two to arrive in Switzerland.[24] As the efficiency of the technology improved, so it became economically attractive even where labour was cheaper and coal scarcer. Between 1820 and 1913 the number of spindles in the world increased four times as fast as the world's population, but the rate of increase was twice as fast abroad as in the United Kingdom. Such were the productivity gains – and the growth of demand – that the gross output of the world cotton industry rose three times as fast as total spindleage.[25] As a result, between 1820 and 1870 a handful of North-west European and North American countries achieved British rates of growth; indeed, Belgium and the United States grew faster.

By the late nineteenth century, then, industrialization was in full swing in two broad bands: one stretching across the American Northeast, with towns like Lowell, Massachusetts at its heart, and another extending from Glasgow to Warsaw and even as far as Moscow. In 1800 seven out of the world's ten biggest cities had still been Asian, and Beijing had still exceeded London in size. By 1900, largely as a result of the Industrial Revolution, only one of the biggest was Asian; the rest were European or American.

The spread around the world of the British-style industrial city inspired some observers but dismayed others. Among the inspired was Charles Darwin who, as he acknowledged in *On the Origin of Species* (1859), had been 'well prepared to appreciate the struggle for existence' by the experience of living through the Industrial Revolution. Much of Darwin's account of natural selection could have applied equally well to the economic world of the mid-nineteenth-century textile business:

> All organic beings are exposed to severe competition ... As more individuals are produced than can possibly survive, there must in every case be a struggle for existence, either one individual with another of the same species, or with the individuals of distinct species, or with the physical conditions of life. Each organic being ... has to struggle for life ... As natural selection acts solely by accumulating slight, successive, favourable variations, it can produce no great or sudden modification ...[26]

In that sense, it might make more sense for historians to talk about an Industrial *Evolution*, in Darwin's sense of the word. As the economists Thorstein Veblen and Joseph Schumpeter would later remark, nineteenth-century capitalism was an authentically Darwinian system, characterized by seemingly random mutation, occasional speciation and differential survival or, to use Schumpeter's memorable phrase, 'creative destruction'.[27]

Yet precisely the volatility of the more or less unregulated markets created by the Industrial Revolution caused consternation among many contemporaries. Until the major breakthroughs in public health described in the previous chapter, mortality rates in industrial cities were markedly worse than in the countryside. Moreover, the advent of a new and far from regular 'business cycle', marked by periodic crises of industrial over-production and financial panic, generally made a stronger impression on people than the gradual acceleration of the economy's average growth rate. Though the Industrial Revolution manifestly improved life over the long run, in the short run it seemed to make things worse. One of William Blake's illustrations for his preface to *Milton* featured, among other sombre images, a dark-skinned figure holding up a blood-soaked length of cotton yarn.* For the composer Richard Wagner, London was 'Alberich's dream come true – Nibelheim, world dominion, activity, work, everywhere the oppressive feeling of steam and fog'. Hellish images of the British factory inspired his depiction of the dwarf's underground realm in *Das Rheingold*, as well as one of the leitmotifs of the entire *Ring* cycle, the insistent, staccato rhythm of multiple hammers:

Steeped in German literature and philosophy, the Scottish writer Thomas Carlyle was the first to identify what seemed the fatal flaw of the industrial economy: that it reduced all social relations to what he called, in his essay *Past and Present*, 'the cash nexus':

> the world has been rushing on with such fiery animation to get work and ever more work done, it has had no time to think of dividing the wages; and has merely left them to be scrambled for by the Law of the Stronger, law of Supply-and-demand, law of Laissez-faire, and other idle Laws and Un-laws. We call it a Society; and go about professing openly the totalest separation, isolation. Our life is not a mutual helpfulness; but rather, cloaked under due laws-of-war, named 'fair competition' and so forth, it is a mutual hostility. We have profoundly forgotten everywhere that *Cash-payment* is not the sole relation of human beings ... [It] is not the sole nexus of man with man, – how far from it! Deep, far deeper than Supply-and-demand, are Laws, Obligations sacred as Man's Life itself.[28]

That phrase – the 'cash nexus' – so much pleased the son of an apostate Jewish lawyer from the Rhineland that he and his co-author, the

---

* The 'dark Satanic mills' of the text may well refer to the Albion Flour Mills, built by Boulton & Watt in London in 1769 and destroyed by fire in 1791.

heir of a Wuppertal cotton mill-owner, purloined it for the outrageous 'manifesto' they published on the eve of the 1848 revolutions.

The founders of communism, Karl Marx and Friedrich Engels, were just two of many radical critics of the industrial society, but it was their achievement to devise the first internally consistent blueprint for an alternative social order. Since this was the beginning of a schism within Western civilization that would last for nearly a century and a half, it is worth pausing to consider the origins of their theory. A mixture of Hegel's philosophy, which represented the historical process as dialectical, and the political economy of Ricardo, which posited diminishing returns for capital and an 'iron' law of low wages, Marxism took Carlyle's revulsion against the industrial economy and substituted a utopia for nostalgia.

Marx himself was an odious individual. An unkempt scrounger and a savage polemicist, he liked to boast that his wife was '*née* Baroness von Westphalen', but nevertheless sired an illegitimate son by their maidservant. On the sole occasion when he applied for a job (as a railway clerk) he was rejected because his handwriting was so atrocious. He sought to play the stock market but was hopeless at it. For most of his life he therefore depended on handouts from Engels, for whom socialism was a hobby, along with fox-hunting and womanizing; his day job was running one of his father's cotton factories in Manchester (the patent product of which was known as 'Diamond Thread'). No man in history has bitten the hand that fed him with greater gusto than Marx bit the hand of King Cotton.

The essence of Marxism was the belief that the industrial economy was doomed to produce an intolerably unequal society divided between the bourgeoisie, the owners of capital, and a propertyless proletariat. Capitalism inexorably demanded the concentration of capital in ever fewer hands and the reduction of everyone else to wage slavery, which meant being paid only 'that quantum of the means of subsistence which is absolutely requisite to keep the labourer in bare existence as a labourer'. In chapter 32 of the first tome of his scarcely readable *Capital* (1867), Marx prophesied the inevitable denouement:

> Along with the constant decrease of the number of capitalist magnates, who usurp and monopolize all the advantages of this process of transformation, the mass of misery, oppression, slavery, degradation and

exploitation grows; but with this there also grows the revolt of the working class . . .

The centralization of the means of production and the socialization of labour reach a point at which they become incompatible with their capitalist integument. This integument is burst asunder. The knell of capitalist private property sounds. The expropriators are expropriated.

It is not unintentional that this passage has a Wagnerian quality, part *Götterdämmerung*, part *Parsifal*. But by the time the book was published the great composer had left the spirit of 1848 far behind. Instead it was Eugène Pottier's song 'The Internationale' that became the anthem of Marxism. Set to music by Pierre De Geyter, it urged the 'servile masses' to put aside their religious 'superstitions' and national allegiances, and make war on the 'thieves' and their accomplices, the tyrants, generals, princes and peers.

Before identifying why they were wrong, we need to acknowledge what Marx and his disciples were right about. Inequality did increase as a result of the Industrial Revolution. Between 1780 and 1830 output per labourer in the UK grew over 25 per cent but wages rose barely 5 per cent. The proportion of national income going to the top percentile of the population rose from 25 per cent in 1801 to 35 per cent in 1848. In Paris in 1820, around 9 per cent of the population were classified as 'proprietors and *rentiers*' (living from their investments) and owned 41 per cent of recorded wealth. By 1911 their share had risen to 52 per cent. In Prussia, the share of income going to the top 5 per cent rose from 21 per cent in 1854 to 27 per cent in 1896 and to 43 per cent in 1913.[29] Industrial societies, it seems clear, grew more unequal over the course of the nineteenth century. This had predictable consequences. In the Hamburg cholera epidemic of 1892, for example, the mortality rate for individuals with an income of less than 800 marks a year was thirteen times higher than that for individuals earning over 50,000 marks.[30] It was not necessary to be a Marxist to be horrified by the inequality of industrial society. The Welsh-born factory-owner Robert Owen, who coined the term 'socialism' in 1817, envisaged an alternative economic model based on co-operative production and utopian villages like the ones he founded at Orbiston in Scotland and New Harmony, Indiana.[31] Even the Irish aesthete and wit Oscar Wilde recognized the foundation of social misery on which the refined world of belles-lettres stood:

> These are the poor; and amongst them there is no grace of manner, or charm of speech, or civilization ... From their collective force Humanity gains much in material prosperity. But it is only the material result that it gains, and the man who is poor is in himself absolutely of no importance. He is merely the infinitesimal atom of a force that, so far from regarding him, crushes him: indeed, prefers him crushed, as in that case he is far more obedient ... Agitators are a set of interfering, meddling people, who come down to some perfectly contented class of the community, and sow the seeds of discontent amongst them. That is the reason why agitators are so absolutely necessary. Without them, in our incomplete state, there would be no advance towards civilization ... [But] the fact is that civilization requires slaves. The Greeks were quite right there. Unless there are slaves to do the ugly, horrible, uninteresting work, culture and contemplation become almost impossible. Human slavery is wrong, insecure, and demoralizing. On mechanical slavery, on the slavery of the machine, the future of the world depends.[32]

Yet the revolution feared by Wilde and eagerly anticipated by Marx never materialized – at least, not where it was supposed to. The *bouleversements* of 1830 and 1848 were the results of short-run spikes in food prices and financial crises more than of social polarization.[33] As agricultural productivity improved in Europe, as industrial employment increased and as the amplitude of the business cycle diminished, the risk of revolution declined. Instead of coalescing into an impoverished mass, the proletariat subdivided into 'labour aristocracies' with skills and a lumpenproletariat with vices. The former favoured strikes and collective bargaining over revolution and thereby secured higher real wages. The latter favoured gin. The respectable working class had their trade unions and working men's clubs.[34] The ruffians – 'keelies' in Glasgow – had the music hall and street fights.

The prescriptions of the *Communist Manifesto* were in any case singularly unappealing to the industrial workers they were aimed at. Marx and Engels called for the abolition of private property; the abolition of inheritance; the centralization of credit and communications; the state ownership of all factories and instruments of production; the creation of 'industrial armies for agriculture'; the abolition of the distinction between town and country; the abolition of the family; 'community of women' (wife-swapping) and the abolition of all nationalities. By contrast, mid-nineteenth-century liberals wanted constitutional government, the freedoms of speech, press and assembly, wider political representation through electoral reform, free trade and, where it was lacking, national self-determination ('Home Rule'). In the half-century after the upheaval of 1848 they got a good many of these things – enough, at any rate, to make the desperate remedies of Marx and Engels seem *de trop*. In 1850 only France, Greece and Switzerland had franchises in which more than a fifth of the population got to vote. By 1900 ten European countries did, and Britain and Sweden were not far below that threshold. Broader representation led to legislation that benefited lower-income groups; free trade in Britain meant cheap bread, and cheap bread plus rising nominal wages thanks to union pressure meant a significant gain in real terms for workers. Building labourers' day wages in London doubled in real terms between 1848 and 1913. Broader representation also led to more progressive taxation. Britain led the way in 1842 when Sir Robert Peel introduced a peacetime income tax; by 1913 the standard rate was 14 pence in the pound (6 per cent). Prior to 1842 nearly all British revenue had come from the indirect taxation of consumption, via customs and excise duties, regressive taxes taking a proportionately smaller amount of your income the richer you are. By 1913 a third of revenue was coming from direct taxes on the relatively rich. In 1842 the central government had spent virtually nothing on education and the arts and sciences. In 1913 those items accounted for 10 per cent of expenditure. By then, Britain had followed Germany in introducing a state pension for the elderly.

Marx and Engels were wrong on two scores, then. First, their iron law of wages was a piece of nonsense. Wealth did indeed become highly concentrated under capitalism, and it stayed that way into the second quarter of the twentieth century. But income differentials began to narrow as real wages rose and taxation became less regressive. Capitalists understood what Marx missed: that workers were also consumers. It therefore made no sense to try to grind their wages down to subsistence levels. On the contrary, as the case of the United States was making increasingly clear, there was no bigger potential market for most capitalist enterprises than their own employees. Far from condemning the masses to 'immiseration', the mechanization of textile production created growing employment opportunities for Western workers – albeit at the expense of Indian spinners and weavers – and the decline in the prices of cotton and other goods meant that Western workers could buy more with their weekly wages. The impact is best captured by the exploding differential between Western and non-Western wages and living standards in this period. Even within the West the gap between the industrialized vanguard and the rural laggards widened dramatically. In early seventeenth-century London, an unskilled worker's real wages (that is, adjusted for the cost of living) were not so different from what his counterpart earned in Milan. From the 1750s until the 1850s, however, Londoners pulled far ahead. At the peak of the great divergence within Europe, London real wages were six times those in Milan. With the industrialization of Northern Italy in the second half of the nineteenth century, the gap began to close, so that by the eve of the First World War it was closer to a ratio of 3:1. German and Dutch workers also benefited from industrialization, though even in 1913 they still lagged behind their English counterparts.[35] Chinese workers, by contrast, did no such catching up. Where wages were highest, in the big cities of Beijing and Canton, building workers received the equivalent of around 3 grams of silver per day, with no upward movement in the eighteenth century and only a slight improvement in the nineteenth and early twentieth (to around 5–6 grams). There was some improvement for workers in Canton after 1900 but it was minimal; workers in Sichuan stayed dirt poor. London workers meanwhile saw their silver-equivalent wages rise from around 18 grams between 1800 and 1870 to 70 grams between 1900 and 1913. Allowing for the cost of maintaining a family, the standard of living of the average Chinese worker fell throughout the nineteenth century, most steeply during the Taiping Rebellion (see Chapter 6). True, subsistence was cheaper in China than in North-western Europe. It should also be remembered that Londoners and Berliners by that time enjoyed a far more variegated diet of bread, dairy products and meat, washed down with copious amounts of alcohol, whereas most East Asians were subsisting on milled rice and small grains. Nevertheless, it seems clear that by the second decade of the twentieth century the gap in living standards between London and Beijing was around six to one, compared with two to one in the eighteenth century.[36]

The second mistake Marx and Engels made was to underestimate the adaptive quality of the nineteenth-century state – particularly when it could legitimize itself as a *nation*-state.

In his *Contribution to a Critique of Hegel's Philosophy of Right*, Marx had famously called religion the 'opium of the masses'. If so, then nationalism was the cocaine of the middle classes. On 17 March 1846 Venice's Teatro La Fenice was the setting for the premiere of a new opera by the already celebrated Italian composer Giuseppe Verdi. Technically, Verdi had in fact been born a Frenchman: his name at birth was formally registered as 'Joseph Fortunin François Verdi' because the village where he was born was then under Napoleonic rule, having been annexed to France along with the rest of the Duchy of Parma and Piacenza. Venice, too, had been conquered by the French, but was handed over to Austria in 1814. The unpopularity of the Habsburg military and bureaucracy explains the rowdy enthusiasm with which the predominantly Italian audience responded to the following lines:

> Tardo per gli anni, e tremulo,
> È il regnator d'Oriente;
> Siede un imbelle giovine
> Sul trono d'Occidente;
> Tutto sarà disperso
> Quand'io mi unisca a te . . .
> *Avrai tu l'universo,*
> *Resti l'Italia a me.*

(Aged and frail / Is the ruler of the Eastern Empire; / A young imbecile sits on the throne of the Western Empire; / All will be scattered / If you and I unite . . . / *You can have the universe / But leave Italy to me.*)

Sung to Attila by the Roman envoy Ezio following the sack of Rome, these words were a thinly veiled appeal to nationalist sentiment. They perfectly illustrate what nationalism always had over socialism. It had style.

Nationalism had its manifestos, to be sure. Another Giuseppe – Mazzini – was perhaps the nearest thing to a theoretician that nationalism produced. As he shrewdly observed in 1852, the Revolution 'has assumed two forms; the question which all have agreed to call social, and the question of nationalities'. The Italian nationalists of the Risorgimento:

> struggled ... as do Poland, Germany, and Hungary, for country and liberty; for a word inscribed upon a banner, proclaiming to the world that they also live, think, love, and labour for the benefit of all. They speak the same language, they bear about them the impress of consanguinity, they kneel beside the same tombs, they glory in the same tradition; and they demand to associate freely, without obstacles, without foreign domination ...[37]

For Mazzini it was simple: 'The map of Europe has to be remade.' In the future, he argued, it would be neatly reordered as eleven nation-states. This was much easier said than done, however, which was why the preferred modes of nationalism were artistic or gymnastic rather than programmatic. Nationalism worked best in the demotic poetry of writers like the Greek Rigas Feraios (Καλλιο'ναι μίας ώρας ελεύθερη ζωή παρά σαράντα χρόνια σκλαβιά και φυλακή – 'It's better to have an hour as a free man than forty years of slavery and prison'), or in the stirring songs of the German student fraternities (*Fest steht und treu die Wacht am Rhein* – 'The Guard on the Rhine stands firm and true'), or even on the sports field, where Scotland played England on St Andrew's Day, 1872, in the world's first international soccer match (result: 0–0). It was more problematic when political borders, linguistic borders and religious borders failed to coincide, as they did most obviously in the fatal triangle of territory between the Baltic, the Balkans and the Black Sea. Between 1830 and 1905 eight new states achieved either independence or unity: Greece (1830), Belgium (1830–39), Romania (1856), Italy (1859–71), Germany (1864–71), Bulgaria (1878), Serbia (1867–78) and Norway (1905). But the American Southerners failed in their bids for statehood, as did the Armenians, the Croats, the Czechs, the Irish, the Poles, the Slovaks, the Slovenes and the Ukrainians. The Hungarians, like the Scots, made do with the role of junior partners in dual monarchies with empires they helped to run. As for such ethno-linguistically distinct peoples as the Roma, Sinti, Kashubes, Sorbs, Wends, Vlachs, Székelys, Carpatho-Rusyns and Ladins, no one seriously thought them capable of political autonomy.

Success or failure in the nation-building game was ultimately about realpolitik. It suited Camillo Benso, conte di Cavour, to turn the rest of Italy into a colonial appendage of Piedmont-Sardinia, just as it suited Otto Eduard Leopold von Bismarck, Count of Bismarck-Schönhausen, to preserve the prerogatives of the Prussian monarchy by making it the most powerful institution in a federal German *Reich*. 'Never did I doubt,' wrote Bismarck in his *Reminiscences*,

> that the key to German politics was to be found in princes and dynasties, not in publicists, whether in parliament and the press, or on the barricades ... The Gordian knot of German circumstance ... could only be cut by the sword: it came to this, that the King of Prussia, conscious or unconscious, and with him the Prussian army, must be gained for the national cause, whether from the 'Borussian' point of view one regarded the hegemony of Prussia or from the national point of view the unification of Germany as the main object: both aims were co-extensive ... The dynasties have at all times been stronger than press and parliament ... In order that German patriotism should be active and effective, it needs as a rule to hang on the peg of dependence upon a dynasty ... It is as a Prussian, a Hanoverian, a Württemberger, a Bavarian or a Hessian, rather than as a German, that [the German] is disposed to give unequivocal proof of patriotism.[38]

The transformation of the thirty-nine-state German *Bund*, which Austria dominated, into a twenty-five-state *Reich*, which Prussia dominated, was Bismarck's masterstroke. What happened when Prussia defeated Austria and the other members of the German Confederation in 1866 is better regarded not as a war of unification, but as the North's victory over the South in a German civil war, for the simple reason that so many German-speakers were excluded from the new Germany. Yet Bismarck's victory was not complete until he had outmanoeuvred his Liberal opponents at home, first by introducing universal suffrage, which cost them seats in the new imperial diet (the Reichstag), then by splitting them over free trade in 1878. The price was to give the South Germans two powerful blocking positions: the Catholic Centre Party's pivotal role in the Reichstag and the South German states' combined veto in the upper house (Bundesrat).

Se vogliamo che tutto rimanga come è, bisogna che tutto cambi – 'If we want everything to stay as it is, everything will have to change.' The most famous line in Giuseppe Tomasi di Lampedusa's historical novel *The Leopard* (1958) is frequently cited to sum up the covertly conservative character of Italian unification. But the new nation-states were about more than just preserving the cherished privileges of Europe's beleaguered landowning elites. Entities like Italy or Germany, composites of multiple statelets, offered all their citizens a host of benefits: economies of scale, network externalities, reduced transaction costs and the more efficient provision of key public goods like law and order, infrastructure and health. The new states could make Europe's big industrial cities, the breeding grounds of both cholera and revolution, finally safe. Slum clearance, boulevards too wide to barricade, bigger churches, leafy parks, sports stadiums and above all more policemen – all these things transformed the capitals of Europe, not least Paris, which Baron Georges Haussmann completely recast for Napoleon III. All the new states had imposing façades; even defeated Austria lost little time in reinventing itself as 'imperial-royal' Austria-Hungary, its architectural identity set in stone around Vienna's Ringstrasse.[39] But behind the façades there was real substance. Schools were built, the better to drum standardized national languages into young heads. Barracks were erected, the better to train the high-school graduates to defend their fatherland. And railways were constructed in places where their profitability looked doubtful, the better to transport the troops to the border, should the need arise. Peasants became Frenchmen – or Germans, or Italians, or Serbs, depending where they happened to be born.

The paradox is that this age of nationalism coincided with a sustained standardization of modes of dress. Military uniforms, to be sure, continued to be nationally distinct so that, in the heat of battle, a *poilu* could be distinguished from a *boche* or a *rosbif*, even in silhouette. Yet the military innovations of the nineteenth century, which greatly improved the accuracy and power of artillery, as well as introducing smokeless gunpowder, necessitated a shift from the bright coats of the eighteenth and nineteenth century to altogether drabber uniforms. The British adopted khaki drill after the 1879 Anglo-Zulu War, an example later followed by the Americans and the Japanese. The Russians also chose khaki, but of a greyer shade, in 1908. The

Italians opted for a grey-green; the Germans and Austrians for field grey and pike grey, respectively. As armies grew in size, too, economy dictated simplification. The face of battle grew plain.

Male civilians also renounced the dandyism of earlier generations. The suit as it had been conceived by Beau Brummell in the Regency era was itself a simplification relative to eighteenth-century fashions. The trend thereafter was inexorably towards bourgeois sobriety. The single-button penguin-like 'Newmarket' frock coat, now seen only at pretentious weddings, displaced Brummell's dress coat and the double-breasted, high-collared coat favoured by Prince Albert. Waistcoats went from colourful Chinese silk to black or grey wool. Breeches yielded to long trousers, and stockings vanished from view, to be replaced by boring black socks. Shirts were uniformly white. Collars seemed to shrink until all that remained were a couple of celluloid chicken wings, wrapped in a necktie that was invariably black. Hats, too, shrank, until only the bowler remained. And hats, too, were black. It was as if a whole society was on its way to a wake.

Of course, there was a great deal more variety and complexity in the female attire of the Victorian period. And there was a different kind of uniformity among the overalled proletariat and the ragged-trousered poor. Nevertheless, the standardization of dress in the Victorian period – which ran the length and breadth of Europe and far beyond the eastern seaboard of the United States – remains a reality and a puzzle, at a time when nationalism was in the ascendant. 'The Internationale' existed, it seemed, but only at the level of the bourgeois dress code. The explanation, as might be expected in the industrial age, was mechanical.

The Singer sewing machine was born in 1850, when Isaac Merritt Singer moved to Boston, Massachusetts, and saw what was wrong with the machine they were making in Orson C. Phelps's workshop. The needle had to be straight not curved. The shuttle needed to be transverse. And the whole thing had to be operated by foot, not by hand. Like Marx, Singer was not a nice man. He had a total of twenty-four children by five different women, one of whom brought an action for bigamy against him, forcing him to flee the United States. Like Marx – and like a disproportionate number of nineteenth- and twentieth-century entrepreneurs, especially in the clothing and cosmetics business* – Singer was of Jewish origin. And, like Marx, he changed the world – though, unlike Marx, for the better.

I. M. Singer & Company, later the Singer Manufacturing Company, completed the process of mechanizing clothes production that James Hargreaves had begun less than a century before. Now even the sewing together of pieces of cloth could be done by machine. The revolutionary nature of this breakthrough is easily overlooked by a generation that has never sewn on more than a couple of buttons. Singer was evidently a man who loved women; has any man done more for womankind in return? Thanks to Singer, the painstaking hours that had previously been needed to stitch the hem of a skirt became mere minutes – and then seconds. The history of the Singer sewing machine perfectly illustrates the evolutionary character of the Industrial Revolution, as one efficiency gain gave way to another. After the initial breakthrough, there was unceasing mutation: the Turtleback model (1856) was followed by the Grasshopper (1858), the New Family (1865) and the electric 99K (1880). By 1900 there were forty different models in production. By 1929 that had increased to 3,000.

Few nineteenth-century inventions travelled faster. From its New York headquarters at 458 (later 149) Broadway, Singer spread with astonishing speed to become one of the world's first truly global brands, with manufacturing plants in Brazil, Canada, Germany, Russia and Scotland; at its peak, the Kilbowie factory at Clydebank covered a million square feet and employed 12,000 people. In 1904 global sales passed 1.3 million machines a year. By 1914 that figure had more than doubled. The brand logo – the 'S' wrapped around a sewing woman – was ubiquitous, to be seen even (according the firm's advertising copywriters) on the summit of Mount Everest. In a rare concession to modernity, Mahatma Gandhi acknowledged that it was 'one of the few useful things ever invented' – praise indeed from the man who disdained even modern medicine.[40]

---

* The following list of names speaks for itself: Donna Karan, Calvin Klein, Estée Lauder, Ralph Lauren, Helena Rubenstein, Levi Strauss. So does the list of department stores: Abraham & Straus, Bergdorf Goodman, Bloomingdale's, Macy's, Neiman Marcus, Saks and Sears, not forgetting the British clothing retailer Marks & Spencer.

Singer exemplified the American advantage. Not only was the United States still attracting, as it always had, the world's natural-born risk-takers. Now there were enough of them to constitute a truly unmatched internal market. Between 1870 and 1913 the United States overtook the United Kingdom. In 1820 there had been twice as many people in the UK as in the US. By 1913 it was the other way round. Between 1870 and 1913 the American growth rate was 80 per cent higher.[41] Already by 1900 the US accounted for a larger share of world manufacturing output: 24 per cent to Britain's 18 per cent.[42] By 1913 even in per-capita terms the United States was the world's number-one industrial economy.[43] Perhaps more importantly, American productivity was poised to overtake British (though it would not actually do so until the 1920s).[44] And, just as in the case of British industrialization, cotton and textiles were front and centre of America's 'gilded age'. In the years before the First World War, raw cotton from the South still accounted for 25 per cent of US exports.[45] Most American cloth, however, was produced for domestic consumption. Britain's net exports of cotton goods in 1910 were worth $453 million; those of the United States just $8.5 million. But perhaps the most surprising statistic of all is that the second-largest exporter of cotton goods by that time was a non-Western country – the first member of the Rest to work out how to compete successfully with the West. That country was Japan.[46]

TURNING WESTERN

By 1910 the world had been economically integrated in a way never seen before. The different bonds that linked it together – railways, steamship lines and telegraphs – were almost entirely Western-invented and Western-owned. The West shrank the world. If all the railways of the United States had been laid end to end, the length would have been thirteen times the earth's circumference. A man could travel from Versailles to Vladivostok by train. And sustained improvements in steamships – the screw propeller, iron hulls, compound engines and surface condensers – made crossing the oceans faster and cheaper than crossing land. The gross tonnage of the *Mau-*

retania (1907) was forty-six times that of the *Sirius* (1838) but the horsepower of its engines was 219 times greater, so it was more than three times faster and crossed the Atlantic with a far larger cargo in nine and half days instead of sixteen.[47] Ocean freight costs fell by more than a third from 1870 to 1910. It cost 8 shillings to send a ton of cotton goods by rail from Manchester to Liverpool, just 30 miles away, but only 30 shillings to ship the same goods a further 7,250 miles to Bombay. The cost of shipping cloth amounted to less than 1 per cent of the cost of the goods. The opening of the Suez Canal (1869) and the Panama Canal (1914) shrank the world still further, the former reducing the distance of the London–Bombay route by more than two-fifths, the latter cutting the cost of shipping from the East to the West Coast of the United States by a third.[48] By the late 1860s, thanks to the introduction of gutta-percha coating, undersea cables could be laid and telegrams sent from London to Bombay or to Halifax.[49] News of the Indian Mutiny had taken forty-six days to reach London in 1857, travelling at an effective speed of 3.8 miles an hour. News of the huge Nobi earthquake in Japan in 1891 took a single day, travelling at 246 miles an hour, sixty-five times faster.[50]

Labour flowed across borders as never before. Between 1840 and 1940, up to 58 million Europeans migrated to the Americas, 51 million Russians to Siberia, Central Asia and Manchuria, and 52 million Indians and Chinese to South-east Asia, Australasia or the Indian Ocean rim.[51] Up to 2.5 million migrants from South and East Asia also travelled to the Americas. One in seven of the US population was foreign-born in 1910, a record that has yet to be surpassed.[52] Capital, too, flowed around the globe. Britain was the world's banker, exporting prodigious amounts of capital to the rest of the world; perhaps contemporaries should have praised the English 'savings glut' rather than grumbled about imperialism. In the peaks of the overseas invest-ment booms – 1872, 1887 and 1913 – the British current-account surplus exceeded 7 per cent of GDP.[53] British firms stood ready to export not just cotton, but the machinery to manufacture cotton and the capital necessary to buy it.

Yet perhaps the most remarkable expression of this first globaliza-tion was sartorial. With extraordinary speed, a mode of dressing that was distinctly Western swept the rest of the world, consigning traditional garb to the dressing-up basket of history. To be sure, that was not the avowed intention of the Singer Manufacturing Company. For the Chicago 'Great Colombian' World's Fair in 1892 – the 400th anniversary of the discovery of the New World – Singer commissioned a series of thirty-six trade cards called 'Costumes of the World' which depicted people of every skin colour, all dressed in traditional costumes, happily using Singer machines. From a Hungarian smock to a Japanese kimono,* any kind of costume could benefit from a stitch in time under the distinctive metal arm of a Singer. Bosnians and Burmese alike were the beneficiaries of Isaac Merritt's ingenuity; everyone, in fact, from Algeria to Zululand. Small wonder the Singer became the gift of choice for foreign potentates like the King of Siam, Dom Pedro II of Brazil and the Japanese Emperor Hirohito. Yet here is the twist in the tale. Far from using their Singer machines to patch up traditional forms of clothing, the grateful recipients used them for a completely different purpose – namely, to copy and wear Western clothing. The crucial new garments were, for men, the frock coat, the stiff-collared white shirt, the felt hat and the leather boot; and for women, the corset, the petticoat and the ankle-length dress.

In 1921 two royal and imperial heirs – the Crown Prince Hirohito of Japan, the future Shōwa Emperor, and Edward, Prince of Wales, the future Edward VIII – posed next to one another for a photographer. The thrones they stood to inherit could scarcely have been more geographically distant. Yet here they both were, on the steps of Henry Poole & Co., the Savile Row tailor,† more or less identically dressed. The Japanese Prince was in London on a pre-wedding shopping spree. A Henry Poole representative had already sailed all the way to Gibraltar to take his measurements, which were then cabled ahead to London. Henry Poole's ledger for the year in question shows the enormous order placed in Hirohito's name: military uniforms, embroidered waistcoats, dinner jackets, morning coats. A typical line in the list

---

* In reality, a kimono does not require the kind of tight stitching produced by a sewing machine.
† James Poole, the father of Henry Poole, had begun working in London as a 'taylor' in the early 1800s, establishing his premises at 4 Old Burlington Street, with an additional entrance at 32 Savile Street, in 1828. He started making military uniforms. His son's coup was to devise a royally acceptable court outfit for civilians.

reads: 'A fancy cashmere suit, a blue cloth suit, and a striped flannel suit'.[54] Hirohito was far from being the only foreign dignitary in the market for an immaculately tailored English suit. Preserved in Henry Poole's basement are thousands of suit patterns for clients ranging from the last Emperor of Ethiopia, Haile Selassie, to the last Tsar of Russia, Nicholas II. Poole's most devoted customer was Jitendra Narayan, Maharaja of Cooch Behar, whose lifetime purchases of bespoke suits exceeded a thousand. In every case, the aim was the same: to be as well dressed as the perfect English gentleman – and 'costumes of the world' be damned. It is revealing that the Japanese word for a suit is *sebiro*: 'Savile Row'. Even today the smartest suits in Tokyo are English in design, hence the popularity of the Eikokuya brand, which means literally 'England Store'. Discerning Anglophiles in Ginza, the West End of Tokyo, still seek out Ichibankan, founded by a tailor who learned his craft in Savile Row.

The Japanese revolution in dress dated back to the 1870s. In the name of *bunmei kaika* ('civilization and enlightenment') and *fukoku-kyōhei* ('rich country, strong army'), the imperial elite of the Meiji era had shed their samurai garb and kimonos in favour of replica European suits and dresses. The inspiration for this makeover came from a two-year tour of the United States and Europe by a delegation led by the Meiji minister Iwakura Tomomi, which had to acknowledge that, after centuries of self-imposed isolation, 'in many respects our civilization is inferior to theirs'.[55] Ever since 1853–4, when their economy had been forcibly reopened to trade by the threatening 'black ships' of the American Commodore Matthew C. Perry, the Japanese had struggled to work out what it was that made the West so much richer and stronger than the Rest. Touring the West – a practice so common that it inspired a *sugoroku* (board game) – only raised more questions. Was it their political system? Their educational institutions? Their culture? Or the way they dressed? Unsure, the Japanese decided to take no chances. They copied everything. From the Prussian-style constitution of 1889 to the adoption of the British gold standard in 1897, Japan's institutions were refashioned on Western models. The army drilled like Germans; the navy sailed like Britons. An American-style system of state elementary and middle schools was also introduced. The Japanese even started eating beef, hitherto taboo, and some reformers went so far as to propose abandoning Japanese in favour of English.

The most visible change, however, was in the way the Japanese looked. It began in 1870, with a formal ban on the blackening of teeth and shaving of eyebrows at court. At around the same time, ministers began to cut their hair in the Western style. An imperial decree of 1871 ordered high officials to don *yōfuku*, the European frock coat worn over a high-collared white shirt; by 1887 it was standard wear for all public servants.[56] A year later, on the advice of his reform-minded advisers, the hitherto closeted Meiji Emperor appeared for the first time in public, wearing (according to the Austrian ambassador) 'a peculiar European uniform, half sailor and half ambassador!' – a swallow-tailed coat with a great deal of gold braid.[57] The armed forces were also required to adopt European uniforms. The new sailor's outfit was based on that of the Royal Navy, while the army's was initially French in inspiration, though it later switched to a Prussian look.[58] Elite Japanese women also started wearing Western dress in 1884, when they began hosting foreign guests at the newly built Roku-meikan,* though the kimono endured in private. Even children's clothing was Westernized, with the adoption of Prussian-style uniforms for boys at elite private schools; girls' uniforms followed in the 1920s (and have not changed much since). No one embraced the new Western look more zealously than Ōkubo Toshimichi, one of the principal architects of the Meiji makeover. Once photographed as a sword-bearing samurai, proudly sitting cross-legged in flowing robes, he now perched stiffly on a chair in a smartly cut black tailcoat, his top hat in his hand. When the delegation he led arrived in England in 1872, the *Newcastle Daily Chronicle* reported that 'the gentlemen were attired in ordinary morning costume and except for their complexion and the oriental cast of their features, they could scarcely be distinguished from their English companions.' Seventeen years later, on the day the new Japanese constitution was formally adopted, the Emperor

---

* It was here, in the Deer Cry Pavilion, designed by the Englishman Josiah Conder, that the Japanese elite donned their ballgowns and frock coats and danced the quadrille, waltz, polka and mazurka to the latest European tunes. Ironically, this wholesale adoption of Western culture coincided with a Western fashion for Japanese art – which even Vincent van Gogh briefly embraced – though this was altogether more transient.

wore the uniform of a European field marshal, his consort a fetching blue and pink evening dress, and the government ministers black military tunics with gold epaulettes.[59]

There were those who were repelled by this aping of Western modes; indeed some Western cartoonists portrayed the Westernized Japanese precisely as apes.[60] The element of self-abasement disgusted Japanese traditionalists too. On 14 May 1878, as he made his way to a meeting of the Council of State at the Akasaka Palace in Tokyo, Ōkubo was attacked and brutally murdered by seven samurai, the death blow delivered to his throat with such force that the sword remained stuck in the ground below.[61] Ōmura Masujirō, whose reforms Westernized Japan's army, was another Meiji-era victim of traditionalist assassins, who posed a recurrent threat to pro-Western ministers until the 1930s. Yet there was no turning back. Attached though the Japanese remained to the samurai code of *bushido*, most accepted Ōkubo's argument that Westernization was indispensable if Japan was to achieve parity with the European and American empires, beginning with equal treatment in trade treaties and international law generally.[62] In the words of one Western observer who knew the country well, the Japanese motive was perfectly rational:

> Their great ambition is to be treated as men, as gentlemen, and as the equal[s] of Occidentals. In their antiquated garb they knew that they or their country would never be taken seriously. Very soon we saw a change of dress, not only among soldiers and Samurai but [also] among all the government officers and even in the Mikado itself . . . This revolution in clothes helped powerfully in the recognition by the whole world of Japan as an equal in the brotherhood of nations.[63]

The Japanese had understood what a potent agent of development Western clothes were. For this was much more than just an outward makeover. It was part of a pivotal breakthrough in world history as Japan became the first non-Western society to experience the transformative power of the Industrial Revolution.

The spread of the new dress code coincided with the rapid growth of the Japanese textile industry. Between 1907 and 1924 the number of cotton mills in Japan doubled from 118 to 232, the number of spindles more than trebled and the number of looms rose sevenfold.[64]

By 1900 textile factories employed 63 per cent of all Japan's factory workers.[65] Ten years later Japan was Asia's sole net exporter of thread, yarn and cloth; indeed, its exports exceeded those of Germany, France and Italy. Japanese textile workers were by far the most productive in Asia. From 1907 to 1924 the Japanese cotton industry increased output per worker by 80 per cent – despite the fact that, as is clear from Adachi Ginkō's 1887 picture of *Ladies Sewing*, the workforce was overwhelmingly young women, with an average age of just seventeen.[66] For firms like Kanegafuchi, the years down to the Depression were boom years, with profits in excess of 44 per cent of capital.[67] By not merely wearing Western clothes but also making them, Japan had ended the West's monopoly on modern manufacturing.

As in the West, one industrial breakthrough was followed by another. The first British-designed Japanese railway was built between Tokyo and Yokohama in the early 1870s. Soon, beginning with the Ginza district of Tokyo, the country's distinctive cities began to acquire telegraph wires, street lamps, iron bridges and brick walls in place of paper ones. Four business conglomerates – the *zaibatsu* – emerged as the dominant players in the economy: Mitsui, Mitsubishi, Sumitomo and Yasuda. Swiftly, under British instruction, the Japanese moved from buying steam locomotives to building them.* By 1929 Platt Brothers of Oldham – for the better part of a century the leading manufacturers of textile machinery – were paying a royalty to the Japanese inventors of the automatic Toyoda loom.[68]

No other Asian country embraced the Western way of life with the same enthusiasm as the Japanese. As India emerged from under British rule, by contrast, there was a conscious effort on the part of nationalists to retain Indian modes of dress, from Gandhi's loincloth to Nehru's collarless jackets and later Indira Gandhi's saris. This symbolic rejection of Western norms was understandable. British protectionism and productivity had devastated India's traditional hand-produced textile industry. Unlike the Japanese, however, the Indians were slow to adopt and exploit the technology of the Indus-

* It was Richard and Francis Trevithick, grandsons of Richard Trevithick, who helped the Japanese build their first locomotive at Kobe in 1893. They were among the so-called *yatoi* (live machines) whose expertise the Japanese hungrily imbibed in the Meiji era.

trial Revolution. Here is one of the many puzzles of nineteenth-century history. The British did not seek to monopolize their new technology; on the contrary, they spread it throughout their empire. The Indians were introduced to the textile mill, the steam engine and the railway long before the Japanese. By the early 1900s, textile equipment was no more expensive in Asia than in continental Europe. Nor was coal. Wage costs were 16 per cent of those in England. Asian factory hours were not restricted by law as British factory hours were. Raw cotton was much closer to hand than in England. Yet industrial development failed to take off in India or, for that matter, in China (where labour costs were even lower).[69] The explanation is that, cheap though labour was in India and China, the advantage was wiped out by dismally low productivity. An American worker was, on average, six to ten times more productive than an Indian using exactly the same equipment.[70] British and American experts offered various explanations for this, ranging from inherent racial inferiority to chronic absenteeism and idling. 'Everywhere it was apparent that there was little or poor supervision, and an entire lack of discipline,' lamented one American visitor to a Bombay mill. 'Empty spindles and loose reels or bobbins rolled about underfoot, waste and spool boxes were piled in heaps, while the basket boys, and even some of the older millhands, gathered in groups chewing *bhang* and *chunam*. Overseers, Mahrattas mostly, strolled indolently about.'[71] A modern explanation might be the abysmal working conditions: the usual poor ventilation and excessive hours combined with temperatures and diseases unknown in Lancashire or Lowell.[72] What was harder to explain was why one Asian country – Japan – was making such rapid gains in productivity that by the later 1930s it had forced 15 per cent of Bombay textile mills to close down altogether.

British clothes were, of course, about more than economic modernity. Nowhere were the subtle gradations of the British class system more clearly expressed than in carefully tailored cloth. This was a world in which you naturally judged a man's social status by the cut of his suit. Unfortunately for Hirohito, and for the Japanese in general, it was a world in which it was no less natural to judge a person's worth by the colour of his skin and the set of his features.

While Hirohito returned to Japan with his bespoke Western suits, the future King Edward VIII went to a fancy-dress ball with his chum Major Edward Dudley 'Fruity' Metcalfe. They were both dressed as 'Japanese coolies'. As far as they were concerned, such costumes were just as absurd as the Japanese dressing up in Western clothes. Indeed, in a letter to his mistress, Edward referred to Hirohito as a 'prize monkey' and observed that the Japanese people 'breed like rabbits'. The Japan in which Hirohito grew to adulthood was a country that both admired the West for its modernity and resented it for its arrogance. To be treated as an equal, it seemed, Japan would have to acquire the ultimate Western accessory: an empire. It did not take long. In 1895 Japan's European-style navy comprehensively defeated the ineptly led Chinese Beiyang Fleet at Weihaiwei. In Japanese illustrations of the time, the victors appear almost entirely European (even facially); the vanquished Chinese, with their outsized sleeves and pigtails, are dressed for defeat.[73] But this was merely the beginning. Disappointed that they had been forced to settle for cash reparations rather than territory as the spoils of war, the Japanese began to realize that their European role models might be reluctant to grant them equal imperial status. As the Foreign Minister Inoue Kaoru put it candidly:

We have to establish a new European-style Empire on the Eastern Sea ... How can we impress upon the minds of our thirty-eight million people this daring spirit and attitude of independence and self-government? In my opinion, the only course is to have them clash with Europeans, so that they will personally feel inconvenienced, realize their disadvantage, and absorb an awareness of Western vigorousness ... I consider that the way to do this is to provide for truly free intercourse between Japanese and foreigners ... Only thus can our Empire achieve a position equal to that of the Western countries with respect to treaties. Only thus can our Empire be independent, prosperous, and powerful.[74]

The first clash with Westerners duly came in 1904 with the Russo-Japanese War over Manchuria. Japan's decisive victory at sea and on land sent a signal to the world: there was nothing divinely ordained about Western predominance. With the right institutions and technology – not to mention the right clothes – an Asian empire could defeat a European one. An economic forecaster in 1910 might already have projected that Japan would overtake even Britain itself before the end of the century, which indeed it did; in 1980 Japanese per-capita GDP exceeded British for the first time. Regrettably, the line from 1910 to 1980 was anything but straight.

RAGTIME TO RICHES

The First World War, as we have seen, was a struggle between empires whose motives and methods had been honed overseas. It toppled four dynasties and shattered their empires. The American President Woodrow Wilson – the first of four Democratic holders of the office to embroil their country in a major overseas war – sought to recast the conflict as a war for national self-determination, a view that was never likely to be endorsed by the British and French empires, whose flagging war effort had been salvaged by American money and men. Czechs, Estonians, Georgians, Hungarians, Lithuanians, Latvians, Poles, Slovaks and Ukrainians were not the only ones who scented freedom; so did Arabs and Bengalis, to say nothing of the Catholic Irish. Aside from the Irish one, not one of the nation-states that emerged in the wake of the war retained meaningful independence by the end of 1939 (except possibly Hungary). The Mazzinian map of Europe appeared and then vanished like a flash in the pan.

The alternative post-war vision of Vladimir Ilyich Lenin was of a Union of Soviet Socialist Republics, potentially expanding right across Eurasia. This gained its traction from the exceptional economic circumstances of the war. Because all governments financed the fighting to some degree by issuing short-term debt and exchanging it for cash at their central banks – printing money, in short – inflation gathered momentum during the war. Because so many men were under arms, labour shortages empowered the workers on the Home Front to push for higher wages. By 1917 hundreds of thousands of workers were involved in strikes in France, Germany and Russia. First Spanish influenza then Russian Bolshevism swept the world. As in 1848 urban order broke down, only this time the contagion spread as far as Buenos Aires and Bengal, Seattle and Shanghai. Yet the proletarian revolution failed everywhere but in the Russian Empire, which was reassembled by the Bolsheviks in the wake of a brutal civil war. No other socialist leaders were as ruthless as Lenin in adopting 'democratic centralism' (which was the opposite of democratic), rejecting parliamentarism and engaging in terrorism against opponents. Some of what the Bolsheviks did (the nationalization of banks, the confiscation of land) was straight out of Marx and Engels's *Manifesto*. Some of what they did ('the greatest ferocity and savagery of suppression . . . seas of blood')[75] owed more to Robespierre. The 'dictatorship of the proletariat' – which in fact meant the dictatorship of the Bolshevik leadership – was Lenin's original contribution. This was even worse than the resurrection of Bazarov, the nihilist in Ivan Turgenev's *Fathers and Sons* (1856). It was what his estranged friend Fyodor Dostoevsky had warned Russia about in the epilogue of *Crime and Punishment* (1866) – the murderer Raskolnikov's nightmare of a 'terrible, unprecedented and unparalleled plague' from Asia:

> Those infected were seized immediately and went mad. Yet people never considered themselves so clever and unhesitatingly right as these infected ones considered themselves. Never had they considered their decrees, their scientific deductions, their moral convictions and their beliefs more firmly based. Whole settlements, whole cities and nations, were infected and went mad . . . People killed each other with senseless rage . . . soldiers flung themselves upon each other, slashed and stabbed, ate and devoured each other.

To the east there was almost no stopping the Bolshevik epidemic. To the west it could not get over the Vistula, nor south of the Caucasus, thanks to a gifted trio of political entrepreneurs who devised that synthesis of nationalism and socialism which was the true manifestation of the *Zeitgeist*: Józef Piłsudski in Poland, Kemal Atatürk in Turkey and Benito Mussolini in Italy. The defeat of the Red Army outside Warsaw (August 1920), the expulsion of the Anatolian Greeks (September 1922) and the fascist March on Rome (October 1922) marked the advent of a new era – and a new look.

With the exception of Mussolini, who wore a three-piece suit with a winged collar and spats, most of those who participated in the publicity stunt that was the March on Rome were in makeshift uniforms composed of black shirts, jodhpurs and knee-high leather riding boots. The idea was that the manly, martial virtues of the Great War would now be carried over into peacetime, beginning with a smaller war fought in the streets and fields against the left. Uniformity was the order of the day – but a uniformity of dress without the tedious discipline of a real army. Even the famous March was more of a stroll, as the many press photographs make clear. It had been the Italian nationalist Giuseppe Garibaldi who had first used red-coloured shirts as the basis for a political movement. By the 1920s dyed tops were mandatory on the right; the Italian fascists opted for black while, as we have seen, the German National Socialist Sturmabteilung adopted colonial brown.

Such movements might have dissolved into ill-tailored obscurity had it not been for the Great Depression. After the inflation of the early 1920s, the deflation of the early 1930s dealt a lethal blow to the Wilsonian vision of a Europe based on national identity and democracy. The crisis of American capitalism saw the stock market slump by 89 per cent, output drop by a third, consumer prices fall by a quarter and the unemployment rate pass a quarter. Not all European countries were so severely affected, but none was unscathed.[76] As governments scrambled to protect their own industries with higher tariffs – the American Smoot-Hawley tariff bill raised the effective *ad valorem* rate on imported cotton manufactures to 46 per cent – globalization simply broke down. Between 1929 and 1932 world trade shrank by two-thirds. Most countries adopted some combination of debt default, currency depreciation, protectionist tariffs, import quotas and prohibitions, import monopolies and export premia. The day had dawned, it seemed, of the nationalist-socialist state.

This was an illusion. Though the US economy seemed to be imploding, the principal cause was the disastrous monetary policy adopted by the Federal Reserve Board, which half wrecked the banking system.[77] Innovation, the mainspring of industrial advance, did not slacken in the 1930s. New automobiles, radios and other consumer durables were proliferating. New companies were developing these products, like DuPont (nylon), Revlon (cosmetics), Proctor & Gamble (Dreft soap powder), RCA (radio and television) and IBM (accounting machines); they were also evolving and disseminating a whole new style of business management. Nowhere was the creativity of capitalism more marvellous to behold than in Hollywood, home of the motion-picture industry. In 1931 – when the US economy was in the grip of blind panic – the big studios released Charlie Chaplin's *City Lights*, Howard Hughes's *The Front Page* and the Marx Brothers' *Monkey Business*. The previous decade's experiment with the Prohibition of alcohol had been a disastrous failure, spawning a whole new economy of organized crime. But it was only more grist for the movie mills. Also in 1931, audiences flocked to see James Cagney and Edward G. Robinson in the two greatest gangster films of them all: *The Public Enemy* and *Little Caesar*. No less creative was the live, recorded and broadcast music business, once white Americans had discovered that black Americans had nearly all the best tunes. Jazz approached its zenith in the swinging sound of Duke Ellington's big band, which rolled out hit after hit even as the automobile-production lines ground to halt: 'Mood Indigo' (1930), 'Creole Rhapsody' (1931), 'It Don't Mean a Thing (If It Ain't Got That Swing)' (1932), 'Sophisticated Lady' (1933) and 'Solitude' (1934). The grandson of a slave, Ellington took reed and brass instruments where they had never been before, mimicking everything from spirituals to the New York subway. His band's long residence at the Cotton Club was at the very heart of the Harlem Renaissance. And of course, as his aristocratic nickname required, Ellington was always immaculately dressed – courtesy of Anderson & Sheppard of Savile Row.

In short, capitalism was not fatally flawed, much less dead. It was merely a victim of bad management, and the uncertainty that followed from it. The cleverest economist of the age, John Maynard Keynes, sneered at the stock exchange as a 'casino', comparing investors' decisions to a newspaper beauty contest. President Franklin D. Roosevelt – elected just as the Depression was ending – inveighed against 'the unscrupulous money changers'. The real culprits were the central bankers who had first inflated a stock-exchange bubble with excessively lax monetary policy and had then proceeded to tighten (or failed adequately to loosen) after the bubble had burst. Between 1929 and 1933, nearly 15,000 US banks – two-fifths of the total – failed. As a result, the money supply was savagely reduced. With prices collapsing by a third from peak to trough, real interest rates rose above

10 per cent, crushing any indebted institution or household. Keynes summed up the negative effects of deflation:

> Modern business, being carried on largely with borrowed money, must necessarily be brought to a standstill by such a process. It will be to the interest of everyone in business to go out of business for the time being; and of everyone who is contemplating expenditure to postpone his orders so long as he can. The wise man will be he who turns his assets into cash, withdraws from the risks and the exertions of activity, and awaits in country retirement the steady appreciation promised him in the value of his cash. A probable expectation of Deflation is bad.[78]

How to escape from the deflation trap? With trade slumbering and capital imports frozen, Keynes's recommendation – government spending on public works, financed by borrowing – made sense. It also helped to abandon the gold standard, whereby currencies had fixed dollar exchange rates, to let depreciation provide a boost to exports (though increasingly trade went on within regional blocs) and to allow interest rates to fall. Yet parliamentary governments that adopted only these measures achieved at best anaemic recoveries. It was when authoritarian regimes adopted plans for industrial expansion and rearmament that unemployment came down fastest. This was where 'socialism in one country' (in Russia) and 'national socialism' (in Germany) appeared to offer solutions superior to anything available in the two big Anglophone economies. Uniquely in the world, the Soviet Union achieved an increase of industrial production between 1929 and 1932; few asked how many people died for every ton of steel produced under Stalin (the answer was nineteen). It did not take Hitler long to lose patience with the realities propounded by his Economics Minister Hjalmar Schacht; rather than slow the pace of rearmament to take account of balance of payments constraints (in short, the Reichsbank's lack of gold to pay for imports in excess of exports), Hitler drafted a Four Year Plan in imitation of Stalin's Five Year Plans. The two regimes were now in blatant competition, intervening on opposite sides in Spain's civil war, erecting rival pavilions at the Paris World Exposition of 1937. Close scrutiny of the muscular giants atop those two totalitarian towers revealed only two meaningful differences: the superhumans of communism were a couple and were modestly clad in dungarees and a smock; the Aryan supermen were two naked males. The only thing stranger than the prudishness of socialist realism was the sexlessness of the Aryan nude. The naked body has been an integral part of Western art since the ancient Greeks, a reminder that what we do not wear is often as important as what we do wear. Since the Renaissance, Western artists had lovingly depicted women in various states of undress, producing masterworks of eroticism like Edouard Manet's *Déjeuner sur l'herbe* and *Olympia* (both 1863), tributes, respectively, to Giorgione's *The Tempest* (*c.* 1506) and Titian's *Venus of Urbino* (1538). But Nazi nudes infallibly induced detumescence, the men implausibly muscle-bound, the women flat-chested and hipless.

Both Stalin and Hitler promised growth and employment through a combination of nationalism and socialism. They delivered both. In 1938 the output of the American economy was still more than 6 per cent below the pre-crisis peak of 1929; German output was 23 per cent higher, and Soviet output even higher, if the official statistics for 'net material product' are to be believed. As early as April 1937 unemployment in Germany fell below the million mark, compared with 6 million just over four years before. By April 1939 fewer than 100,000 Germans were out of work; as good as full employment. The United States lagged far behind, even if one adjusts the official unemployment figures to count those on federal emergency relief work as employed. By a modern definition the unemployment rate was still 12.5 per cent in 1938. The problem was that totalitarian growth did not translate into significantly higher living standards. The economic model was not really Keynesian; it did not use increased public spending to kick-start aggregate demand through a multiplier effect on consumer spending. Rather, the planned economy mobilized manpower to work on heavy industry, infrastructure and arms; and it financed the process through forced saving. As a result, consumption stagnated. People worked and got paid, but because there was steadily less and less to buy in the shops, they had little option but to put the money in savings accounts, where it was recycled into funding the government. Nazi propaganda was full of images of prosperous nuclear families, well fed, fashionably attired and driving along the

Autobahns in spanking new Volkswagen Beetles. The statistics tell another story. As rearmament was stepped up from 1934, textile production stagnated and imports declined. Precious few civilians owned cars.[79] And, with every passing year of the Third Reich, imported staples like coffee became harder to obtain. If German men wanted to look smart by 1938 they needed to be in uniform. Unlike in the Soviet Union, considerable attention was paid to the elegance of military outfits, with the black-clad Schutzstaffel (SS) enjoying the most sinisterly elegant attire, designed by Karl Diebitsch and Walter Heck and produced by Hugo Boss.* This was the height of fascist fashion.

The raison d'être of the SS, and of National Socialism as a whole, was destruction not consumption. Hitler's economic model, as he made clear in the document we know as the Hossbach Memorandum, necessarily entailed the acquisition of 'living space' – the annexation of adjoining territory – as a way of acquiring the raw materials Germany could no longer afford to import. The forced march to full employment via rearmament thus made war ever more likely. And war in its late 1930s variant, given the state of military technology, was a spectacularly destructive affair. As early as 1937 it was revealed what havoc aerial bombardment could wreak, not only in Guernica, where German and Italian planes dive-bombed Spanish Republican positions, but also in Shanghai, which was severely damaged by Japanese air raids. Air power was a terror weapon, designed to sow panic among soldiers and civilians. On the ground, tanks and other forms of mechanized artillery solved the problem of immobility that had defined the First World War in the West; it thereby revealed the advantages of trench warfare. For 'lightning war' was far more costly in terms of human life, not just to exposed combatants but even more so to civilians, who made up a clear majority of the Second World War's casualties.

Superficially, the Second World War was between four distinct versions of Western civilization: national socialism, Soviet communism, European imperialism (which the Japanese had adopted) and American capitalism. Initially, the first and second joined forces

---

* Boss's Metzingen-based company had been bankrupted by the Depression in 1930. Having joined the Nazi Party the following year, he was soon established as one of the principal suppliers of uniforms to the 'Hitler Movement'.

against the third, while the fourth remained neutral. After the pivotal year 1941, when the Nazis attacked the Soviets and the Japanese attacked the Americans, it was the Axis powers – Germany, Italy and Japan – plus their hastily conquered empires and a few hangers-on, against the Big Three – the Soviet Union, the British Empire and the United States – plus everybody else (hence 'the United Nations', as the Allies liked to call themselves). In reality, however, a remarkable convergence occurred as the industrialization of destruction reached its horrific zenith. All the major combatants evolved highly centralized state apparatuses designed to allocate resources – manpower and matériel – by non-market mechanisms, according to preconceived and highly complex plans. All of them subordinated individual freedom to the goal of total military victory and the unconditional surrender of the enemy. All placed an unprecedented proportion of their able-bodied men under arms. All treated civilian population concentrations as legitimate military targets. All discriminated against selected civilian groups in the territory they controlled, though neither the British nor the Americans – nor the Italians – remotely approached the savagery of the Germans and Russians towards mistrusted ethnic minorities. Even the crimes of the Japanese against Chinese civilians and Allied prisoners of war pale into insignificance alongside Hitler's 'Final Solution of the Jewish Question' and Stalin's earlier 'Liquidation of the Kulaks as a Class', both euphemisms for genocide.[80]

Everyone, it seemed, was in uniform. By 1944 the six biggest combatants had more than 43 million people, nearly all men, under arms. For all combatants, the total certainly exceeded 100 million. That was, at most, between a fifth and a quarter of the population, but it was still a far larger proportion than at any time in modern history, before or since.[81] More than 34 million Soviet citizens served, 17 million Germans, 13 million Americans, nearly 9 million loyal subjects from all over the British Empire and 7.5 million Japanese. Young men from those countries who did not end up in government-issue (hence 'GI') clothes were a minority. As a result, a vast proportion of the world's textile industry was given over to the manufacture of military uniforms. What people did in these uniforms varied widely. The majority of Germans, Japanese and Russians were involved in some form or other of lethal organized violence. The majority of Americans and British were behind the lines, leaving the combat to an unlucky minority. The war against Germany was won by a combination of British intelligence, Soviet manpower and American capital; the British cracked the German codes, the Russians slaughtered the German soldiers and the Americans flattened the German cities. Victory over Japan was preponderantly though not exclusively the achievement of the United States, whose Manhattan Project (named after the Manhattan Engineering District where it began in 1942) produced the three war-ending and world-changing atomic bombs tested in New Mexico and dropped on Hiroshima and Nagasaki in 1945.

Inspired by Albert Einstein's warning to Roosevelt that the Germans might be the first to develop such a weapon, and propelled forward by the British discovery of the fissile properties of the isotope uranium-235 – the significance of which the Americans were slow to grasp – the atomic bomb was an authentically Western achievement. The scientists who devised it were of multiple nationalities: Australians, Britons, Canadians, Danes, Germans, Hungarians, Italians and Swiss as well as Americans. Many (notably Otto Frisch and Edward Teller) were Jewish refugees from Europe, reflecting not only the disproportionate role played by Jews in every area of intellectual life since the emancipation that had followed the French Revolution,* but also the cost to the German war effort of Hitler's anti-Semitism. Two were Soviet spies. It may seem odd to identify the A-bomb as one of the greatest creations of Western civilization. Though it dramatically increased the capacity of man to inflict death, the Bomb's net effect was to reduce the scale and destructiveness of war, beginning by averting the need for a bloody amphibious invasion of Japan. To be sure, it did not abolish conventional warfare; no sooner were the 1940s over than another big and bloody war of planes and tanks was

---

* The Jewish role in Western intellectual life in the twentieth century – especially in the United States – was indeed disproportionate, suggesting a genetic as much as a cultural advantage. Accounting for around 0.2 per cent of the world's population and 2 per cent of the American population, Jews won 22 per cent of all Nobel Prizes, 20 per cent of all Fields Medals for mathematics and 67 per cent of the John Clarke Bates Medals for economists under the age of forty. Jews also won 38 per cent of the Oscars for Best Director, 20 per cent of the Pulitzer Prizes for non-fiction and 13 per cent of Grammy Lifetime Achievement Awards.

under way in Korea. But the atomic bomb, and even more so the vastly more destructive hydrogen bomb tested in 1952 (and a year later by the Soviets), circumscribed that war and all subsequent conflicts, by deterring the United States and the Soviet Union from colliding head on. All the wars waged by the two superpowers, as they came to be known, were limited wars waged against, and sometimes through, proxies. Though the risk of a nuclear war was never zero, with hindsight we can see that the age of total war ended with the surrender of Japan.

If the Cold War had ever become hot, the Soviet Union would very likely have won it. With a political system far better able to absorb heavy war losses (the Second World War death rate as a percentage of the pre-war population had been fifty times higher than that for the United States), the Soviet Union also had an economic system that was ideally suited to the mass production of sophisticated weaponry. Indeed, by 1974 the Soviets had a substantially larger arsenal of strategic bombers and ballistic missiles. Scientifically, they lagged only a little way behind. They were also armed with an ideology that was a great deal more appealing than the American alternative in post-colonial societies all over what became known as the Third World, where poor peasantries contemplated a life of drudgery under the heel of corrupt elites who owned all the land and controlled the armed forces.[82] Indeed, it could be argued that the Soviets actually won 'the Third World's War'. Where there was a meaningful class war, communism could prevail.[83]

Yet the Cold War turned out to be about butter more than guns, ballgames more than bombs. Societies living in perpetual fear of Armageddon nevertheless had to get on with civilian life, since even the large armies of the 1950s and 1960s were still much smaller than the armies of the 1940s. From a peak of 8.6 per cent of the population in 1945, the US armed forces were down below 1 per cent by 1948 and never rose above 2.2 per cent thereafter, even at the height of the American interventions in Korea and Vietnam. The USSR remained more militarized, but the military share of the population nevertheless declined from a post-war peak of 7.4 per cent in 1945 and remained consistently below 2 per cent after 1957.[84] The problem for the Soviet

Union was simple: the United States offered a far more attractive version of civilian life than the Soviets could. And this was not just because of an inherent advantage in terms of resource endowment. It was because centralized economic planning, though indispensable to success in the nuclear arms race, was wholly unsuited to the satisfaction of consumer wants. The planner is best able to devise and deliver the ultimate weapon to a single client, the state. But the planner can never hope to meet the desires of millions of individual consumers, whose tastes are in any case in a state of constant flux. This was one of the many insights of Keynes's arch-rival, the Austrian economist Friedrich von Hayek, whose *Road to Serfdom* (1945) had warned Western Europe to resist the chimera of peacetime planning. It was in meeting (and creating) consumer demands that the American market model, revitalized during the war by the biggest fiscal and monetary stimulus of all time, and sheltered by geography from the depredations of total war, proved to be unbeatable.

A simple example illustrates the point. Before the war most clothes were made to measure by tailors. But the need to manufacture tens of millions of military uniforms encouraged the development of standard sizes. In truth, the range of human proportions is not that wide; human height and width are normally distributed, which means that most of us are clustered around a median shape. During 1939 and 1940, about 15,000 American women participated in a national survey conducted by the National Bureau of Home Economics of the US Department of Agriculture. It was the first large-scale scientific study of female proportions ever undertaken. A total of fifty-nine measurements were taken from each volunteer. The results of were published in 1941 as USDA Miscellaneous Publication 454, *Women's Measurements for Garment and Pattern Construction*. Standardized sizes allowed civilian clothes, as well as uniforms, to be mass-produced and sold 'off the peg' or 'ready to wear'. Within a matter of a few decades, it was only the clothes of the wealthy elite that were tailor-made: men's suits from Savile Row and women's haute couture from Paris and Milan.

In the post-war United States the consumer society became a phenomenon of the masses, significantly diminishing the sartorial differences between the social classes. This was part of a generalized levelling up that followed the war. In 1928 the top 1 per cent of the population had received nearly 20 per cent of income. From 1952 until 1982 it was consistently less than 9 per cent, below the equivalent share going to the top 1 per cent in France.[85] Better educational opportunities for the returning soldiers coupled with a wave of house-building in the suburbs translated into a marked improvement in the quality of life. The parents of the baby boomers were the first generation to have significant access to consumer credit. They bought their homes on credit, their cars on credit and their household appliances – refrigerators, televisions and washing machines – on credit.[86] In 1930, as the Depression struck, more than half of American households had electricity, an automobile and a refrigerator. By 1960 around 80 per cent of Americans not only had these amenities, they also had telephones. And the speed with which the new consumer durables spread just kept rising. The clothes-washing machine was a pre-Depression invention dating back to 1926. By 1965, thirty-nine years later, half of households had one. Air conditioning was invented in 1945. It passed the 50 per cent mark in 1974, twenty-nine years later. The clothes dryer came along in 1949; it passed the halfway mark in 1972, twenty-three years later. (The dishwasher, also invented in 1949, was slower to take off; it was not until 1997 that every second household owned one.) Colour television broke all records; invented in 1959, it was in half of all homes by 1973, just fourteen years later. By 1989, when the Cold War effectively ended, two-thirds or more of all Americans had all of these things, with the exception of the dishwasher. They had also acquired microwave ovens (invented in 1972) and video cassette recorders (1977). Fifteen per cent already had the personal computer (1978). A pioneering 2 per cent owned mobile telephones. By the end of the millennium these, too, were in half of all homes, as was the internet.[87]

To societies for whom this trajectory seemed attainable, the appeal of Soviet communism quickly palled. Western Europe, its post-war recovery underwritten by American aid, rapidly regained the growth path of the pre-Depression years (though the biggest recipients of the programme named after George Marshall did not in fact grow fastest). The fascist years had weakened trade unions in much of Europe; labour relations were accordingly less fractious than before the war. Strikes were shorter (though they had higher participation). Only in

Britain, France and Italy did industrial action increase in frequency. Corporatist collective bargaining, economic planning, Keynesian demand management and welfare states: the West Europeans took multiple vaccinations against the communist threat, adding cross-border economic integration with the signing of the Treaty of Rome in 1957. In fact the menace from Moscow had largely receded by that date. The Soviet exactions, the unrelenting emphasis on heavy industry, the collectivization of agriculture and the emergence of what Milovan Djilas called 'The New Class' of Party hacks – all of these things had already sparked revolts in Berlin (1953) and Budapest (1956). The real economic miracles happened in Asia, where not only Japan but also Hong Kong, Indonesia, Malaysia, Singapore, South Korea, Taiwan and Thailand all achieved sustained and in most cases accelerating growth in the post-war period. Asia's share of global GDP rose from 14 per cent to 34 per cent between 1950 and 1990 and, crucially, Asia kept on growing in the 1970s and 1980s when other regions of the world slowed or, in the case of Africa and Latin America, suffered economic contraction. The performance of South Korea was especially impressive. A country that, in terms of per-capita income, had ranked below Ghana in 1960 was sufficiently advanced by 1996 to join the Organization of Economic Co-operation and Development, the rich countries' club. Between 1973 and 1990 it was the world's fastest-growing economy.

The East Asian economic miracle was the key to the Cold War. If Vietnam rather than Korea had been the norm – in other words, if US military interventions had mostly failed – the outcome might have been less happy. What made the difference? First, the United States and its allies (notably Britain in Malaysia) were able to provide credible security guarantees to governments following military interventions. Secondly, post-conflict reforms created secure institutional foundations for growth, a perfect example being the 1946 land reform in Japan, which swept away the remnants of feudalism and substantially equalized property-ownership (something the Meiji reformers had omitted to do). Thirdly, the increasingly open global economic order upheld by the United States very much benefited these Asian countries. Finally, they used various forms of state direction to ensure that savings were channelled into export industries, of which the key first-stage sector was, of course, textiles. The consumer society provided not only a role model for East Asians; it also provided a market for their cheap cloth.

It should be noted that almost none of the 'Asian tigers' that followed Japan's example, industrializing themselves through exports of staples like cotton goods, did so with the help of democratic institutions. South Korea was steered through its industrial revolution by Generals Park Chung-hee (1960–79) and Chun Doo-hwan (1980–87), while Lee Kuan Yew in Singapore and Suharto in Indonesia were essentially absolutists (the former an enlightened one), and monopoly parties ruled in Taiwan and Japan. Hong Kong remained a British colony until 1997. However, in each case, economic success was followed after some lag by democratization. East Asia, in short, spun out of the Soviet gravitational field because it became a stakeholder in the American consumer society. It was a very different story in those countries – Iran, Guatemala, Congo, Brazil, the Dominican Republic and Chile – where US interventions were shorter in duration, and even worse in those – Cuba, Vietnam, Angola and Ethiopia – where Soviet intervention or assistance was more effective.

That mass consumerism, with all the standardization it implied, could somehow be reconciled with rampant individualism was one of the smartest tricks ever pulled by Western civilization. But the key to understanding how it was done lies in that very word: Western. The Soviet Union could perhaps be forgiven for its failure to invent and disseminate the colour television or the microwave oven. But not all the defining products of the consumer society were technologically complex. The simplest of all were in fact a kind of workman's trousers invented on the West Coast of the United States. Perhaps the greatest mystery of the entire Cold War is why the Worker's Paradise could not manage to produce a decent pair of jeans.

THE JEANS GENIE

It was once upon a time in the Wild West that the universal garment was born. Jeans started life as the no-nonsense trousers of miners and cowpokes. By the 1970s they were the most popular article of clothing in the world – and a politically potent symbol of what was wrong with the Soviet economic system. Why? Why could the Soviets not replicate Levi 501s the way they had replicated the atomic bomb?

Jeans as we know them today were invented in 1873, when the Bavarian-born dry-goods merchant Levi Strauss and the Reno tailor Jacob Davis secured the patent for using copper rivets to strengthen the pockets on miners' 'waist overalls'. The fabric they used was denim (originally 'serge de Nîmes', just as 'jeans' probably derives from 'Genoa') manufactured at the Amoskeag Mill in Manchester, New Hampshire, using American-grown cotton dyed with American-grown indigo. The original Levi's factories were in San Francisco and it was there that the familiar leather label was first used in 1886, showing two horses failing to pull a pair of Levi's apart; the red tab was added in 1936. Blue jeans are cheap to make, easy to clean, hard to ruin and comfortable to wear. But then so are workmen's overalls of the sort that used to be worn in Britain (most famously by Churchill during the war), as are dungarees, named after cloth from Dongri in India. Why was it that Californian jeans – which were also issued to convicts in many state penitentiaries – came to dominate the world of fashion? The answer lies in two of the twentieth century's most successful industries: movies and marketing

It began when the young John Wayne traded in the elaborate fringed leather chaps of the early cowboy films for the plain jeans he wore in *Stagecoach* (1939). Then came Marlon Brando's jeans and leathers in *The Wild One* (1953), followed by James Dean's red (jacket), white (T-shirt) and blue (jeans) outfit in *Rebel without a Cause* (1955) and Elvis Presley's black jeans in *Jailhouse Rock* (1957). The marketing men provided further support for the rugged new look with 'Marlboro Man', the cigarette-smoking, denim-clad cowboy devised by the advertising executive Leo Burnett in 1954. Marilyn Monroe was another early adopter of denim; one of her first modelling shoots featured a less than flattering convict suit. The key from the outset was the association between jeans and youthful misbehaviour. As early as the 1830s the Mormon leader Brigham Young had denounced trousers with button flies as 'fornication pants'. In 1944 *Life* magazine caused a storm by publishing a photograph of two Wellesley College women in jeans.[88] By the time Levi's competitor Lee introduced zippers, the reputation of jeans as sexually arousing was established – a curious outcome, considering how very difficult it is to have sex with someone wearing tight-fitting jeans. Jeans were upwardly mobile. They began on the backsides of ranch-hands and convicts; were mandatory for defence workers during the war; moved on to the biker gangs of the post-war years; were adopted by West Coast and then Ivy League students; graduated to 'beat' writers, folk singers and pop groups in the 1960s; and ended up being worn publicly by all presidents after Richard Nixon. Levi's growth was spectacular. In 1948 the company sold 4 million pairs of jeans; by 1959 it was 10 million. Sales of Levi's increased tenfold between 1964 and 1975, passing the $1 billion mark. By 1979 they had reached $2 billion. And Levi's was only one of several successful brands, with Lee and Wrangler also in contention.

These all-American clothes were just as attractive to non-Americans, as became clear when Levi's launched an export drive in the 1960s and 1970s. For young people all over the world, jeans symbolized a generational revolt against the stuffy sartorial conventions of the post-war era. The jean genie was out of the bottle, and the bottle was more than probably the distinctively curved glass container of the Coca-Cola soft drink. It seemed only a matter of time before Levi Strauss & Co. would fulfil their stated ambition of 'clothing the world'. 'The World is Blue Jeans Country Now', proclaimed *Life* in 1972.[89] In expanding overseas, Levi's was taking a leaf out of the Coca-Cola playbook. The brown fizzy liquid, invented in 1886 when John Pemberton carbonated a mixture of cocaine from the coca leaf and caffeine from the kola nut, managed to outdo even Singer as a global brand. Coca-Cola was already calling itself 'the International Beverage' as early as 1929, when it was for sale in seventy-eight different countries, including even Burma – where its distinctive Spencerian script logo could be seen, incongruously, at the entrance to the Schwe Dagon Pagoda in Rangoon.[90] In the Second World War, Coke managed to run sixty-four different bottling plants in six theatres of war. It even managed to establish a bottling plant in Laos in 1973, at the height of the Vietnam War.

For Levi's and Coca-Cola alike, however, there was no more impenetrable barrier than the Iron Curtain drawn across Europe by the Cold

War. Indeed, Coke boss Robert W. Woodruff refused on principle to be involved with the American National Exhibition in Moscow, personally blaming Vice-President Richard Nixon when Pepsi pulled off the coup of getting the Soviet leader Nikita Khrushchev to test their rival soft drink after the two leaders' televised debate at the opening of the Exhibition in July 1959.[91]

In Cold War rhetoric, it was always clear who the 'West' was and who the 'East' was. The East began where the River Elbe marked the end of the Federal Republic of Germany and the beginning of the German Democratic Republic. It ended at the border between the Democratic People's Republic of Korea and the Republic of Korea. But from the vantage point of the real East – from the Middle East to the Far East – the world seemed simply to have been carved up between two rival Wests, a capitalist one and a communist one. The people in charge looked roughly similar. Indeed, in many ways the Soviet Union longed to imitate the United States, to build the same weapons – and also the same consumer goods. As Khrushchev made abundantly clear in his 'kitchen debate' with Nixon, the Soviets aspired to match the Americans product for product. Sartorially there was little to choose between the two men. Clad in perfect black and white, as if to confound the colour television technology he was supposed to be marketing, Nixon looked like the dour Californian lawyer he was. In his light-coloured suit and hat, Khrushchev looked more like a Dixiecrat Congressman who had consumed one too many Martinis at lunch.

Like young people all over the world, teenagers in the Soviet Union and its satellites in Eastern Europe were crying out for jeans. So it really is bizarre that the United States' principal rival in the post-war world failed to replicate these supremely straightforward items of apparel. It might have been thought that the Western craze for denim had made life easier for the Soviets. After all, the Soviet Union was supposed to be the proletarian paradise and jeans are a lot easier to make than, say, Sta-Prest trousers (another Levi Strauss invention, introduced in 1964). Yet somehow the communist bloc failed to understand the appeal of a garment that could equally well have symbolized the virtues of the hard-working Soviet worker. Instead, blue jeans, and the pop music with which they were soon inextricably linked, became the quintessential symbols of Western superiority. And, unlike nuclear warheads, jeans were actually launched against the Soviets: there were displays of Levi's in Moscow in 1959 and again in 1967.

If you were a student living behind the Iron Curtain in the Sixties – in East Berlin, for example – you did not want to dress in the sub-Boy Scout uniform of a Young Pioneer. You wanted to dress like all the young dudes in the West. Stefan Wolle was an East German student at the time. As he recalls:

> Initially, it wasn't possible [to buy jeans in the GDR]. Jeans were seen as the embodiment of the Anglo-Saxon cultural imperialism. And it was strongly frowned upon to wear them. And you couldn't buy them. [But] many got their relatives from the West to bring them over ... They wore them and that caused teachers, employers and policemen in the street to be angry. It gave rise to a black market in Western goods that seemed to threaten the state.[92]

Such was the desirability of this article of clothing that Soviet law-enforcement officials coined the phrase 'jeans crimes', which referred to 'law violations prompted by a desire to use any means to obtain articles made of denim'. In 1986 the French leftist philosopher and former comrade in arms of Che Guevara, Régis Debray, remarked: 'There is more power in rock music, videos, blue jeans, fast food, news networks and TV satellites than in the entire Red Army.'[93] That much was becoming clear by the mid-1980s. In 1968, however, it was anything but certain.

Nineteen-sixty-eight was a year of revolution in all kinds of ways, from Paris to Prague, from Berlin to Berkeley, and even in Beijing.[94] But the common factor in all these disruptions to the Cold War duopoly of power was youth. Rarely in modern times have people aged between fifteen and twenty-four accounted for so large a share of the population as in the decade after 1968. Having dropped as low as 11 per cent of the US population in the mid-1950s, the youth share reached a peak of 17 per cent in the mid-1970s. In Latin America and Asia it rose above 20 per cent. At the same time, the expansion of higher education, especially in the United States, meant that a higher proportion than ever of young men and women went to university. By 1968 university students made up more than 3 per cent of the entire American population, compared with less than 1 per cent in 1928. A more modest expansion had happened in Europe too. These were the post-war baby boomers – young, numerous, educated and prosperous. They had every reason to be grateful to their fathers' generation, which had fought for freedom and bequeathed them opportunity. Instead they revolted.

On 22 March 1968 French students occupied the eighth-floor faculty lounge of the University of Paris X Nanterre – 'mad Nanterre' as the ugly concrete campus became known. By May tens of thousands of students, including those from the elite Sorbonne, were clashing with police on the streets of Paris.[95] A general strike swept the country as the trade unions seized the opportunity to press a weakened government for higher wages. Similar scenes played out at the University of California, Berkeley, the Free University, Berlin – even at Harvard, where members of the organization Students for a Democratic Society occupied the President's house, and members of the Worker-Student Alliance stormed University Hall (temporarily renamed Che Guevara Hall), evicting the deans working there.

Superficially, this campus revolt was directed against the US war to preserve the independence of South Vietnam, a war which by 1968 had cost the lives of more than 30,000 Americans and had lost majority public approval. The 68ers also lent their support to the African-American Civil Rights movement, a classically liberal challenge to the remaining impediments to racial equality in the American South. Yet much of the language of 1968 was Marxist, representing almost every conflict from Israel to Indo-China as an anti-imperialist struggle. According to the more doctrinaire student leaders like Daniel ('Danny le Rouge') Cohn-Bendit and Rudi Dutschke, the aim was 'insurrection in the centres of capitalism'. 'Humanity won't be happy', the *enragés* declared, 'until the last capitalist is hung with the entrails of the last bureaucrat.' As anarchists, the Situationists wanted the abolition of labour itself, urging their student supporters: *Ne travaillez jamais* – Never Work.[96] Yet there was one very practical demand that spoke volumes about the revolution's true aims, and that was for unlimited male access to the female dormitories – hence the injunction to 'unbutton your mind as often as your fly'. As one graffiti artist put it: 'The more I want to make love, the more I want to make revolution. The more I want to make revolution, the more I want to make love.'[97] Female students were encouraged to experiment with hitherto taboo degrees of exposure. From the shapeless pyjamas of Mao's Red Guards to the hippies' denim bell-bottoms, the 1968 revolution was all about clothes. From mini-skirts to bikinis, the sexual revolution was all about the lack of them. 'Women must reject their role as the principal consumers in the capitalist state,' declared the Australian-born feminist Germaine Greer, who loved to party more than she loved the Party.[98]

The irony was that the 68ers, who routinely denounced American imperialism in Vietnam and symbolically smashed the windows of the American Express office in Paris, remained chronically addicted to American popular culture. Blue jeans – now reshaped with low-slung waists and flared legs – remained the uniform of youth rebellion. The record companies continued to supply the soundtrack: the Rolling Stones' 'Street Fightin' Man' (released by Decca in December 1968) and the Beatles' 'Revolution' (released by the band's own Apple label four months before) – both songs notably sceptical about the benefits of revolution. Denim pants and vinyl discs: these were among the most successful products of late twentieth-century capitalism. And, as in the 1920s, a policy of prohibition – this time of narcotics – offered a new field of opportunity to 'Crime Inc.'. The French Situationists might pile opprobrium on the consumer society with its culture of crass materialism and ubiquitous advertising (what Guy Debord sneeringly called 'the society of the spectacle'), but those who rioted against capitalism in Paris were grossly underestimating the benefits they themselves reaped from the system. Give or take the occasional baton charge by redneck and blue-collar policemen, who despised the privileged middle-class 'longhairs', the authorities in the Western world generally allowed the students the freedom to protest. Indeed, most universities caved in to student demands. Another irony was that a youth movement that favoured making 'love not war' ended up being associated with so much violence: race riots in American cities, a surge in the homicide rate and terrorism in Western Europe and the Middle East. A new era began on 23 July 1968, with the hijacking by the Palestine Liberation Organization of an El Al aircraft bound from Rome to Tel Aviv. It was not long before the Keffiyeh headscarf favoured by the PLO leader Yasser Arafat became as chic as Che Guevara's beret.

Going through the Iron Curtain in 1968 was like going through the looking glass. The visitor from Western Europe found much that was familiar. The urban planners in both halves of Europe had made the same mistake, decanting people from city centres and marooning them in repulsive, shoddy apartment blocks in the brutally functional Bauhaus style that had entranced post-war architects. But some familiar things could have diametrically different meanings. In Prague, long hair and jeans were also favoured by the country's youth over the Communist Party's ideal of short back and sides, polyester suits and red ties. But they were favoured precisely because they were redolent of the capitalist West. The Czechs even called jeans *Texasskis* – Texan trousers.[99] With the planners reluctant to manufacture such garments, the only way to get them was through smuggling. The pop singer Petr Janda, whose group Olympic aspired to be the Czech Beatles,* acquired his first pair of Levi 501s that way; they were too short, but his friends were still consumed with envy.[100] As in Paris, so in Prague: universities became flashpoints for a clash of the generations. The beatnik poet Allen Ginsberg visited the Charles University in the spring of 1965; he was expelled in early May for the 'lewd and morally dangerous' nature of his writings. In November 1967 students at the Charles University gathered during a blackout and marched into the centre of Prague holding candles. One of the students involved in the protest was Ivan Touška. As he recalled:

> There were so many power cuts at the time – and the candles were a practical symbol during the first protest – we had candles but we wanted electric light. However 'We want light' obviously had a wider general meaning: 'light' against the 'darkness' of the highest political body of that time – the Central Committee of the Communist Party of Czechoslovakia.[101]

---

* Their biggest hit, 'Zelva' (Tortoise), had lyrics evidently inspired by late John Lennon: 'If you don't pay attention to turtles / They can trick you. / It is hard to catch turtles / When they are in the water.'

In April 1968 Alexander Dubček launched his 'Action Programme' of economic and political liberalization. Significantly, his economic policy shifted the emphasis from heavy industry to consumer goods. But the Soviet leadership in Moscow saw the Prague Spring as an unacceptable threat. At 4 a.m. on 21 August 1968, Soviet tanks and troops surrounded the building that housed the Central Committee of the Czechoslovak Communist Party. Threatened by an angry crowd, the tanks opened fire, killing one young man. At around 9 a.m. troops stormed the building. Dubček was flown to the Soviet Union, whence he was lucky to return alive. A focal point of resistance was Wenceslas Square, where Czechs gathered daily around the equestrian statue of Wenceslas, the beatified tenth-century Duke of Bohemia. In Paris the students had thrown flaming Molotov cocktails at the riot police. In Prague, on 19 January 1969, a Czech student named Jan Palach doused his clothes in kerosene and set himself alight. He died three days later. In the West students indulged themselves with Marxist rhetoric, but what they were really after was free love. On the other side of the Iron Curtain the stakes were higher. What was at issue was freedom itself.

After 1968 the restored communist regime required all Czech rock musicians to sit a written exam in Marxism-Leninism. An idiosyncratic avant-garde band called the Plastic People of the Universe, formed just a month after the Soviet invasion, hit back with songs like '100 Points' ('They are afraid of freedom. / They are afraid of democracy. / They are afraid of the [United Nations] Human Rights' Charter. / They are afraid of socialism. / So why the hell are we afraid of them?').[102] It soon became clear. In January 1970 their professional musicians' licence was revoked. Two years later they were banned from playing in Prague, forcing them to perform at private parties in the Bohemian countryside. It was after one of these underground events – the Second Music Festival of the Second Culture at Bojanovice in February 1976 – that all of the band's members, including their Canadian lead singer Paul Wilson, were arrested. Two of them, Vratislav Brabenec and Ivan Jirous, were put on trial charged with 'extreme vulgarity ... anti-socialism ... nihilism ... and decadence' and sentenced to terms of eighteen and eight months in jail. It was their trial that inspired the founding of Charter 77, the dissident group spearheaded by Václav Havel, the playwright and future President of Czechoslovakia. Never in its history was rock music more political than it was in Prague in the 1970s.*

So why not just let Czechoslovakian students have all the jeans and rock 'n' roll they wanted? The answer is that the consumer society posed a lethal threat to the Soviet system itself. It was market-based. It responded to signals from consumers themselves – their preference for jeans over flannel trousers, or for Mick Jagger over Burt Bacharach. And it devoted an increasing share of resources to satisfying those preferences. This the Soviet system simply could not do. The Party knew what everyone needed – brown polyester suits – and placed its orders with the state-owned factories accordingly. The alternative was inherently subversive. Significantly, the East German authorities blamed the 1953 workers' revolt on Western provocateurs 'with cowboy pants and Texas shirts'.[103] Khrushchev may have yearned to copy the colour television; he most certainly did not want the Beatles. 'The youth of the Soviet Union do not need this cacophonous rubbish,' he declared. 'It's just a small step from saxophones [sic] to switchblades.'[104] In any case, for the Soviets to keep pace with the much richer Americans in the Cold War arms race, tanks had to take precedence over tank-tops, strategic bombers over Stratocasters. One Soviet critic observed, revealingly, that 'every ounce of energy used on the dance floor was energy which could and should have been invested in building a hydroelectric plant'.[105] It did not stop jeans being smuggled into Russia itself by black-market dealers known as *fartsovshchiki*, who specialized in bartering denim for fur hats and caviar, the only souvenirs that Western visitors to Moscow ever wanted to buy. A pair of black-market jeans could fetch between 150 and 250 roubles, at a time when the average monthly salary was under 200 roubles and an ordinary pair of state-manufactured trousers sold for 10 or 20 roubles.

With the crushing of the Prague Spring, the communist system in Eastern Europe seemed unassailable. In Berlin the division of the city into East and West looked like a permanent fact. But while the communists

---

* Among the first official guests Havel invited to Prague after his appointment as president on 29 December 1989 were Frank Zappa and Lou Reed.

were good at crushing political opposition, their resistance to the West's consumer society was altogether weaker. The influence of Western fashion proved impossible to keep out, especially once East Germans were able to watch West German television (they had long had access to Western radio). Designers like Ann Katrin Hendel started making their own Western-style clothes, selling them from car boots. Hendel even made her own jeans:

> We tried to sew them, from tarpaulin or from bed sheets or from fabric that wasn't jeans fabric. We also tried to dye them but it was also very difficult to get your hands on dye . . . They were so popular that people snatched them from our hands.[106]

The critical point was that the success of Western consumer industries was now matched, mirror-like, by the miserable underperformance of their Soviet counterparts. Not only was growth now vanishingly low after 1973 (below 1 per cent); total factor productivity was declining. Some state enterprises were actually subtracting value from the raw materials they processed. Just as Hayek had warned, in the absence of meaningful prices, resources were misallocated; corrupt officials restricted output to maximize their own illicit gains; workers pretended to work and, in return, managers pretended to pay them. Not only the industrial capital stock but also the human capital stock was not being maintained; nuclear power stations crumbled; alcoholism soared. Far from challenging the United States for economic supremacy, as Khrushchev had threatened, the Soviet Union had achieved per-capita consumption of around 24 per cent of the American level – a challenge to Turkey, at best.[107] At the same time, the shift in superpower relations towards détente and disarmament made the Soviets' ability to mass-produce missiles a good deal less valuable. High oil prices in the 1970s had given the system a stay of execution; as oil fell in the 1980s the Soviet bloc was left with nothing but hard-currency debts – money borrowed from the very system Khrushchev had promised to 'bury'. Mikhail Gorbachev, appointed general secretary of the Soviet Communist Party in March 1985, felt there was now no alternative but to reform both the economic and the political system, including the Soviet empire in Eastern Europe. With *perestroika* and *glasnost* the new watchwords in Moscow, hard-liners in East Berlin were left high and dry – forced into censoring publications and reports not only from the West but from the Soviet Union as well.

As in 1848, as in 1918, the revolutions of 1989 spread contagiously. In Warsaw in February 1989 the Polish government agreed to talks with the free trade union Solidarity; soon the country was preparing for free elections. In Budapest in May the Hungarian communists decided to open their border with Austria. The Iron Curtain began to rust away. Around 15,000 East Germans set off via Czechoslovakia to 'holiday' in Hungary on what was in reality a one-way trip to the West. In June Solidarity won the Polish elections and set about forming a democratic government. In September the Hungarian communists followed the Polish example by agreeing to free elections. The following month, as Erich Honecker honed his plans to celebrate the GDR's fortieth anniversary, hundreds, then thousands, then tens of thousands, then hundreds of thousands of people poured on to the streets in Leipzig, first chanting 'Wir sind das Volk' (We are the People), later amending that to 'Wir sind ein Volk' (We are One People). This time, unlike in Budapest in 1956 and Prague in 1968 – not forgetting Gdánsk in December 1981 and Beijing in June 1989 – the troops remained in their barracks. Within the East German Party, where the extent of the GDR's bankruptcy was becoming clear, Honecker was forced aside by younger 'reformers'. But it was all much too late for reform. Other, nimbler apparatchiks, notably in Romania, were already switching sides, calculating the likely benefits to themselves of market reforms.

On 9 November 1989 a bemused East Berlin press corps were informed that 'the decision [had been] taken to make it possible for all citizens to leave the country through the official border crossing points . . . to take effect at once', news that prompted a flood of East Berliners to the border checkpoints. Unprepared, guards opted not to resist. By midnight all the checkpoints had been forced to open and one of the greatest parties of the century was under way, closely followed by one of its biggest shopping sprees. With the fall of the Berlin Wall, the Cold War was essentially over, though it was not until the failed Moscow coup of August 1991 and the subsequent dissolution of the Soviet Union that the Baltic states, Ukraine and Belarus, along with the three big Caucasian republics and the five 'stans' of Central Asia, became independent states.

Few had seen it coming.* For some it was 'the end of history', the definitive victory of the liberal capitalist model.[108] For others it was the 'triumph of the West', the political achievement of three charismatic leaders: Ronald Reagan, Pope John Paul II and Margaret Thatcher.[109] A third view gave the credit to nationalism. But the analyst who was closest to the mark was the Italian apparel executive who started marketing a line in skintight 'perestroika jeans'. It was above all as consumer societies that the Soviet Union and its satellites had failed. It was no accident that the popular protests of 2006 against the incorrigibly authoritarian regime in Belarus took the form of wearing jeans – though Minsk still awaits its Denim Revolution.[110]

PYJAMAS AND SCARVES

In the wake of Mao Zedong's Communist Revolution in 1949 China became the drabbest society on earth. Gone were the last vestiges of Qing-era silk. Gone were the Western outfits favoured by the nationalists between the wars. In the pursuit of strict equality everyone was issued with what looked very much like pyjamas. Grey ones. Yet today when you walk down a typical Chinese street what you see is a kaleidoscope of Western styles of clothing. Advertising hoardings in all the major cities extol the virtues of Western brands from Armani to Ermenegildo Zegna. Like every other industrial revolution, China's began with textile production. Until recently, most of the garments manufactured in the coastal Special Economic Zones were intended for export to the West. Now, with demand down in depressed Western economies, the principal challenge facing policy-makers in Beijing is

---

* The most uncannily accurate prophecy was by the American journalist James P. O'Donnell in an article entitled 'The Ghost Train of Berlin', published in the West German *Reader's Digest* magazine *Das Beste* in January 1979, which foresaw the destruction of the wall ten years later and even the sale of pieces of the wall as souvenirs. Sadly, the rewards for such foresight are paltry – as were the penalties that should have been paid by a generation of clueless academic 'Sovietologists'. The business of political prognostication remains a highly inefficient market.

how to make the Chinese worker save less and consume more; in other words, buy more clothes. It seems as if the triumph of the West's consumer society is close to being complete. Or is it?

Istanbul is a cosmopolitan city, where the outward trappings of Western civilization have long been commonplace in the streets. Stroll down the main shopping thoroughfare of İstiklâl Caddesi and you could be almost anywhere in the Mediterranean world. But go elsewhere in the same city – in the Fatih area near Sultan Ahmet, for example – and things look very different. For devout Muslims, Western norms of female attire are unacceptable because they reveal far more than is prescribed by their religion.* And that is why, in a country that is overwhelmingly Muslim, the headscarf, the veil (*niqāb* or *khimār*) and the loose black body covering (*abaya*) have been making a comeback.

This represents a major change in direction for Turkey. As we saw in Chapter 2, the founder of the Turkish Republic, Kemal Atatürk, set out to Westernize the way Turks dressed, banning the wearing of religious clothing in all state institutions. The secularist military government that came to power in 1982 revived this policy by prohibiting female students from wearing headscarves at university. This ban was not rigorously enforced until after 1997, however, when the Constitutional Court explicitly ruled that the wearing of headscarves on academic premises – including schools as well as universities – violated article 2 of the constitution, which enshrines the secular character of the republic. (The wearing of long beards by male students was also pronounced unconstitutional.) When university and school authorities called in riot police to enforce this ruling, the country was plunged into

---

* The ideal of covering the female head (the Arabic term is *hijāb*) and body (*jilbāb*) derives from the Koran, which commands women to 'subdue their eyes, and maintain their chastity. They shall not reveal any parts of their bodies, except that which is necessary. They shall cover their chests, and shall not relax this code in the presence of other than their husbands, their fathers, the fathers of their husbands, their sons, the sons of their husbands, their brothers, the sons of their brothers, the sons of their sisters, other women, the male servants or employees whose sexual drive has been nullified, or the children who have not reached puberty' (Sura 24 (Al-Nur): 31). The *hadith*, which recounts the acts of Muhammad, goes further, requiring the covering of the neck, ankles and wrists. Zealous Muslims promote the wearing of the *burqa*, a term usually taken to refer to the *niqāb* and the *abaya*.

crisis. In October 1998 around 140,000 people protested against the ban by linking hands to form a human chain in more than twenty-five provinces. In Istanbul thousands of girls opted to miss classes rather than remove their headscarves; some held daily vigils outside their school gates. At Inönü University in Eastern Anatolia a demonstration against the ban turned violent, leading to the arrest of 200 protesters. A number of young women in the eastern city of Kars even committed suicide over the issue,* while a judge who upheld the ban was shot dead in court in May 2006. In 2008 the Islamist government, led since 2003 by Recep Tayyip Erdoğan's Justice and Development Party, amended the constitution to allow headscarves in universities, only to have the decision overturned by the Constitutional Court. The European Court of Human Rights has also upheld the headscarf ban.

The issue illustrates, once again, how our outward trappings can have a deeper significance. Is the headscarf or the veil merely an expression of personal faith, which any Westernized society should tolerate on the principle of freedom of expression? Or is it an antiquated symbol of the sexual inequality ordained by Islam, which a secular society should prohibit? The question is represented by Islamists like the journalist Nihal Bengisu Karaca as a matter of individual freedom and human rights:

> We want to be treated the same as the women who do not wear the scarf. We are the same, nothing is different, we want to be treated the same. We have all the rights that they have ... We just want a democracy between the ladies who don't wear a scarf and those who do wear the scarf.[111]

The Islamist argument is that covering up is no more than a harmless option, which some women freely choose to exercise. The veil, they say, is just another form of feminine attire, available in Istanbul stores in all kinds of colours and styles, with diamanté for the more flamboyantly inclined. The reality, of course, is that promoting the headscarf is

---

* These events inspired Orhan Pamuk's seminal novel *Snow* (2002). Anyone wishing to understand the psychology of Islamic terrorism must read Pamuk's imagined last conversation between the Kars Director of Education and his murderer.

part of a wider agenda to limit women's rights by introducing sharia law in Turkey, achieving gradually what was achieved much more suddenly in Iran after the 1979 Revolution – a backlash against the Shah's 'Westoxification' (*gharbzadegi*) of Iran, which the Ayatollah Khomeini converted into a drastic sexual counter-revolution.[112] Already you can see *burqas* in the streets of Istanbul, covering their wearers in black from head to foot, leaving them with only a tiny slit to see out of – concealing their identities so totally that in 2010 the French National Assembly voted to prohibit such garments altogether. It is no accident that this sartorial shift has been accompanied by a change in Turkish foreign policy. Once a pro-American pillar of NATO and a candidate for membership of the European Union, Turkey is increasingly turning eastwards, vying with the Iranian Islamic Republic for leadership of the Muslim world, reviving memories of the days of Ottoman power.

In short (or in long, if you prefer), what people wear matters. The West's two great economic leaps forward – the industrial evolution and the consumer society – were to a huge extent about clothes: first making them more efficiently, and then wearing them more revealingly. The spread of the Western way of dress was inseparable from the spread of the Western way of life, just as the backlash against Western dress in the Muslim world is a symptom of a global Islamic revival. The Iranian revolutionaries disparaged Westernizers as *fokoli*, from the French word *faux-col* (bow tie), and men in Tehran today pointedly eschew ties.[113] With the growth of Muslim communities in Western Europe, veiled women are now as common a sight on the streets of London as Manchester United football strips are on the streets of Shanghai. Should Britain follow the French in banning the *burqa*? Or does the West's consumer society have an antidote to the veil as effective as blue jeans once were to Maoist pyjamas?

Perhaps, on reflection, these are the wrong questions to ask. For they imply that all the achievements of Western civilization – capitalism, science, the rule of law and democracy – have been reduced to nothing more profound than a spot of shopping. Retail therapy may not be the answer to all our problems. Maybe the ultimate threat to the West comes not from radical Islamism, or any other external source, but from our own lack of understanding of, and faith in, our own cultural heritage.

6

Work

Christianity will go. It will vanish and shrink. I needn't argue about that; I'm right and I will be proved right. We're more popular than Jesus now; I don't know which will go first – rock 'n' roll or Christianity. Jesus was all right but his disciples were thick and ordinary. It's them twisting it that ruins it for me.

John Lennon

In the past twenty years, we have realized that the heart of your culture is your religion: Christianity. That is why the West has been so powerful. The Christian moral foundation of social and cultural life was what made possible the emergence of capitalism and then the successful transition to democratic politics. We don't have any doubt about this.

Anonymous Fellow of the Chinese
Academy of the Social Sciences

WORK ETHIC AND WORD ETHIC

In the course of roughly 500 years, as we have seen, Western civilization rose to a position of extraordinary dominance in the world. Western institutional structures like the corporation, the market and the nation-state became the global standards for competitive economics and politics – templates for the Rest to copy. Western science shifted the paradigms; others either followed or were left behind. Western systems of law and the political models derived from them, including democracy, displaced or defeated the non-Western alternatives.

Western medicine marginalized the witch doctors and other faith-healers. Above all, the Western model of industrial production and mass consumption left all alternative models of economic organization floundering in its wake. Even in the late 1990s the West was still clearly the dominant civilization of the world. The five leading Western powers – the United States, Germany, the United Kingdom, France and Canada – accounted for 44 per cent of total global manufacturing between them. The scientific world was dominated by Western universities, employees of which won the lion's share of Nobel prizes and other distinctions. A democratic wave was sweeping the world, most spectacularly in the wake of the 1989 revolutions. Western consumer brands like Levi's and Coca-Cola flourished almost everywhere; the golden arches of McDonald's were likewise to be seen in all the major cities in the world. Not only had the Soviet Union collapsed; Japan, which some had predicted would overtake the United States, had stumbled and slid into a lost decade of near-zero growth and deflation. Analysts of international relations struggled to find words sufficiently grand to describe the ascendancy of the United States, the leading power of the Western world: was it an empire? A hegemon? A *hyperpuissance*?

At the time of writing, in the wake of two burst financial bubbles, two unexpectedly difficult wars, one great recession – and above all in the wake of China's remarkable ascent to displace Japan as the world's second-largest economy – the question is whether or not the half-millennium of Western predominance is now finally drawing to a close.

Are we living through the descent of the West? It would not be the first time. Here is how Edward Gibbon described the Goths' sack of Rome in August 410 AD:

> in the hour of savage license, when every passion was inflamed, and every restraint was removed ... a cruel slaughter was made of the Romans; and ... the streets of the city were filled with dead bodies, which remained without burial during the general consternation ... Whenever the Barbarians were provoked by opposition, they extended the promiscuous massacre to the feeble, the innocent, and the helpless ... The matrons and virgins of Rome were exposed to injuries

more dreadful, in the apprehension of chastity, than death itself ... The brutal soldiers satisfied their sensual appetites, without consulting either the inclination or the duties of their female captives ... In the pillage of Rome, a just preference was given to gold and jewels ... but, after these portable riches had been removed by the more diligent robbers, the palaces of Rome were rudely stripped of their splendid and costly furniture ...

The acquisition of riches served only to stimulate the avarice of the rapacious Barbarians, who proceeded, by threats, by blows, and by tortures, to force from their prisoners the confession of hidden treasure ... It was not easy to compute the multitudes, who, from an honourable station and a prosperous fortune, were suddenly reduced to the miserable condition of captives and exiles ... The calamities of Rome ... dispersed the inhabitants to the most lonely, the most secure, the most distant places of refuge.[1]

The History of the Decline and Fall of the Roman Empire, published in six volumes between 1776 and 1788, tells the story of the last time the West collapsed. Today, many people in the West fear we may be living through a kind of sequel. When you reflect on what caused the fall of ancient Rome, such fears appear not altogether fanciful. Economic crisis; epidemics that ravaged the population; immigrants overrunning the imperial borders; the rise of a rival empire – Persia's – in the East; terror in the form of Alaric's Goths and Attila's Huns. Is it possible that, after so many centuries of supremacy, we now face a similar conjuncture? Economically, the West is stagnating in the wake of the worst financial crisis since the Depression, while many of the Rest are growing at unprecedented rates. We live in fear of pandemics and man-made changes to the global climate. There is alarming evidence that some immigrant communities within our societies have become seedbeds for Islamist ideology and terrorist networks. A nuclear terrorist attack would be far more devastating to London or New York than the Goths were to Rome. Meanwhile, a rival empire is on the rise in the East: China, which could conceivably become the biggest economy in the world within the next decades.

Gibbon's most provocative argument in the *Decline and Fall of the Roman Empire* was that Christianity was one of the fatal solvents of the first version of Western civilization. Monotheism, with its emphasis on the hereafter, was fundamentally at odds with the variegated paganism of the empire in its heyday. Yet it was a very specific form of Christianity – the variant that arose in Western Europe in the sixteenth century – that gave the modern version of Western civilization the sixth of its key advantages over the rest of the world: Protestantism – or, rather, the peculiar ethic of hard work and thrift with which it came to be associated. It is time to understand the role God played in the rise of the West, and to explain why, in the late twentieth century, so many Westerners turned their backs on Him.

If you were a wealthy industrialist living in Europe in the late nineteenth century, there was a disproportionate chance that you were a Protestant. Since the Reformation, which had led many northern European states to break away from the Roman Catholic Church, there had been a shift of economic power away from Catholic countries like Austria, France, Italy, Portugal and Spain and towards Protestant countries such as England, Holland, Prussia, Saxony and Scotland. It seemed as if the forms of faith and ways of worship were in some way correlated with people's economic fortunes. The question was: what was different about Protestantism? What was it about the teaching of Luther and his successors that encouraged people not just to work hard but also to accumulate capital? The man who came up with the most influential answer to these questions was a depressive German professor named Max Weber – the father of modern sociology and the author who coined the phrase 'the Protestant ethic'.

Weber was a precocious youth. Growing up in Erfurt, one of the strongholds of the German Reformation, the thirteen-year-old Weber gave his parents as a Christmas present an essay entitled 'About the Course of German History, with Special Reference to the Positions of the Emperor and the Pope'. At the age of fourteen, he was writing letters studded with references to classical authors from Cicero to Virgil and already had an extensive knowledge of the philosophy of, among others, Kant and Spinoza. His early academic career was one triumph after another: at the age of twenty-two he was already a qualified barrister. Within three years he had a doctorate for a thesis on 'The History of Medieval Business Organizations' and at twenty-seven his

Habilitation on 'Roman Agrarian History and its Significance for Private Law' secured him a lectureship at the University of Berlin. He was appointed professor of economics at Freiburg at the age of thirty, winning fame and notoriety for his inaugural lecture, which called for a more ambitious German imperialism.

This arc of academic ascent was painfully interrupted in 1897, when Weber suffered a paralysing nervous breakdown, precipitated by the death of his father following a bitter row between them. In 1899 he felt obliged to resign his academic post. He spent three years recuperating, in the course of which he became increasingly preoccupied with religion and its relationship to economic life. His parents had both been Protestants; indeed, his maternal grandfather was a devout Calvinist, while his other grandfather was a successful linen merchant. His mother was a true Calvinist in her asceticism; his father, by contrast, was a bon vivant, living life to the full thanks to an inherited fortune. The link between religious and economic life was the puzzle at the heart of Weber's own existence. Which of his parents had the right attitude to worldly wealth?

Until the Reformation, Christian religious devotion had been seen as something distinct from the material affairs of the world. Lending money at interest was a sin. Rich men were less likely than the poor to enter the Kingdom of Heaven. Rewards for a pious life lay in the afterlife. All that had changed after the 1520s, at least in the countries that embraced the Reformation. Reflecting on his own experience, Weber began to wonder what it was about the Reformation that had made the north of Europe more friendly towards capitalism than the south. It took a transatlantic trip to provide the answer.

In 1904 Weber travelled to St Louis, Missouri, to attend the Congress of Arts and Sciences at the World Fair.[2] The park where the World Fair was held covered more than 200 acres and yet still seemed to overflow with everything that American capitalism had to offer. Weber was dazzled by the shining lights of the Palace of Electricity. The Direct Current King, Thomas Edison himself, was on hand, the personification of American entrepreneurship. St Louis was brimming with marvels of modern technology, from telephones to motion pictures. What could possibly explain the dynamism of this society, which made even industrial Germany seem staid and slow moving?

Almost manically restless, Weber rushed around the United States in search of an answer. A caricature of the absent-minded German professor, he made a lasting impression on his American cousins Lola and Maggie Fallenstein, who were especially struck by his rather bizarre outfit, a checked brown suit with plus-fours and brown knee-socks. But that was nothing compared with the impression America made on Weber. Travelling by train from St Louis to Oklahoma, passing through small Missouri towns like Bourbon and Cuba, Weber finally got it:

> This kind of place is really an incredible thing: tent camps of the workers, especially section hands for the numerous railroads under construction; 'streets' in a natural state, usually doused with petroleum twice each summer to prevent dust, and smelling accordingly; wooden churches of at least 4–5 denominations . . . Add to this the usual tangle of telegraph and telephone wires, and electrical trainlines under construction, for the 'town' extends into the unbounded distance.[3]

The little town of St James, about 100 miles west of St Louis, is typical of the thousands of new settlements that sprang up along the railroads as they spread westwards across America. When Weber passed through it a hundred years ago, he was amazed at the town's huge number of churches and chapels of every stripe. With the industrial extravaganza of the World Fair still fresh in his memory, he began to discern a kind of holy alliance between America's material success and its vibrant religious life.

When Weber returned to his study in Heidelberg he wrote the second part of his seminal two-part essay, 'The Protestant Ethic and the Spirit of Capitalism'. It contains one of the most influential of all arguments about Western civilization: that its economic dynamism was an unintended consequence of the Protestant Reformation. Whereas other religions associated holiness with the renunciation of worldly things – monks in cloisters, hermits in caves – the Protestant sects saw industry and thrift as expressions of a new kind of hardworking godliness. The capitalist 'calling' was, in other words, religious in origin: 'To attain . . . self-confidence [in one's membership of the Elect] intense worldly activity is recommended . . . [Thus] Christian asceticism . . . strode into the market-place of life.'[4] 'Tireless labour', as Weber called it, was the surest sign that you belonged to the Elect, that select band of people predestined by God for salvation. Protestantism, he argued, 'has the effect of liberating the *acquisition of wealth* from the inhibitions of traditionalist ethics; it breaks the fetters on the striving for gain not only by legalizing it, but ... by seeing it as directly willed by God'. The Protestant ethic, moreover, provided the capitalist with 'sober, conscientious, and unusually capable workers, who were devoted to work as the divinely willed purpose of life'.[5] For most of history, men had worked to live. But the Protestants lived to work. It was this work ethic, Weber argued, that gave birth to modern capitalism, which he defined as 'sober, bourgeois capitalism with its rational organization of free labour'.[6]

Weber's thesis is not without its problems. He saw 'rational conduct on the basis of the idea of the calling' as 'one of the fundamental elements of the spirit of modern capitalism'.[7] But elsewhere he acknowledged the irrational character of 'Christian asceticism': 'The ideal type of the capitalistic entrepreneur ... gets nothing out of his wealth for himself, except the irrational sense of having done his job well'; he 'exists for the sake of his business, instead of the reverse', which 'from the view-point of personal happiness' was once again 'irrational'.[8] Even more problematic was Weber's scathing sideswipe at the Jews, who posed the most obvious exception to his argument.* 'The Jews', according to Weber, 'stood on the side of the politically and speculatively oriented adventurous capitalism; their ethos was ... that of pariah-capitalism. Only Puritanism carried the ethos of the rational organization of capital and labour.'[9] Weber was also mysteriously blind to the success of Catholic entrepreneurs in France, Belgium and elsewhere. Indeed, his handling of evidence is one of the more glaring defects of his essay. The words of Martin Luther and the Westminster Confession sit uneasily alongside quotations from Benjamin

---

* Jews have in fact outperformed Protestants in the United States over the past century, with significantly higher earnings and rates of self-employment. Of the chief executive officers of *Fortune* magazine's 100 largest companies in 2003, at least 10 per cent were Jews as were no fewer than 23 per cent of CEOs of the Forbes 400. Not only have Jews been disproportionately successful in starting financial firms; they were also founders or co-founders of some of the world's biggest technology companies, for example Dell, Google, Intel and Oracle.

Franklin and some distinctly unsatisfactory data from the German state of Baden about Protestant and Catholic educational attainment and income. Later scholars, notably the Fabian economic historian R. H. Tawney, have tended to cast doubt on Weber's underlying argument that the direction of causation ran from religious doctrine to economic behaviour.[10] On the contrary, much of the first steps towards a spirit of capitalism occurred before the Reformation, in the towns of Lombardy and Flanders; while many leading reformers expressed distinctly anti-capitalist views. At least one major empirical study of 276 German cities between 1300 and 1900 found 'no effects of Protestantism on economic growth', at least as measured by the growth of city size.[11] Some cross-country studies have arrived at similar conclusions.[12]

Nevertheless, there are reasons to think that Weber was on to something, even if he was right for the wrong reasons. There was indeed, as he assumed, a clear tendency after the Reformation for Protestant countries in Europe to grow faster than Catholic ones, so that by 1700 the former had clearly overtaken the latter in terms of per-capita income, and by 1940 people in Catholic countries were on average 40 per cent worse off than people in Protestant countries.[13] Protestant former colonies have also fared better economically than Catholic ones since the 1950s, even if religion is not a sufficient explanation for that difference.[14] Because of the central importance in Luther's thought of individual reading of the Bible, Protestantism encouraged literacy, not to mention printing, and these two things unquestionably encouraged economic development (the accumulation of 'human capital') as well as scientific study.[15] This proposition holds good not just for countries such as Scotland, where spending on education, school enrolment and literacy rates were exceptionally high, but for the Protestant world as a whole. Wherever Protestant missionaries went, they promoted literacy, with measurable long-term benefits to the societies they sought to educate; the same cannot be said of Catholic missionaries throughout the period from the Counter-Reformation to the reforms of the Second Vatican Council (1962–5).[16] It was the Protestant missionaries who were responsible for the fact that school enrolments in British colonies were, on average, four to five times higher than in other countries' colonies. In

1941 over 55 per cent of people in what is now Kerala were literate, a higher proportion than in any other region of India, four times higher than the Indian average and comparable with the rates in poorer European countries like Portugal. This was because Protestant missionaries were more active in Kerala, drawn by its ancient Christian community, than anywhere else in India. Where Protestant missionaries were not present (for example, in Muslim regions or protectorates like Bhutan, Nepal and Sikkim), people in British colonies were not measurably better educated.[17] The level of Protestant missionary activity has also proved to be a very good predictor of post-independence economic performance and political stability. Recent surveys of attitudes show that Protestants have unusually high levels of mutual trust, an important precondition for the development of efficient credit networks.[18] More generally, religious belief (as opposed to formal observance) of any sort appears to be associated with economic growth, particularly where concepts of heaven and hell provide incentives for good behaviour in this world. This tends to mean not only hard work and mutual trust but also thrift, honesty and openness to strangers, all economically beneficial traits.[19]

Religions matter. In earlier chapters, we saw how the 'stability ethic' of Confucianism played a part in imperial China's failure to develop the kind of competitive institutional framework that promoted innovation in Western Europe – even if China was far from the static, unchanging society described by Weber in his sequel to 'The Protestant Ethic', *Confucianism and Taoism* (1916). We saw how the power of the imams and mullahs snuffed out any chance of a scientific revolution in the Islamic world. And we saw how the Roman Catholic Church acted as one of the brakes on economic development in South America. But perhaps the biggest contribution of religion to the history of Western civilization was this. Protestantism made the West not only work, but also save and read. The Industrial Revolution was indeed a product of technological innovation and consumption. But it also required an increase in the intensity and duration of work, combined with the accumulation of capital through saving and investment. Above all, it depended on the accumulation of human capital. The literacy that Protestantism promoted was vital to all of this. On reflection, we would do better to talk about the Protestant *word* ethic.

The question is: has the West today – or at least a significant part of it – lost both its religion and the ethic that went with it?

GET YOUR KICKS

Europeans today are the idlers of the world. On average, they work less than Americans and a lot less than Asians. Thanks to protracted education and early retirement, a smaller share of Europeans are actually available for work. For example, 54 per cent of Belgians and Greeks aged over fifteen participate in the labour force, compared with 65 per cent of Americans and 74 per cent of Chinese.[20] Of that labour force, a larger proportion was unemployed in Europe than elsewhere in the developed world on average in the years 1980 to 2010. Europeans are also more likely to go on strike.* Above all, thanks to shorter workdays and longer holidays, Europeans work fewer hours.[21] Between 2000 and 2009 the average American in employment worked just under 1,711 hours a year (a figure pushed down by the impact of the financial crisis, which put many workers on short time). The average German worked just 1,437 hours – fully 16 per cent less. This is the result of a prolonged period of divergence. In 1979 the differentials between European and American working hours were minor; indeed, in those days the average Spanish worker put in more hours per year than the average American. But, from then on, European working hours declined by as much as a fifth. Asian working hours also declined, but the average Japanese worker still works as many hours a year as the average American, while the average South Korean works 39 per cent more. People in Hong Kong and Singapore also work roughly a third more hours a year than Americans.[22]

---

* These transatlantic differences are smaller than used to be the case, however. Unemployment has risen much higher in the United States than in most of the European Union as a result of the financial crisis; within the OECD, at the time of writing, only Hungary, Ireland, Portugal, Slovakia and Spain have a higher jobless rate than the US. Measured as a five-year (1996–2000) average of days not worked due to strike action per 1,000 employees, Denmark, Spain, Ireland, Italy and France are all more strike-prone than the United States, but the other members of the European Union are less so.

Work Ethics: Hours Worked per Year in the West and the East, 1950–2009

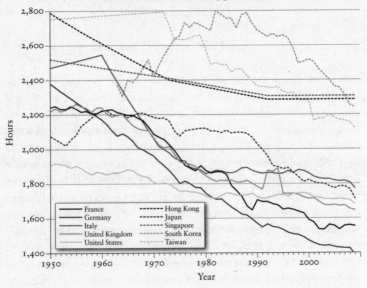

The striking thing is that the transatlantic divergence in working patterns has coincided almost exactly with a comparable divergence in religiosity. Europeans not only work less; they also pray less – and believe less. There was a time when Europe could justly refer to itself as 'Christendom'. Europeans built the continent's loveliest edifices to accommodate their acts of worship. They quarrelled bitterly over the distinction between transubstantiation and consubstantiation. As pilgrims, missionaries and conquistadors, they sailed to the four corners of the earth, intent on converting the heathen to the true faith. Now it is Europeans who are the heathens. According to the most recent (2005–8) *World Values Survey*, 4 per cent of Norwegians and Swedes and 8 per cent of French and Germans attend a church service at least once a week, compared with 36 per cent of Americans, 44 per cent of Indians, 48 per cent of Brazilians and 78 per cent of sub-Saharan Africans. The figures are significantly higher for a number of predominantly Catholic countries like Italy (32 per cent) and Spain (16 per cent). The only countries where religious observance is lower than in Protestant

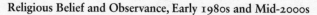

Religious Belief and Observance, Early 1980s and Mid-2000s

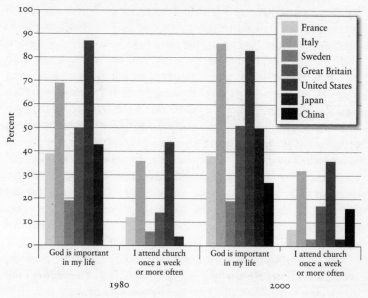

Europe are Russia and Japan. God is 'very important' for just one in ten German and Dutch people; the French proportion is only slightly higher. By comparison, 58 per cent of Americans say He is very important in their lives. The importance of God is higher still in Latin America and sub-Saharan Africa, and highest of all in the Muslim countries of the Middle East. Only in China is God important to fewer people (less than 5 per cent) than in Europe. Just under a third of Americans regard politicians who do not believe in God as unfit for public office, compared with 4 per cent of Norwegians and Swedes, 9 per cent of Finns, 11 per cent of Germans and Spaniards and 12 per cent of Italians. Fully half of Indians and Brazilians would not tolerate an atheist politician.[23] Only in Japan does religious faith matter less in politics than in Western Europe.

The case of Britain is especially interesting in view of the determination with which Britons sought to spread their own religious faith in the nineteenth century. Today, according to the *World Values Survey*, 17 per cent of Britons claim they attend a religious service at least once a week – higher than in continental Europe, but still less than half the American figure. Fewer than a quarter of Britons say God is very important in their lives, again less than half the American figure. True, the UK figures are up slightly since 1981 (when only 14 per cent said they attended church once a week, and under a fifth said God was important to them). But the surveys do not distinguish between religions, so they almost certainly understate the decline of British Christianity. A 2004 study suggested that, in an average week, more Muslims attend a mosque than Anglicans go to church. And nearly all of the recent increase in church attendance is explained by the growth of non-white congregations, especially in Evangelical and Pentecostal churches. When Christian Research conducted a census of 18,720 churches on Sunday 8 May 2005, the real rate of attendance was just 6.3 per cent of the population, down 15 per cent since 1998. On closer inspection, Britain seems to exemplify the collapse both of observance and of faith in Western Europe.

The de-Christianization of Britain is a relatively recent phenomenon. In his *Short History of England* (1917), G. K. Chesterton took it as almost self-evident that Christianity was synonymous with civilization:

> If anyone wishes to know what we mean when we say that Christendom was and is one culture, or one civilization, there is a rough but plain way of putting it. It is by asking what is the most common ... of all the uses of the word 'Christian' ... It has long had one meaning in casual speech among common people, and it means a culture or a civilization. Ben Gunn on Treasure Island did not actually say to Jim Hawkins, 'I feel myself out of touch with a certain type of civilization'; but he did say, 'I haven't tasted Christian food.'[24]

British Protestants were in truth never especially observant (compared, for example, with Irish Catholics) but until the late 1950s Church membership, if not attendance, was relatively high and steady. Even in 1960 just under a fifth of the population of the United Kingdom were Church members. But by 2000 the fraction was down to a tenth.[25] Prior to 1960, most marriages in England and Wales were solemnized in a church; then the slide began, down to around 40 per cent in the late 1990s. For most of the first half of the twentieth century, Anglican Easter Day communicants accounted for around 5 or 6 per cent of the population of England; it was only after 1960 that the proportion slumped to 2 per cent. Figures for the Church of Scotland show a similar trend: steady until 1960, then falling by roughly half. Especially striking is the decline in confirmations. There were 227,135 confirmations in England in 1910; in 2007 there were just 27,900 – and that was 16 per cent fewer than just five years previously. Between 1960 and 1979 the confirmation rate among twelve- to twenty-year-olds fell by more than half, and it continued to plummet thereafter. Fewer than a fifth of those baptized are now confirmed.[26] For the Church of Scotland the decline has been even more precipitous.[27] No one in London or Edinburgh today would use the word 'Christian' in Ben Gunn's sense.

These trends seem certain to continue. Practising Christians are ageing: 38 per cent of Methodists and members of the United Reformed Church were sixty-five or over in 1999, for example, compared with 16 per cent of the population as a whole.[28] Younger Britons are markedly less likely to believe in God or heaven.[29] By some measures, Britain is already one of the most godless societies in the world, with 56 per cent of people never attending church at all – the highest rate in Western Europe.[30] The 2000 'Soul of Britain' survey conducted for Michael Buerk's television series revealed an astounding degree of religious atrophy. Only 9 per cent of those surveyed thought the Christian faith was the best path to God; 32 per cent considered all religions equally valid. Although only 8 per cent identified themselves as atheists, 12 per cent confessed they did not know what to believe. More than two-thirds of respondents said they recognized no clearly defined moral guidelines, and fully 85 per cent of those aged under twenty-four. (Bizarrely, 45 per cent of those surveyed said that this decline in religion had made the country a worse place.)

Some of the finest British writers of the twentieth century anticipated Britain's crisis of faith. The Oxford don C. S. Lewis (best known today for his allegorical children's stories) wrote *The Screwtape Letters* (1942) in the hope that mocking the Devil might keep him at bay. Evelyn Waugh knew, as he wrote his wartime *Sword of Honour* trilogy (1952–61), that he was writing the epitaph of an ancient form of English Roman Catholicism. Both sensed that the Second World War posed a grave threat to Christian faith. Yet it was not until the 1960s that their premonitions of secularization came true. Why, then, did the British lose their historic faith? Like so many difficult questions, this seems at first sight to have an easy answer. But before we can simply blame it, as the poet Philip Larkin did, on 'The Sixties' – the Beatles, the contraceptive pill and the mini-skirt – we need to remind ourselves that the United States enjoyed all these earthly delights too, without ceasing to be a Christian country. Ask many Europeans today, and they will say that religious faith is just an anachronism, a vestige of medieval superstition. They will roll their eyes at the religious zeal of the American Bible Belt – not realizing that it is their own lack of faith that is the real anomaly.

Who killed Christianity in Europe, if not John Lennon?[31] Was it, as Weber himself predicted, that the spirit of capitalism was bound to destroy its Protestant ethic parent, as materialism corrupted the original asceticism of the godly (the 'secularization hypothesis')?[32] This was quite close to the view of the novelist and (in old age) holy man Leo Tolstoy, who saw a fundamental contradiction between Christ's teachings and 'those habitual conditions of life which we call civilization, culture, art, and science'.[33] If so, what part of economic development was specifically hostile to religious belief? Was it the changing role of women and the decline of the nuclear family – which also seems to explain the collapse in family size and the demographic decline of the West? Was it scientific knowledge – what Weber called 'the demystification of the world', in particular Darwin's theory of evolution, which overthrew the biblical story of divine creation? Was it improving life expectancy, which made the hereafter a much less alarmingly proximate destination? Was it the welfare state, a secular shepherd keeping watch over us from the cradle to the grave? Or could it be that European Christianity was killed by the chronic self-obsession of modern culture? Was the murderer of Europe's Protestant work ethic none other than Sigmund Freud?

In *The Future of an Illusion* (1928) Freud, the Moravian-born founding father of psychoanalysis, set out to refute Weber. For

Freud, a lapsed Jew, religion could not be the driving force behind the achievements of Western civilization because it was essentially an 'illusion', a 'universal neurosis' devised to prevent people from giving way to their basic instincts – in particular, their sexual desires and violent, destructive impulses. Without religion, there would be mayhem:

> If one imagined its prohibitions removed, then one could choose any woman who took one's fancy as one's sexual object, one could kill without hesitation one's rival or whoever interfered with one in any other way, and one could seize what one wanted of another man's goods without asking his leave.[34]

Religion not only prohibited rampant sexual promiscuity and violence. It also reconciled men to 'the cruelty of fate, particularly as shown in death' and the 'sufferings and privations' of daily life.[35] When the monotheistic religions fused the gods into a single person, 'man's relations to him could recover the intimacy and intensity of the child's relation to the father. If one had done so much for the father, then surely one would be rewarded – at least the only beloved child, the chosen people, would be.'[36]

Freud had little hope that mankind could wholly emancipate itself from religion, least of all in Europe. As he put it:

> If you want to expel religion from our European civilization, you can only do it by means of another system of doctrines; and such a system would from the outset take over all the psychological characteristics of religion – the same sanctity, rigidity and intolerance, the same prohibition of thought – for its own defence.[37]

That certainly seemed plausible in the 1930s, when both Stalin and Hitler propagated their own monstrous cults. Yet in both cases the totalitarian political religions failed to rein in the primal instincts described in Freud's theory of religion. By 1945 Europe lay exhausted from an orgy of violence – including shocking sexual violence in the form of mass rape – unlike anything seen since the time of Timur. The initial response in many countries, particularly those (like the Soviet Union) most traumatized by mass murder, was to revert to real religion, and to use its time-honoured comforts to mourn the dead.

By the 1960s, however, a generation too young to remember the years of total war and genocide sought a new post-Christian outlet for their repressed desires. Freud's own theories, with their negative view of repression and their explicit sympathy with the erotic impulse, surely played a part in tempting Europeans to exit the churches and enter the sex shops. In *Civilization and its Discontents* (1929–30, but first published in the United States only in 1961), Freud had argued that there was a fundamental 'antithesis' between civilization as it then existed and man's most primal urges:

> The existence of this inclination to aggression, which we can detect in ourselves and justly assume to be present in others, is the factor which disturbs our relations with our neighbour and which forces civilization into such a high expenditure [of energy]. In consequence of this primary mutual hostility of human beings, civilized society is perpetually threatened with disintegration. The interest of work in common would not hold it together; instinctual passions are stronger than reasonable interests. Civilization has to use its utmost efforts in order to set limits to man's aggressive instincts and to hold the manifestations of them in check by psychical reaction-formations. Hence . . . the restriction upon sexual life, and hence too the . . . commandment to love one's neighbour as oneself – a commandment which is really justified by the fact that nothing else runs so strongly counter to the original nature of man . . . Civilization is a process in the service of Eros, whose purpose is to combine single human individuals, and after that families, then races, peoples and nations, into one great unity, the unity of mankind. Why this has to happen, we do not know; the work of Eros is precisely this . . . Men are to be libidinally bound to one another . . . But man's natural aggressive instinct, the hostility of each against all and of all against each, opposes this programme of civilization. This aggressive instinct is the derivative and the main representative of the death instinct which we have found alongside of Eros and which shares world-dominion with it. And now, I think, the meaning of the evolution of civilization is no longer obscure to us. It must present the struggle between Eros and Death, between the instinct of life and the instinct of destruction, as it works itself out in the human species. This struggle is what all life essentially consists of.[38]

Reading this, one sees what the Viennese satirist Karl Kraus meant when he said that psychoanalysis was 'the disease of which it pretends to be the cure'.[39] But this was the message interpreted by the hippies as a new commandment: let it all hang out. And so they did. The Hombres' 'Let It All Hang Out' (1967) was one of the lesser anthems of the 1960s, but its opening lines – 'A preachment, dear friends, you are about to receive / On John Barleycorn, nicotine, and the temptations of Eve' – summed up nicely what was now on offer.* For the West's most compelling critics today (not least radical Islamists), the Sixties opened the door to a post-Freudian anti-civilization, characterized by a hedonistic celebration of the pleasures of the self, a rejection of theology in favour of pornography and a renunciation of the Prince of Peace for grotesquely violent films and video games that are best characterized as 'warnography'.

The trouble with all the theories about the death of Protestantism in Europe is that, whatever they may explain about Europe's de-Christianization, they explain nothing whatsoever about America's continued Christian faith. Americans have experienced more or less the same social and cultural changes as Europeans. They have become richer. Their knowledge of science has increased. And they are even more exposed to psychoanalysis and pornography than Europeans. But Protestantism in America has suffered nothing like the decline it has experienced in Europe. On the contrary, God is in some ways as big in America today as He was forty years ago.[40] The best evidence is provided by the tens of millions of worshippers who flock to American churches every Sunday.

Paradoxically, the advent of the new 1960s trinity of sex, drugs and rock 'n' roll coincided, in the United States, with a boom in Evangelical Protestantism. The Reverend Billy Graham vied with the Beatles to see who could pack more young people into a stadium. This was not so much a reaction, more a kind of imitation. Speaking at the Miami Rock Festival in 1969, Graham urged the audience to 'tune

* The song was later covered by the British singer, record producer and convicted paedophile Jonathan King (Charterhouse and Trinity, Cambridge), also noteworthy for having produced 'Leap Up and Down (Wave your Knickers in the Air)' and the original cast album of *The Rocky Horror Show*.

into God ... Turn on to His power.'[41] In 1972 the college Christian group Campus Crusade organized an Evangelical conference in Dallas called Explo '72 that ended with a concert intended to be the Christian Woodstock (the 1969 rock festival that came to encapsulate the hippy counter-culture).* When Cynthia 'Plaster Caster', a Catholic teenager from Chicago, made plaster casts of the erect penises of Jimi Hendrix, Robert Plant and Keith Richards (though most definitely not of Cliff Richard's), she was merely fulfilling Freud's vision of the triumph of Eros over Thanatos. God was love, as the bumper stickers said, after all. At one and the same time, America was both born again and porn again.

How can we explain the fact that Western civilization seems to have divided in two: to the east a godless Europe, to the west a God-fearing America? How do we explain the persistence of Christianity in America at a time of its steep decline in Europe? The best answer can be found in Springfield, Missouri, the town they call the 'Queen of the Ozarks' and the birthplace of the inter-war highway between Chicago and California, immortalized in Bobby Troup's 1946 song, '(Get Your Kicks on) Route 66'. If Max Weber was impressed by the diversity of Protestant sects when he passed through here a century ago, he would be astonished today. Springfield has roughly one church for every thousand citizens. There are 122 Baptist churches, thirty-six Methodist chapels, twenty-five Churches of Christ and fifteen Churches of God – in all, some 400 Christian places of worship. Now it's not your kicks you get on Route 66; it's your crucifix.

The significant thing is that all these churches are involved in a fierce competition for souls. As Weber saw it, individual American Baptists, Methodists and others competed within their local religious communities to show one another who among them was truly godly. But in Springfield today the competition is *between* churches, and it is just as fierce as the competition between car-dealerships or fast-food joints. Churches here have to be commercially minded in order to attract and retain worshippers and, on that basis, the clear winner is the James River Assembly. To European eyes, it may look more like a shopping mall or

---

* Even at the real Woodstock, the Who had premiered parts of *Tommy*, Pete Townsend's rock opera about a deaf, dumb and blind messiah.

business park, but it is in fact the biggest church in Springfield – indeed, one of the biggest in the entire United States. Its pastor, John Lindell, is a gifted and charismatic preacher who combines old-time scriptural teaching with the kind of stagecraft more often associated with rock 'n' roll. Indeed, at times he seems like the natural heir of the Jesus Revolution identified by *Time* magazine in 1971, a rock-inspired Christian youth movement in the spirit of the British rock opera *Jesus Christ Superstar* (1970). Yet there is also a lean and hungry quality to Lindell; as he makes his pitch for God ('God, You are so awesome') he seems less like Ian Gillan (the shaggy Deep Purple singer who sang the part of Jesus on the original *Superstar* album) and more like Steve Jobs, unveiling the latest handheld device from Apple: iGod, maybe. For Lindell, the Protestant ethic is alive and well and living in Springfield. He has no doubt that their faith makes the members of his congregation harder working than they would otherwise be. He himself is quite a worker: three hyperkinetic services in one Sunday is no light preaching load. And the Holy Ghost seems to fuse with the spirit of capitalism as the collection buckets go around – though thankfully not in the brazen manner favoured by Mac Hammond of the Living Word Christian Centre in Minneapolis, who promises 'Bible principles that will enhance your spiritual growth and help you to win at work, win in relationships, and win in the financial arena'.[42]

A visit to James River makes obvious the main difference between European and American Protestantism. Whereas the Reformation was nationalized in Europe, with the creation of established Churches like the Church of England or Scotland's Kirk, in the United States there was always a strict separation between religion and the state, allowing an open competition between multiple Protestant sects. And this may be the best explanation for the strange death of religion in Europe and its enduring vigour in the United States. In religion as in business, state monopolies are inefficient – even if in some cases the existence of a state religion increases religious participation (where there is a generous subsidy from government and minimal control of clerical appointments).[43] More commonly, competition between sects in a free religious market encourages innovations designed to make the experience of worship and Church membership more fulfilling. It is this that has kept religion alive in America.[44] (The insight is not entirely novel. Adam Smith made a similar argument in *The Wealth of Nations*, contrasting countries with established Churches with those allowing competition.)[45]

Yet there is something about today's American Evangelicals that would have struck Weber, if not Smith, as suspect. For there is a sense in which many of the most successful sects today flourish precisely because they have developed a kind of consumer Christianity that verges on Wal-Mart worship.[46] It is not only easy to drive to and entertaining to watch – not unlike a trip to the multiplex cinema, with soft drinks or Starbucks served on the premises. It also makes remarkably few demands on believers. On the contrary, they get to make demands on God,[47] so that prayer at James River often consists of an extended series of requests for the deity to solve personal problems. God the Father, the Son and the Holy Ghost has been displaced by God the Analyst, the Agony Uncle and the Personal Trainer. With more than two-fifths of white Americans changing religion at some point in their lives, faith has become paradoxically fickle.[48]

The only problem with turning religion into just another leisure pursuit is that it means Americans have drifted a very long way from Max Weber's version of the Protestant ethic, in which deferred gratification was the corollary of capital accumulation. In his words:

> Protestant asceticism works with all its force against the uninhibited enjoyment of possessions; it discourages consumption ... And if that restraint on consumption is combined with the freedom to strive for profit, the result produced will inevitably be the creation of capital through the ascetic compulsion to save.[49]

By contrast, we have just lived through an experiment: capitalism without saving. In the United States the household savings rate fell below zero at the height of the housing bubble, as families not only consumed their entire disposable income but also drew down the equity in their homes. The decline of thrift turned out to be a recipe for financial crisis. When house prices began to decline in 2006, a chain reaction began: those who had borrowed more than the value of their homes stopped paying their mortgage interest; those who had invested in securities backed by mortgages suffered large losses; banks that had borrowed large sums to invest in such securities suffered first illiquidity and then insolvency; to avert massive bank failures governments stepped in with bailouts; and a crisis of private debt mutated into a crisis of public debt. Today the total private and public debt burden in the United States is more than three and a half times the size of gross domestic product.[50]

This was not a uniquely American phenomenon. Variations on the same theme were played in other English-speaking countries: Ireland, the United Kingdom and, to a lesser extent, Australia and Canada – this was the fractal geometry of the age of leverage, with the same-shaped problem recurring in a wide range of sizes. There were bigger real-estate bubbles in most European countries – in the sense that house prices rose further relative to income than in the United States – and much more severe crises of public debt in Portugal, Ireland and Greece, which made the mistake of running very large deficits while in a monetary union with Germany. But the financial crisis of 2007–9, though global in its effects, was not global in its origins. It was a crisis made in the Western world as a result of over-consumption and excess financial leverage. Elsewhere – and especially in Asia – the picture was quite different.

It is generally recognized that savings rates are much higher in the East than in the West. Private debt burdens are much lower; houses are often bought outright or with relatively small mortgages. Other forms of consumer credit play a much smaller role. It is also well known, as we have seen, that Asians work many more hours per year than their Western counterparts – average annual hours worked range from 2,120 in Taiwan to 2,243 in South Korea. What is less appreciated is that the rise of thrift and industry in Asia has gone hand in hand with one of the most surprising side-effects of Westernization: the growth of Christianity, above all in China.

THE CHINESE JERUSALEM

The rise of the spirit of capitalism in China is a story everyone knows. But what about the rise of the Protestant ethic? According to separate surveys by China Partner and East China Normal University in Shanghai, there are now around 40 million Protestant Christians in China, compared with barely half a million in 1949. Some estimates put the maximum even higher, at 75 or 110 million.[51] Include 20 million Catholics, and there could be as many as 130 million Christians in China. Today, indeed, there may already be more practising Christians in China than in Europe.[52] Churches are being built at a faster rate in China than anywhere else in the world. And more Bibles are being printed here than in any other country. The Nanjing Amity Printing Company is the biggest Bible manufacturer in the world. Its vast printworks has produced more than 70 million Bibles since the company was founded in 1986, including 50 million copies in Mandarin and other Chinese languages.[53] It is possible that, within three decades, Christians will constitute between 20 and 30 per cent of China's population.[54] This should strike us as all the more remarkable when we reflect on how much resistance there has been to the spread of Christianity throughout Chinese history.

The failure of Protestantism to take root in China earlier is something of a puzzle. There were Nestorian Christian missionaries in Tang China as early as the seventh century. The first Roman Catholic church was built in 1299 by Giovanni da Montecorvino, appointed archbishop of Khanbalik in 1307. By the end of the fourteenth century, however, these Christian outposts had largely disappeared as a result of Ming hostility. A second wave of missionaries came in the early seventeenth century, when the Jesuit Matteo Ricci was granted permission to settle in Beijing. There may have been as many as 300,000 Christians in China by the 1700s. Yet 1724 brought another crackdown with the Yongzheng Emperor's Edict of Expulsion and Confiscation.[55]

The third Christian wave were the Protestant missions of the nineteenth century. Organizations like the British Missionary Societies sent literally hundreds of evangelists to bring the Good News to the most populous country on earth. The first to arrive was a twenty-five-year-old Englishman named Robert Morrison of the London Missionary Society, who reached Canton (Guangzhou) in 1807. His first step, even before arriving, was to start learning Mandarin and to transcribe the Bible into Chinese characters. Once in Canton, he set to work on a Latin–Chinese dictionary. By 1814, now in the employment of the East India Company, Morrison had completed translations of the Acts of the Apostles (1810), the Gospel of St Luke (1811), the New Testament (1812) and the Book of Genesis (1814), as well as *A Summary of the Doctrine of Divine Redemption* (1811) and *An Annotated Catechism in the Teaching of Christ* (1812). This was enough to persuade the East India Company to permit the import of a printing press and a mechanic to operate it.[56] When the Company later dismissed him, for fear of incurring the wrath of the Chinese authorities, Morrison pressed on undaunted, moving to Malacca to set up an Anglo-Chinese College for the 'cultivation of European and Chinese literature and science, but chiefly for the diffusion of Christianity through the Eastern Archipelago', finishing his translation of the Bible, a joint effort with William Milne (published in 1823), and producing an English grammar for Chinese students as well as a complete English–Chinese dictionary. By the time Morrison followed his first wife and son to the grave in Canton in 1834 he had added a *Vocabulary of the Canton Dialect* (1828). Here truly was the Protestant word ethic made flesh.

Yet the efforts of the first British missionaries had unintended consequences. The imperial government had sought to prohibit – on pain of death – Christian proselytizing on the ground that it encouraged popular attitudes 'very near to bring [*sic*] a rebellion':

> The said religion neither holds spirits in veneration, nor ancestors in reverence, clearly this is to walk contrary to sound doctrine; and the common people, who follow and familiarize themselves with such delusions, in what respect do they differ from a rebel mob?[57]

This was prescient. One man in particular responded to Christian proselytizing in the most extreme way imaginable. Hong Xiuquan had hoped to take the traditional path to a career in the imperial civil service, sitting one of the succession of gruelling examinations that determined a man's fitness for the mandarinate. But he flunked it, and, as so often with exam candidates, failure was followed in short order by complete collapse. In 1833 Hong met William Milne, the co-author with Robert Morrison of the first Chinese Bible, whose influence on him coincided with his emergence from post-exam depression. Doubtless to Milne's alarm, Hong now announced that he was the younger brother of Jesus Christ. God, he declared, had sent him to rid

China of Confucianism – that inward-looking philosophy which saw competition, trade and industriousness as pernicious foreign imports. Hong created a quasi-Christian Society of God Worshippers, which attracted the support of tens of millions of Chinese, mostly from the poorer classes, and proclaimed himself leader of the Heavenly Kingdom of Great Peace. In Chinese he was known as Taiping Tianguo, hence the name of the uprising he led – the Taiping Rebellion. From Guangxi, the rebels swept to Nanjing, which the self-styled Heavenly King made his capital. By 1853 his followers – who were distinguished by their red jackets, long hair and insistence on strict segregation of the sexes – controlled the entire Yangzi valley. In the throne room there was a banner bearing the words: 'The order came from God to kill the enemy and to unite all the mountains and rivers into one kingdom.'

For a time it seemed that the Taiping would indeed overthrow the Qing Empire altogether. But the rebels could not take Beijing or Shanghai. Slowly the tide turned against them. In 1864 the Qing army besieged Nanjing. By the time the city fell, Hong was already dead from food poisoning. Just to make sure, the Qing exhumed his cremated remains and fired them out of a cannon. Even after that, it was not until 1871 that the last Taiping army was defeated. The cost in human life was staggering: more than twice that of the First World War to all combatant states. Between 1850 and 1864 an estimated 20 million people in central and southern China lost their lives as the rebellion raged, unleashing famine and pestilence in its wake. By the end of the nineteenth century, many Chinese had concluded that Western missionaries were just another disruptive alien influence on their country, like opium-trading Western merchants. When British missionaries returned to China after the Taiping Rebellion they thus encountered an intensified hostility to foreigners.[58]

It did not deter them. James Hudson Taylor was twenty-two when he made his first trip to China on behalf of the Chinese Evangelization Society. Unable, as he put it, 'to bear the sight of a congregation of a thousand or more Christian people rejoicing in their own security [in Brighton] while millions were perishing for lack of knowledge' overseas, Taylor founded the China Inland Mission in 1865. His preferred strategy was for CIM missionaries to dress in Chinese clothing

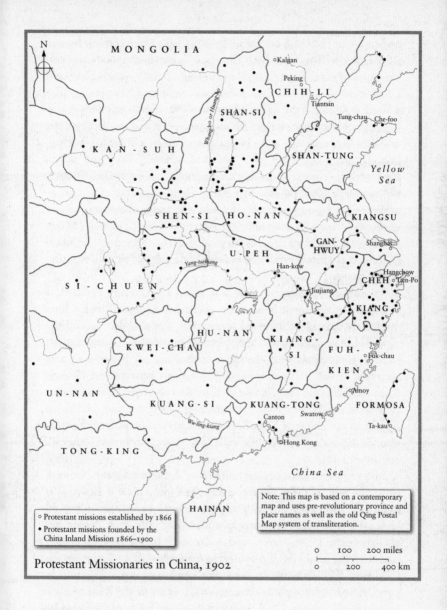

N

MONGOLIA

○Kalgan

Peking
Tiantsin

CHIH-LI

Tung-chau ○Che-foo

SHAN-SI

KAN-SUH

Whang-ho or Huang-ho

SHAN-TUNG

*Yellow
Sea*

SHEN-SI   HO-NAN

KIANGSU

GAN-
HWUY   Shanghai

U-PEH

Han-kow

Yang-tse-kiang

Jiujiang

CHEH   Hangchow
Ning-Po

SI-CHUEN

KIANG

HU-NAN   KIANG-
SI   FUH-

KWEI-CHAU   KIEN

UN-NAN   Fuh-chau

KUANG-SI   KUANG-TONG   Amoy

Canton   Swatow   FORMOSA

Wu-ling-kiang   Ta-kau

○Hong Kong

TONG-KING

China Sea

HAINAN

Note: This map is based on a contemporary
map and uses pre-revolutionary province and
place names as well as the old Qing Postal
Map system of transliteration.

○ Protestant missions established by 1866
• Protestant missions founded by the
  China Inland Mission 1866–1900

0   100   200 miles

0   200   400 km

Protestant Missionaries in China, 1902

and to adopt the Qing-era queue (pigtail). Like David Livingstone in Africa, Taylor dispensed both Christian doctrine and modern medicine at his Hangzhou (Hangchow) headquarters.[59] Another intrepid CIM fisher of men was George Stott, a one-legged Aberdonian who arrived in China at the age of thirty-one. One of his early moves was to open a bookshop with an adjoining chapel where he harangued a noisy throng, attracted more by curiosity than by a thirst for redemption. His wife opened a girls' boarding school.[60] They and others sought to win converts by using an ingenious new evangelical gadget: the Wordless Book, devised by Charles Haddon Spurgeon to incorporate the key colours of traditional Chinese colour cosmology. In one widely used version, devised by the American Dwight Lyman Moody in 1875, the black page represented sin, the red represented the blood of Jesus, the white represented holiness, and the gold or yellow represented heaven.[61]

An altogether different tack was taken by Timothy Richard, a member of the Baptist Missionary Society, who argued that 'China needed the gospel of love and forgiveness, but she also needed the gospel of material progress and scientific knowledge.'[62] Targeting the Chinese elites rather than the impoverished masses, Richard became secretary of the Society for the Diffusion of Christian and General Knowledge among the Chinese in 1891 and was an important influence on Kang Yu Wei's Self-Strengthening Movement, as well as an adviser to the Emperor himself. It was Richard who secured the creation of China's first Western-style university, at Shanxi (Shansi), opened in 1902.

By 1877 there were eighteen different Christian missions active in China as well as three Bible societies. The idiosyncratic Taylor was especially successful at recruiting new missionaries, including an unusually large number of single women, not only from Britain but also from the United States and Australia.[63] In the best Protestant tradition, the rival missions competed furiously with one another, the CIM and BMS waging an especially fierce turf war in Shanxi. In 1900, however, xenophobia erupted once again in the Boxer Rebellion, as another bizarre cult, the Righteous and Harmonious Fist (*yihe quan*), sought to drive all 'foreign devils' from the land – this time with the explicit approval of the Empress Dowager. Before the intervention of a multinational force and the suppression of the Boxers, fifty-eight CIM missionaries perished, along with twenty-one of their children.

The missionaries had planted many seeds but, in the increasingly chaotic conditions that followed the eventual overthrow of the Qing dynasty, these sprouted only to wither. The founder of the first Chinese Republic, Sun Yat-sen, was a Christian from Guandong, but he died in 1924 with China on the brink of civil war. Then the nationalist leader Chiang Kai-shek and his wife – both Christians* – lost out to the communists in China's long civil war and ended up having to flee to Taiwan. Shortly after the 1949 Revolution, Zhou Enlai and Y. T. Wu drew up a 'Christian Manifesto' designed to undercut the position of missionaries on the grounds of both ideology and patriotism.[64] Between 1950 and 1952 the CIM opted to evacuate its personnel from the People's Republic.[65] With the missionaries gone, most churches were closed down or turned into factories. They remained closed for the next thirty years. Christians like Wang Mingdao, Allen Yuan and Moses Xie, who refused to join the Party-controlled Protestant Three-Self Patriotic Movement, were jailed (in each case for twenty or more years).[66] The calamitous years of the misnamed Great Leap Forward (1958–62) – in reality a man-made famine that claimed around 45 million lives[67] – saw a fresh wave of church closures. There was full-blown iconoclasm during the Cultural Revolution (1966–76), which also led to the destruction of many ancient Buddhist temples. Mao himself, 'the Messiah of the Working People', became the object of a personality cult even more demented than those of Hitler and Stalin.[68] His leftist wife Jiang Qing declared that Christianity in China had been consigned to the museum.[69]

To Max Weber and many later twentieth-century Western experts, then, it is not surprising that the probability of a Protestantization of China and, therefore, of its industrialization seemed negligibly low – almost as low as a de-Christianization of Europe. The choice for China seemed to be a stark one between Confucian stasis and chaos.

---

* Chiang had converted to Christianity in 1930. His wife was one of the daughters of the Methodist millionaire Charlie Soong. I have used the more familiar Wade-Giles form of his name and also of Sun Yat-sen's (pinyin: Jiang Jeshi and Sūn Yixiān).

That makes the immense changes of our own time all the more breath-taking.

The city of Wenzhou, in Zhejiang province, south of Shanghai, is the quintessential manufacturing town. With a population of 8 million people and growing, it has the reputation of being the most entrepreneurial city in China – a place where the free market rules and the role of the state is minimal. The landscape of textile mills and heaps of coal would have been instantly recognizable to a Victorian; it is an Asian Manchester. The work ethic animates everyone from the wealthiest entrepreneur to the lowliest factory hand. Wenzhou people not only work longer hours than Americans; they also save a far larger proportion of their income. Between 2001 and 2007, at a time when American savings collapsed, the Chinese savings rate rose above 40 per cent of gross national income. On average, Chinese households save more than a fifth of the money they make; corporations save even more in the form of retained earnings.

The truly fascinating thing, however, is that people in Wenzhou have imported more than just the work ethic from the West. They have imported Protestantism too. For the seeds the British missionaries planted here 150 years ago have belatedly sprouted in the most extraordinary fashion. Whereas before the Cultural Revolution there were 480 churches in the city, today there are 1,339 – and those are only the ones approved by the government. The church George Stott built a hundred years ago is now packed every Sunday. Another, established by the Inland Mission in 1877 but closed during the Cultural Revolution and only reopened in 1982, now has a congregation of 1,200. There are new churches, too, often with bright red neon crosses on their roofs. Small wonder they call Wenzhou the Chinese Jerusalem. Already in 2002 around 14 per cent of Wenzhou's population were Christians; the proportion today is surely higher. And this is the city that Mao proclaimed 'religion free' back in 1958. As recently as 1997, officials here launched a campaign to 'remove the crosses'. Now they seem to have given up. In the countryside around Wenzhou, villages openly compete to see whose church has the highest spire.

Christianity in China today is far from being the opium of the masses.[70] Among Wenzhou's most devout believers are the so-called Boss Christians, entrepreneurs like Hanping Zhang, chairman of Aihao (the Chinese character for which can mean 'love', 'goodness' or 'hobby'), one of the three biggest pen-manufacturers in the world. A devout Christian, Zhang is the living embodiment of the link between the spirit of capitalism and the Protestant ethic, precisely as Max Weber understood it. Once a farmer, he started a plastics business in 1979 and eight years later opened his first pen factory. Today he employs around 5,000 workers who produce up to 500 million pens a year. In his eyes, Christianity is thriving in China because it offers an ethical framework to people struggling to cope with a startlingly fast social transition from communism to capitalism. Trust is in short supply in today's China, he told me. Government officials are often corrupt. Business counterparties cheat. Workers steal from their employers. Young women marry and then vanish with hard-earned dowries. Baby food is knowingly produced with toxic ingredients, school buildings constructed with defective materials. But Zhang feels he can trust his fellow Christians, because he knows they are both hard working and honest.[71] Just as in Protestant Europe and America in the early days of the Industrial Revolution, religious communities double as both credit networks and supply chains of creditworthy, trustworthy fellow believers.

In the past, the Chinese authorities were deeply suspicious of Christianity, and not just because they recalled the chaos caused by the Taiping Rebellion. Seminary students played an important part in the Tiananmen Square pro-democracy movement; indeed, two of the most wanted student leaders back in the summer of 1989 subsequently became Christian clergymen. In the wake of that crisis there was yet another crackdown on unofficial churches.[72] Ironically, the utopianism of Maoism created an appetite that today, with a Party leadership that is more technocratic than messianic, only Christianity seems able to satisfy.[73] And, just as in the time of the Taiping Rebellion, some modern Chinese are inspired by Christianity to embrace decidedly weird cults. Members of the Eastern Lightning movement, which is active in Henan and Heilongjiang provinces, believe that Jesus has returned as a woman. They engage in bloody battles with their arch-rivals, the Three Grades of Servants.[74] Another radical quasi-Christian movement is Peter Xu's Born-Again Movement, also known as the Total Scope Church or the Shouters because of their noisy style of worship, in which weeping is mandatory. Such sects are seen by the authorities as *xiejiao*, or (implicitly evil) cults, like the banned Falun Gong breathing-practice movement.[75] It is not hard to see why the Party prefers to reheat Confucianism, with its emphasis on respect for the older generation and the traditional equilibrium of a 'harmonious society'.[76] Nor is it surprising that persecution of Christians was stepped up during the 2008 Olympics, a time of maximum exposure of the nation's capital to foreign influences.[77]

Even under Mao, however, an official Protestantism was tolerated in the form of the Three-Self Patriotic Movement based on the principles of self-governance, self-support and self-propagation – in other words no foreign influences.[78] Today, St Paul's in Nanjing is typical of official Three-Self churches; here, the Reverend Kan Renping's congregation has grown from a few hundred when he took over in 1994 to some 5,000 regular worshippers. It is so popular that newcomers have to watch the proceedings on closed-circuit television in four nearby satellite chapels. Since the issue of Party Document Number 19 in 1982 there has also been intermittent official tolerance of the 'house churches' movement, congregations that meet more or less secretly in people's homes and often embrace American forms of worship.[79] In Beijing itself, worshippers flock to the Reverend Jin Mingri's Zion Church, an unofficial church with 350 members, nearly all drawn from the entrepreneurial or professional class and nearly all under the age of forty. Christianity has become chic in China. The former Olympic soccer goalkeeper Gao Hong is a Christian. So are the television actress Lu Liping and the pop singer Zheng Jun.[80] Chinese academics like Tang Yi openly speculate that 'the Christian faith may eventually conquer China and Christianize Chinese culture' – though he thinks it more likely either that 'Christianity may eventually be absorbed by Chinese culture, following the example of Buddhism . . . and become a sinless religion of the Chinese genre' or that 'Christianity [will] retain its basic Western characteristics and settle down to be a sub-cultural minority religion.'[81]

After much hesitation, at least some of China's communist leaders now appear to recognize Christianity as one of the West's greatest sources of strength.[82] According to one scholar from the Chinese Academy of the Social Sciences:

> We were asked to look into what accounted for the . . . pre-eminence of the West all over the world . . . At first, we thought it was because you had more powerful guns than we had. Then we thought it was because you had the best political system. Next we focused on your economic system. But in the past twenty years, we have realized that the heart of your culture is your religion: Christianity. That is why the West has been so powerful. The Christian moral foundation of social and cultural life was what made possible the emergence of capitalism and then the successful transition to democratic politics. We don't have any doubt about this.[83]

Another academic, Zhuo Xinping, has identified the 'Christian understanding of transcendence' as having played 'a very decisive role in people's acceptance of pluralism in society and politics in the contemporary West':

> Only by accepting this understanding of transcendence as our criterion can we understand the real meaning of such concepts as freedom, human rights, tolerance, equality, justice, democracy, the rule of law, universality, and environmental protection.[84]

Yuan Zhiming, a Christian film-maker, agrees: 'The most important thing, the core of Western civilization . . . is Christianity.'[85] According to Professor Zhao Xiao, himself a convert, Christianity offers China a new 'common moral foundation' capable of reducing corruption, narrowing the gap between rich and poor, promoting philanthropy and even preventing pollution.[86] 'Economic viability requires a serious moral ethos,' in the words of another scholar, 'more than just hedonistic consumerism and dishonest strategy.'[87] It is even said that, shortly before Jiang Zemin stepped down as China's president and Communist Party leader, he told a gathering of high-ranking Party officials that, if he could issue one decree that he knew would be obeyed everywhere, it would be to 'make Christianity the official religion of China'.[88] In 2007 his successor Hu Jintao held an unprecedented Politburo 'study session' on religion, at which he told China's twenty-five most powerful leaders that 'the knowledge and strength of religious people must be mustered to build a prosperous society'. The XIVth Central Committee of the Chinese Communist Party was presented with a report specifying three requirements for sustainable economic growth: property rights as a foundation, the law as a safeguard and morality as a support.

LANDS OF UNBELIEF

If that sounds familiar, it should. As we have seen, those used to be among the key foundations of Western civilization. Yet in recent years we in the West have seemed to lose our faith in them. Not only are the churches of Europe empty. We also seem to doubt the value of much of what developed in Europe after the Reformation. Capitalist competition has been disgraced by the recent financial crisis and the rampant greed of the bankers. Science is studied by too few of our children at school and university. Private property rights are repeatedly violated by governments that seem to have an insatiable appetite for taxing our incomes and our wealth and wasting a large portion of the proceeds. Empire has become a dirty word, despite the benefits conferred on the rest of the world by the European imperialists. All we risk being left with are a vacuous consumer society and a culture of relativism – a culture that says any theory or opinion, no matter how outlandish, is just as good as whatever it was we used to believe in.

Contrary to popular belief, Chesterton did not say: 'The trouble with atheism is that when men stop believing in God, they don't believe in nothing. They believe in anything.' But he has Father Brown say something very like it in 'The Miracle of Moon Crescent':

> You all swore you were hard-shelled materialists; and as a matter of fact you were all balanced on the very edge of belief – of belief in almost anything. There are thousands balanced on it today; but it's a sharp, uncomfortable edge to sit on. You won't rest until you believe something.[89]

To understand the difference between belief and unbelief, consider the conversation between Muktar Said Ibrahim, one of the Islamists whose plot to detonate bombs in the London transport system was discovered in 2005, and a former neighbour of his in Stanmore, a suburb in the northern outskirts of London. Born in Eritrea, Ibrahim had moved to Britain at the age of fourteen and had just been granted UK citizenship, despite a conviction and prison sentence for his involvement in an armed robbery. 'He asked me', Sarah Scott recalled, 'if I was Catholic because I have Irish family. I said I didn't believe in anything and he said I should. He told me he was going to have all these virgins when he got to Heaven if he praises Allah. He said if you pray to Allah and if you have been loyal to Allah you would get 80 virgins, or something like that.' It is the easiest thing in the world to ridicule the notion, apparently a commonplace among jihadis, that this is the reward for blowing up infidels. But is it significantly stranger to believe, like Sarah Scott, in nothing at all? Her recollected conversation with Ibrahim is fascinating precisely because it illuminates the gulf that now exists in Western Europe between a minority of fanatics and a majority of atheists. 'He said', Scott recalled after her former neighbour's arrest, 'people were afraid of religion and people should not be afraid.'[90]

What Chesterton feared was that, if Christianity declined in Britain, 'superstition' would 'drown all your old rationalism and scepticism'. From aromatherapy to Zen and the Art of Motorcycle Maintenance, the West today is indeed awash with post-modern cults, none of which offers anything remotely as economically invigorating or socially cohesive as the old Protestant ethic. Worse, this spiritual vacuum leaves West European societies vulnerable to the sinister ambitions of a minority of people who do have religious faith – as well as the political ambition to expand the power and influence of that faith in their adopted countries. That the struggle between radical Islam and Western civilization can be caricatured as 'Jihad vs McWorld' speaks volumes.[91] In reality, the core values of Western civilization are directly threatened by the brand of Islam espoused by terrorists like Muktar Said Ibrahim, derived as it is from the teachings of the nineteenth-century Wahhabist Sayyid Jamal al-Din and the Muslim Brotherhood leaders Hassan al-Banna and Sayyid Qutb.[92] The separation of church and state, the scientific method, the rule of law and the very idea of a free society – including relatively recent

Western principles like the equality of the sexes and the legality of homosexual acts – all these things are openly repudiated by the Islamists.

Estimates of the Muslim population of West European countries vary widely. According to one, the total population has risen from around 10 million in 1990 to 17 million in 2010.[93] As a share of national populations, Muslim communities range in size from as much as 9.8 per cent in France to as little as 0.2 per cent in Portugal.[94] Such figures seem to belie the warnings of some scholars of a future 'Eurabia' – a continent Islamicized by the end of the twenty-first century. However, if the Muslim population of the UK were to continue growing at an annual rate of 6.7 per cent (as it did between 2004 and 2008), its share of the total UK population would rise from just under 4 per cent in 2008 to 8 per cent in 2020, to 15 per cent in 2030 and to 28 per cent in 2040, finally passing 50 per cent in 2050.[95]

Mass immigration is not necessarily the solvent of a civilization, if the migrants embrace, and are encouraged to embrace, the values of the civilization to which they are moving. But in cases where immigrant communities are not successfully assimilated and then become prey to radical ideologues, the consequences can be profoundly destabilizing.[96] The crucial thing is not sheer numbers so much as the extent to which some Muslim communities have been penetrated by Islamist organizations like the Arab Muslim Brotherhood, the Pakistani Jama'at-i Islami, the Saudi-financed Muslim World League and the World Assembly of Muslim Youth. In Britain, to take perhaps the most troubling example, there is an active Muslim Brotherhood offshoot called the Muslim Association of Britain, two Jama'at-i Islami spin-offs, the Islamic Society of Britain and its youth wing, Young Muslims UK, as well as an organization called Hizb ut-Tahrir ('Party of Liberation'). Hizb ut-Tahrir openly proclaims its intention to make 'Britain ... an Islamic state by the year 2020!'[97] Also known to be active in recruiting terrorists are al-Qaeda and the equally dangerous Harakat ul-Mujahideen. Such infiltration is by no means unique to the UK.*

* Comparable organizations in the United States include the Islamic Society of North America (ISNA), the Council on American-Islamic Relations (CAIR) and the Muslim American Society (MAS). There are also American branches of the Muslim World League and the World Assembly of Muslim Youth.

The case of Shehzad Tanweer illustrates how insidious the process of radicalization is. Tanweer was one of the suicide bombers who wreaked havoc in London on 7 July 2005, detonating a bomb aboard a Circle Line Underground train between Aldgate and Liverpool Street that killed himself and six other passengers. Born in Yorkshire in 1983, Tanweer was not poor; his father, an immigrant from Pakistan, had built up a successful takeaway food business, selling fish and chips and driving a Mercedes. He was not uneducated, in so far as a degree in sports science from Leeds Metropolitan University counts as education. His case suggests that no amount of economic, educational and recreational opportunity can prevent the son of a Muslim immigrant from being converted into a fanatic and a terrorist if the wrong people get to him. In this regard, a crucial role is being played at universities and elsewhere by Islamic 'centres', some of which are little more than recruiting agencies for jihad. Often, such centres act as gateways to training camps in countries like Pakistan, where the new recruits from *bilad al-kufr* (the lands of unbelief) are sent for more practical forms of indoctrination. Between 1999 and 2009 a total of 119 individuals were found guilty of Islamism-related terrorist offences in the UK, more than two-thirds of them British nationals. Just under a third had attended an institute of higher education, and about the same proportion had attended a terrorist training camp.[98] It has been as much through luck as through effective counter-terrorism that other attacks by British-based jihadis have been thwarted, notably the plot in August 2006 by a group of young British Muslims to detonate home-made bombs aboard multiple transatlantic planes, and the attempt by a Nigerian-born graduate of University College London to detonate plastic explosive concealed in his underwear as his flight from Amsterdam was nearing Detroit airport on Christmas Day 2009.

THE END OF DAYS?

In his *Decline and Fall*, Gibbon covered more than 1,400 years of history, from 180 to 1590. This was history over the very long run, in which the causes of decline ranged from the personality disorders of individual emperors to the power of the Praetorian Guard and the rise of monotheism. After the death of Marcus Aurelius in 180, civil war became a recurring problem, as aspiring emperors competed for the spoils of supreme power. By the fourth century, barbarian invasions or migrations were well under way and only intensified as the Huns moved west. Meanwhile, the challenge posed by Sassanid Persia to the Eastern Roman Empire was steadily growing. The first time Western civilization crashed, as Gibbon tells the story, it was a very slow burn.

But what if political strife, barbarian migration and imperial rivalry were all just integral features of late antiquity – signs of normality, rather than harbingers of distant doom? Through this lens, Rome's fall was in fact quite sudden and dramatic. The final breakdown in the Western Roman Empire began in 406, when Germanic invaders poured across the Rhine into Gaul and then Italy. Rome itself was sacked by the Goths in 410. Co-opted by an enfeebled emperor, the Goths then fought the Vandals for control of Spain, but this merely shifted the problem south. Between 429 and 439, Genseric led the Vandals to victory after victory in North Africa, culminating in the fall of Carthage. Rome lost its southern Mediterranean breadbasket and, along with it, a huge source of tax revenue. Roman soldiers were barely able to defeat Attila's Huns as they swept west from the Balkans. By 452, the Western Roman Empire had lost all of Britain, most of Spain, the richest provinces of North Africa, and south-western and south-eastern Gaul. Not much was left besides Italy. Basiliscus, brother-in-law of Emperor Leo I, tried and failed to recapture Carthage in 468. Byzantium lived on, but the Western Roman Empire was dead. By 476, Rome was the fiefdom of Odoacer, King of the Scirii.[99]

What is most striking about this more modern reading of history is the speed of the Roman Empire's collapse. In just five decades, the population of Rome itself fell by three-quarters. Archaeological evidence from the late fifth century – inferior housing, more primitive pottery, fewer coins, smaller cattle – shows that the benign influence of Rome diminished rapidly in the rest of Western Europe. What one historian has called 'the end of civilization' came within the span of a single generation.[100]

Could our own version of Western civilization collapse with equal suddenness? It is, admittedly, an old fear that began haunting British intellectuals from Chesterton to Shaw more than a century ago.[101]

Today, however, the fear may be better grounded. A large majority of scientists subscribe to the view that, especially as China and other big Asian as well as South American countries narrow the economic gap between the West and the Rest, humanity is running the risk of catastrophic climate change. Without question there has been an unprecedented increase in the amount of carbon dioxide in the earth's atmosphere. And there is some evidence that this has caused an increase in average temperatures. What is less clear is how a continuation of these trends will impact on the earth's weather. However, it does not seem entirely fanciful to imagine further melting of the polar icecaps leading to changes in the direction of ocean currents or flooding of low-lying coastal regions; or the further desertification of areas hitherto capable of sustaining agriculture. Quite apart from climate change, some environmentalists also fear that, as Asia's more populous nations follow the Western route out of poverty, the strain on global supplies of energy, food and fresh water will become unbearable. Sceptics about the risks of climate change should spend some time in China, where the biggest and fastest industrial revolution in history is causing measurable – indeed, unmissable – environmental damage.

Most people who discuss these issues – myself among them – are not scientifically qualified to weigh the evidence. What attracts us to the idea of an environmental disaster is not so much the data as the familiarity of the prediction. Since the earliest recorded myths and legends, mankind has been fascinated by the idea of a spectacular end of the world, from the 'twilight of the gods' in the Nibelung saga to the key text of Christian eschatology, the Book of Revelation, written by the Evangelist John of Patmos. In this version of the apocalypse, the Messiah or Lamb of God will return to earth and defeat the Antichrist in the Battle of Armageddon, after which Satan will be confined to a bottomless pit for a thousand years. The culmination will come when Satan re-emerges from the abyss and summons together the people of Gog and Magog. This will be the cue for 'voices, and thunders, and lightnings; and . . . a great earthquake, such as was not since men were upon the earth' (Revelation 16:18). Jehovah's Witnesses and Seventh-Day Adventists both subscribe to a literal interpretation of this prophecy, but they are by no means alone. A remarkably large number of Evangelical Christians in the United States say they share the belief that we are nearing the End of Days. For many, the only question is who will be left behind when the 'Rapture' comes. Some say the phase of tribulation has already started. On 14 December 2008, it is said, the First Trumpet sounded, as the financial crisis neared its nadir. Once the Second, Third and Fourth Trumpets have sounded, the United States will collapse as a world power. When the Fifth Trumpet sounds, the Third World War will break out, killing billions of people. Then, on the last day of this great tribulation, Jesus Christ will return to redeem the true believers, as foreseen in the Book of Revelation. On a trip to the barren hill at Megiddo in Israel, commonly held to be the site of the coming Battle of Armageddon, I was not wholly surprised to encounter a party of Americans drawn there by precisely this kind of millenarian belief. Like those unreconstructed Marxists who continue to yearn for the collapse of capitalism, interpreting each new financial crisis as the beginning of the end, they feel a certain frisson at the thought that the End might come on their watch.

This idea that we are doomed – that decline and fall are inevitable, that things can only get worse – is deeply connected with our own sense of mortality. Because as individuals we are bound to degenerate, so, we instinctively feel, must the civilizations in which we live. All flesh is grass. In the same way, all vainglorious monuments end up as ruins. The wind blows through the melancholy relics of our former achievements.

But what we struggle to decide is how exactly this process of decline and fall unfolds in the realm of complex social and political structures. Do civilizations collapse with a bang, on the battlefield of Armageddon, or with a long, lingering whimper? The only way to answer that concluding question is to return to the first principles of historical explanation itself.

Conclusion: The Rivals

Well, Sir Anthony, since you desire it, we will not anticipate
the past! – So mind, young people – our retrospection be all to
the future.

Sheridan

He felt that in the electric flame department of the infernal
regions there should be a special gridiron, reserved exclusively
for the man who invented these performances [amateur theat-
ricals], so opposed to the true spirit of civilization.

P. G. Wodehouse

There is no better illustration of the life cycle of a civilization than
The Course of Empire, a series of five paintings by Thomas Cole that
hang in the gallery of the New York Historical Society. A founder of
the Hudson River School and one of the pioneers of nineteenth-century
American landscape painting, Cole beautifully captured a theory to
which most people remain in thrall to this day: the theory of cycles of
civilization.

Each of the five imagined scenes depicts the mouth of a great river
beneath a rocky outcrop. In the first, *The Savage State*, a lush wilderness is populated by a handful of hunter-gatherers eking out a primitive
existence at the break of a stormy dawn. The second picture, *The
Arcadian or Pastoral State*, is of an agrarian idyll: the inhabitants
have cleared the trees, planted fields and built an elegant Greek temple.
The third and largest of the paintings is *The Consummation of Empire*.
Now the landscape is covered by a magnificent marble entrepôt, while

the contented farmer-philosophers of the previous tableau have been replaced by a throng of opulently clad merchants, proconsuls and citizen-consumers. It is midday in the life cycle. Then comes *Destruction*. The city is ablaze, its citizens fleeing an invading horde that rapes and pillages beneath a brooding evening sky. Finally, the moon rises over *Desolation*. There is not a living soul to be seen, only a few decaying columns and colonnades overgrown by briars and ivy.

Conceived in the mid-1830s, Cole's pentaptych has a clear message: all civilizations, no matter how magnificent, are condemned to decline and fall. The implicit suggestion was that the young American republic of Cole's age would do better to stick to its bucolic first principles and resist the temptations of commerce, conquest and colonization.

For centuries, historians, political theorists, anthropologists and the public at large have tended to think about the rise and fall of civilizations in such cyclical and gradual terms. In Book VI of Polybius' *Histories*, which relate the rise of Rome, the process of political *anacyclosis* goes as follows:

1. Monarchy
2. Kingship
3. Tyranny
4. Aristocracy
5. Oligarchy
6. Democracy
7. Ochlocracy (mob rule)

This idea was revived in the Renaissance, when Polybius was rediscovered, and passed, meme-like, from the writing of Machiavelli to that of Montesquieu.[1] But a cyclical view also arose quite separately in the writings of the fourteenth-century Arab historian Ibn Khaldun and in Ming Neo-Confucianism.[2] In his book *Scienza nuova* (1725), the Italian philosopher Giambattista Vico describes all civilizations as passing through a *ricorso* with three phases: the divine, the heroic and the human or rational, which reverts back to the divine through what Vico called 'the barbarism of reflection'. 'The best instituted governments, like the best constituted animal bodies,' wrote the British political philosopher Henry St John, Viscount Bolingbroke, in 1738, 'carry in them the seeds of their destruction: and, though they grow and improve for a time, they will soon tend visibly to their dissolution. Every hour they live is an hour the less that they have to live.'[3] In *The Wealth of Nations* Adam Smith conceived of economic growth – 'opulence' as he put it – ultimately giving way to the 'stationary state'.

Idealists and materialists agreed on this one thing. For Hegel and Marx alike, it was the dialectic that gave history its unmistakable beat. History was seasonal for Oswald Spengler, the German historian, who wrote in *The Decline of the West* (1918–22) that the nineteenth century had been 'the winter of the West, the victory of materialism and scepticism, of socialism, parliamentarism, and money'. The British historian Arnold Toynbee's twelve-volume *Study of History* (1936–54) posited a cycle of challenge, response by 'creative minorities', then decline – civilizational suicide – when leaders stop responding with sufficient creativity to the challenges they face. Another grand theory was that of the Russian émigré sociologist Pitrim Sorokin, who argued that all major civilizations passed through three phases: 'ideational' (in which reality is spiritual), 'sensate' (in which reality is material) and 'idealistic' (a synthesis of the two).[4] The American historian Carroll Quigley taught his students at the Georgetown School of Foreign Service (among them the future President Bill Clinton) that civilizations had, like man, seven ages: mixture, gestation, expansion, conflict, universal empire, decay and invasion. It was, Quigley explained in a classic statement of the life-cycle theory:

> a process of evolution ... each civilization is born ... and ... enters a period of vigorous expansion, increasing its size and power ... until gradually a crisis of organization appears. When this crisis has passed and the civilization been reorganized ... its vigor and morale have weakened. It becomes stabilized and eventually stagnant. After a Golden Age of peace and prosperity, internal crises again arise. At this time there appears, for the first time, a moral and physical weakness, which raises ... questions about the civilization's ability to defend itself against external enemies ... The civilization grows steadily weaker until it is submerged by outside enemies, and eventually disappears.[5]

Each of these models is different, but all share the assumption that history has rhythm.

Although hardly anyone reads Spengler, Toynbee or Sorokin today – Quigley is still enjoyed by conspiracy theorists* – similar strains of thought are legible in the work of more modern authors. Paul Kennedy's *The Rise and Fall of the Great Powers* (1987) is another work of cyclical history, in which great powers rise and fall according to the growth rates of their industrial bases and the costs of their imperial commitments relative to their economies. Just as in Cole's *Course of Empire*, imperial expansion carries the seeds of future decline. As Kennedy writes: 'If a state overextends itself strategically ... it runs the risk that the potential benefits from external expansion may be outweighed by the great expense of it all.'[6] This phenomenon of 'imperial overstretch', he argues, is common to all great powers. When Kennedy's book was published, many people in the United States shared his fear that their own country might be succumbing to this disease.

More recently, it is the anthropologist Jared Diamond who has captured the public imagination with a grand theory of rise and fall. His book, *Collapse: How Societies Choose to Fail or Succeed* (2005), is cyclical history for the Green Age: tales of societies, from seventeenth-century Easter Island to twenty-first-century China, that risked, or now risk, destroying themselves by abusing their natural environments. Diamond quotes John Lloyd Stevens, the American explorer and amateur archaeologist who discovered the eerily dead Mayan cities of Mexico: 'Here were the remains of a cultivated, polished, and peculiar people, who had passed through all the stages incident to the rise and fall of nations, reached their golden age, and

* In his 1966 book, *Tragedy and Hope*, Quigley attributed great power to a mysterious Anglo-American 'secret society' allegedly founded by Cecil Rhodes, Alfred Milner and the journalist William T. Stead and devoted to 'extend[ing] the British Empire' and converting it into a federation. The 'Rhodes–Milner group' and its Round Table affiliates, Quigley claimed, were responsible for the Boer War, the weakening of the Versailles Treaty and the appeasement of Nazi Germany. After Milner's death in 1925, this group continued to exert a malign influence through the Rhodes Trust, the Royal Institute for International Affairs (Chatham House) and the Council on Foreign Relations in New York. Quigley exaggerated both the secrecy and the success of Milner's activities.

perished.'[7] According to Diamond, the Maya fell into a classic Malthusian trap as their population grew larger than their fragile and inefficient agricultural system could support. More people meant more cultivation, but more cultivation meant deforestation, erosion, drought and soil exhaustion. The result was civil war over dwindling resources and, finally, collapse.

Diamond's inference is of course that today's world could go the way of the Maya.[8] The critical point is that environmental suicide is a slow and protracted process. Unfortunately, political leaders in almost any society – primitive or sophisticated – have little incentive to address problems that are unlikely to manifest themselves for a hundred years or more. As the United Nations Climate Change Conference in Copenhagen in December 2009 made clear, rhetorical pleas to 'save the planet' for future generations are insufficient to overcome the conflicts over economic distribution between rich and poor countries that exist in the here and now. We love our grandchildren. But our great-great-grandchildren are harder to relate to.

Yet it is possible that this whole conceptual framework is, in fact, flawed. Perhaps Cole's artistic representation of a civilizational super-cycle of birth, growth and eventual death is a misrepresentation of the historical process. What if history is not cyclical and slow-moving but arrhythmic – sometimes almost stationary, but also capable of violent acceleration? What if historical time is less like the slow and predictable changing of the seasons and more like the elastic time of our dreams? Above all, what if collapse is not centuries in the making but strikes a civilization suddenly, like a thief in the night?

Civilizations, as I have endeavoured to show in this book, are highly complex systems, made up of a very large number of interacting components that are asymmetrically organized, so that their construction more closely resembles a Namibian termite mound than an Egyptian pyramid. They operate somewhere between order and disorder – on 'the edge of chaos', in the phrase of the computer scientist Christopher Langton. Such systems can appear to operate quite stably for some time, apparently in equilibrium, in reality constantly adapting. But there comes a moment when they 'go critical'. A slight perturbation can set off a 'phase transition' from a benign equilibrium to a crisis – a single grain of sand causes an apparently stable sandcastle to fall in on itself.

To understand complexity, it is helpful to examine how natural scientists use the concept.[9] Think of the spontaneous self-organization of half a million termites, which allows them to construct a complex mound, or the fractal geometry of the snowflakes formed by water molecules, with their myriad variants of sixfold symmetry. Human intelligence itself is a complex system, a product of the interaction of billions of neurons in the central nervous system – what the neuroscientist Charles Sherrington called the 'enchanted loom'. Our immune system is also a complex system in which antibodies mobilize themselves to wage a defensive war against alien antigens. All complex systems in the natural world share certain characteristics. A small input to such a system can produce huge, often unanticipated changes – what scientists call 'the amplifier effect'.[10] Causal relationships are often non-linear, which means that traditional methods of generalizing from observations (such as trend analysis and sampling) are of little use. Indeed, some theorists would go so far as to say that certain complex systems are wholly non-deterministic, meaning that it is next to impossible to make predictions about their future behaviour based on past data. There is no such thing as a typical or average forest fire, for example. To use the jargon of modern physics, a forest before a fire is in a state of 'self-organized criticality'; it is teetering on the verge of a breakdown, but the size of the breakdown is unknown, because the distribution of forest fires by magnitude does not follow the familiar bell curve, with most fires clustered around a mean value, the way most adult male heights are clustered around five foot nine. Rather, if you plot the size of fires against the frequency of their occurrence, you get a straight line. Will the next fire be tiny or huge, a bonfire or a conflagration? The most that can be said is that a forest fire twice as large as last year's is roughly four (or six or eight, depending on the forest) times less likely to happen this year. This kind of pattern – known as a 'power-law distribution' – is remarkably common in the natural world. It can be seen not just in forest fires but also in earthquakes and epidemics. Only the steepness of the line varies.[11]

The political and economic structures made by humans share many of the features of complex systems. Indeed, heterodox economists such as W. Brian Arthur have been arguing along these lines for decades, going far beyond Adam Smith's notion of an 'Invisible Hand', seeming to guide multiple profit-maximizing individuals, or Friedrich von Hayek's later critique of economic planning and demand management.[12] To Arthur, a complex economy is characterized by the interaction of dispersed agents, a lack of any central control, multiple levels of organization, continual adaptation, incessant creation of new market niches and no general equilibrium. In contradiction to the core prediction of classical economics that competition causes diminishing returns, in a complex economy increasing returns are quite possible. Viewed in this light, Silicon Valley is economic complexity in action; so is the internet itself. And the financial crisis that began in 2007 can also be explained in similar terms. As Nassim Taleb has argued, the global economy by the spring of 2007 had come to resemble an over-optimized electricity grid. The relatively small surge represented by defaults on subprime mortgages in the United States sufficed to tip the entire world economy into the financial equivalent of a blackout, which for a time threatened to cause a complete collapse of international trade.[13] Researchers at the Santa Fe Institute are currently exploring how such insights can be applied to other aspects of collective human activity, including 'metahistory'.[14]

This is less esoteric than it seems, since wars are even less normally distributed than financial crises. The physicist and meteorologist Lewis Fry Richardson* grouped 'deadly quarrels', ranging from homicides to world wars, according to their magnitudes, using the base-10 logarithm of the total number of deaths. Thus a terrorist act that kills 100 people has a magnitude of 2, while a war with a million victims is a magnitude-6 conflict. (Note that a war of magnitude 6 ± 0.5 could cause anywhere from 316,228 to 3,162,278 deaths.) Considering only the period from 1815 to 1945, Richardson found more than 300 conflicts of magnitude 2.5 or higher (in other words, responsible for

---

* Born in Yorkshire in 1881, Richardson was a Quaker, a conscientious objector during the First World War (though he did drive ambulances on the Western Front) and a proponent of Esperanto. It depressed him that he could find no evidence of a trend towards less war, nor any strong statistical predictor of when and where war would occur, beyond two relatively weak relationships: wars were more common between neighbouring states and more likely between states with different religions.

upwards of 300 deaths). Of these, two magnitude-7 wars (the world wars) killed at least 36 million (60 per cent of the total), excluding victims of war-related famine or disease, and millions of magnitude-0 homicides (with one, two or three victims) claimed 9.7 million lives (16 per cent). These data appear at first sight to be completely random. But they, too, obey a power law.[15]

If the incidence of war is as unpredictable as the incidence of forest fires, the implications for any theory of the rise and fall of civilizations are immense, given the obvious causal role played by wars in both the ascent and descent of complex social organizations. A civilization is by definition a highly complex system. Whatever nominal central authority exists, in practice it is an adaptive network of dynamic economic, social and political relations. It is not surprising, then, that civilizations of all shapes and sizes exhibit many of the characteristics of complex systems in the natural world – including the tendency to move quite suddenly from stability to instability.

As we saw in the last chapter, Western civilization in its first incarnation – the Roman Empire – did not decline and fall sedately. It collapsed within a generation, tipped over the edge of chaos by barbarian invaders in the early fifth century. Comparably swift collapses have been a leitmotif of this book. In 1530 the Incas were the masters of all they surveyed from their lofty Andean cities. Within less than a decade, foreign invaders with horses, gunpowder and lethal diseases had smashed their empire to smithereens. The Ming dynasty's rule in China also fell apart with extraordinary speed in the mid-seventeenth century. Again, the transition from equipoise to anarchy took little more than a decade. In much the same way, the Bourbon monarchy in France passed from triumph to terror with astonishing rapidity. French intervention on the side of the colonial rebels against British rule in North America seemed like a good idea in the 1770s, but it served to push French finances into a critical state. The summoning of the Estates General in May 1789 unleashed a political chain reaction and a collapse of royal legitimacy so swift that within four years the King had been decapitated by guillotine, a device invented only in 1791. At the time of the Young Turk movement, which came to power in 1908, the Ottoman Empire still seemed capable of being reformed. By 1922, when the last Sultan

Empire departed Istanbul aboard a British warship, it was gone. Japan's empire reached its maximum territorial extent in 1942, after Pearl Harbor. By 1945 it too was no more.

The sun set on the British Empire with comparable suddenness. In February 1945 Prime Minister Winston Churchill bestrode the world stage as one of the 'Big Three', deciding the fates of nations with US President Franklin Roosevelt and Soviet leader Joseph Stalin at Yalta. No sooner had the war ended than he was swept from office. Within a dozen years, the United Kingdom had conceded independence to Burma, Egypt, Ghana, India, Israel, Jordan, Malaya, Pakistan, Ceylon and Sudan. The Suez Crisis in 1956 proved that the United Kingdom could not act in defiance of the United States in the Middle East, setting the seal on the end of empire. Although it took until the 1960s for Harold Macmillan's 'wind of change' to blow through sub-Saharan Africa and the remnants of colonial rule east of Suez, the United Kingdom's age of hegemony was effectively over less than a dozen years after its victories over Germany and Japan.

The most recent and familiar example of precipitous decline is, of course, the collapse of the Soviet Union. With the benefit of hindsight, historians have traced all kinds of rot within the Soviet system back to the Brezhnev era and beyond. According to one recent account, it was only the high oil prices of the 1970s that 'averted Armageddon'.[16] But this was not apparent at the time. In March 1985, when Mikhail Gorbachev became general secretary of the Soviet Communist Party, the CIA (wrongly) estimated the Soviet economy to be approximately 60 per cent the size of the US economy. The Soviet nuclear arsenal was genuinely larger than the US stockpile. And governments in what was then called the Third World, from Vietnam to Nicaragua, had been tilting in the Soviets' favour for most of the previous twenty years. Yet less than five years after Gorbachev took power, the Soviet imperium in Central and Eastern Europe had fallen apart, followed in 1991 by the Soviet Union itself. If ever an empire fell off a cliff – rather than gently declining – it was the one founded by Lenin.

If civilizations are complex systems that sooner or later succumb to sudden and catastrophic malfunctions, rather than cycling sedately from Arcadia to Apogee to Armageddon, what are the implications for

Western civilization today? First, we need to remind ourselves of how the West came to dominate the rest of the world after around 1500.

Recent research has demolished the fashionable view that China was economically neck and neck with the West until as recently as 1800. Per-capita gross domestic product essentially stagnated in the Ming era and was significantly lower than in pre-industrial Britain. The main reason for this was that China was still overwhelmingly an agricultural economy, with 90 per cent of GDP accounted for by low-productivity cultivation, a much higher share than in early-modern Britain. Moreover, for a century after 1520, the Chinese national savings rate was negative. There was no capital accumulation in late Ming China; rather the opposite.[17] The story of what Kenneth Pomeranz has called 'the Great Divergence' between East and West therefore began much earlier than Pomeranz asserted. Even the late Angus Maddison may have been over-optimistic when he argued that in 1700 the average inhabitant of China was slightly better off than the average inhabitant of the future United States. Maddison was closer to the mark when he estimated that in 1600 British per-capita GDP was already 60 per cent higher than Chinese.[18]

What happened after that was that China's output and population grew in lockstep, causing individual income to stagnate, while the English-speaking world, closely followed by North-western Europe, surged ahead. By 1820 US per-capita GDP was twice that of China; by 1870 it was nearly five times greater; by 1913 the ratio was nearly ten to one. Despite the painful interruption of the Great Depression, the United States suffered nothing so devastating as China's wretched twentieth-century ordeal of revolution, civil war, Japanese invasion, more revolution, man-made famine and yet more ('cultural') revolution. In 1968 the average American was thirty-three times richer than the average Chinese, using figures calculated on the basis of purchasing-power parity (allowing for the different costs of living in the two countries). Calculated in current dollar terms the differential at its peak was more like seventy to one.

The Great Divergence manifested itself in various ways. In 1500 the world's ten biggest cities had nearly all been in the East, with Beijing by far the biggest (more than ten times the size of wretched little London). In 1900 the biggest cities were nearly all in the West, with

44. A scene of death and destruction from the Taiping Rebellion

45. Mass-producing scripture: the Nanjing Amity Bible Printing Company

46. Industrial Revelation: China today

47. The end of Western predominance: President Barack Obama bows to Chinese Premier Wen Jiabao, November 2009

Patents Granted by Country of Origin of Applicant, 1995–2008

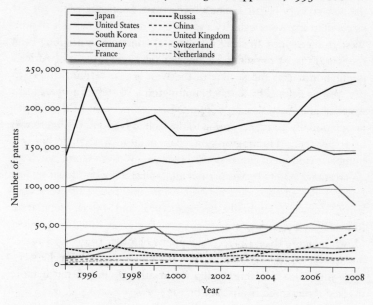

there in 1975. According to the Conference Board, Singapore's per-capita GDP is currently 21 per cent higher than that of the US, Hong Kong's is about the same, Japan's and Taiwan's are about 25 per cent lower and South Korea's 36 per cent lower.[20] It would be a brave man who bet against China following the same trajectory in the decades ahead. China's is the biggest and fastest of all the industrial revolutions. In the space of twenty-six years, its GDP grew by a factor of ten. It took the UK seventy years after 1830 to grow by a factor of four. According to the International Monetary Fund, China's share of global GDP (measured in current prices) will pass the 10 per cent mark in 2013. Before the financial crisis, economists at Goldman Sachs forecast that China would overtake the United States in terms of GDP in 2027.[21] But the financial crisis reduced US growth more than Chinese. If present rates persist, China's economy could surpass America's in 2014 in terms of domestic purchasing power and by 2020 in current dollar terms.[22] Indeed, in some ways the Asian century has already arrived. China is on the brink of surpassing the American share of global manufacturing, having overtaken Germany and Japan since the new century began. China's biggest city, Shanghai, is already far larger than any American city and sits atop a new league table of non-Western megacities. In sheer numbers, of course, Asia has long been the world's most populous region. But the rapid growth of Africa's population makes the decline of the West a near certainty. In 1950 the West as defined by Samuel Huntington – Western Europe, North America and Australasia – accounted for 20 per cent of the world's population. By 2050, according to the United Nations, the figure will be 10 per cent.[23] Huntington's own data point to Western decline in a number of different dimensions: language (Western share down by 3 percentage points between 1958 and 1992); religion (down by just under 1 percentage point between 1970 and 2000); territory controlled (down fractionally between 1971 and 1993); population (down by 3 percentage points since 1971); gross domestic product (down by more than 4 percentage points between 1970 and 1992);* and military manpower (down by nearly 6 percentage points between 1970 and 1991). In most cases, the relative decline is much more marked if measured from 1913 or 1938.[24]

The financial crisis that began in the summer of 2007 should therefore be understood as an accelerator of an already well-established trend of relative Western decline. This was very nearly a Great Depression. The reasons it has been just a Slight Depression are threefold. First, China's huge expansion of bank lending, which mitigated the effect of slumping exports to the West. Second, the massive expansion of the US monetary base implemented by Federal Reserve Chairman Ben Bernanke. Third, the immense fiscal deficits run by nearly all developed countries, with the United States out in front, borrowing in excess of 9 per cent of GDP in three consecutive years. These policies – the diametric opposite of what was done in the early 1930s – pulled the world economy out of a tailspin from June 2009 onwards. But now the developed world is in the hangover phase that follows all

---

* In fact the total current dollar gross domestic product for all the countries defined by Huntington as Western has remained remarkably constant at between 61 and 69 per cent of the global total since 1960.

forms of excessive stimulus. For various reasons, the fiscal policies of three Eurozone countries, Greece, Ireland and Portugal, have lost credibility in the eyes of bond investors, driving up their borrowing costs and deepening their fiscal difficulties. Looking at the long-term trend of public debt in these countries, as the Bank for International Settlements did in early 2010, one can see why.[25] The financial crisis came on top of an already serious structural problem of debt accumulation. Yet the same could be said for both the United Kingdom and the United States. And, at the time of writing, only the former has taken any steps to address the problem.

It is important to remember that most cases of civilizational collapse are associated with fiscal crises as well as wars. All the examples of collapse discussed above were preceded by sharp imbalances between revenues and expenditures, as well as by difficulties with financing public debt. Think of Spain in the sixteenth century: already by 1543 nearly two-thirds of ordinary revenue was going on interest on the *juros*, the loans by which the Habsburg monarchy financed itself. As early as 1559 total interest payments on the *juros* exceeded ordinary Spanish revenue; and the situation was little better in 1584 when 84 per cent of ordinary revenue went on interest. By 1598 the proportion was back to 100 per cent. Or think of France in the eighteenth century: between 1751 and 1788, the eve of Revolution, interest and amortization payments rose from just over a quarter of tax revenue to 62 per cent. Then there is the case of Ottoman Turkey in the nineteenth century: debt service rose from 17 per cent of revenue in 1868 to 32 per cent in 1871 to 50 per cent in 1877, two years after the enormous default which ushered in the disintegration of the Ottoman Empire in the Balkans. Finally, consider the case of Britain in the twentieth century. By the mid-1920s, debt charges were absorbing 44 per cent of total government expenditure, exceeding defence expenditure every year until 1937, when rearmament finally got under way in earnest. But note that Britain's real problems came after 1945, when a substantial proportion of its now immense debt burden was in foreign hands. Of the £21 billion national debt at the end of the war, around £3.4 billion was owed to foreign creditors – equivalent to around a third of GDP.[26]

From 2001, in the space of just ten years, the US federal debt in public hands doubled as a share of GDP from 32 per cent to a projected 66 per cent in 2011. According to the Congressional Budget Office's 2010 projections (using the 'Alternative Fiscal Scenario', which the CBO regards as more politically likely than its 'Extended Baseline Scenario'), the debt could rise above 90 per cent of GDP by 2021 and could reach 150 per cent by 2031 and 300 per cent by 2047.[27] Note that these figures do not take account of the estimated $100 trillion of unfunded liabilities of the Medicare and Social Security systems. Nor do they include the rapidly growing deficits of the states, nor the burgeoning liabilities of public employees' pension schemes. On this basis, the fiscal position of the United States in 2009 was worse than that of Greece. With a debt-to-revenue ratio of 312 per cent, Greece was manifestly in dire straits. According to calculations by Morgan Stanley, however, the debt-to-revenue ratio of the United States was 358 per cent.[28]

These numbers are bad, but in the realm of financial stability the role of perception is in many ways more important. For now, the world still expects the United States to muddle through, eventually doing the right thing when, in a phrase commonly attributed to Churchill, all other possibilities have been exhausted. Past alarms about the deficit in the 1980s were overblown; by the late 1990s the federal government was running surpluses. So why worry? Such complacency can persist for a surprisingly long time – long after the statistical indicators have started flashing red. But one day, a seemingly random piece of bad news – perhaps a negative report by a rating agency – will make the headlines during an otherwise quiet news cycle. Suddenly, it will be not just a few specialists who worry about the sustainability of US fiscal policy but also the public at large, not to mention investors abroad. It is this shift that is crucial, for a complex adaptive system is in big trouble when a critical mass of its constituents loses faith in its viability. Beginning in the summer of 2007, the complex system of the global economy flipped from boom to bust because investors' expectations about the probability of sub-prime defaults suddenly changed, blowing huge holes in the business models of thousands of highly leveraged financial institutions. The next phase of the current crisis may begin when the same investors reassess the creditworthiness of the US government itself. Neither interest rates at zero nor fiscal stimulus can achieve a sustainable recovery if people in the United States and abroad collectively decide that such measures will lead to much higher inflation rates or outright default. As the economist Thomas Sargent demonstrated two decades ago, such decisions are self-fulfilling, because it is not the supply of base money that determines inflation but the velocity of its circulation, which in turn is a function of expectations.[29] In the same way, it is not the debt-to-GDP ratio that determines government solvency but the interest rate that investors demand. Bond yields can shoot up if expectations change about future government solvency or currency stability, intensifying an already bad fiscal crisis by driving up the cost of interest payments on new debt. The result is a kind of death spiral of falling confidence, rising yields and rising deficits. This is precisely what happened to Greece, Ireland and Portugal in 2010.

It is of course true that Japan has been able to increase its public debt to even higher levels relative to GDP without triggering such a crisis of confidence. However, nearly all the Japanese debt is in the hands of Japanese investors and institutions, whereas half the US federal debt in public hands is in the hands of foreign creditors, of which just over a fifth is held by the monetary authorities of the People's Republic of China. Only the American 'exorbitant privilege' of being able to print the world's premier reserve currency gives the US breathing space.[30] Yet this very privilege is under mounting attack from the Chinese government. 'Because the United States' issuance of dollars is out of control and international commodity prices are continuing to rise,' declared the Chinese Commerce Minister Chen Deming in October 2010, 'China is being attacked by imported inflation.'[31] The United States is engaged in 'uncontrolled' and 'irresponsible' money printing, according to Xia Bin, an economic adviser to the People's Bank of China: 'As long as the world exercises no restraint in issuing global currencies such as the dollar ... then the occurrence of another crisis is inevitable.'[32] Quantitative easing (purchases of Treasury securities by the Federal Reserve) was a form of 'financial protectionism', declared Su Jingxiang, a researcher with the China Institute of Contemporary International Relations.[33] In November 2010 the Dagong credit rating agency downgraded the US to A+ from AA, with a negative outlook.

Chinese anxieties are understandable. The prices of all but a few commodities have surged upward since the trough of the crisis.* Nor is it surprising that China's official holdings of US Treasuries were apparently reduced by around 10 per cent between July 2009 and June 2010.[34] Even with the price of an ounce of gold at an unprecedented $1,400, the Chinese began to buy it in 2010 as a time-honoured hedge against inflation. Yet the United States fears not inflation but deflation. Prices are rising at the lowest rate since the 1950s, when the consumer price index was created. Despite the Federal Reserve's best efforts, broad money is contracting and credit stubbornly refuses to grow. Even if nominal ten-year bond yields stay low, that means real long-term interest rates are likely to stay positive in the foreseeable future, which means no easy inflationary exit from the colossal debt burden weighing down on households, banks and government alike, of the sort that was achieved by many countries in the 1920s and the 1970s. Growth will stay sluggish, which also means that the federal government will continue to run deficits, albeit smaller ones. And that means a rising interest bill. According to the Congressional Budget Office's alternative fiscal scenario, interest payments on the federal debt will rise from 9 per cent of federal tax revenues to 20 per cent in 2020, to 36 per cent in 2030 and to 58 per cent in 2040.[35]

Figures like these imply, among other things, a rapid reduction in American military commitments overseas. The CBO is already projecting the savings that would be made if the number of troops deployed overseas were slashed to 30,000 by 2013.[36] This is exactly what we would expect to see as interest payments outstrip military expenditure as a share of federal revenue, which they soon will.

Does the shift of the world's centre of gravity from West to East imply future conflict? In a seminal essay, Samuel Huntington predicted that the twenty-first century would be marked by a 'clash of civilizations', in which the West would be confronted by a 'Sinic' East and a Muslim Greater Middle East, and perhaps also the Orthodox civilization of

---

* The only commodities in the comprehensive International Monetary Fund database that have not gone up in price since February 2009 are natural gas, wood, olive oil, shrimp and chicken – good news for anyone planning a surf and turf barbecue.

the former Russian Empire.[37] 'The principal conflicts of global politics', he wrote, 'will occur between nations and groups of different civilizations. The clash of civilizations will dominate global politics. The fault lines between civilizations will be the battle lines of the future.'[38] Numerous objections were raised to this prediction in the wake of its publication.[39] It nevertheless seems a better description of the post-Cold War world than the competing theories Huntington discarded: that there would be a post-historical (or neo-conservative) 'one world' under American leadership, or a realist free-for-all between nearly 200 nation-states, or just downright 'apolarity', otherwise known as chaos.

Yet there is one major defect in Huntington's model. As a prophecy it has failed – thus far – to come true. Huntington claimed that 'conflicts between groups in different civilizations will be more frequent, more sustained and more violent than conflicts between groups in the same civilization.' This has not been the case. There has been no increase in inter-civilizational war since the end of the Cold War. Nor do wars between members of different civilizations appear to last longer than other conflicts.[40] Most wars in the past two decades have been civil wars, but only a minority of them have conformed to Huntington's model. More often than not, the wars of the New World Disorder have been fought between ethnic groups within one of Huntington's civilizations. To be precise: of thirty major armed conflicts that were either still going on or had recently ended in 2005 – twelve years after the publication of Huntington's original essay – only nine could be regarded as being in any sense between civilizations, in the sense that one side was predominantly Muslim and the other non-Muslim. Nineteen were essentially ethnic conflicts, the worst being the wars that continue to bedevil Central Africa, closely followed by the wars in the Greater Middle East, where the vast majority of victims have been Muslims killed by other Muslims.[41] Furthermore, many of those conflicts that have a religious dimension are also ethnic conflicts; religious affiliation often has more to do with the localized success of missionaries in the relatively recent past than with long-standing membership of a Christian or Muslim civilization. The future therefore looks more likely to bring multiple local wars – most of them ethnic conflicts in Africa, South Asia and the Middle East – than a global collision of civilizations. Indeed, these centrifugal tendencies may end up tearing apart the very civilizations identified by Huntington. In short, for 'the clash of civilizations', read 'the *crash* of civilizations'.

In the successful computer game *Civilization*, created by Sid Meier in 1991 and now in its fifth version, players could choose between sixteen rival civilizations, ranging from American to Zulu. The challenge was then to 'build an empire to stand the test of time' in competition with between two and six of the others. The game can now be won in one of three ways: reaching the end of the modern era with the highest score, winning the space race by reaching the star system of Alpha Centauri – or by destroying all the other civilizations. But is that really how the historical process works? As we have seen, Western civilization, in the form of the kingdoms and republics of Western Europe, did indeed destroy or subjugate most of the rest of the world's civilizations after around 1500. Yet much of this was achieved with a minimum of outright conflict, at least compared with the number and scale of the wars the Western powers fought with one another.[42] China's economic stagnation and geopolitical marginalization were the consequences not of the Opium Wars, but of a protracted internal sclerosis that was inherent in the Far Eastern system of cultivation and in the imperial system of rule. The Ottoman Empire's retreat from the European continent, and its decline from great power to 'sick man', was due only superficially to military defeats; the defeats themselves were due to a chronic failure to participate in the Scientific Revolution. There was no large-scale clash between North and South American civilizations; the former was simply superior institutionally to the latter and quickly acquired the means to intervene at will in Southern affairs. Likewise, the wars fought by the European empires in Africa were trivially small compared with the wars they fought with each other back home in Europe. Africa's subjugation was as much the achievement of the mission school, the telegraph office and the laboratory as of the Maxim gun. The Industrial Revolution and the consumer society did not need to be imposed on non-Western countries; if they had any sense, they adopted both voluntarily, like the Japanese. As for the work ethic, that was spread to the East not by the sword but by the word – above all, by the major improvement in public health and education achieved from the mid-twentieth century onwards.

It is in this light that we should understand the rise of China in our time. Despite the oft-stated Chinese preference for a 'quiet rise', some commentators already detect the first signs of Huntington's civilizational clash. In late 2010 the resumption of quantitative easing by the Federal Reserve appeared to spark a currency war between the US and China. If 'the Chinese don't take actions' to end the manipulation of their currency, President Obama declared in New York in September of that year, 'we have other means of protecting US interests'.[43] The Chinese Premier Wen Jiabao was not slow to respond: 'Do not work to pressure us on the renminbi rate ... Many of our exporting companies would have to close down, migrant workers would have to return to their villages. If China saw social and economic turbulence, then it would be a disaster for the world.'[44] Such exchanges did not, however, vindicate Huntington, any more than the occasional Sino-American naval incidents or diplomatic spats over Taiwan or North Korea. They were in truth a form of *pi ying xi*, the traditional Chinese shadow puppet theatre. The real currency war was between Chimerica – the united economies of China and America – and the rest of the world. If the US printed money while China effectively still pegged its currency to the dollar, both parties benefited. The losers were countries like Indonesia and Brazil, whose real trade-weighted exchange rates appreciated between January 2008 and November 2010 by, respectively, 18 per cent and 17 per cent.

No doubt, Chimerica has passed its prime; as an economic marriage between a spender and a saver it already shows all the signs of being on the rocks.[45] With China's output in mid-2010 around 20 per cent above its pre-crisis level and that of the US still 2 per cent below, it seems clear that the symbiosis has become more beneficial to the creditor than to the debtor. American policy-makers utter the mantra 'They need us as much as we need them' and refer back to Lawrence Summers's famous phrase about 'mutually assured financial destruction'. Unbeknown to them, China's leaders already have a plan to wind up Chimerica and reduce their dependence on dollar-reserve accumulation and subsidized exports. It is not so much a plan for world domination on the model of Western imperialism as a strategy to re-establish China as the Middle Kingdom – the dominant tributary state in the Asia-Pacific region.[46] If one had to summarize China's new grand strategy, the best way to do it might be, Mao-fashion, as the 'Four Mores':

1. Consume more
2. Import more
3. Invest abroad more
4. Innovate more

In each case, a change of economic strategy promises to pay a handsome geopolitical dividend.

By consuming more, China can and will reduce its trade surplus and in the process endear itself to its major trading partners, especially the other emerging markets. China has just overtaken the United States as the world's biggest automobile market (14 million sales a year to 11 million) and its demand is projected to rise tenfold in the years ahead. By 2035, according to the International Energy Agency, China will be using a fifth of all global energy, a 75 per cent increase since 2008.[47] It accounted for about 46 per cent of global coal consumption in 2009, the World Coal Institute estimates, and consumes a similar share of the world's aluminium, copper, nickel and zinc production. Such figures translate into major gains for the exporters of these and other commodities. China is already Australia's biggest export market, accounting for 22 per cent of Australian exports in 2009. It buys 12 per cent of Brazil's exports and 10 per cent of South Africa's. It has also become a big purchaser of high-value manufactures from Japan and Germany. Once China was mainly an exporter of low-price manufactures. Now that it accounts for fully a fifth of global growth, it has become the most dynamic new market for other people's stuff. And that wins friends.

However, the Chinese are justifiably nervous of the vagaries of world market prices for commodities – how could they feel otherwise after the huge price-swings of the period 2004–10? So it makes sense for them to invest abroad to acquire commodity-producing assets, from oil fields in Angola to copper mines in Zambia. In just a single month (January 2010), Chinese investors made direct investments worth a total of $2.4 billion in 420 overseas enterprises in seventy-five countries and regions. The overwhelming majority of the investments were in Asia (45 per cent) and Africa (42 per cent). The biggest sectors were mining, petrochemical and communications infrastructure.[48] The Chinese mode of operation is now well established across Africa. Typical deals exchange highway and other infrastructure investment for long leases of mines or agricultural land, with few questions asked about human rights abuses or political corruption.[49] When challenged about China's economic relations with Sudan, at the height of the genocide in Darfur, China's Deputy Foreign Minister said simply: 'Business is business.'[50] In July 2008 the Chinese special envoy Liu Guijin restated China's policy on aid to Africa: 'We don't attach political conditions. We have to realize the political and economic environments [in Africa] are not ideal. But we don't have to wait for everything to be satisfactory or human rights to be perfect.'[51]

Growing overseas investment in natural resources not only makes sense as a diversification strategy to reduce China's exposure to the risk of dollar depreciation. It also allows China to increase its financial power, not least through its vast and influential sovereign wealth fund, China Investment Corporation, which has around $200 billion of assets. And investment abroad justifies China's ambitious plans for naval expansion. In the words of Rear Admiral Zhang Huachen, Deputy Commander of the East Sea Fleet: 'With the expansion of the country's economic interests, the navy wants to better protect the country's transportation routes and the safety of our major sea-lanes.'[52] The South China Sea is increasingly regarded as a 'core national interest' and deepwater ports are projected in Pakistan – in the former Omani enclave of Gwadar – as well as in Burma and Sri Lanka. This is a very different maritime model from Admiral Zheng He's (see Chapter 1). It comes straight from the playbook of the Victorian Royal Navy.

Finally, and contrary to the view that China is condemned to remain an assembly line for products 'designed in California', China is innovating more, aiming to become (for example) the world's leading manufacturer of wind turbines and photovoltaic panels. In 2007 China overtook Germany in terms of the number of new patent applications. It will soon do the same in terms of patents granted, having overtaken Britain in 2004, Russia in 2005 and France in 2006. Since

1995 the number of new patents granted to Chinese innovators has increased by a factor of twenty-nine.[53] This is part of a wider story of Eastern ascendancy. China has increased expenditure on research and development by a factor of six in the past decade, has more than doubled the number of its scientists and is now second only to the United States in its annual output of scientific papers and its supercomputing capability. There remains a significant gap in terms of international citations of Chinese research, but there is good reason to expect this to close.[54] Perhaps the most compelling evidence that the shift from West to East is real lies in the realm of education. In a 2005 study of academic attainment by people aged twenty-five to thirty-four, the Organization for Economic Co-operation and Development found a startling differential between the top countries, South Korea and Japan, and the laggards, Britain and Italy.[55] The same gulf manifests itself in standardized tests of mathematical aptitude among fourteen-year-olds, where students from Singapore far outperform students

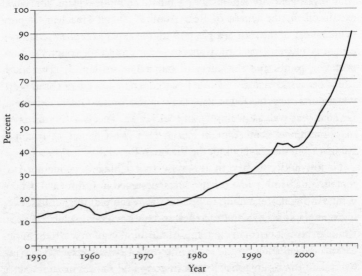

GDP of Greater China (People's Republic plus Hong Kong, Singapore and Taiwan) as a Percentage of US GDP, 1950–2009

Average Mathematics Score of 8th Grade (~14-year-old) Students, 2007 (International mean = 500)

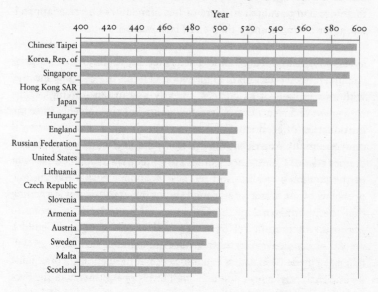

from Scotland. The former are 19 per cent above the international average; the latter 3 per cent below it.[56]

What could go wrong for the ascending Chinese dragon? There are at least four different hypotheses proposed by those who expect it to stumble. The first is that similar projections of inexorable ascent used to be made for Japan. It too was supposed to overtake the United States and to become the number one global economic superpower. So, the argument goes, China could one day suffer the fate of Japan after 1989. Precisely because the economic and political systems are not truly competitive, a real-estate or stock-market bubble and bust could saddle the country with zombie banks, flat growth and deflation – the plight of Japan for the better part of two decades now. The counter-argument is that an archipelago off the east coast of Eurasia was never likely to match a continental power like the United States. It was credible to predict even a century ago that Japan would catch up with the United Kingdom, its Western analogue – as it duly did – but not that it would overhaul the United States. In addition, Japan's defeat in 1945 meant that throughout the period of its economic ascent it was dependent on the United States for its security, and therefore had to submit to more or less mandatory currency appreciation, for example under the 1985 Plaza Accord.

A second possibility is that China might succumb to social unrest, as has so often happened in its past. After all, China remains a poor country, ranked eighty-sixth in the world in terms of per-capita income, with 150 million of its citizens – nearly one in ten – living on the equivalent of $1.50 a day or less. Inequality has risen steeply since the introduction of economic reforms, so that the income distribution is now essentially American (though not quite Brazilian). An estimated 0.4 per cent of Chinese households currently own around 70 per cent of the country's wealth. Add to these economic disparities chronic problems of air, water and ground pollution, and it is not surprising that the poorer parts of the Chinese rural hinterland are prone to outbreaks of protest. Yet only a fevered imagination could build a revolutionary scenario on these slender foundations. Economic growth may have made China a less equal society, but the capitalist-communist regime currently enjoys uniquely high levels of legitimacy in the eyes of its own people.[57] Indeed, survey data suggest that Chinese people today are more committed to the idea of the free market than Americans. The real social threat to China's stability is demographic. As a result of the One-Child policy introduced in 1979, China by 2030 will have a significantly more elderly population than its comparably large neighbour India. The share of the population aged sixty-five and over will be 16 per cent, compared with 5 per cent in 1980. And the gender imbalance in provinces like Anhui, Hainan, Guangdong and Jiangxi is already quite without parallel in a modern society, with between 30 and 38 per cent more males than females.[58] The next Chinese revolution, if there is going to be one, will be led by frustrated bachelors. But history suggests that young men without women are as likely to embrace radical nationalism as revolution.

A third plausible scenario is that a rising middle class could, as so often in Western history, demand a bigger political say than they currently have. China was once a rural society. In 1990 three out of four Chinese lived in the countryside. Today 45 per cent of people are city-dwellers and by 2030 it could be as high as 70 per cent. Not only is a middle class rapidly growing in urban China; the spread of mobile telephony and the internet means that they can form their own spontaneous horizontal networks as never before. The challenge this represents is personified not by the jailed dissident Liu Xiaobo, awarded the 2010 Nobel Peace Prize, who belongs to an earlier generation of activists, but by the burly, bearded artist Ai Weiwei, who has used his public prominence to agitate on behalf of the victims of the 2008 Sichuan earthquake. The counter-argument here comes from a young Beijing-based television producer I got to know while researching this book. 'My generation feels like it's the lucky one,' she told me one night. 'Our grandparents had the Great Leap Forward, our parents had the Cultural Revolution. But we get to study, to travel, to make money. So I guess we really don't think that much about the Square thing.' At first I didn't know what she meant by that. And then I realized: she meant the *Tiananmen* Square 'thing' – the pro-democracy protest crushed by military force in 1989.

The fourth and final pitfall is that China may so antagonize its neighbours that they gravitate towards a balancing coalition led by an increasingly realist United States. There is certainly no shortage of resentment in the rest of Asia about the way China throws its weight about these days. Chinese plans to divert the water resources of the Qinghai-Tibetan plateau have troubling implications for Bangladesh, India and Kazakhstan. In Hanoi patience is wearing thin with the Chinese habit of employing their own people in Vietnamese bauxite mines. And relations with Japan took such a turn for the worse in a dispute over the tiny Senkaku/Diaoyu Islands that China imposed an embargo on rare-earth exports, in retaliation for the arrest of a stray Chinese fisherman.[59] Yet these frictions are very far from sufficient grounds for what would be the biggest shift in US foreign policy since Richard Nixon and Henry Kissinger reopened diplomatic communications with China in 1972. And the forty-fourth occupant of the White House seems a long way removed from the realist tradition in American foreign policy, despite the impression left by his visits to India and Indonesia in late 2010.

The dilemma posed for the 'going' power by the 'coming' power is always agonizing. The cost of resisting Germany's rise was heavy indeed for Britain; it was much easier quietly to slide into the role of

Europe, America, China and India, Estimated Shares of Global GDP, Selected Years, 1500–2008

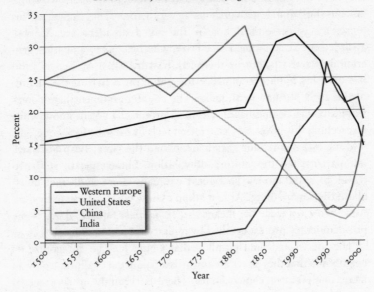

junior partner to the United States. Should America seek to contain China? Or appease China? Opinion polls suggest that ordinary Americans are no more certain how to respond than the President. In a recent survey by the Pew Research Center, 49 per cent of respondents said they did not expect China to 'overtake the U.S. as the world's main superpower', but 46 per cent took the opposite view.[60] Coming to terms with a new global order was hard enough after the collapse of the Soviet Union, which went to the heads of many commentators. But the Cold War lasted little more than four decades and the Soviet Union never came close to overtaking the US economy. What we are living through now is the end of 500 years of Western predominance. This time the Eastern challenger is for real, both economically and geopolitically. It is too early for the Chinese to proclaim 'We are the masters now.' But they are clearly no longer the apprentices. Nevertheless, civilizational conflict in Huntington's sense still seems a distant prospect. We are more likely to witness the kind of shift that in the past 500 years nearly always went in favour of the West. One civilization grows weaker, another stronger. The critical question is not whether the two will clash, but whether the weaker will tip over from weakness to outright collapse.

Retreat from the mountains of the Hindu Kush or the plains of Mesopotamia has long been a harbinger of decline and fall. It is significant that the Soviet Union withdrew from Afghanistan in the *annus mirabilis* of 1989 and ceased to exist in 1991. What happened then, like the events of the distant fifth century, is a reminder that civilizations do not in fact appear, rise, reign, decline and fall according to some recurrent and predictable life cycle. It is historians who retrospectively portray the process of dissolution as slow-acting, with multiple over-determining causes. Rather, civilizations behave like all complex adaptive systems. They function in apparent equilibrium for some unknowable period. And then, quite abruptly, they collapse. To return to the terminology of Thomas Cole, the painter of *The Course of Empire*, the shift from consummation to destruction and then to desolation is not cyclical. It is sudden. A more appropriate visual representation of the way complex systems collapse may be the old poster, once so popular in thousands of college dorm rooms, of a runaway steam train that has crashed through the wall of a Victorian railway terminus and hit the street below nose first. A defective brake or a sleeping driver can be all it takes to go over the edge of chaos.

Can anything be done to save Western civilization from such a calamity? First, we should not be too fatalistic. True, the things that once set the West apart from the Rest are no longer monopolized by us. The Chinese have got capitalism. The Iranians have got science. The Russians have got democracy. The Africans are (slowly) getting modern medicine. And the Turks have got the consumer society. But what this means is that Western modes of operation are not in decline but are flourishing nearly everywhere, with only a few remaining pockets of resistance. A growing number of Resterners are sleeping, showering, dressing, working, playing, eating, drinking and travelling like Westerners.[61] Moreover, as we have seen, Western civilization is more than just one thing; it is a package. It is about political pluralism (multiple states and multiple authorities) as well as capitalism; it is about the freedom of thought as well as the scientific method; it is about the rule of law and property rights as well as democracy. Even today, the West still has more of these institutional advantages than the Rest. The Chinese do not have political competition. The Iranians do not have freedom of conscience. They get to vote in Russia, but the rule of law there is a sham. In none of these countries is there a free press. These differences may explain why, for example, all three countries lag behind Western countries in qualitative indices that measure 'national innovative development' and 'national innovation capacity'.[62]

Of course Western civilization is far from flawless. It has perpetrated its share of historical misdeeds, from the brutalities of imperialism to the banality of the consumer society. Its intense materialism has had all kinds of dubious consequences, not least the discontents Freud encouraged us to indulge in. And it has certainly lost that thrifty asceticism that Weber found so admirable in the Protestant ethic.

Yet this Western package still seems to offer human societies the best available set of economic, social and political institutions – the ones most likely to unleash the individual human creativity capable of solving the problems the twenty-first century world faces. Over the past half-millennium, no civilization has done a better job of finding and educating the geniuses that lurk in the far right-hand tail of the distribution of talent in any human society. The big question is whether or not we are still able to recognize the superiority of that package. What makes a civilization real to its inhabitants, in the end, is not just the splendid edifices at its centre, nor even the smooth functioning of the institutions they house. At its core, a civilization is the texts that are taught in its schools, learned by its students and recollected in times of tribulation. The civilization of China was once built on the teachings of Confucius. The civilization of Islam – of the cult of submission – is still built on the Koran. But what are the foundational texts of Western civilization, that can bolster our belief in the almost boundless power of the free individual human being?* And

* I would suggest the King James Bible, Isaac Newton's *Principia*, John Locke's *Two Treatises of Government*, Adam Smith's *Moral Sentiments* and *Wealth of Nations*, Edmund Burke's *Reflections on the Revolution in France* and Charles Darwin's *Origin of Species* – to which should be added William Shakespeare's plays and selected speeches of Abraham Lincoln and Winston Churchill. If I had to select just a single volume as my Koran, it would be Shakespeare's complete works.

how good are we at teaching them, given our educational theorists' aversion to formal knowledge and rote-learning? Maybe the real threat is posed not by the rise of China, Islam or CO_2 emissions, but by our own loss of faith in the civilization we inherited from our ancestors.

Our civilization is more than just (as P. G. Wodehouse joked) the opposite of amateur theatricals (see the epigraph above). Churchill captured a crucial point when he defined the 'central principle of [Western] Civilization' as 'the subordination of the ruling class to the settled customs of the people and to their will as expressed in the Constitution':

> Why [Churchill asked] should not nations link themselves together in a larger system and establish a rule of law for the benefit of all? That surely is the supreme hope by which we should be inspired . . .
>
> But it is vain to imagine that the mere . . . declaration of right principles . . . will be of any value unless they are supported by those qualities of civic virtue and manly courage – aye, and by those instruments and agencies of force and science [–] which in the last resort must be the defence of right and reason.
>
> Civilization will not last, freedom will not survive, peace will not be kept, unless a very large majority of mankind unite together to defend them and show themselves possessed of a constabulary power before which barbaric and atavistic forces will stand in awe.[63]

In 1938 those barbaric and atavistic forces were abroad, above all in Germany. Yet, as we have seen, they were as much products of Western civilization as the values of freedom and lawful government that Churchill held dear. Today, as then, the biggest threat to Western civilization is posed not by other civilizations, but by our own pusillanimity – and by the historical ignorance that feeds it.

Notes

INTRODUCTION: RASSELAS'S QUESTION

1. Clark, *Civilisation*.
2. Braudel, *History of Civilizations*.
3. See also Bagby, *Culture and History*; Mumford, *City in History*.
4. On manners see Elias, *Civilizing Process*.
5. See Coulborn, *Origins of Civilized Societies* and, more recently, Fernández-Armesto, *Civilizations*.
6. Quigley, *Evolution of Civilizations*.
7. Bozeman, *Politics and Culture*.
8. Melko, *Nature of Civilizations*.
9. Eisenstadt, *Comparative Civilizations*.
10. McNeill, *Rise of the West*.
11. Braudel, *History of Civilizations*, pp. 34f.
12. See Fernández-Armesto, *Millennium*; Goody, *Capitalism and Modernity* and *Eurasian Miracle*; Wong, *China Transformed*.
13. McNeill, *Rise of the West*. See also Darwin, *After Tamerlane*.
14. Based on data in Maddison, *World Economy*. The historic figures for global output (gross domestic product) must be treated with even more caution than those for population because of the heroic assumptions Maddison had to make to construct his estimates, and also because he elected to calculate GDP in terms of purchasing-power parity to allow for the much lower prices of non-traded goods in relatively poor countries.
15. Details in Fogel, *Escape from Hunger*, tables 1.2, 1.4.
16. Figures from Chandler, *Urban Growth*.
17. Calculated in terms of current dollars, from the World Bank's World Development Indicators online database.
18. For an illuminating discussion, see Scruton, *The West and the Rest*.
19. See e.g. Laue, 'World Revolution of Westernization'.

20. Acemoglu et al., 'Reversal of Fortune'; Putterman and Weil, 'Post-1500 Population Flows'.
21. Pomeranz, *Great Divergence*.
22. Elvin, *Pattern of the Chinese Past*.
23. Clark, *Farewell to Alms*.
24. Johnson, *Rasselas*, pp. 56f.
25. Murray, *Human Accomplishment*.
26. Landes, *Wealth and Poverty*.
27. Hibbs and Olsson, 'Geography'; Bockstette et al., 'States and Markets'.
28. Diamond, *Guns, Germs and Steel*.
29. Diamond, 'How to Get Rich'.
30. See e.g. Roberts, *Triumph of the West*.
31. See North, *Understanding the Process of Economic Change*; North et al., *Violence and Social Orders*.
32. Clark, *Farewell to Alms*, pp. 337–42.
33. Rajan and Zingales, 'Persistence of Underdevelopment'; Chaudhary et al., 'Big BRICs, Weak Foundations'.
34. Huntington, *Clash of Civilizations*.
35. Wallerstein, *Modern World-System*.
36. Huntington, *Clash of Civilizations*.
37. See e.g. Kagan, *Paradise and Power* and, more recently, Schuker, 'Sea Change'.
38. See most recently Osborne, *Civilization*.
39. Morris, *Why the West Rules*.
40. Brownworth, *Lost to the West*.
41. Cahill, *How the Irish Saved Civilization*. At the time of writing, it remains to be seen if the compliment will be returned.
42. Dawson, *Making of Europe*; Woods, *How the Catholic Church Built Western Civilization*.
43. Matthews, 'Strange Death'; Guyver, 'England'.
44. Amanda Kelly, 'What Did Hitler Do in the War, Miss?', *Times Educational Supplement*, 19 January 2001.
45. MacGregor, *History of the World*.

CHAPTER I: COMPETITION

1. Smith, *Wealth of Nations*, Book I, chs. 8, 11, Book IV, ch. 9.
2. Montesquieu, *Spirit of the Laws*, Book VIII, ch. 21. See also Book VII, ch. 7, Book XIX, chs. 17–20.
3. See in general Bishop, *China's Imperial Way*.

4. Tsai, *Perpetual Happiness*, p. 123.

5. Brook, *Confusions of Pleasure*.

6. Pinker, *Better Angels*.

7. Castor, *Blood and Roses*.

8. Fogel, *Escape from Hunger*, tables 1.2, 1.4.

9. Clark, *Farewell to Alms*.

10. Dardess, 'Ming Landscape', pp. 323f.

11. Needham (ed.), *Science and Civilization*, vol. V, pp. 52, 313.

12. Ibid., vol. VI, pp. 558, 571, 581. Cf. Hobson, *Eastern Origins*, p. 201.

13. Mokyr, *Lever of Riches*, pp. 209ff.

14. Needham (ed.), *Science and Civilization*, vol. IV, p. 184.

15. Ibid., vol. V, pp. 61, 157, 354, 421. Cf. Hobson, *Eastern Origins*, pp. 207–12.

16. Levathes, *When China Ruled the Seas*.

17. Ray, 'Analysis', p. 82.

18. Ibid., pp. 82–4.

19. Duyvendak, 'True Dates'.

20. Cotterell, *Imperial Capitals*, p. 222. See also Fernández-Armesto, *Millennium*, ch. 4; *Pathfinders*, ch. 4.

21. Landes, *Wealth and Poverty*, pp. 95f.

22. Keay, *China: A History*, p. 385.

23. According to Nicholas D. Kristof, '1492: The Prequel', *New York Times*, 6 June 1999.

24. Finlay, 'Portuguese and Chinese Maritime Imperialism', pp. 240f.

25. Flynn and Giraldez, 'Born with a "Silver Spoon"', p. 204.

26. Chirot, 'Rise of the West', pp. 181ff.

27. Cipolla, *Guns and Sails*, pp. 77–82.

28. Hoffman, 'Why Was It that Europeans Conquered the World?' On the deficiencies of the Ming tax system, see Huang, *1587*, p. 64.

29. Jones, *European Miracle*, p. 67.

30. Ibid., p. 120.

31. Birch, *Historical Charters*, pp. 3f.

32. Ibid., pp. 19f.

33. Ibid., pp. 61f.

34. Details from Inwood, *History of London*.

35. Burrage and Corry, 'At Sixes and Sevens'.

36. Landes, *Revolution in Time*, pp. 34–42.

37. Barmé, *Forbidden City*.

38. Cotterell, *Imperial Capitals*, p. 222.

39. Cotterell, *China: A History*, p. 178.

40. Catto, 'Written English'.

41. Flynn and Giraldez, 'Arbitrage, China, and World Trade'.

42. Ebrey, *Cambridge Illustrated History of China*, esp. p. 215.

43. For a good summary, see Goody, *Capitalism and Modernity*, pp. 103–17.

44. Guan and Li, 'GDP and Economic Structure'.

45. See Mintz, *Sweetness and Power*, p. 191; Higman, 'Sugar Revolution'.

46. Clark, *Farewell to Alms*, p. 57.

47. Pelzer and Pelzer, 'Coffee Houses of Augustan London'.

48. For a revisionist view, which downplays the social damage done by exports of opium from British India, see Newman, 'Opium Smoking in Late Imperial China'.

49. Barrow, *Life of Macartney*, vol. I, pp. 348f.

CHAPTER 2: SCIENCE

1. See in general Bakar, *Tawhid and Science*; Morgan, *Lost History*; Lyons, *House of Wisdom*.

2. Freely, *Aladdin's Lamp*, p. 163.

3. Lyons, *House of Wisdom*, p. 5.

4. İhsanoglu, *Science, Technology and Learning*, pp. 16f.

5. Mansel, *Constantinople*, p. 62.

6. Hamdani, 'Ottoman Response'.

7. Forster and Daniel (eds.), *Life and Letters*, p. 221.

8. Hess, 'Ottoman Seaborne Empire'.

9. İnalcik and Quataert, *Economic and Social History of the Ottoman Empire*, p. xviii.

10. Stoye, *Siege of Vienna*, p. 32.

11. Ibid., p. 119. Cf. Panaite, *Ottoman Law*.

12. Goodwin, *Lords of the Horizons*, p. 229.

13. Lewis, *What Went Wrong?*, pp. 18f.

14. Özmucur and Pamuk, 'Real Wages'; Quataert, *Ottoman Manufacturing*. As in India, traditional textile manufacturing was hard hit by European competition in the early nineteenth century, but the Ottoman economy fared better in the period after 1850.

15. Rafeq, 'Making a Living'; Pamuk, 'Institutional Change'.

16. Grant, 'Rethinking the Ottoman "Decline"'.

17. Steinberg, *Five Hundred Years*, pp. 22–5.

18. Eisenstein, *Printing Revolution*, p. 168.

19. Luther, *Concerning Christian Liberty* (1520).

20. Crofts, 'Printing, Reform and Catholic Reformation', p. 376.

21. Holborn, 'Printing and the Growth of a Protestant Movement', pp. 134f.
22. Dittmar, 'Ideas, Technology, and Economic Change'.
23. Walsham, 'Unclasping the Book?', p. 156.
24. Hall, 'Intellectual Tendencies', pp. 390f.
25. Bohnstedt, 'Infidel Scourge of God', p. 24.
26. Clark, 'Publication of the Koran', p. 9.
27. Thomas, *Religion and the Decline of Magic*; Levack, *Witch-Hunt*.
28. Kuhn, *Structure of Scientific Revolutions*.
29. Henry, *Scientific Revolution*, p. 74.
30. Shank, *Newton Wars*, p. 239.
31. Murray, *Human Accomplishment*, esp. pp. 257f., 297f. See also Basalla, 'Spread of Western Science'.
32. Smith, 'Science and Technology'. Cf. Clark, 'Aristotle and Averroes'.
33. Deen, *Science under Islam*, pp. 122ff.; Huff, *Rise of Early Modern Science*, p. 92.
34. Huff, *Rise of Early Modern Science*, p. 75.
35. Deen, *Science under Islam*, pp. 4f.; Faroqhi, *Subjects of the Sultan*.
36. Mansel, *Constantinople*, p. 45.
37. Lewis, *What Went Wrong?*, p. 43.
38. Barkey, *Empire of Difference*, pp. 232f.; İhsanoglu, *Science, Technology and Learning*, p. 20. See also Mansel, *Constantinople*, p. 46; Vlahakis et al., *Imperialism and Science*, p. 79.
39. İhsanoglu, *Science, Technology and Learning*, p. 4.
40. Barkey, *Empire of Difference*, p. 233.
41. Sprat, *History of the Royal Society*, pp. 63f.
42. Fernández-Armesto, *Pathfinders*, p. 281.
43. Gribbin, *Fellowship*, pp. 253f.
44. Hall, *Philosophers at War*.
45. Stewart, *Rise of Public Science*, p. 258.
46. Allen, *Steam Engine*; Allen, *1715 and Other Newcomen Engines*.
47. Goldstone, *Revolution and Rebellion*, p. 367. Cf. Gerber, 'Monetary System'; Pamuk, 'Prices'.
48. Goffman, *Ottoman Empire and Early Modern Europe*, p. 119.
49. Shaw, *History of the Ottoman Empire*, p. 207.
50. Lewis, *Middle East*, p. 126. See also Goldstone, *Revolution and Rebellion*, pp. 378f.
51. Lewis, *Modern Turkey*, p. 23.
52. Coles, *Ottoman Impact*, p. 163.
53. Mansel, *Constantinople*, pp. 86–96; Goodwin, *Lords of the Horizons*, p. 168.
54. Clark, *Iron Kingdom*, p. 240.

55. T. R. Ybarra, 'Potsdam of Frederick the Great – After William II', *New York Times*, 10 September 1922.
56. Clark, *Iron Kingdom*, p. 189.
57. Chakrabongse, *Education of the Enlightened Despots*, pp. 52f.
58. Fraser, *Frederick the Great*, pp. 29f.
59. Clark, *Iron Kingdom*, p. 215.
60. Frederick, *Anti-Machiavel*, ch. 26.
61. Clark, *Iron Kingdom*, p. 231.
62. Ibid., pp. 241f.
63. Haffner, *Rise and Fall of Prussia*, pp. 37, 43f.
64. Gerber, 'Jews and Money-Lending'. See also Quataert, *Manufacturing and Technology Transfer*.
65. Clark, *Iron Kingdom*, p. 187.
66. Blanning, *Culture of Power*, pp. 108f.
67. Darnton, *Literary Underground*, p. 25.
68. Terrall, *Man Who Flattened the Earth*, pp. 181–5.
69. Aldington (ed.), *Letters of Voltaire and Frederick the Great*, p. 179.
70. Frederick, *Anti-Machiavel*, pp. 400–405.
71. Terrall, *Man Who Flattened the Earth*, p. 235.
72. Shank, *Newton Wars*, p. 475; Fraser, *Frederick the Great*, p. 259.
73. Kant, '"What is Enlightenment?"'
74. Clark, *Iron Kingdom*, p. 215.
75. Ibid., p. 195.
76. Palmer, 'Frederick the Great', p. 102.
77. Bailey, *Field Artillery*, pp. 165ff.
78. Duffy, *Frederick the Great*, p. 264.
79. Kinard, *Weapons and Warfare*, pp. 157f.
80. Steele, 'Muskets and Pendulums', pp. 363ff.
81. Ibid., pp. 368f.
82. Agoston, 'Early Modern Ottoman and European Gunpowder Technology'.
83. Coles, *Ottoman Impact*, p. 186.
84. Montesquieu, *Persian Letters*, Letter XIX.
85. Mansel, *Constantinople*, pp. 185f.
86. Shaw, *History of the Ottoman Empire*, pp. 236–8.
87. Lewis, *What Went Wrong?*, p. 27.
88. Aksan, *Ottoman Statesman*.
89. İhsanoglu, *Science, Technology and Learning*, p. 56. See also Levy, 'Military Reform'.
90. Reid, *Crisis of the Ottoman Empire*, pp. 59–64.
91. Mansel, *Constantinople*, pp. 237ff.

92. Araci, 'Donizetti', p. 51.

93. İhsanoglu, *Science, Technology and Learning*, pp. 170ff.

94. Clarke, 'Ottoman Industrial Revolution', pp. 67f.

95. Findley, 'Ottoman Occidentalist'.

96. Weiker, 'Ottoman Bureaucracy', esp. pp. 454f.

97. Pamuk, 'Bimetallism', p. 16; Davison, *Essays*, pp. 64–7. Cf. Farley, *Turkey*, pp. 121f.

98. Pamuk, *Ottoman Empire*, pp. 55–9.

99. Kinross, *Atatürk*, p. 386.

100. Mango, *Atatürk*, p. 396.

101. Kinross, *Atatürk*, pp. 442f.

102. Mango, *Atatürk*, p. 412.

103. World Intellectual Property Organization, *World Intellectual Property Indicators 2010* (Geneva, 2010): http://www.wipo.int/ipstats/en/statistics/patents/.

104. Senor and Singer, *Start-Up Nation*.

105. Ferguson, *High Financier*, pp. 317f.

CHAPTER 3: PROPERTY

1. Fernández-Armesto, *Americas*, p. 66.

2. The classic statements are Pomeranz, *Great Divergence*; Williams, *Capitalism and Slavery*. For a modified version of the argument, see Acemoglu et al., 'Rise of Europe'.

3. Barrera-Osorio, *Experiencing Nature*.

4. Churchill, 'Civilization', pp. 45f.

5. Hemming, *Conquest of the Incas*, p. 28.

6. Markham (ed.), *Reports*, pp. 113–27.

7. Wood, *Conquistadors*, p. 134.

8. Hemming, *Conquest of the Incas*, p. 121.

9. Bingham, *Lost City*.

10. Burkholder, *Colonial Latin America*, p. 46.

11. Ibid., p. 126.

12. Findlay and O'Rourke, *Power and Plenty*, figure 4.4.

13. Lanning, *Academic Culture*.

14. Barrera-Osorio, *Experiencing Nature*.

15. Fernández-Armesto, *Americas*, p. 95.

16. South Carolina Department of Archives and History, Charleston.

17. Tomlins, 'Indentured Servitude'.

18. Engerman and Sokoloff, 'Once upon a Time in the Americas'.

19. See in general Egnal, *New World Economies*.

20. Elliott, *Empires of the Atlantic World*, p. 411.

21. Adamson, 'England without Cromwell'.

22. Clark, 'British America'.

23. Acemoglu et al., 'Reversal of Fortune'.

24. Clark, *Farewell to Alms*.

25. Emmer, *Colonialism and Migration*, p. 35.

26. North et al., *Violence and Social Orders*, ch. 3.

27. Fernández-Armesto, *Americas*, p. 159.

28. The classic statement is by North and Weingast, 'Constitutions and Commitment'. See also on the role of fiscal strength and overseas expansion O'Brien, 'Inseparable Connections'.

29. Hobbes, *Leviathan*, Part I, ch. 13.

30. Ibid., ch. 18.

31. Ibid., Part II, chs. 17, 19.

32. Locke, *Two Treatises*, Book II, ch. 3.

33. Ibid., ch. 11.

34. Ibid., ch. 6.

35. Ibid., ch. 9.

36. Ibid., ch. 13.

37. Full text at http://avalon.law.yale.edu/17th_century/nc05.asp.

38. Engerman and Sokoloff, 'Once upon a Time in the Americas'.

39. Arneil, *John Locke and America*, p. 98.

40. Locke, *Two Treatises*, Book II, ch. 5.

41. Elliott, *Empires of the Atlantic World*, p. 135.

42. Ibid., p. 40. See also Sato, *Legal Aspects of Landownership*.

43. Engerman and Sokoloff, 'Once upon a Time in the Americas'.

44. Ibid.

45. See Clark, *Language of Liberty*.

46. Clark, 'British America'.

47. George Washington to William Crawford, 20 September 1767, in Washington and Crawford, *Washington–Crawford Letters*, pp. 3f.

48. See Jasanoff, *Liberty's Exiles*.

49. Lynch, *Bolívar*, p. 63.

50. http://faculty.chass.ncsu.edu/slatta/hi216/documents/bolivar/sbwar1813.htm.

51. Ortega, 'Earthquakes'.

52. Lynch, 'Bolívar and the Caudillos', pp. 6f.

53. King, 'Royalist View'.

54. Lynch, 'Bolívar and the Caudillos', pp. 16f.

55. Woodward, 'Spanish Army'.
56. Ulrick, 'Morillo's Attempt', p. 553.
57. Hamnett, 'Counter Revolution'.
58. Lynch, *Bolívar*, p. 99.
59. See in general Langley, *Americas in the Age of Revolution*, esp. pp. 243–84.
60. http://web.archive.org/web/19970615224356/www.umich.edu/~proflame/mirror/etext/bol5.html.
61. Williamson, *Penguin History*, p. 218.
62. http://web.archive.org/web/19970615224356/www.umich.edu/~proflame/mirror/etext/bol5.html.
63. Bolívar to Sir Henry Cullen, 6 September 1815, in Bolívar (ed.), *Selected Writings*, vol. I, p. 114.
64. http://web.archive.org/web/19970615224356/www.umich.edu/~proflame/mirror/etext/bol2.html.
65. http://web.archive.org/web/19970615224356/www.umich.edu/~proflame/mirror/etext/bol5.html.
66. Lynch, *Bolívar*, p. 218.
67. Engerman and Sokoloff, 'Once upon a Time in the Americas'.
68. Brown, *Adventuring*, figure 2.2.
69. Lynch, 'Bolívar and the Caudillos', pp. 16ff.
70. Data from Engerman and Sokoloff, 'Once upon a Time in the Americas'.
71. Lynch, 'Bolívar and the Caudillos', p. 34.
72. Lynch, *Bolívar*, p. 276.
73. Cordeiro, 'Constitutions'.
74. Engerman and Sokoloff, 'Once upon a Time in the Americas'.
75. Fage, 'Slavery and the Slave Trade', p. 395.
76. Curtin, *Plantation Complex*, pp. 4–26.
77. Thornton and Heywood, *Central Africans*.
78. Curtin, *Plantation Complex*, p. 26; Klein and Luna, *Slavery in Brazil*, p. 28. See also Prado, *Colonial Background*; Poppino, *Brazil*.
79. Schwartz, 'Colonial Past', p. 185.
80. Schwartz, *Slaves, Peasants and Rebels*, p. 46.
81. Graham, *Patronage and Politics*, p. 26.
82. Elkins, *Slavery*, p. 76.
83. Davis, 'Slavery', p. 72.
84. Thomas, *Slave Trade*, p. 633.
85. Davis, 'Slavery', p. 78.
86. Schwartz, *Slaves, Peasants and Rebels*, p. 42.
87. Elkins, *Slavery*, p. 40.
88. Ibid., p. 50.

89. Elliott, *Empires of the Atlantic World*, p. 283.
90. Davis, 'Slavery', p. 125.
91. Walvin, *Black Ivory*, pp. 16f.
92. See Rostworowski, *Doña Francisca Pizarro*.
93. Wang et al., 'Geographic Patterns'.
94. Carvajal-Carmona et al., 'Strong Amerind/White Sex Bias'; Bedoya et al., 'Admixture Dynamics'.
95. Ferguson, *War of the World*, pp. 20–22.
96. Creel, *Peculiar People*.
97. Eltis, 'Volume and Structure', table 1.
98. Schaefer, *Genealogical Encyclopaedia*; Thornton and Heywood, *Central Africans*.
99. Langley, *Americas in the Age of Revolution*, p. 240. Emphasis added.
100. Sam Roberts, 'Projections Put Whites in Minority in U.S. by 2050', *New York Times*, 18 December 2009.
101. Haber, 'Development Strategy'.

CHAPTER 4: MEDICINE

1. For a classic formulation, see Jules Ferry's speech of 28 July 1885, quoted in Brunschwig, *French Colonialism*, pp. 76f.
2. Gandhi, *Hind Swaraj*, ch. VI.
3. Twain, *Following the Equator*, p. 321.
4. Lenin, *Imperialism*, ch. X.
5. Collier, *Bottom Billion*.
6. Moyo, *Dead Aid*. See also Easterly, *White Man's Burden*.
7. Gandhi, *Collected Works*, vol. LIV, pp. 233f. http://www.gandhiserve.org/cwmg/VOL054.PDF.
8. Riley, 'Health Transitions', esp. figure 2, table 1.
9. Ibid., pp. 750, 752.
10. Shaw, 'Preface on Doctors', pp. lxvii–lxviii.
11. Burke, *Reflections*, p. 151.
12. Ferguson, *Ascent of Money*, p. 154.
13. http://avalon.law.yale.edu/18th_century/rightsof.asp.
14. Burke, *Reflections*, pp. 190f.
15. Rousseau, *Social Contract*.
16. Burke, *Reflections*, p. 291.
17. Schama, *Citizens*, remains the most readable English account.
18. Tocqueville, *Democracy in America*, pp. 148–51.
19. Ibid., p. 153.

20. Carter et al., (eds.), *Historical Statistics of the United States*, table Ed1-5.
21. http://users.erols.com/mwhite28/wars18c.htm.
22. All quotations from Clausewitz, *On War*, Book I, chs. 1, 2, 7; Book III, ch. 17; Book VII, chs. 4, 5, 6, 22; Book VIII, chs. 1–9.
23. Acemoglu et al., 'Consequences of Radical Reform'.
24. McLynn, *Napoleon*, p. 664.
25. Lieven, *Russia against Napoleon*.
26. Ferguson, *Ascent of Money*, pp. 81f.
27. Taylor, '1848 Revolutions'.
28. Blanton et al., 'Colonial Style'.
29. Crowder, *Senegal*, pp. 6f., 14f.; Cruise O'Brien, *White Society*, p. 39.
30. Klein, *Islam and Imperialism*, p. 118.
31. R. L. Buell, *The Native Problem in Africa* (1928), quoted in Crowder, *Senegal*, p. 23.
32. Cruise O'Brien, *White Society*, p. 33.
33. Gifford and Louis, *France and Britain*, p. 672.
34. Cohen, *Rulers of Empire*, ch. 1.
35. Brunschwig, 'French Exploration and Conquest'.
36. Conklin, *Mission*, p. 13.
37. Fonge, *Modernization without Development*, p. 66.
38. Ibid.
39. Berenson, *Heroes of Empire*, pp. 197f.
40. Joireman, 'Inherited Legal Systems'.
41. Cohen, *Rulers of Empire*, pp. 79f.
42. Asiwaju, *West African Transformations*, p. 60.
43. Taithe, *Killer Trail*.
44. Echenberg, *Colonial Conscripts*, p. 18.
45. Cohen, *Rulers of Empire*, p. 38.
46. Lunn, *Memoirs of the Maelstrom*, p. 62.
47. Marr, *Vietnamese Anticolonialism*. For full English text, see www.fsmitha.com/h2/y14viet.html.
48. Gardiner, 'French Impact on Education', p. 341.
49. Sabatier, '"Elite" Education in French West Africa'.
50. See in general Acemoglu et al., 'Disease and Development'.
51. Iliffe, *Africans*, p. 70.
52. Cohen, *Rulers of Empire*, p. 23.
53. MacLeod and Lewis (eds.), *Disease, Medicine and Empire*, p. 7.
54. *Punch*, 16 September 1903.
55. MacLeod and Lewis (eds.), *Disease, Medicine and Empire*.
56. Echenberg, 'Medical Science'; Marcovich, *French Colonial Medicine*.

57. See e.g. Beck, 'Medicine and Society'.

58. Conklin, *Mission*, pp. 56f.

59. Ibid., pp. 51ff.

60. Ibid., pp. 48ff.

61. Robiquet (ed.), *Discours et opinions*, pp. 199–201, 210–11.

62. Cohen, *Rulers of Empire*, p. 74.

63. Ibid., p. 77.

64. Van Beusekom, *Negotiating Development*, p. 6.

65. Schneider, 'Smallpox in Africa'.

66. Ngalamulume, 'Keeping the City Totally Clean', p. 199.

67. Wright, *Conflict on the Nile*. See also Daly, 'Omdurman and Fashoda'; Chipman, *French Power*, p. 53.

68. Gide, *Travels in the Congo*, p. 35.

69. Crowder, *Senegal*, pp. 4ff.

70. Yansané, 'Impact of France', p. 350; Gifford and Louis, *France and Britain*, p. 697.

71. Betts, 'Establishment of the Medina'; Cruise O'Brien, *White Society*, p. 54. Cf. Smith, *Vietnam*, pp. 88f.

72. Cohen, *Rulers of Empire*, p. 49. Cf. Betts, *Assimilation and Association*, pp. 64, 152.

73. Echenberg, *Black Death*.

74. Rohrbach, *Deutsche Kolonialwirtschaft*, vol. I, pp. 330–33. Cf. Steer, *Judgment*, p. 61.

75. Madley, 'Patterns', p. 169.

76. Deutsch, *Emancipation without Abolition*.

77. Steer, *Judgment*, pp. 55ff.

78. Seiner, *Bergtouren*, pp. 267–78.

79. Olusoga and Erichsen, *Kaiser's Holocaust*, p. 118.

80. Gewald, *Herero Heroes*, pp. 146ff.

81. Rust, *Krieg und Frieden*, pp. 6–15; Anon., *Rheinische Mission*, pp. 10–16; Leutwein, *Elf Jahre Gouverneur*, pp. 466–7; Kuhlmann, *Auf Adlers Flügeln*, pp. 42f.

82. Olusoga and Erichsen, *Kaiser's Holocaust*, p. 139.

83. Full text in Gewald, 'Great General', p. 68.

84. Zimmerer, 'First Genocide', p. 37.

85. Gewald, *Herero Heroes*, p. 173. For a contemporary German account, Bayer, *Mit dem Hauptquartier*, pp. 161–7.

86. Drechsler, *Südwestafrika unter deutscher Kolonialherrschaft*, pp. 251–79. Cf. Olusoga and Erichsen, *Kaiser's Holocaust*, p. 235.

87. Ibid., p. 224.

88. Fischer, *Rehobother Bastards*, pp. 302f.
89. Eiermann, 'The Good, the Bad, and the Ugly'.
90. Rohrbach, *Aus Südwest-Afrikas schweren Tagen*, pp. 177f.
91. For a good overview of a now large literature, see Madley, 'From Africa to Auschwitz'.
92. The point is well made in Mazower, *Dark Continent*.
93. Strachan, *First World War in Africa*.
94. Strachan, *To Arms*, p. 95.
95. Conklin, *Mission*, pp. 146–59.
96. Lunn, *Memoirs of the Maelstrom*, p. 78.
97. Ibid., p. 69.
98. Ibid., p. 71.
99. Ibid., p. 139.
100. Eichacker, 'Blacks Attack!'
101. Smith et al., *France and the Great War*, p. 128.
102. Lunn, *Memoirs of the Maelstrom*, p. 140.
103. Winter, *Great War*, p. 75; Beckett and Simpson (eds.), *Nation in Arms*, p. 11.
104. Kipling, 'France at War', pp. 341f.
105. See in general McCullum, *Military Medicine*.
106. Olusoga and Erichsen, *Kaiser's Holocaust*, pp. 284f.
107. Evans, 'Anthropology at War'.
108. Madley, 'From Africa to Auschwitz', pp. 453ff. See in general Weindling, *Health, Race and German Politics*.
109. Mazower, *Hitler's Empire*, pp. 147, 584.
110. Levine, 'Film and Colonial Memory'.
111. Riley, 'Health Transitions', table 4.
112. Iliffe, *Africans*, pp. 251–3.
113. Singer and Langdon, *Cultured Force*, p. 20.
114. Tai, 'Politics of Compromise'.
115. Saxe, 'Changing Economic Structure'.
116. Centre d'Informations Documentaires, *Work of France*, p. 17.
117. Hochschild, *Leopold's Ghost*.
118. Mazower, *Hitler's Empire*, p. 205.
119. Ibid., pp. 152, 286.
120. Ibid., p. 137.
121. Ibid., p. 149.
122. Ibid., p. 256.
123. Ibid., p. 248.
124. Fieldhouse, *Black Africa*.

CHAPTER 5: CONSUMPTION

1. Okuefuna, *Wonderful World of Albert Kahn*.
2. Galeano, *Open Veins*, p. 47.
3. Crafts, 'British Economic Growth', table 6.1.
4. Clark, *Farewell to Alms*, figure 9.2.
5. Gildea, *Barricades and Borders*, pp. 6, 145, 181.
6. Mokyr, *Industrial Revolution*, p. 109.
7. Esteban, 'Factory Costs', figure 1.
8. Allen, *British Industrial Revolution*, p. 156.
9. Morris, *Why the West Rules*, p. 497.
10. Jones, 'Living the Enlightenment'.
11. Morris, *Why the West Rules*, p. 491.
12. See especially McKendrick et al., *Birth of a Consumer Society*.
13. Berg, 'Pursuit of Luxury'.
14. Vries, 'Purchasing Power'.
15. Berg, 'Imitation to Invention'.
16. Findlay and O'Rourke, *Power and Plenty*, tables 6.2 and 6.4.
17. La Porta et al., 'Law and Finance', 'Investor Protection' and 'Economic Consequences'.
18. O'Brien et al., 'Political Components'. See also Leunig, 'British Industrial Success', p. 93.
19. Guinnane et al., 'Putting the Corporation in its Place'; Lamoreaux, 'Scylla or Charybdis?'
20. Allen, *British Industrial Revolution*.
21. Parthasarathi, 'Rethinking Wages'.
22. Pollard, *Peaceful Conquest*.
23. See Fowler Mohanty, *Labor and Laborers of the Loom*, esp. p. 76. On the wider ramifications of cotton cultivation, see Dattel, *Cotton and Race*.
24. Clark, *Farewell to Alms*, p. 267.
25. Farnie, 'Role of Merchants', pp. 20ff.
26. Darwin, *Origin*, chs. 3, 4 and 14.
27. Ferguson, 'Evolutionary Approach'.
28. Carlyle, *Past and Present*, Book I, chs. 1–4, Book IV, chs. 4, 8.
29. Kaelble, *Industrialization and Social Inequality*.
30. Evans, *Death in Hamburg*.
31. Grayling, *Light of Liberty*, pp. 189–93.
32. Wilde, *De Profundis*, pp. 21, 23, 33.
33. Berger and Spoerer, 'Economic Crises'.
34. See e.g. Fowler, *Lancashire Cotton Operatives*.

35. Allen, 'Great Divergence in European Wages'. I am grateful to Robert Allen for sharing his wage data with me.
36. Allen et al., 'Wages, Prices, and Living Standards'.
37. Mazzini, 'To the Italians'.
38. Bismarck, *Reminiscences*, Vol. I, ch. 13.
39. Schorske, *Fin-de-Siècle Vienna*.
40. H. C. Martin, 'Singer Memories': http://www.singermemories.com/index.html.
41. Maddison, *World Economy*, tables B-10, B-21.
42. Kennedy, *Rise and Fall*, p. 190.
43. Bairoch, 'International Industrialization Levels'.
44. Broadberry, 'Total Factor Productivity'.
45. Fordham, '"Revisionism" Reconsidered'.
46. Clark and Feenstra, 'Technology in the Great Divergence', table 8.
47. Dyos and Aldcroft, *British Transport*, table 4.
48. Maurer and Yu, *Big Ditch*, p. 145.
49. Clark and Feenstra, 'Technology in the Great Divergence'.
50. Clark, *Farewell to Alms*, table 15.3.
51. McKeown, 'Global Migration', p. 156.
52. Carter et al. (eds.), *Historical Statistics of the United States*, tables Ad354–443.
53. Mitchell, *Abstract of British Historical Statistics*, pp. 333f.
54. I am grateful to Simon Cundey of Henry Poole for giving me sight of the firm's old order books and other useful documents.
55. Beasley, *Japan Encounters the Barbarian*.
56. See Hirano, *State and Cultural Transformation*, p. 124.
57. Keene, *Emperor of Japan*, p. 12. See the 1873 photograph of the Emperor by Uchida Kyuichi: http://ocw.mit.edu/ans7870/21f/21f.027j/throwing_off_asia_01/emperor_02.html.
58. Malony, 'Modernity, Gender and Empire'.
59. See *Illustration of the Ceremony Promulgating the Constitution*, unknown artist (1890).
60. Penn State University, *Making Japanese* online resource, http://www.east-asian-history.net/textbooks/MJ/ch3.htm.
61. Keene, *Emperor of Japan*, p. 295.
62. Gong, *Standard of 'Civilization'*.
63. Keene, *Emperor of Japan*, p. 194.
64. Japan Cotton Spinners' Association, *Cotton Statistics of Japan: 1903–1924*, table 1.
65. Wall, *Japan's Century*, p. 17.

66. Kamisaka, *Cotton Mills and Workers*.
67. Moser, *Cotton Textile Industry*, p. 30.
68. Ibid.
69. Farnie, 'Role of Cotton Textiles'.
70. Clark and Feenstra, 'Technology in the Great Divergence'. On American productivity, see Copeland, 'Technical Development'.
71. See e.g. Moser, *Cotton Textile Industry*, p. 102. See also Wolcott and Clark, 'Why Nations Fail'.
72. Upadhyay, *Existence, Identity and Mobilization*.
73. A fine example is Mizono Toshikata's woodblock print in the Museum of Fine Arts, Boston.
74. Meech-Pekarik, *World of the Meiji Print*, p. 145.
75. From Lenin, *The State and Revolution* (1918).
76. Cole et al., 'Deflation and the International Great Depression'.
77. Friedman and Schwartz, *Monetary History of the United States*.
78. Keynes, *Tract on Monetary Reform* (1924).
79. Tooze, *Wages of Destruction*.
80. For further details, see Ferguson, *War of the World*.
81. Harrison, *Economics of World War II*.
82. Westad, *Global Cold War*.
83. Ferguson, *War of the World*, pp. 606–17.
84. Data from Singer and Small, Correlates of War.
85. Piketty and Saez, 'Income Inequality', esp. figure 20.
86. Hyman, 'Debtor Nation'.
87. I am grateful to my colleague Diego Comin for these figures.
88. Sullivan, *Jeans*, pp. 9, 77.
89. Ibid., pp. 214f.
90. 'Coca-Cola as Sold Throughout the World', *Red Barrel*, 8, 3 (March 1929).
91. See Allen, *Secret Formula*, p. 325.
92. Interview with the author, 2009. See also Wolle, *Traum von der Revolte*, esp. pp. 56–61.
93. Debray, 'The Third World', http://www.digitalnpq.org/archive/1986_spring/kalashnikov.html
94. Suri, *Power and Protest*.
95. Kurlansky, *1968*.
96. Marshall, *Demanding the Impossible*, pp. 551ff.
97. For 1968 graffiti, see http://www.bopsecrets.org/CF/graffiti.htm.
98. Greer, *Female Eunuch*, p. 322.
99. Sullivan, *Jeans*, p. 131.
100. Interview with author, 2009.
101. Interview with author, 2009.

102. Ramet, 'Rock Music in Czechoslovakia', pp. 59, 63.
103. Poiger, *Jazz, Rock and Rebels*, pp. 62ff.
104. Safanov, 'Revolution'.
105. Siefert, 'From Cold War to Wary Peace'.
106. Interview with author, 2009.
107. Bergson, 'How Big was the Soviet GDP?' See in general Cox (ed.), *Rethinking the Soviet Collapse*.
108. Fukuyama, *End of History*.
109. Gaddis, *Cold War*.
110. Charlotte Sector, 'Belarusians Wear Jeans in Silent Protest', ABC News, 13 January 2006.
111. Interview with author, 2009.
112. Ferdows, 'Women and the Islamic Revolution'; Nashat, 'Women in the Islamic Republic'.
113. Ebadi, *Iran Awakening*, pp. 41f.

CHAPTER 6: WORK

1. Gibbon, *Decline and Fall*, ch. 31, Parts III and IV.
2. Scaff, 'Remnants of Romanticism'.
3. Weber, *Max Weber*, p. 292.
4. Weber, *Protestant Ethic*, pp. 112, 154.
5. Ibid., p. 119.
6. Ibid., p. 24. For a modern restatement, see Koch and Smith, *Suicide of the West*, pp. 184f.
7. Weber, *Protestant Ethic*, p. 180.
8. Ibid., pp. 70f.
9. Ibid., p. 166. See Chiswick, 'Economic Progress'.
10. Tawney, *Religion and the Rise of Capitalism*.
11. Cantoni, 'Economic Effects'.
12. Delacroix and Nielsen, 'Beloved Myth'. See also Iannaccone, 'Introduction'.
13. Young, 'Religion and Economic Growth'.
14. Grier, 'Effect of Religion on Economic Development'.
15. Becker and Wössmann, 'Was Weber Wrong?'
16. Trevor-Roper, 'Religion, the Reformation and Social Change'.
17. Woodberry, 'Shadow of Empire'.
18. Guiso et al., 'People's Opium?'
19. Barro and McCleary, 'Religion and Economic Growth'.
20. World Bank, World Development Indicators online.
21. Ferguson, 'Economics, Religion and the Decline of Europe'.

22. Data from the Conference Board Total Economy Database, September 2010, http://www.conference-board.org/data/economydatabase/. See also OECD.Stat and various OECD publications.

23. World Values Survey Association, *World Values Survey*.

24. Chesterton, *Short History*, p. 104.

25. Bruce, *God is Dead*, p. 67.

26. Data from http://www.cofe.anglican.org/news/pr2009.html.

27. See Brown, *Death of Christian Britain*, esp. p. 191. See also the essays in McLeod and Ustorf (eds.), *Decline of Christendom*.

28. Bruce, *God is Dead*, p. 65.

29. Davie, *Religion in Britain*, pp. 119, 121.

30. Davie, *Europe: The Exceptional Case*, pp. 6f.

31. The celebrated interview quoted in the first epigraph was by Maureen Cleave, 'How Does a Beatle Live? John Lennon Lives Like This', *Evening Standard*, 4 March 1966.

32. See Barro and McCleary, 'Religion and Political Economy'.

33. Tolstoy, *Kingdom of God*, p. 301.

34. Freud, *Future of an Illusion*, p. 25.

35. Ibid., p. 30.

36. Ibid., p. 34.

37. Ibid., p. 84.

38. Freud, *Civilization*, pp. 55, 59, 69.

39. Szasz, *Anti-Freud: Karl Kraus's Criticism of Psychoanalysis and Psychiatry*.

40. Attendance is down from 25–55 per cent in the 1970s to 18–22 per cent today, but religion is clearly consumed in myriad ways (television and internet evangelists) undreamt of forty years ago: Putnam and Campbell, *American Grace*, pp. 74, 105.

41. Sheehan, 'Liberation and Redemption', p. 301.

42. Putnam and Campbell, *American Grace*, p. 326.

43. Barro and McCleary, 'Which Countries Have State Religions?'

44. Iannaconne, 'Introduction'; Davie, *Europe: The Exceptional Case*, pp. 43ff. For a popular account, see Micklethwait and Wooldridge, *God is Back*, esp. p. 175.

45. Smith, *Wealth of Nations*, Book V, ch. I.

46. Micklethwait and Wooldridge, *God is Back*, p. 175.

47. Zakaria, *Future of Freedom*, pp. 199ff.

48. Putnam and Campbell, *American Grace*, p. 137.

49. Weber, *Protestant Ethic*, pp. 115, 117.

50. For an historically informed account of the crisis, see Ferguson, *Ascent of Money*.

51. Different estimates in Aikman, *Beijing Factor*, pp. 7f.
52. Bays, 'Chinese Protestant Christianity', p. 182.
53. Aikman, *Beijing Factor*, pp. 141f.
54. Ibid., p. 285.
55. Ibid., pp. 20–34.
56. Morrison, *Memoirs*, pp. 77f., 288f.
57. Ibid., pp. 335ff.
58. Cohen, *China and Christianity*.
59. Taylor, *Hudson Taylor*, pp. 144f.
60. Stott, *Twenty-six Years*, pp. 26–54.
61. Austin, *China's Millions*, pp. 4–10, 86–90, 167–9.
62. Ng, 'Timothy Richard', p. 78.
63. Austin, *China's Millions*, p. 192. See also Steer, *J. Hudson Taylor*.
64. See in general Kuang-sheng, *Antiforeignism*.
65. Thompson, *Reluctant Exodus*, esp. pp. 45–50.
66. Aikman, *Beijing Factor*, pp. 53f.
67. Dikötter, *Mao's Great Famine*.
68. Zuo, 'Political Religion', p. 101.
69. Aikman, *Beijing Factor*, pp. 159, 162, 215.
70. See Chen and Huang, 'Emergence', pp. 189, 196; Bays, 'Chinese Protestant Christianity', pp. 194–6.
71. Interview with the author, 2010. See also Fenggang, 'Lost in the Market', p. 425.
72. Jianbo and Fenggang, 'The Cross Faces the Loudspeakers'.
73. Jiwei, *Dialectic of the Chinese Revolution*, pp. 150ff.
74. Simon Elegant, 'The War for China's Soul', *Time*, 20 August 2006. See also Bays, 'Chinese Protestant Christianity'.
75. Aikman, *Beijing Factor*, pp. 73–89.
76. Fenggang, 'Cultural Dynamics', p. 49. See also Sheila Melvin, 'Modern Gloss on China's Golden Age', *New York Times*, 3 September 2007; Timothy Garton Ash, 'Confucius Can Speak to Us Still – And Not Just about China', *Guardian*, 9 April 2009.
77. Christian Solidarity Worldwide, *China: Persecution of Protestant Christians in the Approach to the Beijing 2008 Olympic Games* (June 2008); Bureau of Democracy, Human Rights and Labor, *International Religious Freedom Report, 2007* (2007).
78. Hunter and Chan, *Protestantism in Contemporary China*, p. 23. See also Yihua, 'Patriotic Protestants'.
79. Simon Elegant, 'The War for China's Soul', *Time*, 20 August 2006. See also Potter, 'Belief in Control'.

80. Evan Osnos, 'Jesus in China: Christianity's Rapid Rise', *Chicago Tribune*, 22 June 2008.

81. Hunter and Chan, *Protestantism in Contemporary China*, p. 6.

82. Peng, 'Unreconciled Differences', pp. 162f.; Zhao, 'Recent Progress of Christian Studies'.

83. Aikman, *Beijing Factor*, p. 5.

84. Zhuo, 'Significance of Christianity', p. 258.

85. Aikman, *Beijing Factor*, pp. 245ff.

86. Evan Osnos, 'Jesus in China: Christianity's Rapid Rise', *Chicago Tribune*, 22 June 2008.

87. Bao, 'Intellectual Influence of Christianity', p. 274.

88. Aikman, *Beijing Factor*, p. 17.

89. Chesterton, 'Miracle of Moon Crescent', p. 116.

90. Craig Whitlock, '2 British Suspects Came from Africa', *Washington Post*, 27 July 2005.

91. Barber, *Jihad vs. McWorld*.

92. Cox and Marks, *The West, Islam and Islamism*.

93. Pew Forum, *Muslim Networks*, p. 6.

94. Tony Barber, 'Tensions Unveiled', *Financial Times*, 16 November 2010, p. 9.

95. Calculated from figures in the UK Labour Force Survey and the United Nations Population Prospects middle projection. See also 'Muslim Population "Rising 10 Times Faster than Rest of Society"', *The Times*, 30 January 2009.

96. Caldwell, *Reflections*.

97. Pew Forum, *Muslim Networks*, pp. 20–56.

98. Simcox et al., *Islamist Terrorism*.

99. See Goldsworthy, *How Rome Fell*; Heather, *Fall of the Roman Empire*.

100. Ward-Perkins, *Fall of Rome*.

101. Chesterton, 'Patriotic Idea', p. 618; Shaw, *Back to Methuselah*, pp. xv–xvi.

CONCLUSION: THE RIVALS

1. Hexter, 'Seyssel, Machiavelli, and Polybius'.

2. Goldstone, 'Cultural Orthodoxy', pp. 129f.; Goldstone, *Revolution and Rebellion*, p. 354.

3. Bolingbroke, *Patriot King*, p. 273.

4. Sorokin, *Social and Cultural Dynamics*.

5. Quigley, *Tragedy and Hope*, pp. 3f. See also Quigley, *Evolution of Civilizations*.

6. Kennedy, *Rise and Fall*, p. xvi.

7. Diamond, *Collapse*, p. 158.

8. For an interesting critique, see Joseph A. Tainter's review in *Current Anthropology*, 46 (December 2005).

9. For an introduction see Mitchell, *Complexity*.

10. Ibid., p. 5. See also Holland, *Emergence*.

11. Buchanan, *Ubiquity*.

12. Waldrop, *Complexity*.

13. Taleb, 'Fourth Quadrant'.

14. Krakauer et al. (eds.), *History, Big History and Metahistory*. Cf. Holland, *Hidden Order*.

15. Richardson, *Statistics of Deadly Quarrels*. For a modern review, see Hayes, 'Statistics of Deadly Quarrels' and the discussion in Pinker, *Better Angels*.

16. Kotkin, *Armageddon Averted*.

17. Guan and Li, 'GDP and Economic Structure'.

18. Maddison, *World Economy*.

19. http://gcr.weforum.org/gcr2010/.

20. http://www.conference-board.org/data/economydatabase/.

21. I am grateful to Jim O'Neill at Goldman Sachs for providing me with the relevant dataset.

22. Martin Wolf, 'Will China's Rise Be Peaceful?', *Financial Times*, 16 November 2010.

23. Population Division of the Department of Economic and Social Affairs of the United Nations Secretariat, World Population Prospects: The 2008 Revision, http://esa.un.org/unpp, 27 November 2010.

24. Huntington, *Clash of Civilizations*, tables 3.1, 3.2, 3.3, 4.3, 4.5, 4.6.

25. Cecchetti et al., 'Future of Public Debt'.

26. All details from Ferguson, *Cash Nexus*.

27. Congressional Budget Office, 'Supplemental Data for the Congressional Budget Office's Long-Term Budget Outlook' (June 2010).

28. Marès, 'Sovereign Subjects', Exhibit 2.

29. Sargent, 'Ends of Four Big Inflations'.

30. Eichengreen, *Exorbitant Privilege*.

31. http://english.peopledaily.com.cn/90001/90776/90883/7179010.html.

32. http://www.reuters.com/article/idUSTOE6A301Q20101104.

33. http://www.businessweek.com/news/2010–11–09/china-researcher-says-u-s-s-qe2-is-financial-protectionism.html.

34. http://www.ustreas.gov/tic/mfh.txt.

35. Author's calculations from CBO data.

36. Congressional Budget Office, 'The Budget and Economic Outlook: An Update' (August 2010), table 1.7.

37. Huntington, *Clash of Civilizations*.
38. Huntington, 'Clash of Civilizations', p. 22.
39. Sen, *Identity and Violence*; Berman, *Terror and Liberalism*. See also Edward Said, 'The Clash of Ignorance', *Nation*, 22 October 2001.
40. Tusicisny, 'Civilizational Conflicts'.
41. Marshall and Gurr, *Peace and Conflict*, appendix, table 11.1.
42. See e.g. Luard, *War in International Society*.
43. David E. Sanger, 'With Warning, Obama Presses China on Currency', *New York Times*, 23 September 2010.
44. Alan Beattie, Joshua Chaffin and Kevin Brown, 'Wen Warns against Renminbi Pressure', *Financial Times*, 6 October 2010.
45. Ferguson and Schularick, 'End of Chimerica'.
46. Jacques, *When China Rules the World*.
47. International Energy Agency, *World Energy Outlook 2010* (London, 2010).
48. http://en.china.cn/content/d732706,cd7c6d,1912_6577.html.
49. Collier, *Plundered Planet*.
50. Raine, *China's African Challenges*, p. 97.
51. Ibid., p. 164.
52. Economy, 'Game Changer', p. 149.
53. World Intellectual Property Organization, *World Intellectual Property Indicators 2010* (Geneva, 2010): http://www.wipo.int/ipstats/en/statistics/patents/.
54. Mu Rongping, 'China', in *UNESCO Science Report 2010*, pp. 379-98.
55. Organization for Economic Co-operation and Development, *Economic Survey of the UK* (October 2005).
56. Institution of Education Sciences, *Trends in International Mathematics and Science Study* (2007).
57. Pew Global Attitudes Project, 'The Chinese Celebrate their Roaring Economy, as They Struggle with its Costs', 22 July 2008: http://pewglobal.org/2008/07/22/.
58. Nicholas Eberstadt, 'China's Family Planning Policy Goes Awry', American Enterprise Institute for Public Policy Research, 23 November 2010: http://www.aei.org/article/101389.
59. Economy, 'Game Changer'.
60. Pew Research Center for People and the Press, 'Public Sees a Future Full of Promise and Peril', 22 June 2010: http://people-press.org/report/?pageid=1740.
61. Zakaria, *Post-American World*.
62. Rongping, 'China', p. 395.
63. Churchill, 'Civilization', pp. 45f.

Bibliography

INTRODUCTION: RASSELAS'S QUESTION

Acemoglu, Johnson and Robinson, 'Reversal of Fortune: Geography and Institutions in the Making of the Modern World Income Distribution', *Quarterly Journal of Economics*, 117 (2002), 1231–94

Bagby, Philip, *Culture and History: Prolegomena to the Comparative Study of Civilizations* (Berkeley/Los Angeles, 1959)

Bayly, C. A., *The Birth of the Modern World, 1780–1914* (Blackwell, 2004)

Bockstette, Valerie, Areendam Chanda and Louis Putterman, 'States and Markets: The Advantage of an Early Start', *Journal of Economic Growth* (2002), 347–69

Bozeman, Adda B., *Politics and Culture in International History: From the Ancient Near East to the Opening of the Modern Age* (New York, 1994 [1960])

Braudel, Fernand, *A History of Civilizations*, trans. Richard Mayne (New York, 1993)

Brownworth, Lars, *Lost to the West: The Forgotten Byzantine Empire that Rescued Western Civilization* (New York, 2009)

Cahill, Thomas, *How the Irish Saved Civilization* (New York, 1995)

Chandler, T., *Four Thousand Years of Urban Growth: A Historical Census* (Lewiston/Queenstown, 1987)

Chaudhary, Latika, Aldo Musacchio, Steven Nafziger and Se Yan, 'Big BRICs, Weak Foundations: The Beginning of Public Elementary Education in Brazil, Russia, India, and China, 1880–1930', draft working paper (2010)

Clark, Gregory, *A Farewell to Alms: A Brief Economic History of the World* (Princeton, 2007)

Clark, Kenneth, *Civilisation: A Personal View* (London, 2005 [1969])

Coulborn, Rushton, *The Origin of Civilized Societies* (Princeton, 1959)

Darwin, John, *After Tamerlane: The Rise and Fall of Global Empires* (London, 2007)

Dawson, Christopher, *The Making of Europe: An Introduction to the History of European Unity* (London, 1932)

Diamond, Jared, *Guns, Germs and Steel: A Short History of Everybody for the Last 13,000 Years* (London, 1998)

——, 'How to Get Rich: A Talk', *Edge*, 56, June 7, 1999

Eisenstadt, S. N., *Comparative Civilizations and Multiple Modernities* (Leiden, 2003)

Elias, Norbert, *The Civilizing Process*, 2 vols. (Oxford, 1969, 1982 [1939])

Elvin, Mark, *The Pattern of the Chinese Past* (London, 1973)

Fernández-Armesto, Felipe, *Civilizations: Culture, Ambition and the Transformation of Nature* (New York/London/Toronto/Sydney/Singapore, 2001)

——, *Millennium: A History of our Last Thousand Years* (London, 1997)

Findlay, Ronald and Kevin H. O'Rourke, *Power and Plenty: Trade, War, and the World Economy in the Second Millennium* (Princeton, 2007)

Fogel, Robert W., *The Escape from Hunger and Premature Death, 1700–2100: Europe, America, and the Third World* (Cambridge, 2003)

Goody, Jack, *Capitalism and Modernity* (Cambridge/Malden, MA, 2004)

——, *The Eurasian Miracle* (Cambridge/Malden, MA, 2009)

Guyver, Robert, 'England and the Battle for the Centre Ground: The History Working Group and the First History War (1988–1991) as an Archetype for Subsequent Wars', in Tony Taylor and Robert Guyver (eds.), *History Wars in the Classroom: Global Perspectives* (forthcoming)

Hibbs, Douglas A. Jr. and Ola Olsson, 'Geography, Biogeography, and Why Some Countries are Rich and Others are Poor', *Proceedings of the National Academy of Sciences of the United States*, 101, 10 (2004), 3715–20

Huntington, Samuel, *The Clash of Civilizations and the Remaking of World Order* (New York/London/Toronto/Sydney, 1996)

Johnson, Samuel, *The History of Rasselas, Prince of Abissinia* (Boston, 1811 [1759])

Jones, Eric, *The European Miracle: Environments, Economies and Geopolitics in the History of Europe and Asia* (Cambridge, 2003)

Kagan, Robert, *Of Paradise and Power: America and Europe in the New World Order* (New York, 2003)

Kennedy, Paul, *The Rise and Fall of the Great Powers: Economic Change and Military Conflict from 1500 to 2000* (New York, 1989)

Landes, David S., *The Wealth and Poverty of Nations: Why Some are So Rich and Some So Poor* (New York, 1998)

Laue, Theodore H. von, 'The World Revolution of Westernization', *History Teacher*, 20, 2 (1987), 263–79

MacGregor, Neil, *A History of the World in 100 Objects* (London, 2010)

McNeill, William H., *The Pursuit of Power: Technology, Armed Force and Society since AD 1000* (Chicago, 1982)

———, *The Rise of the West: A History of the Human Community* (Chicago, 1991 [1963])

Maddison, Angus, *The World Economy: A Millennial Perspective* (Paris, 2001)

Melko, Matthew, *The Nature of Civilizations* (Boston, 1969)

Matthews, Derek, 'The Strange Death of History Teaching (Fully Explained in Seven Easy-to-Follow Lessons', unpublished pamphlet (January 2009)

Morris, Ian, *Why the West Rules – For Now: The Patterns of History, and What They Reveal About the Future* (New York, 2010)

Mumford, Lewis, *The City in History* (New York, 1961)

Murray, Charles A., *Human Accomplishment: The Pursuit of Excellence in the Arts and Sciences, 800 B.C. to 1950* (New York, 2003)

North, Douglass C., *Understanding the Process of Economic Change* (Princeton, 2005)

———, John Joseph Wallis and Barry R. Weingast, *Violence and Social Orders: A Conceptual Framework for Interpreting Recorded Human History* (Cambridge, 2009)

Osborne, Roger, *Civilization: A New History of the Western World* (New York, 2008)

Pomeranz, Kenneth, *The Great Divergence: China, Europe and the Making of the Modern World Economy* (Princeton, 2000)

Putterman, L. and David N. Weil, 'Post-1500 Population Flows and the Long Run Determinants of Economic Growth and Inequality', working paper (September 2008)

Quigley, Carroll, *The Evolution of Civilizations* (New York, 1961)

Rajan, Raghuram G. and Luigi Zingales, 'The Persistence of Underdevelopment: Institutions, Human Capital, or Constituencies?', NBER working paper no. 12093 (February 2006)

Roberts, John, *The Triumph of the West* (London, 1985)

Schuker, Stephen A., 'A Sea Change in the Atlantic Economy? How the West Pulled Ahead of the Rest and Why It May Cease to Do So', in William Anthony Hay and Harvey Sicherman (eds.), *Is There Still a West? The Future of the Atlantic Alliance* (Columbia, MO, 2007), 89–124

Scruton, Roger, *The West and the Rest: Globalization and the Terrorist Threat* (London/New York, 2002)

Wallerstein, Immanuel, *The Modern World-System* (New York, 1974, 1980 and 1989)

Wong, R. Bin, *China Transformed: Historical Change and the Limits of European Experience* (Ithaca/London, 2000)

Woods, Thomas E. Jr., *How the Catholic Church Built Western Civilization* (Washington, DC, 2001)

CHAPTER 1: COMPETITION

Barmé, G. R., *The Forbidden City* (London, 2008)

Barrow, Sir John, *Some Account of the Public Life, and a Selection from the Unpublished Writings, of the Earl of Macartney*, 2 vols. (London, 1807)

Birch, W., *The Historical Charters and Constitutional Documents of the City of London* (Charleston, SC, 2009)

Bishop, K., *China's Imperial Way* (Hong Kong, 1997)

Brook, Timothy, *The Confusions of Pleasure: Commerce and Culture in Ming China* (Berkeley, 1999)

Burrage, M. C. and Corry, D., 'At Sixes and Sevens: Occupational Status in the City of London from the Fourteenth to the Seventeenth Century', *American Sociological Review*, 46, 1 (1981), 375–93

Castor, Helen, *Blood and Roses: The Paston Family and the War of the Roses* (London, 2004)

Catto, Jeremy, 'Written English: The Making of the Language, 1370–1400', *Past & Present*, 179 (2003), 24–59

Chirot, Daniel, 'The Rise of the West', *American Sociological Review*, 50, 2 (1985), 181–95

Clark, Gregory, *A Farewell to Alms: A Brief Economic History of the World* (Princeton, 2007)

Cipolla, Carlo M., *Guns and Sails in the Early Phase of European Expansion, 1400–1700* (London, 1965)

Cotterell, A., *The Imperial Capitals of China: An Inside View of the Celestial Empire* (London, 2008)

Dardess, J. W., 'A Ming Landscape: Settlement, Land Use, Labor and Estheticism in T'ai-Ho County, Kiangsi', *Harvard Journal of Asiatic Studies*, 49, 2 (1989), 295–364

Dreyer, E. L., *Zheng-He: China and the Oceans in the Early Ming Dynasty, 1405–33* (London, 2006)

Duyvendak, J. J. L., 'The True Dates of the Chinese Maritime Expeditions in the Early Fifteenth Century', *T'oung Pao*, 34, 5, Second Series (1939), 378–9

Ebrey, Patricia Buckley, *The Cambridge Illustrated History of China* (Cambridge, 1996)

Fernández-Armesto, Felipe, *Millennium: A History of our Last Thousand Years* (London, 1997)

———, *Pathfinders: A Global History of Exploration* (Oxford, 2007)

Finlay, Robert, 'Portuguese and Chinese Maritime Imperialism: Camoes's Lusiads and Luo Maodeng's Voyage of the San Bao Eunuch', *Comparative Studies in Society and History*, 34, 2 (1992), 232–41

Flynn, Dennis O. and Arturo Giraldez, 'Arbitrage, China, and World Trade in the Early Modern Period', *Journal of the Economic and Social History of the Orient*, 38, 4 (1995), 429–48

———, 'Born with a "Silver Spoon": The Origin of World Trade in 1571', *Journal of World History*, 6, 2 (1995), 201–21

Fogel, Robert W., *The Escape from Hunger and Premature Death, 1700–2100: Europe, America, and the Third World* (Cambridge, 2003)

Goody, Jack, *Capitalism and Modernity* (Cambridge/Malden, MA, 2004)

Guan Hanhui and Li Daokui, 'The GDP and Economic Structure of the Ming Dynasty' (forthcoming)

Higman, B. W., 'The Sugar Revolution', Economic History Review, 53, 2 (2000), 213–36

Hobson, John, *The Eastern Origins of Western Civilisation* (Cambridge, 2004)

Hoffman, Philip T., 'Prices, the Military Revolution, and Western Europe's Comparative Advantage in Violence', *Economic History Review* (forthcoming)

Huang, Ray, *1587: A Year of No Significance: The Ming Dynasty in Decline* (New Haven, 1977)

Inwood, S., *A History of London* (London, 1998)

Jones, Eric, *The European Miracle: Environments, Economies and Geopolitics in the History of Europe and Asia* (Cambridge, 2003)

Keay, John, *China: A History* (London, 2009)

Landes, David S., *Revolution in Time: Clocks and the Making of the Modern World*, 2nd edn (New York, 2000)

———, *The Wealth and Poverty of Nations: Why Some are So Rich and Some So Poor* (New York, 1998)

Levathes, Louise, *When China Ruled the Seas: The Treasure Fleet of the Dragon Throne, 1405–1433* (Oxford, 1994)

Menzies, Gavin, *1421: The Year China Discovered the World* (London, 2002)

Mintz, Sidney W., *Sweetness and Power: The Place of Sugar in Modern History* (London, 1985)

Mokyr, Joel, *Lever of Riches* (Oxford, 1990)

Montesquieu, Charles de Secondat, baron de, *The Spirit of the Laws*, trans. Thomas Nugent and J. V. Prichard (London, 1914 [1748])

Needham, Joseph (ed.), *Science and Civilization in China*, 7 vols. (Cambridge, 1954–)

Newman, R., 'Opium Smoking in Late Imperial China: A Reconsideration', *Modern Asian Studies,* 29 (1995), 765–94

Pelzer, John and Linda, 'The Coffee Houses of Augustan London', *History Today,* 32, (1982) 40–44

Pinker, Steven, *The Better Angels of our Nature: The Decline of Violence and its Psychological Roots* (forthcoming)

Ray, Haraprasad, 'An Analysis of the Chinese Maritime Voyages into the Indian Ocean during Early Ming Dynasty, and their Raison d'Etre', *China Report,* 23, 1 (1987), 65–87

Smith, Adam, *An Inquiry into the Nature and Causes of the Wealth of Nations* (London, 1904, [1776])

Tsai, Shih-shan Henry, *Perpetual Happiness: The Ming Emperor Yongle* (Seattle/London, 2002)

Wong, R. Bin, *China Transformed: Historical Change and the Limits of European Experience* (Ithaca/London, 2000)

CHAPTER 2: SCIENCE

Agoston, G., 'Early Modern Ottoman and European Gunpowder Technology', in E. Ihsanoglu, K. Chatzis and E. Nicolaidis, *Multicultural Science in the Ottoman Empire* (Turnhout, 2003), 13–27

Aksan, V. H., *An Ottoman Statesman in War and Peace: Ahmed Resmî Efendi, 1700–1783* (New York, 1995)

Aldington, Richard (ed.), *Letters of Voltaire and Frederick the Great* (New York, 1927)

Allen, J. S., *The 1715 and Other Newcomen Engines at Whitehaven, Cumberland* (London, 1972)

————, *The Steam Engine of Thomas Newcomen* (New York, 1977)

Araci, Emre, 'Giuseppe Donizetti at the Ottoman Court: A Levantine Life', *Musical Times, 143,* 1880 (Autumn 2002), 49–56

Bailey, Jonathan, *Field Artillery and Firepower* (Oxford, 1989)

Bakar, O., *Tawhid and Science: Essays on the History and Philosophy of Islamic Science* (Kuala Lumpur, 1991)

Barkey, K., *Empire of Difference: The Ottomans in Comparative Perspective* (Cambridge, 2008)

Basalla, George, 'The Spread of Western Science', *Science,* 156, 3775 (5 May 1967), 611–22

Blanning, T. C. W., *The Culture of Power and the Power of Culture* (Oxford, 2002)

Bohnstedt, John W., 'The Infidel Scourge of God: The Turkish Menace as Seen by German Pamphleteers of the Reformation Era', *Transactions of the American Philosophical Society*, New Series 58, 9 (1968), 1–58

Chakrabongse, C. [Prince of Siam], *The Education of the Enlightened Despots* (London, 1948)

Cizacka, M., 'Price History and the Bursa Silk Industry: A Study in Ottoman Industrial Decline, 1550–1650', *Journal of Economic History*, 40, 3 (1960), 533–50

Clark, Carol Lea, 'Aristotle and Averroes: The Influences of Aristotle's Arabic Commentator upon Western European and Arabic Rhetoric', *Review of Communication*, 7, 4 (October 2007), 369–87

Clark, Christopher, *Iron Kingdom: The Rise and Downfall of Prussia 1600–1947* (London, 2006)

Clark, Harry, 'The Publication of the Koran in Latin: A Reformation Dilemma', *The Sixteenth Century Journal*, 15, 1 (Spring 1984), 3–12

Clarke, E. C., 'The Ottoman Industrial Revolution', *International Journal of Middle East Studies*, 5, 1 (1974), 65–76

Coles, Paul, *The Ottoman Impact on Europe* (London, 1968)

Crofts, Richard A., 'Printing, Reform and Catholic Reformation in Germany (1521–1545)', *Sixteenth Century Journal*, 16, 3 (Autumn 1985), 369–81

Darnton, Robert, *The Literary Underground of the Old Regime* (Cambridge, MA/London, 1982)

Davison, Roderic H., *Essays in Ottoman and Turkish History, 1774–1923: The Impact of the West* (Austin, TX, 2001)

Deen, S. M., *Science under Islam: Rise, Decline and Revival* (Keele, 2007)

Dittmar, Jeremiah, 'Ideas, Technology, and Economic Change: The Impact of the Printing Press', American University working paper (September 2009)

Duffy, C., *Frederick the Great: A Military Life* (London, 1988)

Eisenstein, Elizabeth L., *The Printing Revolution in Early Modern Europe*, 2nd edn (Cambridge, 2005)

Farley, James L., *Turkey* (London, 1866)

Faroqhi, Suraiya, *Subjects of the Sultan: Culture and Daily Life in the Ottoman Empire* (London, 2005)

Ferguson, Niall, *High Financier: The Lives and Time of Siegmund Warburg* (London, 2010)

Fernández-Armesto, Felipe, *Pathfinders: A Global History of Exploration* (Oxford, 2007)

Findley, C. V., 'An Ottoman Occidentalist in Europe: Ahmed Midhat Meets Madame Gülnar, 1889', *American Historical Review*, 103, 1 (1998), 15–49

Forster, C. T. and F. H. B. Daniel (eds.), *The Life and Letters of Ogier Ghiselin de Busbecq* (London, 1881)

Fraser, David, *Frederick the Great* (London, 2000)

Frederick the Great, *Anti-Machiavel*, ed. Werner Bahner and Helga Bergmann, *Les Oeuvres complètes de Voltaire*, vol. XIX (Oxford, 1996)

Freely, J., *Aladdin's Lamp: How Greek Science Came to Europe through the Islamic World* (New York, 2009)

———, *The Emergence of Modern Science, East and West* (Istanbul, 2004)

Gerber, H., 'Jews and Money-Lending in the Ottoman Empire', *Jewish Quarterly Review*, 72, 2 (1981), 100–118

———, 'The Monetary System of the Ottoman Empire', *Journal of Economic and Social History of the Orient*, 25, 3 (1982), 308–24

Goffman, D., *The Ottoman Empire and Early Modern Europe* (Cambridge, 2002)

Goldstone, Jack A., *Revolution and Rebellion in the Early Modern World* (Berkeley/Los Angeles/Oxford, 1991)

Goodwin, Jason, *Lords of the Horizons: A History of the Ottoman Empire* (London, 1999)

Grant, J., 'Rethinking the Ottoman "Decline": Military Technology Diffusion in the Ottoman Empire, Fifteenth to Eighteenth Centuries', *Journal of World History*, 10, 1 (1999), 179–201

Gribbin, J., *The Fellowship: The Story of a Revolution* (London, 2005)

Haffner, Sebastian, *The Rise and Fall of Prussia* (London, 1998)

Hall, A. R., 'Intellectual Tendencies: Science', in *The New Cambridge Modern History*, vol. II: *The Reformation, 1520–59* (Cambridge, 1962), 422–52

———, *Philosophers at War* (Cambridge 1980)

Hamdani, A., 'The Ottoman Response to the Discovery of America and the New Route to India', *Journal of the American Oriental Society*, 101, 3 (1981) 323–30

Henry, John, *The Scientific Revolution and the Origins of Modern Science* (Basingstoke, 1997)

Hess, A. C., 'The Evolution of the Ottoman Seaborne Empire in the Age of the Oceanic Discoveries, 1453–1525', *American Historical Review*, 75, 7 (1970), 1892–1919

Holborn, Louise W., 'Printing and the Growth of a Protestant Movement in Germany from 1517 to 1524', *Church History*, 11, 2 (June 1942), 122–37

Huff, Toby E., *The Rise of Early Modern Science* (Cambridge, 1995)

İhsanoğlu, E., *Science, Technology and Learning in the Ottoman Empire* (Aldershot, 2004)

İnalcik, H. and D. Quataert (eds.), *An Economic and Social History of the Ottoman Empire*, vol. II, *1600–1914* (Cambridge, 1994)

Kant, Immanuel, 'Answer to the Question: "What is Enlightenment?"' (Königsberg, 1784): philosophy.eserver.org/kant/what-is-enlightenment.txt

Kinard, J., *Weapons and Warfare: Artillery* (Santa Barbara, 2007)

Kinross, Patrick, *Atatürk: The Rebirth of a Nation* (London, 2001)

Kuhn, Thomas, *The Structure of Scientific Revolutions*, 2nd edn (Chicago, 1970)

Levack, Brian, *The Witch-Hunt in Early Modern Europe*, 2nd edn (London, 1995)

Levy, A., 'Military Reform and the Problem of Centralization in the Ottoman Empire in the Eighteenth Century', *Journal of Middle Eastern Studies*, 18, 3 (July, 1982), 227–49

Lewis, Bernard, *The Emergence of Modern Turkey* (New York/Oxford, 2001)

——, *The Middle East: Two Thousand Years of History from the Rise of Christianity to the Present Day* (London, 2001)

——, *What Went Wrong? The Clash between Islam and Modernity in the Middle East* (London, 2002)

Lyons, Jonathan, *The House of Wisdom: How the Arabs Transformed Western Civilization* (London, 2010)

McCarthy, J., *The Ottoman Turks: An Introductory History to 1923* (London, 1997)

Mango, Andrew, *Atatürk* (London, 1999)

Mansel, Philip, *Constantinople: City of the World's Desire, 1453–1924* (London, 2006)

Montesquieu, *Persian Letters*, transl. Margaret Mauldon (Oxford, 2008 [1721])

Morgan, Michael Hamilton, *Lost History: The Enduring Legacy of Muslim Scientists, Thinkers and Artists* (New York, 2008)

Murray, Charles A., *Human Accomplishment: The Pursuit of Excellence in the Arts and Sciences, 800 B.C. to 1950* (New York, 2003)

Özmucur, S. and S. Pamuk, 'Real Wages and Standards of Living in the Ottoman Empire, 1489–1914', *Journal of Economic History*, 62, 2 (2002), 292–321

Palmer, R. R., 'Frederick the Great, Guibert, Bülow: From Dynastic to National War', in Peter Paret (ed.), *Makers of Modern Strategy: From Machiavelli to the Nuclear Age* (Oxford, 1986), 91–123

Pamuk, S., 'From Bimetallism to the "Limping Gold Standard": The Ottoman Monetary System in the Nineteenth Century', in Philip L. Cottrell (ed.), *East Meets West: Banking, Commerce and Investment in the Ottoman Empire* (Aldershot, 2008), 11–24

——, 'Institutional Change and the Longevity of the Ottoman Empire, 1500–1800', *Journal of Interdisciplinary History*, 35, 2 (2004), 225–47

——, *The Ottoman Empire and European Capitalism, 1820–1913: Trade, Investment and Production* (Cambridge, 1987)

——, 'Prices in the Ottoman Empire, 1469–1914', *International Journal of Middle East Studies*, 36 (2004), 451–68

Panaite, V., *The Ottoman Law of War and Peace: The Ottoman Empire and Tribute Payers* (Boulder, CO/New York, 2000)

Quataert, D., *Manufacturing and Technology Transfer in the Ottoman Empire, 1800–1914* (Istanbul, 1992)

——, *Ottoman Manufacturing in the Age of the Industrial Revolution* (Cambridge, 1993)

Rafeq, Abdul-Karim, 'Making a Living or Making a Fortune', in Nelly Hanna (ed.), *Money, Land and Trade: An Economic History of the Muslim Mediterranean* (London and New York, 2002), 101–23

Reid, James J., *Crisis of the Ottoman Empire: Prelude to Collapse, 1839–1878* (Stuttgart, 2000)

Senor, Dan and Saul Singer, *Start-Up Nation: The Story of Israel's Economic Miracle* (New York, 2009)

Shank, J. B., *The Newton Wars and the Beginning of the French Enlightenment* (Chicago/London, 2008)

Shaw, Stanford J., *History of the Ottoman Empire and Modern Turkey* (Cambridge, 1976)

Smith, W. G. C., 'Science and Technology in Early Modern Islam, c. 1450–c. 1850', London School of Economics working paper (n.d.)

Sprat, T., *The History of the Royal Society of London, for the Improving of Natural Knowledge*, 2nd edn (London, 1702)

Steele, B. D., 'Muskets and Pendulums: Benjamin Robins, Leonhard Euler, and the Ballistics Revolution', *Technology and Culture Journal*, 35, 2 (1994), 348–82

Steinberg, S. H., *Five Hundred Years of Printing* (London, 1959)

Stewart, L. *The Rise of Public Science: Rhetoric, Technology and Natural Philosophy in Newtonian Britain, 1660–1750* (Cambridge, 1992)

Stoye, John, *The Siege of Vienna* (Edinburgh, 2006)

Sturdy, D. J., *Fractured Europe 1600–1721* (Oxford, 2002)

Terrall, M., *The Man Who Flattened the Earth: Maupertuis and the Sciences in the Enlightenment* (Chicago, 2002)

Thomas, Keith, *Religion and the Decline of Magic* (London, 1971)

Vlahakis, George N. et al., *Imperialism and Science: Social Impact and Interaction* (Santa Barbara, 2006)

Walsham, Alexandra, 'Unclasping the Book? Post-Reformation English Catholicism and the Vernacular Bible,' *Journal of British Studies*, 42, 2 (2003), 141–66

Weiker, Walter F., 'The Ottoman Bureaucracy: Modernization and Reform', *Administrative Science Quarterly*, 13, 3 (1968), 451–70

CHAPTER 3: PROPERTY

Acemoglu, Daron, Simon Johnson and James A. Robinson, 'Reversal of Fortune: Geography and Institutions in the Making of the Modern World Income Distribution', *Quarterly Journal of Economics*, 117, 4 (2002), 1231–94

——, 'The Rise of Europe: Atlantic Trade, Institutional Change and Economic Growth', *American Economic Review*, 95, 3 (2005), pp. 546–79

Adamson, J. A. A., 'England without Cromwell: What if Charles I Had Avoided the Civil War?', in Niall Ferguson (ed.), *Virtual History: Alternatives and Counterfactuals* (London, 1993), 91–125

Arneil, Barbara, *John Locke and America: The Defence of English Colonialism* (Oxford, 1996)

Barrera-Osorio, A., *Experiencing Nature: The Spanish American Empire and the Early Scientific Revolution* (Austin, TX, 2006)

Bedoya, Gabriel et al., 'Admixture Dynamics in Hispanics: A Shift in the Nuclear Genetic Ancestry of a South American Population Isolate', *PNAS*, 103, 19 (9 May 2006), 7234–9

Bingham, H., *Lost City of the Incas* (London, 2003)

Bolívar, Simón, *Selected Writings of Bolívar*, ed. Harold A. Bierck Jr, transl. Lewis Bertrand, compiled by Vicente Lecuna, 2 vols. (New York, 1951)

Brown, Matthew, *Adventuring through Spanish Colonies: Simon Bolivar, Foreign Mercenaries and the Birth of New Nations* (Liverpool, 2006)

Burkholder, M. A., *Colonial Latin America*, 2nd edn (Oxford, 1994)

Carvajal-Carmona, Luis G. et al., 'Strong Amerind/White Sex Bias and a Possible Sephardic Contribution among the Founders of a Population in Northwest Colombia', *American Journal of Human Genetics*, 67 (2000), 1287–95

Churchill, Winston S., 'Civilization', in Randolph S. Churchill (ed.), *Blood, Sweat and Tears*, (Whitefish, MT, 2007 [1940]), 45–9

Clark, Gregory, *A Farewell to Alms: A Brief Economic History of the World* (Princeton, 2007)

Clark, J. C. D., 'British America: What If There Had Been No American Revolution?' in Niall Ferguson (ed.), *Virtual History: Alternatives and Counterfactuals* (London, 1993), 125–75

——, *The Language of Liberty, 1660–1832: Political Discourse and Social Dynamics in the Anglo-American World* (Cambridge, 1993)

Cordeiro, Jose Luis, 'Constitutions around the World: A View from Latin

America', Institute of Developing Economies Discussion Paper, 164 (2008)

Creel, Margaret Washington, *A Peculiar People: Slave Religion and Community-Culture among the Gullahs* (New York, 1988)

Curtin, Philip, *The Rise and Fall of the Plantation Complex: Essays in Atlantic History* (Cambridge, 1998)

Davis, David Brion, 'Slavery', in C. Van Woodward (ed.), *The Comparative Approach to American History: Slavery* (New Jersey, 1969), pp. 121–35

Egnal, M., *New World Economies: The Growth of the Thirteen Colonies and Early Canada* (New York/Oxford, 1998)

Elkins, Stanley, *Slavery: A Problem in American Institutional and Intellectual Life* (Chicago, 1968)

Elliott, J. H., *Empires of the Atlantic World* (New Haven, 2006)

Eltis, David, 'The Volume and Structure of the Transatlantic Slave Trade: A Reassessment', *William and Mary Quarterly*, 58, 1 (January 2001), 17–46

Emmer, P. C. (ed.), *Colonialism and Migration: Indentured Labour before and after Slavery* (Dordrecht, 1986)

Engerman, Stanley L. and Kenneth L. Sokoloff, 'Once upon a Time in the Americas: Land and Immigration Policies in the New World', working paper (2008)

Fage, J. D., 'Slavery and the Slave Trade in the Context of West African History', *Journal of African History*, 10, 3 (1969), 393–404

Ferguson, Niall, *The War of the World: History's Age of Hatred* (London, 2006)

Fernández-Armesto, Felipe, *The Americas: A History of Two Continents* (London, 2003)

Findlay, Ronald and Kevin H. O'Rourke, *Power and Plenty: Trade, War, and the World Economy in the Second Millennium* (Princeton, 2007)

Gabai, Rafael Varón, *Francisco Pizarro and his Brothers: The Illusion of Power in Sixteenth-Century Peru* (Norman, 1997)

Graham, R., *Patronage and Politics in Nineteenth-Century Brazil* (Stanford, 1990)

Haber, Stephen, 'Development Strategy or Endogenous Process? The Industrialization of Latin America', Stanford University working paper (2005)

Hamnett, Brian R., 'The Counter Revolution of Morillo and the Insurgent Clerics of New Granada, 1815–1820', *Americas*, 32, 4 (April 1976), 597–617

Hemming, J., *The Conquest of the Incas* (London, 1993)

Hobbes, Thomas, *Leviathan or the Matter, Forme, and Power of a Common Wealth, Ecclesiasticall and Civil* (London, 1651)

Jasanoff, Maya, *Liberty's Exiles: American Loyalists in the Revolutionary World* (forthcoming)

King, James F., 'A Royalist View of Colored Castes in the Venezuelan War of Independence', *Hispanic American Historical Review*, 33, 4 (1953), 526–37

Klein, Herbert F. and Francisco Vidal Luna, *Slavery in Brazil* (Cambridge, 2010)

Langley, Lester D., *The Americas in the Age of Revolution, 1750–1850* (New Haven/London, 1998)

Lanning, John Tate, *Academic Culture in the Spanish Colonies* (Port Washington, NY/London, 1969)

Locke, John, *Two Treatises of Government: In the former, The false Principles and Foundation of Sir Robert Filmer, And his Followers, are Detected and Overthrown. The latter is an Essay concerning The True Original, Extent, and End of Civil Government* (London, 1690)

Lynch, J., 'Bolívar and the Caudillos', *Hispanic American Historical Review*, 63, 1 (1983), 3–35

——, *Simón Bolívar: A Life* (London, 2006)

Markham, Clements R. (ed.), *Reports on the Discovery of Peru* (London, 1872)

North, Douglass C., John Joseph Wallis and Barry R. Weingast, *Violence and Social Orders: A Conceptual Framework for Interpreting Recorded Human History* (Cambridge, 2009)

North, Douglass C. and Barry R. Weingast, 'Constitutions and Commitment: The Evolution of Institutions Governing Public Choice in Seventeenth-Century England', *Journal of Economic History*, 44, 4 (1989), 803–32

O'Brien, Patrick K.,'Inseparable Connections: Trade, Economy, Fiscal State, and the Expansion of Empire, 1688–1815', in P. J. Marshall (ed.), The Oxford History of the British Empire, vol. II: The Eighteenth Century (Oxford/New York, 1998), 53–77

Ortega, F. A., 'Earthquakes during the Colonial Period', *ReVista: Harvard Review of Latin America* (2007): http://www.drclas.harvard.edu/revista/articles/view/907

Pomeranz, Kenneth, *The Great Divergence: China, Europe and the Making of the Modern World Economy* (Princeton, 2000)

Poppino, Rollie E., *Brazil: The Land and the People* (Oxford, 1968)

Prado, C., *The Colonial Background of Modern Brazil* (Berkeley/Los Angeles/London, 1969)

Reid, James J., *Crisis of the Ottoman Empire: Prelude to Collapse, 1839–1878* (Stuttgart, 2000)

Rostworowski, María, *Doña Francisca Pizarro* (Lima, 1989)

Sato, A., *Legal Aspects of Landownership in Colonial Spanish America* (Tokyo, 1976)

Schaefer, Christina, *Genealogical Encyclopaedia of the Colonial Americas* (Baltimore, 1998)

Schwartz, Stuart B., 'The Colonial Past: Conceptualizing Post-*Dependentista* Brazil', in Jeremy Adelman (ed.), *Colonial Legacies: The Problem of Persistence in Latin American History* (New York/London, 1999), 175–92

———, *Slaves, Peasants, and Rebels: Reconsidering Brazilian Slavery* (Champaign, IL, 1995)

Thomas, Hugh, *The History of the Atlantic Slave Trade 1440–1870* (London, 1997)

Thornton John and Linda Heywood, *Central Africans, Atlantic Creoles, and the Foundation of the Americas, 1585* (Cambridge, 2007)

Tomlins, C., 'Indentured Servitude in Perspective: European Migration into North America and the Composition of the Early American Labour Force, 1600–1775', in Cathy Matson (ed.), *The Economy of Early America: Historical Perspectives and New Directions* (Philadelphia, 2007), 146–82

Ullrick, Laura F., 'Morillo's Attempt to Pacify Venezuela', *Hispanic American Historical Review*, 3, 4 (1920), 535–65

Walvin, J., *Black Ivory: Slavery in the British Empire* (Oxford/Malden, MA, 2001)

Wang S., N. Ray, W. Rojas, M. V. Parra, G. Bedoya et al., 'Geographic Patterns of Genome Admixture in Latin American Mestizos', *PLoS Genet*, 4, 3 (2008), 1–9

Washington, George and William Crawford, *The Washington–Crawford Letters. Being the Correspondence between George Washington and William Crawford, from 1767 to 1781, Concerning Western Lands. With an Appendix, Containing Later Letters of Washington on the Same Subject; and Letters from Valentine Crawford to Washington, written in 1774 and 1775, Chronologically Arranged and Carefully Annotated* (Cincinnati, 1877)

Williams, Eric, *Capitalism and Slavery* (London, 1964)

Williamson, E., *The Penguin History of Latin America* (London, 1992)

Wood, Michael, *Conquistadors* (London, 2001)

Woodward, Margaret L., 'The Spanish Army and the Loss of America, 1810–1824', *Hispanic American Historical Review*, 48, 4 (1968) 586–607

CHAPTER 4: MEDICINE

Acemoglu, Daron, Davide Cantoni, Simon Johnson and James A. Robinson, 'The Consequences of Radical Reform: The French Revolution', National Bureau of Economic Research working paper 14831 (April 2009)

Acemoglu, Daron, Simon Johnson and James Robinson, 'Disease and Development in Historical Perspective', *Journal of the European Economic Association*, 1, 2–3 (2003), 397–405

Anon., *Die Rheinische Mission und Der Herero-Aufstand: Erelebnisse und Beobachtungen rheinischer Missionare* (Barmen, 1904)

Asiwaju, A. I., *West African Transformations: Comparative Impact of French and British Colonialism* (Niger, 1991)

Bayer, Hauptmann M., *Mit dem Hauptquartier in Südwestafrika* (Berlin, 1909)

Beck, Ann, 'Medicine and Society in Tanganyika, 1890–1930: A Historical Inquiry', *Transactions of the American Philosophical Society*, 67, 3 (1977), 1–59

Beckett, I. and K. Simpson (eds.), *A Nation in Arms: A Social Study of the British Army in the First World War* (Manchester, 1985)

Berenson, E., *Heroes of Empire: Five Charismatic Men and the Conquest of Africa* (Berkeley/Los Angeles/London, 2011)

Betts, Raymond F., *Assimilation and Association in French Colonial Theory, 1890–1914* (New York/London, 1961)

———, 'The Establishment of the Medina in Dakar', *Africa: Journal of the International African Institute*, 41, 2 (April 1971), 143–52

Blanton, Robert, T. David Mason and Brian Athow, 'Colonial Style and Post-Colonial Ethnic Conflict in Africa', *Journal of Peace Research*, 38, 4 (2001), 473–91

Brunschwig, H., *French Colonialism 1871–1914: Myths and Realities* (London, 1966)

———, 'French Exploration and Conquest in Tropical Africa from 1865 to 1898', in L. H. Gann and P. Duignan (eds.), *Colonialism in Africa, 1870–1960*, vol. I (Cambridge, 1969), 132–64

Buell, R. L., *The Native Problem in Africa* (London, 1965)

Burke, Edmund, *Reflections on the Revolutions in France: A Critical Edition*, ed. J. C. D. Clark (Cambridge, 2001)

Carter, Susan B., Scott Sigmund Gartner, Michael R. Haines, Alan L. Olmstead, Richard Sutch and Gavin Wright (eds.), *Historical Statistics of the United States: Millennial Edition Online* (Cambridge, 2006)

Centre d'Informations Documentaires, *The Work of France in the Cameroons* (Paris, 1939)

Clausewitz, Carl von, *On War*, ed. Michael Howard and Peter Paret (Princeton, 1976)

Cohen, William, *Rulers of Empire: The French Colonial Service in Africa* (Stanford, 1971)

Collier, Paul, *The Bottom Billion: Why the Poorest Countries are Failing and What Can Be Done about It* (Oxford, 2007)

Conklin, Alice L., *A Mission to Civilise: The Republican Idea of Empire in France and West Africa, 1895–1930* (Stanford, 1998)

Crowder, Michael, *Senegal: A Study of French Assimilation Policy* (Oxford, 1962)

Cruise O'Brien, Rita, *White Society in Black Africa: The French of Senegal* (London, 1972)

Daly, M. W., 'Omdurman and Fashoda, 1898: Edited and Annotated Letters of F. R. Wingate', *Bulletin of the British Society for Middle Eastern Studies*, 10, 1 (1983), 21–37

Deutsch, Jan-Georg, *Emancipation without Abolition in German East Africa c. 1884–1914* (Oxford, 2006)

Drechsler, Horst, *Südwestafrika unter deutscher Kolonialherrschaft: Der Kampf der Herero und Nama gegen den deutschen Imperialismus (1884–1915)* (Berlin, 1966)

Easterly, William, *The White Man's Burden: Why the West's Efforts to Aid the Rest Have Done So Much Ill and So Little Good* (London, 2007)

Echenberg, Myron, *Black Death, White Medicine: Bubonic Plague and the Politics of Public Health in Senegal, 1914–1945* (Portsmouth, NH/ Oxford, 2002)

——, *Colonial Conscripts: The Tirailleurs Senegalais in French West Africa, 1857–1960* (London, 1990)

——, 'Medical Science in Colonial Senegal: The Pasteur Institute of Dakar and the Quest for a Yellow Fever Vaccine, 1925–1925', McGill University paper (n.d.)

Eichacker, Captain Rheinhold, 'The Blacks Attack!', *New York Times Current History*, 9 (April–June 1917), 110–12

Eiermann, Martin, 'The Good, the Bad, and the Ugly: Colonial Violence, Domestic Discourses, and the Production of Truths in Imperial Germany, 1904 to 1908', (Harvard University senior thesis, 2010)

Evans, Andrew D., 'Anthropology at War: Racial Studies of Prisoners of War during World War I', in H. Penny and M. Bunzl (eds.), *Worldly Provincialism: German Anthropology in the Age of Empire* (Ann Arbor, MI, 2003), 198–230

Ferguson, Niall, *The Ascent of Money: A Financial History of the World* (London, 2008)

Fieldhouse, D. K., *Black Africa 1945–80: Economic Decolonization and Arrested Development* (London, 1986)

Fischer, Eugen, *Die Rehobother Bastards und das Bastardierungsproblem beim Menschen: Anthropologische und ethnographische Studien am Rehebother Bastardvolk in Deutsch-Südwest-Afrika* (Jena, 1913)

Fonge, Fuabeh P., *Modernization without Development in Africa: Patterns of Change and Continuity in Post-Industrial Cameroonian Public Service* (Trenton, NJ/Asmara, Eritrea, 1997)

Gandhi, Mahatma, *The Collected Works of Mahatma Gandhi* (electronic book) (New Delhi, 1999)

——, *Hind Swaraj*, ed. Jitendra T. Desai (Ahmedabad, 1938)

Gardiner, David E., 'The French Impact on Education in Africa, 1817–1960', in G. Wesley Johnson (ed.), *Double Impact: France and Africa in the Age of Imperialism* (Westport, CT/London, 1985), 333–44

Gewald, Jan-Bart, 'The Great General of the Kaiser', in *Botswana Notes and Records*, 26 (1994), 67–76

——, *Herero Heroes: A Socio-Political History of the Herero of Namibia, 1890–1923* (Oxford/Cape Town/Athens, 1999)

Gide, André, *Travels in the Congo* (Berkeley/Los Angeles, 1929)

Gifford, P. and Louis Wm Roger, *France and Britain in Africa: Imperial Rivalry and Colonial Rule* (New Haven/London, 1971)

Hochschild, A., *King Leopold's Ghost: A Story of Greed, Terror and Heroism in Colonial Africa* (New York, 1999)

Iliffe, J., *Africans: The History of a Continent* (Cambridge, 2007 [1995])

Joireman, Sandra F., 'Inherited Legal Systems and Effective Rule of Law: Africa and the Colonial Legacy', *Journal of Modern African Studies*, 39, 4 (2001), 57196

Kipling, Rudyard, 'France at War: On the Frontier of Civilization', in *The Collected Works of Rudyard Kipling*, vol. II (Charleston, SC, 2008)

Klein, Martin A., *Islam and Imperialism in Senegal: Sine-Saloum, 1847–1914* (Stanford, 1968)

Kuhlmann, A., *Auf Adlers Flügeln* (Barmen, 1911)

Labrousse, Ernest, '1789–1830–1848: How Revolutions are Born', in François Crouzet, William Henry Chaloner and Fritz Stern (eds.), *Essays in European Economic History, 1789–1914* (London, 1969), 1–14

Lenin, Vladimir Ilyich, *Imperialism, the Highest Stage of Capitalism* (Moscow, 1963 [1917])

Leutwein, Theodor, *Elf Jahre Gouverneur in Deutsch-Südwestafrika* (Berlin, 1906)

Levine, Alison Murray, 'Film and Colonial Memory: La Croisière noire, 1924–2004', in Alec G. Hargreaves (ed.) *Memory, Empire and Post-colonialism: Legacies of French Colonialism* (Lanham, MD/Oxford, 2005), 81–97

Lieven, Dominic, Russia against Napoleon: The True Story of the Campaigns of War and Peace (New York, 2010)

Lunn, Joe, *Memoirs of the Maelstrom: A Senegalese Oral History of the First World War* (London, 1999)

McCullum, Jack E., *Military Medicine: From Ancient Times to the 21st Century* (Santa Barbara, 2008)

MacLeod, Roy and M. Lewis (eds.), *Disease, Medicine and Empire: Perspectives on Western Medicine and the Experience of European Expansion* (London /New York, 1988)

McLynn, Frank, *Napoleon: A Biography* (London, 2002)

Madley, Benjamin, 'From Africa to Auschwitz: How German South West Africa Incubated Ideas and Methods Adopted and Developed by the Nazis in Eastern Europe', *European History Quarterly*, 35, 3 (2005), 429–64

———, 'Patterns of Frontier Genocide 1803–1910: The Aboriginal Tasmanians, the Yuki of California, and the Herero of Namibia', *Journal of Genocide Research*, 6, 2 (2004), 167–92

Marcovich, A., *French Colonial Medicine and Colonial Rule: Perspectives on Western Medicine and the Experience of European Expansion* (London/New York, 1988)

Marr, D. G., *Vietnamese Anticolonialism, 1885–1925* (Berkeley/Los Angeles, 1971)

Mazower, Mark, *Dark Continent: Europe's Twentieth Century* (London, 2008)

———, *Hitler's Empire: Nazi Rule in Occupied Europe* (London, 2008)

Moyo, Dambisa, *Dead Aid: Why Aid is Not Working and How There is Another Way for Africa* (London, 2010)

Ngalamulume, K., 'Keeping the City Totally Clean: Yellow Fever and the Politics of Prevention in Colonial Saint-Louis-de-Sénégal', *Journal of African History*, 45 (2004), 183–202

Olusoga, David and Casper W. Erichsen, *The Kaiser's Holocaust: German Forgotten Genocide and the Colonial Roots of Nazis* (London, 2010)

Riley, James C., 'The Timing and Pace of Health Transitions around the World', *Population and Development Review*, 31, 4 (Dec. 2005), 741–64

Robiquet, Paul (ed.), *Discours et opinions de Jules Ferry* (Paris, 1897)

Rohrbach, Paul, *Aus Südwest-Afrikas schweren Tagen: Blätter von Arbeit und Abschied* (Berlin, 1909)

———, *Deutsche Kolonialwirtschaft*, vol. I: *Südwest-Afrika* (Berlin, 1907)

Rousseau, Jean-Jacques, *The Social Contract* (London, 1968)

Rust, Conrad, *Krieg und Frieden im Hereroland: Aufzeichnungen aus dem Kriegsjahre 1904* (Berlin, 1905)

Sabatier, Peggy R., '"Elite" Education in French West Africa: The Era of Limits, 1903–1945', *International Journal of African Historical Studies*, 11, 2 (1978), 247–66

Saxe, Jo W., 'The Changing Economic Structure of French West Africa', *Annals of the American Academy of Political and Social Science*, 298 (1955), 52–61

Schama, Simon, *Citizens: A Chronicle of the French Revolution* (London, 1990)

Schneider, W. H., 'Smallpox in Africa during Colonial Rule', *Medical History Journal*, 53, 2 (April 2009), 193–227

Seiner, Franz, *Bergtouren und Steppenfahrten im Hereroland* (Berlin, 1904)

Shaw, George Bernard, 'Preface on Doctors', in *The Doctor's Dilemma, Getting Married, and the Shewing-Up of Blanco Posnet* (Rockville, MD, 2003 [1911])

Singer, B. and Langdon, J., *Cultured Force: Makers and Defenders of the French Colonial Empire* (Madison, WI, 2004)

Smith, Leonard V., Stéphane Audoin-Rouzeau and Annette Becker, *France and the Great War, 1914–1918* (Cambridge, 2003)

Smith, R., *Vietnam and the West* (London, 1968)

Steer, G. L., *Judgment on German Africa* (London, 1939)

Strachan, Hew, *The First World War*, vol. I: *To Arms* (Oxford, 2001)

———, *The First World War in Africa* (Oxford, 2004)

Tai, Hue-Tam Ho, 'The Politics of Compromise: The Constitutionalist Party and the Electoral Reforms of 1922 in French Cochinchina', *Modern Asian Studies Journal*, 18, 3 (1984), 371–91

Taithe, B., *The Killer Trail: A Colonial Scandal in the Heart of Africa* (Oxford, 2009)

Taylor, Miles, 'The 1848 Revolutions and the British Empire', *Past & Present*, 166 (Feb. 2000), 146–80

Tocqueville, Alexis de, *Democracy in America*, ed. Bruce Frohnan (London, 2002)

Twain, Mark, *Following the Equator: A Journey around the World*, vol. II (New York, 1897)

Van Beusekom, Monica M., *Negotiating Development: African Farmers and Colonial Experts at the Office du Niger, 1920–1960* (London, 2002)

Weindling, Paul, *Health, Race and German Politics between National Unification and Nazism, 1870–1945* (Cambridge, 1989)

Winter, J. M., *The Great War and the British People* (London, 1985)

Wolpert, Stanley, *Gandhi's Passion: The Life and Legacy of Mahatma Gandhi* (Oxford, 2002)

Wright, P., *Conflict on the Nile: The Fashoda Incident of 1898* (London, 1972)

Yansané, A. Y., 'The Impact of France on Education in West Africa', in G. Wesley Johnson (ed.), *Double Impact: France and Africa in the Age of Imperialism* (Westport, CT/London, 1985), 345–62

Zimmerer, 'The First Genocide of the Twentieth Century: The German War of Destruction in South-West Africa (1904–1908) and the Global History of Genocide', in Doris L. Bergen (ed.), *Lessons and Legacies: From Generation to Generation* (Evanston, IL, 2008), 34–51

CHAPTER 5: CONSUMPTION

Allen, Frederick, *Secret Formula: How Brilliant Marketing and Relentless Salesmanship Made Coca-Cola the Best-Known Product in the World* (New York, 1995)

Allen, Robert C., *The British Industrial Revolution in Global Perspective* (Cambridge, 2009)

———, 'The Great Divergence in European Wages and Prices from the Middle Ages to the First World War', *Explorations in Economic History*, 38 (2001), 411–47

Allen, Robert C., Jean-Pascal Bassino, Debin Ma, Christine Moll-Murata and Jan Luiten van Zanden, 'Wages, Prices, and Living Standards in China, Japan, and Europe, 1738–1925', working paper (2005)

Bairoch, Paul, 'International Industrialization Levels from 1750 to 1980', *Journal of Economic History*, 11 (1982), 269–333

Beasley, W. G., *Japan Encounters the Barbarian: Japanese Travellers in America and Europe* (New Haven, 1995)

Berg, Maxine, 'From Imitation to Invention: Creating Commodities in Eighteenth-Century Britain', *Economic History Review*, New Series, 55, 1 (2002), 1–30

———, 'In Pursuit of Luxury: Global History and British Consumer Goods in the Eighteenth Century', *Past & Present*, 182 (2004), 85–142

Berger, Helge and Mark Spoerer, 'Economic Crises and the European Revolutions of 1848', *Journal of Economic History*, 61, 2 (2001), 293–326

Bergson, Abram, 'How Big was the Soviet GDP?', *Comparative Economic Studies* (1997), 1–14

Bismarck, Count Otto von, *Reflections and Reminiscences* (London, 1899)

Broadberry, Stephen N., 'How did the United States and Germany Overtake Britain? A Sectoral Analysis of Comparative Productivity Levels, 1870–1990', *Journal of Economic History*, 58, 2 (1998), 375–407

Buruma, Ian, *Inventing Japan: From Empire to Economic Miracle, 1853–1964* (London, 2003)

Carlyle, Thomas, *Past and Present* (London, 1843)

Clark, Gregory, *A Farewell to Alms: A Brief Economic History of the World* (Princeton, 2007)

Clark, Gregory and Robert C. Feenstra, 'Technology in the Great Divergence', in Michael D. Bordo, Alan M. Taylor and Jeffrey G. Williamson (eds.), *Globalization in Historical Perspective* (Chicago/London, 2003), 277–322

Cole, Harold L., Lee O. Ohanian and Ron Leung, 'Deflation and the International Great Depression: A Productivity Puzzle', Federal Reserve Bank of Minneapolis Research Department staff report, 356 (February 2005)

Copeland, Melvin T., 'Technical Development in Cotton Manufacturing since 1860', *Quarterly Journal of Economics*, 24, 1 (1909), 109–59

Cox, Mick (ed.), *Rethinking the Soviet Collapse: Sovietology, the Death of Communism and the New Russia* (London, 1999)

Crafts, N. F. R., 'British Economic Growth, 1700–1831: A Review of the Evidence, *Economic History Review*, 36, 2 (1983), 177–99

Darwin, Charles, *On the Origin of Species* (Oxford, 2008 [1859])

Dattel, Gene, *Cotton and Race in the Making of America: The Human Costs of Economic Power* (New York, 2009)

Debray, Jules Régis, 'The Third World: From Kalashnikovs to God and Computers', Interview with Nathan Gardels, *New Perspectives Quarterly*, 3, 1 (1986), 25–8

Dyos, H. J. and D. H. Aldcroft, *British Transport: An Economic Survey from the 17th Century to the 20th* (Leicester, 1969)

Ebadi, S., *Iran Awakening* (London, 2006)

Esteban, Javier Cuenca, 'Factory Costs, Market Prices, and Indian Calicos: Cotton Textile Prices Revisited, 1779–1831', *Economic History Review*, 52, 4 (1999), 749–55

Evans, Richard J., *Death in Hamburg: Society and Politics in the Cholera Years, 1830–1910* (Oxford, 1987)

Farnie, Douglas A., 'The Role of Cotton Textiles in the Economic Development of India, 1600–1990', in Douglas A. Farnie and David J. Jeremy (eds.), *The Fiber that Changed the World: The Cotton Industry in International Perspective, 1600–1990s* (Oxford, 2004), 395–430

——, 'The Role of Merchants as Prime Movers in the Expansion of the Cotton Industry, 1760–1990', in Douglas A. Farnie and David J. Jeremy (eds.), *The Fiber that Changed the World: The Cotton Industry in International Perspective, 1600–1990s* (Oxford, 2004), 15–55

Ferdows, A. K., 'Women and the Islamic Revolution', *International Journal of Middle East Studies*, 15, 2 (1983), 283–98

Ferguson, Niall, 'An Evolutionary Approach to Financial History', *Cold Spring Harbor Symposia on Quantitative Biology*, 74 (2009), 449–54

——, *The War of the World: History's Age of Hatred* (London, 2006)

Findlay, Ronald and Kevin H. O'Rourke, *Power and Plenty: Trade, War, and the World Economy in the Second Millennium* (Princeton, 2007)

Fordham, Benjamin O.,'"Revisionism" Reconsidered: Exports and American Intervention in the First World War', unpublished paper, Department of Political Science, Binghamton University (SUNY) (2004)

Fowler, Alan, *Lancashire Cotton Operatives and Work, 1900–1950: A Social History of Lancashire Cotton Operatives in the Twentieth Century* (Farnham, 2003)

Fowler Mohanty, G., *Labor and Laborers of the Loom: Mechanization and Handloom Weavers, 1780–1840* (New York/London, 2006)

Friedman, Milton and Anna J. Schwartz, *A Monetary History of the United States, 1867–1960* (Princeton, 1963)

Fukuyama, Francis, *The End of History and the Last Man* (New York, 1992)

Gaddis, John, *The Cold War: A New History* (London, 2006)

Galeano, Eduardo, *Open Veins of Latin America: Five Centuries of the Pillage of a Continent* (London, 2009)

Gildea, Robert, *Barricades and Borders: Europe, 1815–1914* (Oxford, 1996)

Gong, Gerrit W., *The Standard of 'Civilization' in International Society* (Oxford, 1984)

Grayling, A. C., *Toward the Light of Liberty: The Struggles for Freedom and Rights that Made the Modern Western World* (New York, 2007)

Greer, Germaine, *The Female Eunuch* (New York, 1980 [1970])

Guinnane, Timothy, Ron Harris, Naomi R. Lamoreaux and Jean-Laurent Rosenthal, 'Putting the Corporation in its Place', NBER working paper 13109 (May 2007)

Harrison, Mark (ed.), *The Economics of World War II: Six Great Powers in International Comparison* (Cambridge, 1998)

Hirano Ken'ichiro (ed.), *The State and Cultural Transformation: Perspectives from East Asia* (Tokyo, 1993)

Howarth, S., *Henry Poole, Founders of Savile Row* (Honiton, 2003)

Hunt, Tristan, *The Frock-Coated Communist: The Revolutionary Life of Friedrich Engels* (London, 2009)

Hyman, Louis, 'Debtor Nation: How Consumer Credit Built Postwar America', *Enterprise and Society*, 9, 4 (2008), 614–18

Jones, Peter M.,'Living the Enlightenment and the French Revolution: James Watt, Matthew Boulton, and their Sons', *Historical Journal*, 42, 1 (1999), 157–82

Kaelble, Hartmut, *Industrialization and Social Inequality in 19th-Century Europe*, trans. Bruce Little (Leamington Spa/Heidelberg, 1986)

Kamisaka, S., *Cotton Mills and Workers in Modern Japan* (Osaka, 1919)

Keene, Donald, *Emperor of Japan: Meiji and his World, 1852–1912* (New York, 2005)

Kurlansky, Mark, *1968: The Year that Rocked the World* (New York, 2005)

Lamoreaux, Naomi, 'Scylla or Charybdis? Some Historical Reflections on the Two Basic Problems of Corporate Governance', unpublished paper (2009)

La Porta, Rafael, Florencio Lopez-de-Silanes and Andrei Shleifer, 'The Economic Consequences of Legal Origins', *Journal of Economic Literature*, 46, 2 (2008), 285–332

La Porta, Rafael, Florencio Lopez-de-Silanes, Andrei Shleifer and Robert Vishny, 'Investor Protection and Corporate Governance', *Journal of Financial Economics*, 58, 1 (2000), 1–25

——, 'Law and Finance', *Journal of Political Economy*, 106, 6 (1998), 1113–55

Leggewie, Claus, '1968: A Defining Year in World Politics: A Return from Cultural Nostalgia to Political Analysis', Goethe Institute Online: http://www.goethe.de/ges/pok/dos/dos/wdp/en3045262.htm

Leunig, T., 'A British Industrial Success: Productivity in the Lancashire and New England Cotton Spinning Industries a Century Ago', *Economic History Review* 56, 1 (2003), 90–117

McKendrick, Neil, John Brewer and J. H. Plumb, *The Birth of a Consumer Society: The Commercialization of Eighteenth-Century England* (London, 1982)

McKeown, Adam, 'Global Migration, 1846–1940', *Journal of World History*, 15 (2004), 185–9

Maddison, Angus, *The World Economy: A Millennial Perspective* (Paris, 2001)

Malony, B., 'Modernity, Gender and the Empire: Gender, Citizenship and Dress in Modernizing Japan', *International Institute for Asian Studies Newsletter*, 46 (2008): www.iias.nl/nl/46/IIAS_NL46_0809.pdf

Marshall, Peter, *Demanding the Impossible: A History of Anarchism* (Oakland, 2010)

Maurer, Noel, and Carlos Yu, *The Big Ditch: How America Took, Built, Ran and Ultimately Gave Away the Panama Canal* (Princeton, 2011)

Mazzini, Giuseppe, 'To the Italians', in *The Duties of Man and Other Essays*, trans. Thomas Jones (Charleston, 2010)

Meech-Pekarik, J., *The World of the Meiji Print: Impressions of a New Civilization* (New York, 1986)

Mitchell, B. R., *Abstract of British Historical Statistics* (Cambridge, 1962)

Mokyr, Joel, *The Economics of the Industrial Revolution* (London, 1985)

Morris, Ian, *Why the West Rules – For Now: The Patterns of History, and What They Reveal about the Future* (New York, 2010)

Moser, Charles K., *The Cotton Textile Industry of Far Eastern Countries* (Boston, MA, 1930)

Nashat, G., 'Women in the Islamic Republic of Iran', *Iranian Studies Journal*, 13, 1–4 (1980), 165–94

O'Brien, P. K., T. Griffiths and P. Hunt, 'Political Components of the Industrial Revolution: Parliament and the English Cotton Textile Industry, 1660–1774', *Economic History Review*, 44, 3 (1991), 395–423

Okuefuna, David, *The Wonderful World of Albert Kahn: Colour Photographs from a Lost Age* (London, 2008)

Parthasarathi, Prasannan, 'Rethinking Wages and Competitiveness in the Eighteenth Century: Britain and South India', *Past & Present*, 158 (1998), 79–109

Piketty, Thomas and Emmanuel Saez, 'Income Inequality in the United States, 1913–1998', NBER working paper no. 8467 (2001)

Poiger, Uta G., *Jazz, Rock and Rebels: Cold War Politics and American Culture in a Divided Germany* (Berkeley/Los Angeles, 2000)

Pollard, Sidney, *Peaceful Conquest: The Industrialization of Europe, 1780–1914* (Oxford, 1981)

Ramet, Sabrina Petra, 'Rock Music in Czechoslovakia', in Sabrina Petra Ramet (ed.), *Rocking the State: Rock Music and Politics in Eastern Europe and Russia* (Boulder/San Francisco/Oxford, 1994) 55–72

Safanov, Mikhail, 'You Say You Want a Revolution', *History Today* (Aug. 2003): http://www.historytoday.com

Schorske, Carl E., *Fin-de-Siècle Vienna: Politics and Culture* (New York, 1979)

Siefert, Marsha, 'From Cold War to Wary Peace: American Culture in the USSR and Russia', in Alexander Stephan (ed.), *The Americanization of Europe: Culture, Diplomacy and Anti-Americanism after 1945* (Oxford, 2006), 185–217

Singer, J. David and Melvin Small, Correlates of War Database, University of Michigan, www.umich.edu/~cowproj

Sullivan, James, *Jeans: A Cultural History of an American Icon* (New York, 2006)

Suri, Jeremi, *Power and Protest: Global Revolution and the Rise of Détente* (Cambridge, MA, 2003)

Tooze, Adam J., *The Wages of Destruction: The Making and Breaking of the Nazi Economy* (London, 2006)

Upadhyay, S. B., *Existence, Identity and Mobilization: The Cotton Millworkers of Bombay, 1890–1919* (New Delhi, 2004)

Vries, Jan De, 'Between Purchasing Power and the World of Goods: Understanding the Household Economy in Early Modern Europe', in J. Brewer and R. Porter (eds.), *Consumption and the World of Goods* (London, 1993), 85–132

Wall, Rachel F., *Japan's Century: An Interpretation of Japan's History Since the Eighteen-Fifties* (London, 1964)

Westad, Odd Arne, *The Global Cold War: Third World Interventions and the Making of our Times* (New York, 2005)

Wheen, Francis, *Karl Marx* (London, 2002)

Wilde, Oscar, *De Profundis and Other Writings*, ed. Hesketh Pearson (London, 1986 [1905])

Wolcott, S. and Clark,G., 'Why Nations Fail: Managerial Decisions and Performance in Indian Cotton Textiles, 1890–1938', *Journal of Economic History*, 59, 2 (1999), 397–423

Wolle, Stefan, *Der Traum von der Revolte: Die DDR 1968* (Berlin, 2008)

CHAPTER 6: WORK

Aikman, D., *The Beijing Factor: How Christianity is Transforming China and Changing the Global Balance of Power* (Oxford/Grand Rapids, MI, 2003)

Austin, Alvyn, *China's Millions: The China Inland Mission and Late Qing Society, 1832–1905* (Grand Rapids, MI/Cambridge, 2007)

Bao, Limin, 'The Intellectual Influence of Christianity in a Modern China Society', in H. Yang and Daniel H. N. Yeung (eds.), *Sino-Christian Studies in China* (Newcastle, 2006), 265–79

Barber, Benjamin R., *Jihad vs. McWorld: Terrorism's Challenge to Democracy* (London, 2003)

Barro, Robert J. and Rachel M. McCleary, 'Religion and Economic Growth across Countries', *American Sociological Review* (2003), 760–81

——, 'Religion and Political Economy in an International Panel', Harvard University working paper (Nov. 2003)

——, 'Which Countries Have State Religions?', Harvard University working paper (Feb. 2005)

Bays, D., 'Chinese Protestant Christianity Today', in D. L. Overmyer (ed.), *Religion in China Today* (Cambridge, 2003), 182–99

Becker, Sascha O. and Ludger Wössmann,'Was Weber Wrong? A Human Capital Theory of Protestant Economic History', *Quarterly Journal of Economics*, 124, 2 (2009), 531–96

Brown, Callum G., *The Death of Christian Britain: Understanding Secularization, 1800–2000* (London, 2001)

Bruce, S., *God is Dead: Secularization in the West* (Malden, MA/Oxford, 2002)

Caldwell, Christopher, *Reflections on the Revolution in Europe: Immigration, Islam and the West* (New York, 2009)

Cantoni, David, 'The Economic Effects of the Protestant Reformation: Testing the Weber Hypothesis in the German Lands', Harvard University working paper (September 2009)

Chen Cunfu and Huang Tianhai, 'The Emergence of a New Type of Christians in China Today', *Review of Religious Research*, 46, 2 (2004), 183–200

Chesterton, G. K., *A Short History of England* (Charleston, SC, 2009 [1917])

——, 'The Miracle of Moon Crescent', in *The Collected Works of G. K. Chesterton*, vol. XIII (San Francisco, 2005), 94–117

——, 'The Patriotic Idea: England – A Nation', in James V. Schall (ed.), *The Collected Works of G. K. Chesterton*, vol. XX (San Francisco, 2001), 595–623

Chiswick, Barry, 'The Economic Progress of American Jewry: From 18th Century Merchants to 21st Century Professionals', University of Illinois working paper (Nov. 2009)

Cohen, Paul A., *China and Christianity: The Missionary Movement and the Growth of Chinese Antiforeignism, 1860–1870* (Cambridge, MA, 1963)

Cox, Caroline and John Marks, *The West, Islam and Islamism: Is Ideological Islam Compatible with Liberal Democracy?*, 2nd edn (London, 2006)

Davie, G., *Europe: The Exceptional Case: Parameters of Faith in the Modern World* (London, 2002)

——, *Religion in Britain since 1945* (Malden, MA/Oxford, 1994)

Delacroix, Jacques and François Nielsen, 'The Beloved Myth: Protestantism and the Rise of Industrial Capitalism in Nineteenth-Century Europe', *Social Forces*, 80, 2 (2001), 509–53

Dickson, Tony and Hugh V. McLachlan, 'In Search of "The Spirit of Capitalism": Weber's Misinterpretation of Franklin', *Sociology*, 23, 1 (1989), 81–9

Dikötter, Frank, *Mao's Great Famine: The History of China's Most Devastating Catastrophe* (London, 2010)

Fenggang Yang, 'Cultural Dynamics in China: Today and in 2020', *Asia Policy*, 4 (2007), 41–52

——, 'Lost in the Market, Saved at McDonald's: Conversion to Christianity in Urban China', *Journal for the Scientific Study of Religion*, 44, 4 (2005), 423–41

Ferguson, Niall, *The Ascent of Money: A Financial History of the World* (London, 2008)

——, 'Economics, Religion and the Decline of Europe', *Economic Affairs* (2004), 37–40

Freud, Sigmund, *Civilization and its Discontents*, trans. James Strachey (New York, 1961 [1929–30])

——, *The Future of an Illusion*, trans. W. D. Robson-Scott (New York, 1928)

Gibbon, Edward, *History of the Decline and Fall of the Roman Empire*, ed. David Womersley (London, 1996)

Giddens, Anthony, *Capitalism and Modern Social Theory: An Analysis of the Writings of Marx, Durkheim, and Max Weber* (Cambridge, 1971)

Goldsworthy, Adrian, *How Rome Fell: Death of a Superpower* (New Haven, 2009)

Green, Robert W., *Protestantism and Capitalism: The Weber Thesis and its Critics* (Boston, 1959)

Grier, Robin, 'The Effect of Religion on Economic Development: A Cross National Study of 63 Former Colonies', *Kyklos*, 50, 1 (1997), 47–62

Guiso, Luigi, Paola Sapienza and Luigi Zingales, 'People's Opium? Religion and Economic Attitudes', *Journal of Monetary Economics*, 50 (2003), 225–82

Heather, Peter, *The Fall of the Roman Empire: A New History* (London, 2006)

Hunter, Alan and Kim-Kwong Chan, *Protestantism in Contemporary China* (Cambridge, 1993)

Iannaccone, Laurence R., 'Introduction to the Economics of Religion', *Journal of Economic Literature*, 36, 3 (1998), 1465–96

Jianbo Huang and Fenggang Yang, 'The Cross Faces the Loudspeakers: A Village Church Perseveres under State Power', in Fenggang Yang and Joseph B. Tamney (ed.), *State, Market and Religions in Chinese Societies* (Leiden/Boston, 2005), 41–62

Jiwei Ci, *Dialectic of the Chinese Revolution* (Stanford, 1994)

Kitch, M. J., *Capitalism and the Reformation* (London, 1967)

Koch, R. and C. Smith, *Suicide of the West* (London/New York, 2006)

Kuang-sheng Liao, *Antiforeignism and Modernization in China, 1860–1980: Linkage between Domestic Politics and Foreign Policy* (Hong Kong, 1984)

Lehmann, Hartmut and Guenther Roth, *Weber's Protestant Ethic* (Cambridge, 1993)

McLeod, Hugh and Werner Ustorf (eds.), *The Decline of Christendom in Western Europe, 1750–2000* (Cambridge, 2003)

Marshall, Gordon, *In Search of the Spirit of Capitalism* (New York, 1982)

Micklethwait, John and Adrian Wooldridge, *God is Back* (London, 2009)

Morrison, Eliza A., Mrs Robert, *Memoirs of the Life and Labours of Robert Morrison*, vol. I (London, 1839)

Ng, Peter Tze Ming, 'Timothy Richard: Christian Attitudes towards Other Religions and Cultures', *Studies in World Christianity*, 14, 1 (2008), 73–92

Peng Liu, 'Unreconciled Differences: The Staying Power of Religion', in Jason Kindopp and Carol Lee Hamrin (eds.), *God and Caesar in China: Policy Implications of Church–State Tensions* (Washington, DC, 2004), 149–64

Pew Forum on Religion and Public Life, *Muslim Networks and Movements in Western Europe* (Washington, DC, 2010)

Potter, P. B., 'Belief in Control: Regulation of Religion in China', in D. L. Overmyer (ed.), *Religion in China Today* (Cambridge, 2003), 11–32

Putnam, Robert D. and David E. Campbell, *American Grace: How Religion Divides and Unites Us* (New York/London, 2010)

Roth, Guenther and Wolfgang Schluchter, *Max Weber's Vision of History* (Berkeley, 1979)

Scaff, Lawrence A., 'Remnants of Romanticism: Max Weber in Oklahoma and Indian Territory', *Journal of Classical Sociology*, 5, 53 (2005), 53–72

Shaw, George Bernard, *Back to Methuselah: A Metabiological Pentateuch* (Charleston, 2009 [1921])

Sheehan, Rebecca, 'Liberation and Redemption in 1970s Rock Music', in Niall Ferguson, Charles S. Maier, Erez Manela and Daniel Sargent (eds.), *The Shock of the Global: The 1970s in Perspective* (Cambridge, MA/London), 294–305

Simcox, Robin, Hannah Stuart and Houriya Ahmed, *Islamist Terrorism: The British Connections* (London, 2010)

Smith, Adam, *An Inquiry into the Nature and Causes of the Wealth of Nations* (London, 1904, [1776])

Sprenkel, Otto B. van der, 'Max Weber on China', *History and Theory*, 3, 3 (1964), 348–70

Steer, R., *J. Hudson Taylor: A Man in Christ*, 5th edn (London, 2009)

Stott, Grace, *Twenty-six Years of Missionary Work in China* (London, 1904)

Szasz, Thomas Stephen, *Anti-Freud: Karl Kraus's Criticism of Psychoanalysis and Psychiatry* (Syracuse, 1990)

Tawney, R. H., *Religion and the Rise of Capitalism: A Historical Study* (New York, 1926)

Taylor, James Hudson, *Hudson Taylor: The Autobiography of a Man Who Brought the Gospel to China* (Minneapolis, 1987)

Thompson, Phyllis, *China: The Reluctant Exodus* (Sevenoaks, 1979)

Tolstoy, Leo Nikolayevich, *The Kingdom of God is within You* (Charleston, SC, 2008 [1894])

Trevor-Roper, Hugh, 'Religion, the Reformation and Social Change', in Hugh Trevor-Roper, *Religion, the Reformation and Social Change* (London, 1967), 1–46

Viner, Jacob, *Religious Thought and Economic Society* (Durham, 1978)

Ward-Perkins, Bryan, *The Fall of Rome and the End of Civilization* (Oxford, 2005)

Weber, Marianne, *Max Weber: A Biography* (New Brunswick, 1988)

Weber, Max, *The Protestant Ethic and the Spirit of Capitalism*, trans. P. Baehr and G. C. Wells (London 2002 [1905])

Woodberry, Robert D., 'The Shadow of Empire: Christian Missions, Colonial Policy, and Democracy in Postcolonial Societies', unpublished PhD thesis, University of North Carolina (2004)

World Values Survey Association (www.worldvaluessurvey.org), *World Values Survey 1981–2008 Official Aggregate v.20090901* (2009), Aggregate File Producer: ASEP/JDS, Madrid

Yihua Xi, 'Patriotic Protestants: The Making of an Official Church', in Jason Kindopp and Carol Lee Hamrin (eds.), *God and Caesar in China: Policy Implications of Church–State Tensions* (Washington, DC, 2004), 107–21

Young, Cristobal, 'Religion and Economic Growth in Western Europe: 1500–2000', working paper (Princeton, 2009)

Zakaria, Fareed, *The Future of Freedom: Illiberal Democracy at Home and Abroad* (New York, 2003)

Zhao Dunhua, 'Recent Progress of Christian Studies Made by Chinese Academics in the Last Twenty Years', in H. Yang and Daniel H. N. Yeung (eds.), *Sino-Christian Studies in China* (Newcastle, 2006), 246–51

Zhuo Xinping, 'The Significance of Christianity for the Modernization of Chinese Society', in H. Yang and Daniel H. N. Yeung (eds.), *Sino-Christian Studies in China* (Newcastle, 2006), 252–64

Zuo Jiping, 'Political Religion: The Case of the Cultural Revolution in China', *Sociological Analysis*, 52, 1 (1991), 99–110

CONCLUSION: THE RIVALS

Berman, Paul, *Terror and Liberalism* (New York, 2004)

Bolingbroke, Viscount Henry St John, 'The Idea of a Patriot King', in *The Works of Lord Bolingbroke, with a Life*, vol. II (Philadelphia, 1841), 372–429

Buchanan, Mark, *Ubiquity: The Science of History . . . Or Why the World is Simpler Than We Think* (London, 2005)

Cecchetti, Stephen G., M. S. Mohanty and Fabrizio Zampolli, 'The Future of Public Debt: Prospects and Implications', BIS working papers no. 300 (March 2010)

Churchill, Winston S., 'Civilization', in Randolph S. Churchill (ed.), *Blood, Sweat and Tears*, (Whitefish, MT, 2007 [1940]), 45–9

Collier, Paul, *The Plundered Planet: Why We Must – and How We Can – Manage Nature for Global Prosperity* (Oxford, 2010)

Diamond, Jared, *Collapse: How Societies Choose to Fail or Succeed* (New York, 2005)

Economy, Elizabeth, 'The Game Changer: Coping with China's Foreign Policy Revolution', *Foreign Affairs* (Nov./Dec. 2010), 142–52

Eichengreen, Barry, *Exorbitant Privilege: The Decline of the Dollar and the
Future of the International Monetary System* (Oxford, 2011)

Ferguson, Niall, *The Cash Nexus: Money and Power in the Modern World*
(London, 2001)

Ferguson, Niall and Moritz Schularick, 'The End of Chimerica', *International
Finance* (forthcoming)

Goldstone, Jack A., 'Cultural Orthodoxy, Risk and Innovation: The Divergence of East and West in the Early Modern World', *Sociological Theory*,
5, 2 (1987), 119–35

———, *Revolution and Rebellion in the Early Modern World* (Berkeley/Los
Angeles/Oxford, 1991)

Guan Hanhui and Li Daokui, 'The GDP and Economic Structure of the Ming
Dynasty' (forthcoming)

Hayes, Brian, 'Statistics of Deadly Quarrels', *American Scientist* (Jan.–Feb.
2002)

Hexter, J. H., 'Seyssel, Machiavelli, and Polybius VI: The Mystery of the
Missing Translation', *Studies in the Renaissance*, 3 (1956), 75–96

Holland, John H., *Emergence: From Chaos to Order* (New York, 1998)

———, *Hidden Order: How Adaptation Builds Complexity* (New York, 1995)

Huntington, Samuel, *The Clash of Civilizations and the Remaking of World
Order* (New York/London/Toronto/Sydney, 1996)

———, 'The Clash of Civilizations', *Foreign Affairs* (Summer 1993), 22–49

Jacques, Martin, *When China Rules the World: The Rise of the Middle Kingdom and the End of the Western World* (London, 2009)

Kauffman, Stuart, *At Home in the Universe: The Search for the Laws of Self-
Organization and Complexity* (New York, 1995)

Kennedy, Paul, *The Rise and Fall of the Great Powers: Economic Change and
Military Conflict from 1500 to 2000* (New York, 1989)

Kotkin, Stephen, *Armageddon Averted: The Soviet Collapse, 1970–2000*
(Oxford, 2001)

Krakauer, David, John Gaddis, and Kenneth Pomeranz (eds.), *History, Big
History and Metahistory* (forthcoming)

Luard, Evan, *War in International Society: A Study in International Sociology*
(New Haven/London, 1987)

Maddison, Angus, *The World Economy: A Millennial Perspective* (Paris,
2001)

Marès, Arnaud, 'Sovereign Subjects: Ask Not *Whether* Governments Will
Default, But *How*', Morgan Stanley Research (August 2010)

Marshall, Monty G. and Ted Robert Gurr, *Peace and Conflict 2005: A Global Survey of Armed Conflicts, Self-Determination Movements, and Democracy* (College Park, MD, 2005)

Mitchell, Melanie, *Complexity: A Guided Tour* (New York, 2009)

Pinker, Steven, *The Better Angels of our Nature: The Decline of Violence and its Psychological Roots* (forthcoming)

Quigley, Carroll, *Tragedy and Hope: A History of the World in our Time* (New York/London, 1966)

Raine, Sarah, *China's African Challenges* (Abingdon, 2009)

Richardson, Lewis F., *Statistics of Deadly Quarrels* (Pacific Grove, CA, 1960)

Sargent, Thomas J., 'The Ends of Four Big Inflations', in Thomas J. Sargent, *Rational Expectations and Inflation* (New York, 1993), 43–116

Sen, Amartya, *Identity and Violence: The Illusion of Destiny* (New York, 2006)

Sorokin, Pitrim, *Social and Cultural Dynamics: A Study of Change in Major Systems of Art, Truth, Ethics, Law and Social Relationships* (Boston, 1970 [1957])

Taleb, Nassim Nicholas, 'The Fourth Quadrant: A Map of the Limits of Statistics', *Edge* (15 Sept. 2008)

Tusicisny, Andrej, 'Civilizational Conflicts: More Frequent, Longer, and Bloodier?', *Journal of Peace Research*, 41, 4, (2004), 485–98

Waldrop, M. Mitchell, *Complexity: The Emerging Science at the Edge of Chaos* (New York, 1992)

Zakaria, Fareed, *The Post-American World* (New York, 2008)

Index